Risk Makers
Risk Takers
Risk Breakers

Risk Makers
Risk Takers
Risk Breakers

Reducing the Risks for Young Literacy Learners

Edited by

JoBeth Allen
University of Georgia

Jana M. Mason
University of Illinois at Champaign Urbana

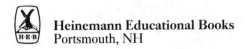

Heinemann Educational Books
Portsmouth, NH

HEINEMANN EDUCATIONAL BOOKS, INC.
361 Hanover Street   Portsmouth, NH   03801-3959
Offices and agents throughout the world

The following have generously given permission to use quotations from copyrighted works:

Page 1: "Remember" from *Horses Make a Landscape Look More Beautiful*, copyright © 1984 by Alice Walker, reprinted by permission of Harcourt Brace Jovanovich, Inc.

Table 4–4: From "Roads to Reading: Studies of Hispanic First Graders at Risk for Reading Failures" by Claude Goldenberg in *NABE Journal* (Vol. II, No. 3), pp. 235–250. Copyright © 1988, Claude Goldenberg.

Pages 151–52: *To Town* and *The Jigaree* by Joy Cowley in the series entitled *The Story Box*[R]. Used by permission of The Wright Group Publishers, 10949 Technology Place, San Diego, CA 92127.

Page 179: From "We Like Colors" — Level 2, Set A from *Special Practice Reading Books*. Copyright © 1979, 1971 by Scott, Foresman and Company. Reprinted by permission.

Page 191: From *Paul* by Glenda Laurence from the Ready-To-Read Series. Copyright © 1983 by the Department of Education, Wellington, New Zealand. Distributed in the United States by Richard C. Owen Publishers, Inc.

Page 192: From *A Pot of Gold* from *Reading Unlimited*, Level 3. Copyright © 1976, 1971 by Scott, Foresman and Company. Reprinted by permission.

Pages 231–32: From *Great Day for Up!* by Dr. Seuss. Copyright © 1974 by Dr. Seuss and A. S. Geisel. Reprinted by permission of Random House, Inc.

Pages 259, 262, 270–72: From *Growing Up Literate*. Copyright © 1988 by Denny Taylor and Catherine Dorsey-Gaines. Reprinted by permission of Heinemann Educational Books, Inc.

Page 260: From "Creating Family Story" by Denny Taylor. In W. Teale and E Sulzby (Eds.) *Emergent Literacy: Writing and Reading*, copyright © 1986. Reprinted by permission of Ablex Publishing Corporation.

Pages 261, 272: From *Family Literacy*. Copyright © 1983 by Denny Taylor. Reprinted by permission of Heinemann Educational Books, Inc.

Page 304: From "Chiefs Urge That States 'Guarantee' School Quality for Those 'At Risk'," *Education Week* (November 18, 1987). Washington, DC: Editorial Projects in Education, 1, 17.

Library of Congress Cataloging-in-Publication Data
Risk makers, risk takers, risk breakers: reducing the risks for young
   literacy learners/edited by JoBeth Allen and Jana M. Mason.
      p.   cm.
   Bibliography: p.
   Includes index.
   ISBN 0–435–08483–6
   1. Socially handicapped children—Education—Reading. 2. Socially
handicapped children—Education—United States. 3. Reading
(Preschool)—United States. 4. Literacy—United States. I. Allen,
JoBeth. II. Mason, Jana.
LC4086.R57 1989
371.9'0973—dc 19   88–27400
                                                       CIP

Designed by Hunter Graphics.
Printed in the United States of America.
10 9 8 7 6 5 4 3 2

Contents

Contributors

JoBeth Allen

JoBeth Allen is an associate professor of language education at the University of Georgia. She collaborates with teachers in developing and studying whole language classrooms. A former preschool and elementary teacher, she is currently working with teachers to develop, implement, and research the effects of a whole language literacy curriculum on high-risk elementary students.

Emily Carr

Emily Carr has taught for ten years, five in classes designed for children at risk. Currently, she teaches kindergarten at Fourth Street Elementary in Athens, Georgia, and is a doctoral student in language education at The University of Georgia. She is interested in how teachers build on the literacy knowledge children bring to school. As teacher/researcher, she is studying the link between child as informant and teacher as instructional decision maker.

Markay Cheyney

A kindergarten teacher at Lamar Elementary School in San Antonio Independent School District, Markay Cheyney has fifteen years of experience as a teacher of primarily at-risk children in Texas, and as an Exchange Teacher in England. Through in-service workshops and courses at San Antonio Community College, she has worked with day-care and elementary teachers on issues in language and literacy development.

Robert G. Delisle

Robert Delisle is an associate professor at Lehman College of The City University of New York, and chair of the Department of Specialized

Services in Education. He has been a professor in residence at the Children's School Project for four years. He works with teachers on new ways of observing literacy development in young children, with a special interest in children and literature.

David K. Dickinson

A former elementary teacher in the Philadelphia public schools, David Dickinson is an assistant professor of education at Clark University. He has studied class meetings in kindergarten, computers in a first-second grade, and book reading styles of preschool teachers. He is beginning a longitudinal study with Catherine Snow of family and school influences on the development of decontextualized language and literacy skills among low-income children.

Marian Wright Edelman

Marian Wright Edelman founded the Washington Research Project in 1968; in 1973 this became the Children's Defense Fund, where she continues as president. She has served as director of the Center for Law and Education at Harvard, and on innumerable national and international committees as an advocate for children. The CDF legislative agenda has targeted education issues including Chapter 1, community learning centers, and especially preschool programs for disadvantaged children.

Patricia A. Edwards

An assistant professor of reading at Michigan State University, Patricia Edwards was a senior researcher at the Center for the Study of Reading during the 1988–89 term. Her work stems from a long-standing commitment to the literacy development of black children in lower socio-economic families. She is currently working with teachers on effective ways to work with parents in a follow-up to the study presented in this volume.

Frederick Erickson

Frederick Erickson is a professor of education and chair of the Educational Leadership Division of the Graduate School of Education, University of Pennsylvania. He also directs the Center for Urban Education. His ethnographic research has focused on issues of equity and reform, especially race, class, and language, in schools and communities. He has pioneered the use of audio-visual aids in the study of social interactions in these settings.

Claude N. Goldenberg

A native Spanish speaker, Claude Goldenberg has taught junior high and first grade in predominantly Hispanic schools in San Antonio and Los Angeles. From 1986–88 he was a Spencer Fellow of the National Academy of Education. He has recently begun a Spencer Foundation study with Ronald Gallimore on home and school effects on literacy development of Hispanic children in kindergarten through third grade.

Jane Hansen

Jane Hansen is an associate professor of reading at the University of New Hampshire and teaches in the UNH summer writing program. She has been an elementary classroom and Chapter 1 reading teacher. Since 1981 she has conducted research in elementary classrooms to learn about how children become readers and writers, how they evaluate themselves as readers and writers, and how teachers teach reading and writing effectively.

Ann Hemmeter

With twenty-two years teaching experience in Indiana and Texas, Ann Hemmeter is currently a kindergarten teacher of disadvantaged children in San Antonio Independent School District. She is a former supervisor of student teachers and a former director of a university-sponsored cooperative nursery school.

Connie McBroom

Connie McBroom was a kindergarten teacher in San Antonio's Northeast Independent School District at the time this chapter was written. She taught kindergarten in Virginia for ten years. She served as cochair of a reading and writing festival in Fairfax, Virginia, and presents workshops for parents.

Beverly McConnell

Beverly McConnell works as a private consultant specializing in program development, evaluation and research of early childhood programs serving minority children. Her research has led to change in federal policies on group care of infants and Head Start programs for migrant workers' children. Since 1970 she has been involved with a longitudinal study of an educational program for migrant, Hispanic, and Laotian children.

Christine E. McCormick

A former school psychologist, Christine McCormick is presently an associate professor of psychology at Eastern Illinois University where she teaches developmental psychology and assessment of preschool children. Her research with Jana Mason over the past ten years combines her interests in early reading with her awareness of the needs of children from homes which do not foster literacy acquisition.

Miriam G. Martinez

Miriam Martinez is currently an assistant professor of reading education at Southwest Texas State University. Her research focuses on teachers' story-book reading styles and on children's emergent literacy behaviors within the classroom context. For the past five years she has codirected the Kindergarten Emergent Literacy Program in San Antonio area schools.

Jana M. Mason

Jana Mason is a professor at the University of Illinois and a member of the Center for the Study of Reading. She has developed preschool programs in Pittsburgh and Champaign, Illinois, and taught in elementary schools in upstate New York and Chicago. Her current work is on reading and writing development in young children, its instruction in preschool and elementary classrooms, and intervention techniques for children who are at academic risk.

Brad Mitchell

Brad Mitchell is an assistant professor of educational policy and leadership at The Ohio State University. He is the codirector of PROBE, an educational policy research enterprise at OSU, where he specializes in the politics of education and policy analysis. He is involved in on-going research on students at risk in Ohio.

Gay Su Pinnell

A former elementary teacher and state-level administrator, Gay Su Pinnell is an associate professor at The Ohio State University. She is the director of the state-wide Ohio Reading Recovery project, an early intervention program to prevent reading failure. She is the director of the Early Literacy Research Project, sponsored by the MacArthur Foundation, which involves research on the at-risk population.

Dorothy S. Strickland

Dorothy Strickland, a professor of education at Rutgers University, has extensive experience working with children in urban areas as a teacher, reading consultant, learning disabilities specialist, and researcher. Her interest in language learning of black children is evidenced by her early research on language diversity and her recent book on the education of black children.

Denny Taylor

Denny Taylor, recently of Teachers College, is currently a research associate with the Family Research Laboratory at the University of New Hampshire. For the past twelve years, she has studied language, literacy, and learning in family, community, and school settings. She is currently studying literacy and socialization in families of working parents.

William H. Teale

Formerly a language arts and reading teacher, William Teale is an associate professor of education at The University of Texas at San Antonio. He is the codirector of the Kindergarten Emergent Literacy Program, a cooperative project of UTSA and local school districts that promotes curriculum development and classroom-based research.

Valora Washington

Valora Washington is the program director of the Kellogg Foundation. She specializes in child development and social policy and has worked at the federal level on Head Start and other educational policies. Her recent work includes books on black children and American institutions, and on Head Start, with particular focus on family needs.

Foreword

Literacy Risks for Students, Parents, and Teachers
Frederick Erickson

This is a book about reducing risks for young learners in literacy instruction. That topic is at once timely, significant, and risky. It is timely and significant because much national attention has been turned to problems of literacy acquisition and to the earliest stages of literacy learning by young children. The topic is risky because the field of inquiry and practice is new, our understandings are necessarily partial, and the stakes for students, parents, and educators are high. I heard a folk singer a few years ago say, "In this life there are some driveways you want to go down with your lights on." Our notions of early literacy acquisition and of what it is to be "at risk" in it are one of the dangerous driveways in American education.

The chapters in this book shed diverse lights on the driveway and its risks. In my judgment, a principal risk lies in assuming it is difficult for many children to learn to read and write. When we consider that through-out the world, regardless of social background, by age three almost every human child has learned to speak a language with fluency and appropriate-ness, which is a task far more cognitively complex than learning to read and write in that language once it has been learned, the concern of American educators over the difficulty of literacy acquisition is puzzling.

Our beliefs about social class play an important role in our beliefs about literacy. Children from low-income families are over-represented in the category of those having difficulty in learning to read, while children from higher income families are under-represented in that category. Various notions explain those social facts. One belief is that children from low-income backgrounds grow up in homes in which they rarely encounter meaningful uses of print. Yet in their chapter in this volume, Taylor and Strickland show low-income black children encountering a wide variety of functional types of printed texts. Another belief is that low-income parents are, at worst, uninterested in their children's academic success, or at best, concerned for their children but lacking the knowledge and skill necessary to assist them in acquiring literacy and the habits of engagement and persistence that are necessary for school success. Yet the chapter by Goldenberg reports that low-income Latino parents took great pains to assist their children's school learning, and a number of them were successful in their attempts, without any special training, when they had been alerted by teachers that their children were having serious trouble in learning to read.

Still another belief is that children are uninterested in and perhaps threatened by the prospect of learning to read unless they have been read to by their parents at home. Yet the chapter by Dickinson reports a dramatic increase in young children's early literacy interests that appears to be the result of changes in classroom practices by teachers, without changes having occurred in literacy-focused interaction in family life. As low-income preschool children were presented by teachers with a much more rich set of classroom encounters with books than they had experienced previously, the children showed increased interest in and engagement with books. The chapter by McConnell reports that literacy acquisition by Native American and Latino Follow Through students improved when classroom aides were hired who came from the same ethnic and linguistic backgrounds as the students. Again, these changes in the classroom learning environment did not involve changes in the daily lives of children at home.

Teachers can do much, in preschool and in the early grades, to make children's engagement with text interesting and appropriate to their developmental level. One of the greatest risks may be to conduct initial literacy instruction in ways that are aversive to children. A powerful source of aversion, as suggested by the Edwards chapter, lies in the hidden curriculum of conventional classroom practice, with its ubiquitous framework of "right answers" for learning to read and write. Edwards reports poignant scenes of a low-income mother paralyzed by anxiety over making mistakes when reading aloud to her child, an anxiety we can assume was acquired during the mother's own childhood experience with fear and shame in school learning environments. Those vignettes give us pause; they caution us from blithely prescribing training for low-income parents in how to read aloud to your child without considering the possible negative side effects of such treatments.

There are risks inherent in highly intrusive interventions to foster early literacy acquisition. Less intrusive interventions may be both more respectful of young children and their parents, an aim that is desirable in itself, and more appropriate and successful educationally than more intrusive interventions, especially those that propose to change customary patterns of family life. Interventions that are minimally intrusive would be appropriate if it were relatively easy for most children to learn to read and write and if schools inadvertently hadn't made it painful and difficult for some kinds of children, especially those whose mothers didn't read bedtime stories to them. Frederick Douglass and Abraham Lincoln didn't have mothers who read them stories: both mothers were illiterate. Moreover, Douglass' mother was a slave and Lincoln's mother was dead, so we could say that they grew up in a mother-absent literacy environment. Yet they both learned to read. As far as we know neither Socrates and Sappho, nor St. Augustine and St. Catherine of Siena, were read aloud to as children. Yet they became literate. Reading aloud to children is, I think, a fine thing. Both my mother and my father read aloud to me a great deal when I was a child, and I treasure the memories of those moments. However, I do not assume that being read aloud to at home is a necessary condition for learning to read and write in school. To believe that is to allow us yet another opportunity to blame low-income parents for their children's school failure. Treating that belief as authoritative truth can be seen as a well-intentioned means of inadvertently putting those children and parents at risk in acquiring literacy.

As a sociolinguistically oriented anthropologist of education my cultural relativism tempts me to say, "Change the classroom if you will, and if you do so, try to increase the amount of rich, intriguing, nonthreatening engagement that children can have with a wide range of texts and their uses, just as children learning to talk in their families encounter oral language in a wide range of forms and functions without externally imposed skill drill or early and swift correction when they make small mistakes in language form. But as teachers of beginning reading and writing, don't try to mess with how parents raise their children. Your job is to teach them in the classroom. Leave the home alone." That may be too extreme a position, a result of my knee-jerk reaction against the dangers of diagnosing by using ethnocentric standards of educational disability and then prescribing culturally inappropriate educational treatments for children and families that are not necessarily sick in the first place. Though I remain inveterately chary of ethnocentrism in educational prescriptions, this book made me think twice before condemning all early childhood intervention as coercive and misguided.

The chapter by McCormick and Mason is suggestive here. They changed Head Start classroom practice so that teachers conducted discussions of "little books" with predictable texts. These were high-interest materials that provided easy access to text for young children. The books were mailed home and the children read them there as well as at school, occasionally engaging their parents with the books. Parents were involved at the child's own initiative, with the child and parent able to find their own level of involvement and their own culturally appropriate ways of interacting around literacy. This is a low-intrusion, low-technology intervention that leaves room for spontaneous engagement and disengagement with text at home; it also leaves room for easy, nonthreatening access to text rehearsal and comprehension by children with the guidance of a teacher in the preschool classroom. No ditto sheets for the preschoolers, no lessons for the parents in how to read bedtime stories effectively. Just do the discussions at school, mail the books home, and something happens. Here, as in a certain style of architecture, less is more. It still makes me nervous, frankly. (I think that if we fundamentally changed instruction in the early grades we wouldn't need Head Start, let alone intervention in family life.) But it gave me ideas to ponder.

There appear to be many ways to reduce the literacy risks for young learners. The biggest risks appear to lie in everybody trying too hard. If learning to read and write is actually easier than learning to talk, then we can all relax a bit—not relaxing our vigilance over student learning or lessening our commitment to broad access to literacy in our society, but relaxing the means and widening the range of cultural and linguistic ways by which educators, together with children and parents, attempt to reach that end. What Wood and Bruner called instructional scaffolding in inter-action between an adult and a child may be of important benefit to the child, whatever the income level of the child's family. Taken as a group, the studies reported in this book suggest that for scaffolding to happen in educationally productive literacy interaction at home and at school, it is not necessary to nail the child to the scaffold or make the scaffold only one shape and size. That is good educational news, if we heed it, for our teachers, our children, and our families.

Preface

A group of us sat in a circle, discussing a proposal for the 1987 meeting of the International Reading Association. Our Special Interest Group, Literacy Development in Young Children (LDYC), sponsors a symposium or pre-convention institute each year. To date, our sessions have focused on how children develop as readers and writers. What, we wondered, were the burning issues surrounding literacy development in young children? We discussed assessment, instruction, home/school connections, until someone asked a question that cut across all of our concerns: "Aren't all of these issues most crucial to the child who is at risk?"

There was immediate concurrence. As a group, we shared some basic assumptions about literacy learning. We believed that children are not inherently "at risk"; school systems put them at risk when they uniformly impose an inflexible curriculum and an invariable timetable for "success." We wanted to focus on reducing risks rather than the "at-risk child," a label that we felt shifted the responsibility unfairly, and unproductively. We had just listened to Denny Taylor describe the "contextual worlds of childhood," and believed that if we came to know children in their worlds, we would be better able to foster their literacy learning.

Based on these assumptions, the group charged JoBeth (the outgoing president of LDYC) and Jana (the new president) with putting together a symposium on "Effective Literacy Experiences for Young Children: Reducing the Risk Factors." We chaired the symposium in Los Angeles the following year (1987). David Dickinson shared his work with Catherine Snow on the relations between language and literacy skills; Claude Goldenberg talked about his research with Hispanic first graders who learned to read despite contrary teacher predictions; and Pat Edwards told us about her work with Head Start mothers who were committed to helping their children succeed in school.

In the process of putting together the symposium, we talked to people all over the country who were involved in and concerned about reducing the risks for young literacy learners. The idea for this book was born.

Nearly all the people we contacted agreed to share their work. Brad Mitchell suggested a dual focus, one that would speak to policy as well as practices. Philippa Stratton, our editor, offered enthusiasm and a contract. Everyone agreed to, and faithfully supported, an ambitious timetable for completion, because we felt the issues we were raising were crucial to the education of children; they couldn't afford our leisure.

We have divided the book into four sections: Learning with Children, Learning with Teachers, Learning with Families, and Literacy Learning for All Children. In the first chapter, JoBeth provides a framework for the book, using Bronfenbrenner's (1979) concept of a *macrosystem*—a multilevel, interactive "system of systems." This concept directs us to look at interaction among children, teachers, and families, among policy makers and those affected by policy. Therefore, our chapter division is based on primary focus (the learner, the educational environment, the home/school connection, and policy) rather than on single focus, recognizing the interaction within and among chapters.

In the three chapters in "Learning with Children," the authors provide detailed accounts of how individual children are learning. Jane Hansen describes Anna's literacy development across two years, emphasizing Anna's evaluation of her own growth. JoBeth Allen and Emily Carr profile James, a kindergarten child who learns how to ask for and respond to help from his peers during daily writing time. Claude Goldenberg shows us how Elena, Karen, and Freddy—Hispanic first graders identified by their teachers as being at risk for reading failure—in fact succeeded.

All of the children in Section I grew, at least in part, because of something their teachers did. In Section II, we look in more detail at teachers and classroom learning environments. Bob Delisle describes the Children's School in New York City. Miriam Martinez, Markay Cheyney, Connie McBroom, Ann Hemmeter, and Bill Teale describe the Kindergarten Emergent Literacy Project in San Antonio. David Dickinson describes implementation of a shared book reading program in a Head Start classroom, part of the Literacy/Curriculum Connection Project in Cambridge, Massachusetts. Gay Su Pinnell discusses the highly successful Reading Recovery Program in Ohio, a short-term first-grade intervention that she believes could be even more effective as part of a systemic approach to risk reduction. Finally, Chris McCormick and Jana Mason describe classroom book reading strategies that, coupled with providing books in the homes, effectively increased the first-grade reading achievement of Head Start children.

In Section III, "Learning with Families," authors focus on the home/school connection. Beverly McConnell describes the powerful effects of involving adults from Cheyenne Indian and Texas migrant communities in the classroom teaching of their children; in these communities, education was a cultural process. Pat Edwards worked with Head Start mothers in her Louisianna community, modeling and instructing them in the parent-child book interaction patterns identified with successful literacy development. Denny Taylor and Dorothy Strickland provide realistic strategies for educators to learn about family and community literacy, and to build upon that knowledge in constructing the literacy curriculum.

Authors in the first three sections have addressed policy issues specific to the practices and programs they describe. In the final section, "Learning for All Children," the authors focus on literacy policy as the only way of ensuring literacy development for all young learners. Valora Washington challenges educators to close the educational gaps between the races without losing sight of the cultural diversity represented by black and other minority groups. Brad Mitchell, drawing on practices and policies discussed in the other chapters, proposes a policy agenda for reducing the risks for young learners; the cornerstone of this agenda is school-based self study to learn about the needs of at-risk students in school, at home, and in the larger community. Marian Wright Edelman leaves us with a challenge to immediate action, ten steps we can take today to begin affecting the broad politics of education.

We invite you to adopt and adapt the practices described in this book, making them your own, molding them to the specific cultures, experiences, and needs of the children in your community. And we challenge you to begin talking, to share this book and other literature on reducing risks with parents, teachers, administrators, researchers, school board members, and legislators, who together must establish the policies that empower all literacy learners.

JOBETH ALLEN
JANA M. MASON

Chapter 1

Introduction: Risk Makers, Risk Takers, Risk Breakers

JoBeth Allen

Remember

by Alice Walker

Remember me?
I am the girl
with the dark skin
whose shoes are thin
I am the girl
with rotted teeth
I am the dark
rotten-toothed girl
with the wounded eye
and the melted ear.

I am the girl
holding their babies
cooking their meals
sweeping their yards
washing their clothes
Dark and rotting
and wounded, wounded.

I would give
to the human race
only hope.

I am the woman
with the blessed dark skin
I am the woman
with teeth repaired
I am the woman
with the healing eye
the ear that hears.

I am the woman: Dark,
repaired, healed
Listening to you.

I would give
to the human race
only hope.

I am the woman
offering two flowers
whose roots
are twin

Justice and Hope

Let us begin.

This is not a poem about two people, one dark and rotting and wounded, the other blessed and repaired and healed. Rather, it is a poem of two ways of seeing, of risk makers and risk takers. We can look at the woman and see her risks—her liabilities, her differences from the bright, healthy, advantaged world—and with subtle persistence, we can make her view herself through our eyes: we can label her "at risk." Or we can look at the woman and see the woman, can accept the flowers of justice and hope, transplanting them to our own life's work—we can take risks with her. We *can* reduce the risks. Let us begin.

A new way of seeing requires hindsight, insight, and foresight. In this chapter I will examine what we have learned from hindsight, especially from inquiries into the *risk makers* of our social and educational systems. Then I will share the insights of the various chapter authors on practices that reduce the risks for young learners; these authors and the people they describe—teachers, researchers, parents, and young learners themselves—are *risk takers*. As with the woman in Walker's poem, we have listened to the human race and proceeded with hope. Individually we are risk takers; collectively, we have recognized that although individual action is crucial, it is not sufficient. We must have foresight, must look beyond our own classrooms, our own schools, our own communities: we must become *risk breakers*. And as several chapter authors argue, breaking the complex pattern of social and educational factors that create risks for children must involve strong, thoughtful policies that address the child's entire ecological environment.

Bronfenbrenner (1979) describes this environment as a macrostructure with four levels, with an underlying belief system of ideology. Level 1 is the child's immediate, primary setting (home, school, etc.); Level 2 is the interaction between immediate settings; Level 3 involves settings beyond the child (e.g., parents' jobs); and Level 4 includes a wide range of developmental influences, such as war or national economic crisis, which produce subcultures. The literature, some of which I will review in the next section, is replete with examples of risk makers within each level: homes without books, classrooms without equity, homes and schools without communication, parents without jobs (or with jobs that leave no time for family), and subcultures without hope created by influences as wide-ranging as weather conditions on the migrant worker's route to drug wars in urban neighborhoods.

We must look at children within their macrostructures, and Bronfenbrenner signals one important place to look. Opportunities for human development (and thus risks for not developing, or underdeveloping) often occur with a change of primary, immediate setting. For young learners, this is usually when they go from spending most of the day at home to most of the day in an educational institution. This can be a time of development, the child's "evolving conception of the ecological environment, and his relation to it, as well as the ... growing capacity to discover, sustain, or alter its properties" (Bronfenbrenner, 1979, p. 10).

But for development to occur, there have to be supported opportunities for this self-in-environment examination. Bronfenbrenner further posits that "the direction and degree of psychological growth are governed by the extent to which opportunities to enter settings conducive to development in various domains are open or closed to the developing person" (p. 288). For the home/school transition, the opportunities must be present for social, academic, and emotional development. Thus it is during the transitional years that risks may begin to develop. If there is no connection between home and school systems, if there is not some mutual respect and understanding and a shared commitment to the individual child, she or he will be at risk of not becoming a confident, literate, contributing member of society. And such children place our society at risk (Pellicano, 1987).

The nature of these transitional risk-making situations, as Bronfenbrenner further explains, has to do with the match between how the child was developing at home and how that development is fostered in school.

> The developmental effect of a transition from one primary setting to another is a function of the match between the developmental trajectory generated in the old setting and the balance between challenge and support presented both by the new setting and its interconnections with the old. The nature of this balance [must take into account] the person's stage of development, physical health, and degree of integration with as opposed to alienation from the existing social order. (p. 288)

This proposition challenges us to gather information from many sources, as Taylor and Strickland suggest in their chapter, about the child's literacy development at home *as well as* to provide a smooth integration with the new social order, school. And we have to figure out how to do that with a balance between challenging children to be all they are capable of being and supporting them during the process of becoming.

By examining Bronfenbrenner's hypotheses through the lens of children whose developmental potential is not realized, we have a way of thinking about risk makers, risk takers, and risk breakers that transcends linear variables, and we have a crucial time period (the early home/school transitional years) where we have chosen to focus our work. We can think about systems (family, societal) interacting with systems (educational, political) within a macrostructure. Such contemplation is complex and confusing, like all real problems; it also offers hope of a new way of seeing, leading to a new way of doing.

RISK MAKERS

The chapters in this book focus on the insights of risk-taking practices and the foresight of risk-breaking policies. However, clear vision dictates hindsight as well, a sense of the history of the problems many young learners face today. That history includes others' attempts to identify and study risk makers, that is, factors that increase the likelihood that a child will "underachieve in school despite adequate intellectual endowment and, as a result, will underachieve as [an adult]" (Comer, 1987, p. 13).

Perhaps the largest collective step the United States has taken in reducing the risks for school children was desegregating the schools following the mandate of *Brown vs. Board of Education of Topeka* (1954). As part of the "crusade to improve urban education" (Boyer, 1987), equal education became a focal point for addressing unequal social conditions. When poor, minority children did not immediately thrive in their newly integrated schools, educators and policy makers instituted another wave of educational reform. Title 1 (now Chapter 1) funding provided compensatory reading and math instruction for school-age children; Head Start provided preschool enrichment opportunities designed to compensate for the nursery school and home experiences of middle-class students. Follow Through programs were designed a few years later to provide continuing support in kindergarten through grade three for children who had begun as Head Start students. P.L. 94–142 gave students with handicapping conditions access to "free, appropriate public education."

During this period of attention to increased educational equity, there was a concomitant interest among researchers in determining what factors increased the risks for children. Pellicano (1987) cites reports of a multitude of factors thus identified: "poverty, alcohol and drug consumption, sexual activity, school attendance, educational failure . . . race and ethnicity . . . the breakdown of the family; the unwillingness or inability of government and schools to meet their responsibilities toward children; the permissiveness of society's value system; . . . the absence of values in the nation's homes or schools; discipline, alienation, curriculum (both hidden and overt), skills and knowledge, technological literacy, or math and science competencies" (p. 47). While many people would argue that a focus on individual factors has been simplistic and unfruitful, we cannot deny that the cumulative literature on risk makers has contributed to our present understanding of the complexity of the problem. Let us explore some of the socio-educational risk makers.

Societal Factors

Socio-economic factors such as family income, parents' educational level, and parents' professions have been related to educational achievement; Washington's chapter (this volume) provides us with an insightful discussion of how the study of these factors has affected policy, especially for poor, black children. Bond (1981) points out that though there is "widespread agreement on the existence of a socio-economic status/academic achievement correlation, there is considerable controversy over the reasons for the correlation" (p. 239). He saw the reasons given by the educational field as falling into four basic categories. The first argument is that lower SES groups are genetically inferior; "the value of explanations based on this argument would appear to be slight," Bond concluded (p. 240). The second argument is that the home experiences of lower SES children are deficient due to the "culture of poverty"; children of poverty do not participate in the linguistic and cognitive experiences that lead to school success. Washington discusses, and dismisses, this argument in her chapter, but both she and Bond point out that most compensatory programs are based on this argument.

The third argument is that lower SES children "receive inferior treatment from the educational system" (Bond, p. 243). This treatment may be based on low teacher expectations for lower SES and minority children and/or on students' low expectations for their own chances of social and economic success in a racist society (Ogbu, 1978). The fourth argument recognizes the third, but places it in the context of "the educational system as a means of maintaining class differences" (p. 245). We will explore the third and fourth arguments more fully later in the next section. However, the gist of Bond's review and analysis of socioeconomic factors is that while researchers recognize SES as an "extremely important aspect" of educational success, we have not studied it with enough sophistication to make reliable interpretations or recommendations.

Perhaps, then, we should be looking at broader societal factors, ones affecting the very makeup of society, not so much as it is but as it is evolving. "Urbanization has reduced the extended family to a nuclear one with only [one or] two adults; and the functioning neighborhood ... has withered to a small circle of friends, most of them accessible only by car or telephone" (Bronfenbrenner, 1970, p. 97). Heath and McLaughlin (1987) concur; we are operating, they believe, on "outdated assumptions about the role of families. Dual career families, like single-parent families, have precious little time or energy to spend working as partners in their children's education" (p. 578). Regardless of parental income or education, children who do not have the opportunity to interact regularly with adults, especially around books and print, enter school with a different literacy set from the mainstream child (Heath, 1982; Mason & Allen, 1986).

Heath and McLaughlin's perspective that changing family dynamics contribute to educational risk means that some children well outside the low socio-economic parameters may be at risk. Elkind extends the concept of risk to children who may have "the best"—but too much of it, and too soon. "When we instruct children in academic subjects, or in swimming, gymnastics, or ballet, at too early an age, we miseducate them; we put them at risk for short-term stress and long-term personality damage for no useful purpose" (Elkind, 1987, p. 3). In a *New York Times* article, Friedman (1986) cites John Levy of the Jung Institute as identifying another afflic- tion—"affluenza"—family wealth that insulates children from "challenge, risk, and consequence." Friedman (1986) reports that psychologists believe that "in some ways the children of the urban rich most resemble the children of the urban poor. Both tend to suffer from broken homes and absentee parents. Both develop hard, streetwise skills that belie the gaping emotional holes within."

Educational Factors

Some educators choose to look within the school society for risk-making factors, assuming the school to be a more manageable and fruitful venue for change than the society as a whole. One inquiry, based on hearings in ten cities around the country held by a citizens Board of Inquiry, found many barriers within the educational system, including inflexible school structures (large classes, rigid scheduling), abuses of tracking and ability grouping, misuse of testing, narrow curriculum and teaching practices, lack of early childhood programs, little or no voice in governance by teachers or students, and lack of support services (National Coalition of Advocates for Students, 1985).

Recognition of such barriers leads us to look carefully at schools in hopes of pinpointing risk-making practices. For example, what happens when children signal us early in their schooling that they are not surviving the transition, that there is not the needed "balance between challenge and support" Bronfenbrenner called for? Of the many responses to their signals, including no response, we will examine two: retention and remedial services.

Administrators in Boulder Valley, Colorado, asked Shepard and Smith (1985) to study the effects of retention practices (including "developmental" and "transitional" kindergarten and first-grade classes) before implementation of a policy for district-wide testing and alternative placement for kindergarten children. They reviewed eight studies of "children who were identified as potential failures but whose parents refused retention" and found that most of them achieved the same or better than children who were retained, especially looking at achievement over time. They concluded, in capital letters, that "THE EXISTING RESEARCH DOES NOT SHOW EITHER ACADEMIC OR SOCIAL-EMOTIONAL BENEFIT FROM RETAINING IMMATURE CHILDREN" (p. 4). Their findings caused the district to stop using the Gesell test for placement and to reexamine retention practices.

But if we do not retain children who have not developed the same skills at the same rate as their peers, shouldn't we be providing them with compensatory instruction? Allington, et al. (1987) suggest that the answer to the question depends on the instruction. In an indepth study of remedial reading programs in six school districts, using multiple data sources including the shadowing of students, they found disheartening practices. Few remedial students got enough instructional time to overcome reading difficulties; some actually got less time than if they had not been in remedial reading programs. Students rarely read anything longer than a paragraph, nor were they asked to comprehend what they read. There was little coordination, or even communication, between the remedial and regular classroom teachers. There was little individualization of instruction. Remedial reading was characterized by "fragmented instruction and inconsistent curriculum."

The problems are more pervasive, and begin earlier, than a focus on retention and remedial issues would indicate. Rist (1973), following children in an all-black, urban school from their first day of kindergarten through the middle of second grade, observed that on the eighth day of kindergarten, the teacher placed children in a permanent seating arrangement, with what she described as her "fast learners" at Table 1 and those who had "no idea what was going on" at Tables 2 and 3. Her placements were determined solely on the basis of observation, a parent questionnaire about "deviant behaviors," welfare notations on the children's folders, and knowledge of the family (especially older siblings). Children at Table 1 were all well-dressed and clean, had better command of standard English, and were from families with incomes above poverty level—much like the teacher herself, and in contrast to children at the other two tables. Table 1 students received more of her time and instruction, her physical presence, and positive expectations. But the most shocking finding of Rist's inquiry was that the children remained in the same basic groupings throughout the study. Their status as learners was determined on their eighth day of school for at least the next three years, and probably throughout their school careers.

A decade later, Grant and Rothenberg (1986) explored in detail the effects of such ability grouping on first and second graders in blue-collar and white-collar communities. They found that teachers were more protective of the higher group's time, allowing fewer disruptions; that when they praised the low group, it was often qualified ("Very good—much better than yesterday"); that when they criticized the high group, it was often buffered ("I must not have explained that very well—you usually get these"); and that teachers formed warmer personal relationships with children in the high groups. The researchers concluded that "for most children in public schools, assignment to an elementary school reading group is a critical first step in an academic sorting process that channels some students toward success, some toward moderate levels of achievement, and some toward failure" (p. 29). Coupled with the sorting procedures Rist observed, these findings show that the school system, as a venue for change, cannot be divorced from the rest of the social system. There is, indeed, a macrostructure.

Interacting Factors

Many of the studies discussed thus far were designed, conducted, and interpreted based on a what's-wrong-with model of children, their homes, their communities, or their schools. As Bronfenbrenner (1979) says, "One begins with the individual, looking for signs of apathy, hyperactivity, learning disabilities, defense mechanisms. . . . If the source of the deficiency is not to be found within the child, it must lie with the parents" (p. 290). From the family, educators turned to social class or ethnic characteristics, because "there must be something wrong with somebody, and somebody usually turns out to be the person or group having the problem in the first place" (Bronfenbrenner, p. 290).

The educational community seems to be moving away from one-dimensional views of risk makers. Some children survive seemingly insurmountable conditions, including those cataloged above. We are learning that children do not always fit into categories, that all poor children do not have impoverished educational environments (e.g., Teale, 1986) any more than all rich children have enriched environments (Friedman, 1986). As Teale concluded, "Home background is a complex of economic, social, cultural, and even personal factors" (Teale, 1986, p. 193). Increasingly, societal conditions, existing within and across the community, the family, and the school (Comer, 1987) are seen as combining to create greater risks for some children. For example, Ogbu (1978) sees not just inferior school-ing for many of today's black children, but the *history* of inferior education for blacks as contributing to poor school performance. Gross factors such as de facto segregation and unequal funding and facilities (Children's Defense Fund, 1987) combine with subtle factors such as teacher attitudes and expectations (e.g., Rist, 1973; Spindler, 1987) to perpetuate social stratification, subordination, and exclusion of caste-like minorities in our educational system. These educational factors are compounded by and interrelated with societal factors such as job ceilings (Ogbu, 1978).

This progression from single factors to multiple factors to interacting factors is an indication of the increased sophistication with which educators are viewing risk makers; but it can leave us feeling overwhelmed and discouraged. What does this hindsight offer? It offers many places to start making a difference in children's lives, and it suggests a more sophisticated way of studying change. We are learning to focus on the child *within* a complex system, not to examine what is wrong, but what is right. In the next section we will examine risk takers, children and others within that complex system willing to take risks, to make changes. In moving from risk makers to risk takers, we explore literacy practices as they actually affect children within their socio-educational systems.

RISK TAKERS

Most of the authors in this volume participated in and/or studied edu-cational change from the vantage point of children, teachers, or parents who were risk takers. In many cases, changes (risk taking) by one person enabled changes by another, as one would expect in an interactive macro-system. The authors recognized the mutuality within the socio-educational system; all the chapters deal in some way with home/school connections. In examining these risk takers, we will first look at those who acted to address home/school relations directly; then we will look at school practices that have been informed by home practices.

Goldenberg studied several first-grade classrooms in a predominantly Hispanic school, focusing on nine children who had been identified by their kindergarten teachers as being at risk for reading failure (see Chapter 4). He observed many complex and interacting factors, but was struck by the rather profound effects of the teachers contacting parents about their children's school performance. This was not part of a systematic parent involvement program; rather, the contact was almost accidental in some cases, spurred by behavior problems or parent inquiry. Yet it prompted action by the parents that seemed to make the crucial difference for the children involved—they became successful readers. This confirms other research findings from studies of children who succeed in reading despite predictions that they will not (e.g., Durkin, 1984). As Chall and Snow (1988) concluded from their study of high-achieving, low-income children, "Across all the grades we studied, children made greater gains where their parents and teachers were in direct contact, regardless of whether the contacts were initiated by parents or by teachers" (p. 7).

Other researchers have been more intentional in their attempts to foster home/school relationships. McCormick and Mason (Chapter 8) supplied "little books" (simple picture books, written by the authors, and reproduced) to homes of Head Start children, so that the children could engage in home literacy experiences similar to their school experiences. The researchers also provided information for both teachers and parents to interact with children in developmentally appropriate ways as they participated in reading the little books with children.

The importance of the availability of books in children's homes is echoed by many of the authors in this volume. It is a component of the Kindergarten Emergent Literacy Program (Martinez et al., Chapter 6), Edwards' project with Head Start mothers (see Chapter 11), and the Literacy/Curriculum Connections Project discussed by Dickinson in Chapter 7. The availability of books for home as well as classroom use was an important component of Morrow's (1987) successful promotion of book involvement among inner-city children (including homeless children). These projects, and others like them, may address a finding by Blom, Jansen, and Allerup (1976), who studied factors related to reading achievement across twelve countries. They learned that the two countries with the lowest literacy rates—England and the United States—were the only two countries that did not give children their beginning reading books to keep.

Edwards was also intentional in her attempt to relate children's home and school experiences. As an advisor to a Head Start program, she responded to parental concern about the achievement lag of their children by working with several mothers on their book reading interactions. She devised a modeling/teaching program, similar to a successful home-based preschool literature program in Pennsylvania (Spewock, 1988), which encouraged parent-child interaction and provided books in the home. In her chapter, we see these mothers taking sometimes painful risks (exposing their own halting reading styles, their insecurities) so that their children might be more successful in school. Like the parents in Goldenberg's study, these parents, far from being disinterested, were hungry for knowledge about how they might help their children.

The parents with whom McConnell worked became even more in-volved, entering the schools themselves (see Chapter 10). Working in American Indian and Spanish-speaking migrant worker communities, McConnell involved parents and other adults in the communities as teacher aides in the local Follow Through programs. She concludes that such involvement minimizes cultural shock and language differences and in-creases early school success and identification with an educational model of one's own culture. Further, the employment of community members helped break the cycle of poverty and alienation from the educational system frequent in such communities.

Sometimes teachers contact parents in an attempt to draw them into the educational process. Sometimes parents intervene, as in the parent-initiated South Providence Tutorial center discussed in the final section of this chapter, where parents disturbed with their children's education took decisive action to connect home and school. These authors included in this volume have demonstrated that in spite of urbanization (Bronfenbrenner, 1970) and the changing role of families (Heath & McLaughlin, 1987), there are fruitful avenues open to educators and parents. Even marginally literate parents—perhaps especially marginally literate parents—have the desire to help their children learn to read and write, and given the oppor-tunity for meaningful partnerships, they *can* help.

Several chapters deal with school practices that, although not directly engaged in fostering home/school connections, are based on what we know about how children learn in facilitative home environments. Four chapters describe programs that have been founded on this knowledge: the Literacy/Curriculum Connections Project in a Cambridge, Massachusetts, Head Start (Dickinson), the Kindergarten Emergent Literacy Project in San Antonio (Martinez et al.), the Children's School Project in New York City (Delisle), and Reading Recovery in Columbus, Ohio (Pinnell).

Each author provides a rich description of how teachers are working to create supportive literacy environments. Dickinson describes the implemen-tation of a Shared Book Reading format, based on Holdaway's (1979) observations of how parents and children interact during home book read-ing. A similar kind of format is also a component of the McCormick and Mason study, Martinez et al., and Delisle. What we gain from Dickinson's study is consistent with the perspective that there are no simple answers. He discovered that while certain desirable literacy activities increased (e.g., interest in books, active interaction with book language), others (topical discussion) decreased. His perspective as a researcher on how the change actually affected children, as opposed to the assumption that it would be better, led to further changes.

Martinez and her fellow teacher/researchers also examined how their

program affected children. Through two case studies of high-risk kindergarteners, they provide insights into how an emergent literacy perspective
and curriculum can affect literacy learning. Further, through studying the
implementation of the program in different settings, they are able to offer
suggestions to teachers who have only students with limited literacy backgrounds, as well as to teachers who have students with a wider variety
of literacy backgrounds. Like Allen and Carr (Chapter 3) and Hansen
(Chapter 2), they found that when there was a mix of literacy proficiencies,
children learned successfully from each other from the very beginning of
school. This finding is consistent with Heath's (1982) recommendations
that the teacher draw on the linguistic and narrative strength of all children
in school settings.

As in all the programs, Delisle stresses the importance of appropriate
literacy instruction not only for the children but for the teachers as well.
The Children's School Project was seen as "facilitating the renewal of
teachers as well as their enculturation into new ways of viewing young
children and . . . themselves" (p. 91). Martinez et al. quote a teacher's
explanation of her positive involvement with KELP: "I can't stand to be
bored." When children become informants about their own literacy development (Harste, Woodward, & Burke, 1984), teachers are never bored
because they, like their students, are risk takers.

Reading Recovery also emphasizes teachers as informed risk takers. In
addition, Pinnell's chapter pushes the concept of literacy communities
beyond the Reading Recovery classroom. "We cannot afford to engage in
piecemeal efforts," Pinnell believes. She proposes an interactive, systemic
approach involving appropriate literacy instruction throughout the school,
book ownership, early intervention, long-term teacher inservice, and a
"policy climate that actively supports the development of literacy in young
children" (p. 196). More people need to take more risks.

The risk takers in the Allen and Carr and the Hansen chapters are
children, James and Anna (respectively). While quite different from each
other, these two children were both potentially at risk, according to their
teachers. However, both entered supportive literacy environments, with
teachers who were also risk takers. James' teacher, aware that most children
come to kindergarten having learned successfully from peers in unstructured
social settings, fostered the same kind of learning during writing time. She
rejected the standard kindergarten workbook curriculum and quiet classroom to create a learning environment where James could be a successful
learner.

Anna's teacher also fostered learning from peers, and in addition
rejected standard evaluation procedures in favor of encouraging self-
evaluation. As Hansen argues, it is especially important that children who
are experiencing difficulty learning to read and write be able to become

independent learners, to know what they need to learn and who can help them, and to "show proof that they are making progress" (p. 27).

How do the effective strategies and practices described throughout this book differ from compensatory programs, with their implicit assumptions of deficits? For the most part, the educators in these chapters are involved with innovation that is developmentally and educationally sound for all children. The authors have provided a rationale for these practices as being particularly beneficial to students who might otherwise risk being failed by the schools; but they are not suggesting that children be separated either by label or by instruction.

One striking feature of many of these practices that reduce the risks for young learners is their relative simplicity. Talk with parents about what they can do to help. Talk with other teachers about what the child could read easily the previous year (a very different question than what reading group she was in); then provide the same books in your room. Read books over and over. Provide an extensive classroom library, and time to read the books. Write and copy books for children to own. Send library books home—yes, even in kindergarten. Allow children to learn from each other. Ask them what they are learning. Involve them in literacy for genuine purposes and share your own love of reading and writing with them.

But don't be lulled into the complacency of simple solutions. As educators and researchers, we recognize what we have learned from hindsight, that complex problems ask questions of us that cannot be answered with one-dimensional practices, no matter how good they are, any more than children with complex problems can be "defined" by one-dimensional descriptors. Each chapter ends with policy implications, because the authors recognize that it is at the policy level where risks can be reduced most thoroughly and permanently, and for the most children.

RISK BREAKERS

We have looked within the macrosystems of children's worlds at risk makers and risk takers, factors that increase the risks and people who reduce them. Let us now return to the larger system of systems to ask what can be done beyond individual practices. Bronfenbrenner believes that "the macrosystem encompasses the blueprint of the ecological environment not only as it is but also *as it might become* if the present social order were altered" (1979, p. 291, emphasis added). To change the existing social order, he suggests that we "reject the deficit model [of human growth] in favor of research, policy, and practice committed to transforming experiments" (p. 291).

What might these transforming experiments look like? The whole concept of macrosystems suggests that such experiments go beyond individual classrooms, individual schools, individual practices. McConnell describes one such endeavor, Follow Through programs that began with an understanding of the cultures of its learners and proceeded to ease the home/school transition for children by making the school more like the home. They accomplished this in part by bringing in members of the child's community. Other attempts to have schools reflect home learning have also been highly successful, most notably the Kamehamaha Early Education Program for native Hawaiian children (Tharp et al., 1984). The element that increases the impact of McConnell's programs beyond the individual schools is that the involvement of parents also changed their lives. Many of the parent aides held regularly paying jobs for the first time through the program. Many became empowered to affect their children's education in real ways for the first time.

Such empowerment was instrumental in the founding of the South Providence Tutorial, where parents organized and founded a community learning center to help their children, as well as themselves. As Chall, Heron, and Hilferty (1987) point out, "solutions to the problem of adult literacy must also be tied to programs for the improvement of literacy among young people" (p. 196). The SPT center began with a few parents attempting to make Title 1 more responsive to children and their families. The SPT staff (mostly community members) works with adults and children in the collaborative identification of strengths and needs, goals, learning plans, and career and family needs. A major component of the center is to educate and support parents in their interactions with the schools.

Another program drawing on the collaborative strength of home/school relationships is the New Haven Project (Comer, 1987). There is an ongoing, intentional effort to learn from and share with parents information about each child's development (as opposed to "skills"). Other components of the program include children staying with the same teacher for two years, teachers who are trained and committed to working with disadvantaged students, more quality contact with many adults within the school, and more teachers from the same minority groups as the children. When the program was instituted in 1969, fourth-grade students in the two elementary schools ranked thirty-second and thirty-third in city-wide achievement comparisons. In 1986, the original project school (with the same SES makeup as in 1969) tied for third. In addition, students ranked about a year above grade level on the ITBS, and were among the best in the city for attendance.

The emphasis on strengthened home/school relationships is the central tenet of Taylor and Strickland's chapter. They state that "reading and writing instruction begins with the children that we teach ... the families of the children that we teach ... and the place in which the children that we teach live" (p. 264). There is a crucial shift in their recommendations from earlier parent involvement emphases: they argue that the school system must enter the family's and child's world, rather than just asking the family and child to enter the school world. We learn from children, families, and communities what they know and value about literacy, two crucial elements in becoming truly literate (Allen & Rubin, in press).

Taylor and Strickland go on to make wide-ranging recommendations for a "socially relevant academic curriculum" that supports and is supported by learners throughout their schooling. They echo Bronfenbrenner's (1970) concern: "Surely, the most needed innovation in the American classroom is the involvement of pupils in responsible tasks on behalf of others within the classroom, the school, the neighborhood, and the community" (p. 156). Again, Taylor and Strickland provide an interactive way of looking at school/community relationships. If it is profitable for members of the community to come into the schools (e.g., the Adopt-a-School program), it may be equally important that students reach out to the community. Such a perspective takes us from the "how to" of literacy to the "what for."

How can we create environments like those just described that break the risk cycle? How can we act upon our environments—social, familial, educational—as they act upon us (Vygotsky, 1978)? How do we move from the vision of a social order as it might be to creating that social order? All of the chapter authors have addressed these questions by discussing policy implications of the practices they feel should be part of a new socio-educational order. The final three chapters of the book focus on policy agendas for moving toward a new order.

Washington challenges educational policy makers to "maximize the cognitive and social skills of children in ways compatible with cultural diversity" (p. 294). Rather than perceiving an amorphous underclass of children at risk, she argues that we need to learn about and base instruction on what we know about the needs of poor, black children and other distinct groups who continue to be affected by socio-educational factors. Like Goldenberg, McConnell, and other chapter authors, she believes genuine involvement between parents and schools is one key avenue for reducing the risks for young learners.

How might we learn about the needs of children who may experience risk in their transition from home to school? Mitchell calls for a systematic, school-wide study to "identify the relationship between the school, its at-risk students, the students' homes, and the larger community" (p. 312). He feels that such study, combined with support for increased teacher professionalism and improved social network infrastructures, will reduce the risks for young learners. His recommendations are consistent with those from the Committee for Economic Development (1985), composed of business executives and educators. In their statement of research and policy, the committee identifies the targeting of high-risk groups, a developmental view of schooling, and well-designed, longitudinal research as educational imperatives for education, especially in the preschool and elementary years.

The final chapter is actually a call to action. Edelman's chapter is abstracted from *A Children's Defense Budget* for 1988 (Children's Defense Fund, 1987). The entire book is must reading for those interested in affecting policy at the legislative level. Edelman outlines ten steps that can be taken immediately to improve the quality of life and education for children. They are first steps in a long journey, but they are possible for all of us.

We guide you into *Risk Makers, Risk Takers, Risk Breakers: Reducing the Risks for Young Literacy Learners* with a challenge, one that many of us are trying to address. The first part of the challenge is to become a risk taker, to do something to reduce the risks for young learners, something based on the kinds of informed practices presented in the following chapters. The second part of the challenge is to study what you do, and to study it in all the complexity implied by our discussion of the child within a macrostructure. In their review of early education programs and policies, White and Buka (1987) stress that "we need a more 'ecologically valid' approach to research on early education—research that looks more directly at the life of the child in the [school] environment" (p. 75). As an example, they cite the Oxford Research Project, directed by Bruner, involving five foci of investigation (children, language, teachers, parents, and management practices). As in some of the chapters in this book, teachers and researchers worked together to establish the research agenda. From our expanded perspective of the child's world, we are learning that the ecology extends beyond the classroom; so must our research.

So as you read, ask yourself two questions: How might these practices benefit the children with whom I work? and How might I study if and how they are of benefit? The answer to the first will reduce the risks for some children immediately. The answer to the second will lead to policies that may one day reduce the risks for all children. Now, let us begin.

Learning with Children

Anna Evaluates Herself
Jane Hansen

IN December 1987 I said to Anna, "You've been in second grade for three months now. What have you learned about yourself as a reader?"

"I'm better," she said through her sideways smile.

"Prove it," I grinned, knowing she could.

"Listen." Anna took *Bread and Jam* by Josephine Wright from her reading folder and read:

> Bread is a kitten.
> Jam is a kitten, too.
> Bread and Jam are brothers.
>
> Mother Cat is going to the store.
> "Be good," she said
> to Bread and Jam.

Anna read the old (1947) paperback's fourteen pages perfectly. She had finally started on the road to becoming a reader, knew she was on her way, and knew how to prove her competence. In other words, Anna could evaluate herself and provide convincing evidence about her progress to others.

She is part of a research project on evaluation and is one of eight case study children in the project. These children's ability to evaluate themselves helps them to become better learners.

19

Even though Anna can now read, she has struggled, creating anxiety for her family, teachers, and most of all herself, as she tried to fit her reading, writing, and relationships with others into an overall situation within which she had some control.

ANNA'S READING

Anna started grade one three years ago but, at the end of September 1985, the school personnel decided to place her in readiness (a classroom in the school for children of grade-one age who are not ready for grade one) because her social skills were immature. Her family disapproved, but finally consented, thinking she would know how to read before she entered first grade.

Not only didn't this happen, but she didn't learn to read in the fall of grade one. In February 1987, her first-grade teacher referred her to Chapter 1. Anna's family (she lives with her aunt and uncle) didn't think this would help, since the readiness program hadn't helped, but they eventually consented.

In the fall of 1987, Anna started second grade and took the Gates McGinite test. Her scores qualified her for Chapter 1 help again. As before, her family said, "No." This time they stayed firm, and Anna does not receive outside help. She receives help, instead, from many children in her classroom at the Stratham Memorial elementary school in Stratham, New Hampshire, where eight of the faculty research their teaching in collaboration with seven doctoral students and faculty from the University of New Hampshire.[1]

Evaluation of reading and writing is the focus of the research, with my emphasis in this chapter being on Anna's evaluation of her own progress in both reading and writing. This focus on self is a new step in the world of evaluation, but one that's due (Brown, 1987; Hornsby, Sukarna, & Perry, 1986; Johnston, 1987). Educators have too long condoned passive students and competitive assessment that creates castes, poor self-concepts, and dishonesty. However, when children choose their own writing genre, writing topics, reading genre, and reading books, they pursue their own purposes and are aware of their own learning (Hansen, 1987).

Anna Tried to Create Meaning When She Read

Anna was monitoring her comprehension in first grade, as I discovered while listening to her read *City Mouse, Country Mouse*, a story from a basal, on March 5, 1987. She always interchanged *city* and *country*, but I never corrected her. This behavior on my part is something I've trained myself to do during this research project, where we are testing the notion of the child as evaluator. I wish I had been more aware of the importance of this years ago, because the effect of my never being the one to say, "Does that make sense?" places the responsibility for creating meaning on the child's shoulders, where it belongs.

Anna started to notice that something didn't make sense in her reading, but at first she didn't know what to do about it. She started to read *city* and *country* correctly, but always "corrected" herself (i.e., she "fixed" the correct rendition of *city* by changing it to *country* because that fit the story she had composed up to that point). Finally, she was confused enough to turn to me. "Which mouse in the picture is the city mouse?"

I told her.

She said, "No."

I explained.

Anna said, "My dad said that's *country*. He could be mixed up." From then on, Anna no longer confused the two mice. Anna had heard and read this story many times, and gradually, as with other early readers (Pappas & Brown, 1987), brought her text to approximate more closely the one in the book. Feedback from several of us helped her. When I was the person with her, I never gave her any words unless she turned to me. In other words, I didn't stop her to put my doubts into her efforts.

When we don't monitor children's word-by-word reading, they have to think constantly about meaning. They don't develop the habit of relying on us to say, "Does that make sense?" Their self-assessment provides the cornerstone of evaluation in a reading program and the instructional program rests on it (Reuning & Sulzby, 1985).

Anna Could Seek Help from Friends in the Midst of Books

The necessity of immediate help became critical as Anna continued to make minimal progress during the spring of grade one. Her teacher, Ms. Doten, had started to change the reading program to complement the writing program, where she based her instruction on what the children needed to know in order to write messages of their choice. Similarly, in reading, on some days each week she now based her teaching on what the children needed to know in order to read books of their choice. Some children quickly adapted to the new procedures, but not Anna. In an effort to make learning more accessible to Anna, Ms. Doten adapted her new procedures for reading class.

On March 24, she announced to the class, "When you are reading your books and come to a word you don't know, ask another child if the adults are busy." Previously, when a child met a word she wanted to know, she signed her name on the chalkboard under the heading: Hard Word

Conference. Ms. Doten and other adults who might be in the room went to those children as soon as they could, but while waiting, children like Anna became less involved with their books. However, on the very day of Ms. Doten's announcement, Anna started to read more.

This enthusiasm was short-lived, though, because Anna usually couldn't find a book to read.

Anna Learns to Choose Books

One day when I was in her room, she spent the entire reading period looking for a book. She started in the classroom library and ended up in the school library. Along the way, I asked, "Why is it hard to find a book?"

She gave me the answer I predicted: "Cuz most are too hard. Seems like they don't want me to read. I'd rather count to 100 than look for a book. I know how to count to 100." And she proceeded to do so!

Anna did learn to read a few books, but at the end of the year when Betty Batchelder, the school librarian who studies Anna with me, interviewed Anna she said, "I don't want to read."

Second grade started out on the same note. She had to choose the books she would learn to read from, and she swept her arm toward her classroom library: "Look at all these books. I can't read any of them." On October 8 she was still frustrated. She repeated the exact words of a month earlier when talking to Ms. Bennett, the intern in her classroom.

Then, on October 13, Anna started to see herself as a reader. When I stopped beside her desk, she had *Bug in a Jug* in her hands and said, "I can read it." This book was a new accomplishment, but it had taken her a long time to muster the nerve to pursue a new book.

During those first six weeks of school she had looked for, and finally found, the familiar books from grade one that she knew she could read. For example, on more than one occasion she sought help from Ms. Batchelder to find *Benjamin Bunny*, the first book she learned how to read. She had to start where she left off, on firm ground, then she could step out into unknown territory. She knew when it was time to move ahead.

This need of Anna's was something we had not predicted, but because we have learned from Anna, we can in the future help at-risk children by making sure they begin a new year surrounded by the books they can read.

On that day in October when Anna said she could read *Bug in a Jug*, I listened to her read it. Then at the top of a sheet of paper I wrote: "Books I Can Read Perfectly." Anna helped me make this list for her, thinking of six titles. I suggested she add to the list whenever she learned a new book. This list, coupled with the familiarity she now had with the books in the classroom library, opened the door. The wonderful world of books wasn't as overwhelming as it had been.

Anna had found her own entryway into the classroom library. Her breakthrough in reading rested, in part, on her own persistence. She is a problem solver. When she was in first grade I had watched her and Melinda build a house for Little Bear. Anna had four cutouts for the side of the house, stood them, and unsuccessfully tried to tape them. She couldn't hold them upright and manipulate the tape. As I observed, I wondered when she'd reach her frustration limit, but she never did. She simply said, "Oh, well. I have to do it another way." She put the pieces down on the carpet, taped them, and stood them as a square.

This determination to figure things out worked to Anna's advantage. She had to learn how to choose books or nothing else could happen. Her achievement also depended on the learning environment in her classroom and home.

ANNA'S SIGNIFICANT OTHERS

Much of Anna's interest on a given day depended on the current status of her relationship with her friends and family.

Anna's Family

As she explained to me on January 22, 1987, "I live with my aunt and uncle. Three people live in my house. Our hobby is roses."

Rhona, Anna's aunt, came to this country from Eastern Europe after World War II. She still does not feel comfortable in this country and never comes to the school. However, she baked delicious strudel for Anna's class this fall from apples they collected on their trip to an orchard.

Fred is Anna's other caretaker. He is a retired military man who spends much time on his roses. He brings some to Anna's classes, and each year, at his invitation, her class comes to their house to see these roses. For a celebration at school this fall, Fred brought fifty roses. He comes to school regularly, usually unannounced, and knows Anna's teachers well.

Fred loves Anna. She is his only child and he would like to adopt her. He believes in being strict and has Anna on a daily regimen. When she comes home from school, she has fifteen minutes to herself, then they do homework for a certain amount of time, then something else. The entire evening is scheduled. One of the things they do is read, he to her and she to him. She brings books from school and Fred has collected a shelf of old classics for her, which he proudly showed to Ms. Batchelder when she accepted his invitation to come with Anna's first-grade class to their house.

Our understanding of Anna's home helps us when we think about how to help her (Taylor, 1983).

Ms. Gagnon, Anna's second-grade teacher, knows that Fred is determined to help Anna learn how to read and has suggested ways for him to respond to her efforts in ways that are consistent with what happens in the classroom. The daily sessions between Anna and Fred come up frequently in Anna's school conversations, as do other home activities.

She sometimes feels excited, such as the day she told me about her new dog, and on other days she feels blue, such as when Rhona wouldn't let her have a birthday party. Because Anna spends her at-home time just with Rhona and Fred, she has developed few social skills to use with other children. Initially, however, she seemed to get along well.

Anna's First-Grade Friends

She volunteered to draw hearts for Melinda, got paper for Melinda when she needed it, stopped to visit with Melinda when she passed by her desk, and drew telephone poles like Melinda's. She walked around the classroom with her arm around Melinda and said to her one day during writing, "I never shared this with anyone, but I'll share with you."

Deana was her other friend. A book I was reading to Anna one day contained a part about special friends, and Anna said, "I love Deana, but one time she bit me and I was very upset."

Spats between Anna and her friends were commonplace but were usually minor and could be called expressions of honesty, she said what she thought. On January 22 when she and Melinda were drawing telephone poles, Anna said, "You don't have the right lines on your telephone pole." Melinda drew another, and Anna did also. Such open, supportive comments and behaviors typically bounce back and forth among young learners and contribute to their academic growth (Dyson, 1987). Frankness doesn't interfere with their work.

Anna expected this same kind of honest appraisal when adults examined her work. One day during handwriting the children were making rows of A's. They then circled their two best A's and the substitute teacher, who was walking among the children, stopped at each child to circle one she thought was good. At Anna, the teacher said, "They're all good. Perfect."

Anna said to me, "She did that with my numbers."

I didn't understand.

Anna explained. "She said that they were all good. They aren't. That one's not." She pointed to an A that floated above the line. As teachers, we often do what Anna's teacher did, thinking we are boosting a child's self-concept. However, we must be honest with children if we expect them to be honest with us.

Anna's Second-Grade Friends

The new classroom assignments at the end of grade one split Anna and her two friends. Anna started grade two with no one. This common practice in schools, to mix up children each year, placed Anna at a loss until late November when a new girl moved into the second-grade classroom next door and the two girls became friends.

By this time Anna could probably only have found a friend in another room because the other children in her class had turned against her. To me, Anna is a cute, charming little girl, but to the other second-grade girls her clothes are not as up-to-date as theirs and her social skills make her different. Whenever the class chooses children for an activity, Ms. Gagnon works skillfully on the sidelines, or "Anna would be the last one chosen." Ms. Gagnon often intervenes in Anna's favor.

One day Anna felt the power of Ms. Gagnon's support, after she had a wetting accident during standardized tests. While she went home to change clothes, Ms. Gagnon told the children not to tease her because the same thing had happened to her, years ago, when she was a child. Later, during recess, one of the children told Anna about Ms. Gagnon's accident. Anna was furious and said to Ms. Gagnon, "You talked to the children about me."

However, this was a turning point in Anna and Ms. Gagnon's relationship. Throughout the fall, Anna pitted Ms. Gagnon and her uncle against each other to get something she wanted. Now she knew Ms. Gagnon was on her side. Her relationship with her teacher could be a productive force, and they both knew it.

For months, Ms. Gagnon's number one goal in working with Anna had been to develop a relationship of trust. Finally, a bond developed. This confidence between them and Anna's new friendship may help her social security return. Coupled with her recent achievements in reading, these improved relationships may help her progress. Despite several problems, a positive note has been constant for Anna ever since her year in readiness.

ANNA'S WRITING

Anna Could Choose Topics

Anna has always felt good about herself as a writer. In June of 1987, when Ms. Batchelder asked for her end-of-the-year evaluation of herself as a writer, she said, "I always know what to write about. I like to write. I'm hoping to be an author."

Anna wrote every day throughout grade one and readiness, and chose what to write about. Like other at-risk children (Avery, 1987), the writing workshop's predictable structure, supportive environment, and choice of topics, gave her the chance she needed to feel good about herself. Even though she was pleased with herself in grade one, she felt better in grade two, as her next self-evaluation shows.

Anna Learned to Create Meaning

On the same day that she read the book I quoted at the beginning of this chapter, I asked her about her writing: "You've been in the second grade for three months now, what have you learned about yourself as a writer?"

"I can write better books than I could in the first grade, better because I put more grown-up words in my books and they make more sense, because a book I wrote last year, I have in my desk and it doesn't make much sense." She surprised me by pulling the book from her desk. This is the text:

The Changing Rainbows!!

page 1	The rainbow changed again!!
page 2	The rainbow changed again!!!
page 3	The rainbow changed again!!
page 4	I love rainbows.
page 5	I love changing rainbows.
page 6	I see another rainbow.

Anna explained. "That doesn't make much sense. The rainbow changes over and over again doesn't sound good."

She then read her latest published book, so I could hear the grown-up words and how they made sense. She read the first words of her book with a truly scary voice:

The Scary Pumpkin and the Scary Ghost and the Scary Cat

"Ohhh! Ohh!" the pumpkin said.
"Let's scare some more kids."
And the scary cat said, "I'm hungry."
And the scary ghost said, "I'm hungry too." And the rest of his family said the
   same.
The scary pumpkin took them all out to eat. They went to Pizza Hut.

Anna's growth as a writer is obvious; she does have a story. She introduces each of the three characters named in the title. First, the pumpkin wants to scare some more children. The cat, however, would rather eat. So would the ghost, who has a family that Anna drew across a double page in bright magic markers, with the mother ghost labeled "Anna" and the father ghost labeled "Fred." The pumpkin, outnumbered, drops the notion of going out to scare children and instead takes everyone to Pizza Hut, Anna's favorite eating place.

More important than *our* assessment of her growth is the fact that Anna can evaluate the comparative quality of pieces of writing. She is on her way toward putting together even more complex texts.

Her interactions with the other writers in her classroom help stretch what she does and knows about writing. Not only do her stories get better, but she learns particular skills, as she did when she wrote *The Changing Rainbows!!* in grade one.

That February when four children met with Ms. Doten at a table with drafts to edit, Anna showed her interest. When Frank read, Anna leaned forward to see his writing. She commented on the content of his draft, and later commented on his illustrations: "They look alive. Freckles all over." She was antsy, but even though she stood, sat, and walked around her chair, she kept her eyes on Frank's paper as Ms. Doten edited it with him. One of the edits was an exclamation mark. Ms. Doten turned to Anna, "Do you know when to use an exclamation mark?"

"There might be a couple of them in here," and she pointed to the draft she would soon share. There were no exclamation marks, but within a few minutes she had added the nine we saw!

Anna continued to write daily throughout grade one and grade two, and even though we adults often felt her stories were sparse, she continued to value herself as a writer. Our knowledge of her self-assessment kept us at bay, very careful not to shatter her confidence. She was growing, and we had to be careful to support her pace and direction.

POLICY ISSUES

The notion of placing children in the center of evaluation is new for most of us. For decades, we have been the ones who decided whether students were doing well, and we thought it was our responsibility, within daily lessons, to motivate children. This, however, may hurt rather than help children.

They may come to rely on us too much, and learned helplessness may set in. We know this often happens because we lament the lack of initiative in at-risk children. The task is to figure out how to move the initiative from our court into theirs. And one way to do that is to set high expectations for all children, especially those at risk. They must be able to show proof that they are making progress, and they must decide what they want to learn how to read (or write, or whatever the case may be). They must know when to ask for help, and must have help readily available to them—and usually, that help must not be us. Our policy supports independent learners.

Anna is still a high-risk child, but much of the risk has shifted from her shoulders to ours. She feels good enough about her learning to take the risks she needs in order to move ahead. We, now, must be very careful to maintain her motivation.

She has far to go to become a competent reader and writer, but she has learned much. In writing, she has "always" known how to choose writing topics and can now make qualitative judgments about her writing. In contrast, she has only begun to know how to choose books to read. I wonder when she'll compare the books others have written in the same way she contrasts the differences in the books she's written.

I wonder what she'll say in June when we ask, "Anna, you've finished second grade now. What have you learned about yourself as a reader?"

NOTE

[1]The eight people from Stratham Memorial School who participated in the Evaluation of Literacy project during 1987–88, the second of its three years, were: Donna Lee, Chip Nelson, Mary Ann Wessels, Nancy Herdecker, Chris Gaudet, Mike Quinn, Betty Batchelder, and Katy Kramer. The seven University of New Hampshire people were: Ann Vibert, Judy Fueyo, Peggy Murray, Mary-Ellen MacMillan, William Wansart, Donald Graves (on sabbatical), and myself. The project is funded by the University of New Hampshire, the School Advisory Unit of which Stratham is a member, and funds generated by the Writing Lab from sales of video tapes produced by Heinemann Educational Books.

In preparation of this manuscript, I reread all my field notes on Anna, recorded on 29 dates beginning in January 1987 and continuing into December 1987. Sometimes I had several pieces of information from one date. I placed the first piece of information on the computer, then the second, and then, for the third, I placed it with the first or second, if it was somehow similar. I tried this with each piece of information, looking for patterns. Initially, I thought I had lots of categories, but I combined similar patterns until four major groups of data emerged: information about things Anna knew, notes in which there was evidence that Anna didn't know something, interactions between Anna and her classmates, and notes about her home.

This exercise brought all my information on Anna to the front of my mind and to my fingertips. The story of her as a reader, writer, and social being emerged.

We saw how Anna grew as a reader and writer because she learned within a community of readers and writers. In Chapter 3 we will meet James, who is also a member of a literacy community, a kindergarten writing group. The children in this group learn collaboratively about the power and peculiarities of writing. We will take a closer look at how James begins to ask his peers for help and to learn from them without sacrificing his concept of himself as a capable learner.

Collaborative Learning Among Kindergarten Writers: James Learns How to Learn at School

JoBeth Allen and Emily Carr

"How you make that house?" James asks Ivan. Rather than waiting for a response, James draws a large three-sided figure. Monica looks up from her writing and comments, "It's supposed to be a square." "I know," he shouts in disgust. "Ga-a! I'm making a spaceship that go up. Ga!" he scowls, verbally rejecting her unsolicited teaching. In fact, however, he accepts the content of her teaching: he draws a four-sided figure on another piece of paper.

Later, he is all charm as he woos Monica to his side and asks her help.

Monica: Okay, I'll help you now, what you want to spell?

James: Help me draw this.

Monica: Draw what—a house? Okay, I'll help you.

[*They work together for some time, discussing their own homes, basements, and stairs.*]

James: Now help me spell this—Monica, Monica, Monica.

Monica: Okay, what?

James: Spell spaceship. [*He poises his pencil under the first drawing.*]

Monica: Spaceship—sp—sp—"s" [*James writes an "s"*] spaceship—sh—sh—"h"

James: sh—sh—sh— [*laughs*] How you make a "h"?

Monica: I'll make it for you—with a monkey tail ... like that. [*Monica writes a D'Nealian "h."*]

James: What else?

Monica: Space—spa—"a."

James: "a" [*He writes an "a."*] Wait—what else, Monica?

Monica: Let's see—"o"—"o"—"o"—I'll make you a "o."

James: I'll make a "o" [*He begins to write, then stops.*] Wait—make me a "o." [*She does.*] Ship—ship—sh—ip.

Monica: "P"—make a good "p" now.

James: "D"? Duh—duh—"d."

Monica: No, spa—a—ace.

James: What else?

Monica [*Thoughtfully, with great exaggeration*]: Sp—a—ce—sh—ip. "O"—it needs another "o."

James [*Writes an "o."*]: Space sh—sh—ship.

Monica: That's all.

[*James then moves on to the picture Monica helped him with.*]

James: House—house—"s." [*James writes an "s."*]

Monica: It doesn't start with a "s."

James: House—hu—hu—house.

Monica: It starts with a "h." James, my little young boy, it starts with hu—hu—"h." [*James erases the "s" and writes an "h." They proceed in a similar fashion.*]

James is learning important aspects of creating a text, of refining his drawing, matching picture and print, and matching sound and letter. It may be less obvious that he is also learning how to learn. This teaching/learning episode near the end of March shows how Monica, James, and the other children in this kindergarten taught and learned from each other. Monica is learning that although her unsolicited teaching is usually rejected by James, he accepts help quite readily when he is the one initiating the teaching/learning sequence. James is learning that he can help determine the kind and amount of assistance he receives from his teachers—both peer and adult. Throughout this teaching/learning episode there is a constant negotiation of appropriate levels of help. These levels range from Monica's writing letters for James, telling him what letters to write, drawing the word out so he can hear sounds, giving feedback that puts the ball back in his court ("It doesn't start with 's'"), to providing a letter when he has isolated the sound (the "p" in ship). When James ventures even more independence and guesses "d," Monica simply sounds the word out again for him, giving him another opportunity to provide his own letter.

Through the analysis of 106 teaching/learning episodes like this one, we began to answer some of the questions that prompted our inquiry, questions about children's language and learning, and questions about children like James who are often at risk of not being educated in our public schools. Emily and JoBeth had been talking for several months about literacy development in kindergarten, Emily from her current perspective as kindergarten teacher at Lumpkin Elementary school and JoBeth from her perspective as a researcher in kindergarten classrooms. Emily invited JoBeth to observe her students during writing time. One casual observation resulted in five months (January through May, 1987) of collaborative research, with JoBeth serving as a participant observer with a group of five children during writing time three days a week, and Emily a constant observer/teacher of the whole class.

We had many questions about literacy development in kindergarten going into the study, but the one that seemed to demand our attention in our regular discussions of the writing group transcripts was, "How do children teach and learn from each other?" We were familiar with numerous reports of children teaching each other from those who research writing development (Calkins, 1983, 1986; Dyson, 1987; Graves, 1983). We observed that our children worked together, and we supposed that that work enhanced their writing and reading development. But like Dyson (1987), we supposed that much of the teaching/learning was unintentional. However, we began to notice very intentional requests and corresponding responses as the children wrote, talked, and read together. We were amazed at the amount and quality of direct instruction children provided each other and at their awareness of their roles as teachers and learners.

In order to share what we learned in the course of our research, we will first depict the learning environment in Emily's kindergarten and then describe in general how children changed as teachers and learners as they interacted with each other. Next we will provide a profile of how James, a child at risk for not learning at school, learned how to learn from his classmates. Finally, we will discuss two policy issues that influenced the kind of environment Emily was able to establish.

A COLLABORATIVE LEARNING ENVIRONMENT

Emily structured her classroom and curriculum to enable children to learn from each other. Of her twenty-one students, twelve were black and nine were Anglo. About half of the children received free or reduced-price lunches. Some of the students, like Monica, came from mainstream socio-economic/educational backgrounds that included extensive opportunities for talking, reading, and writing interactions with adults and other children. Others, like James, had not had similar literacy and language experiences. Such children are often at risk in an educational system geared primarily to children like Monica.

Writing time was part of the classroom structure Emily designed to reduce the risk factors for students like James. During writing time there were frequent opportunities to (1) develop and expand literacy and language skills in a way that builds on children's previous knowledge, regardless of the sophistication of that knowledge, through planning, sharing, talking about, and engaging in personal writing (Allen, 1989); (2) engage in "a lot of talk about nothing," even when this talk does not focus in an obvious way on the task at hand, because as Heath learned from her research in similar communities and classrooms, with these opportunities "children from homes and communities whose uses of language do not match those of the school *can* achieve academic success" (Heath, 1987, p. 48); (3) collaborate as learners in stable groups, where children have an opportunity to learn who can help them, how to ask for help, and how to offer help.

Learning with and from other children extends the way many children have learned language and social skills prior to entering school (Heath, 1983), especially in families where the parents do not have the time or inclination for the informal teaching of language common in mainstream homes (Thomas, 1985; Wells, 1981). Writing was one of many times during the day that was designed to help children make the connection between their school learning and their learning prior to and outside of kindergarten.

During the time of the study, January through May, 1987, the children managed the routine of writing time with confidence. When Emily announced writing time, the children came to their assigned, masking-taped spots in a circle on the floor. There they would listen and talk with Emily for five to ten minutes about some aspect of writing. Emily frequently drew a picture and wrote her own stories on a large chart, with the children helping her invent the spellings. They discussed such issues as what to do when you can't draw what you want to write about, strategies that might help you read your own story more easily, and options when you are tired of writing just books.

After this lesson, the children went immediately to one of four writing tables around the room. Emily had assigned them to writing groups so that each group represented a range of abilities, interests, and personalities. The children worked at their respective tables, but could move around the room to look for supplies, copy a word from various sources, or read to someone at a different table.

Most children began composing immediately, some with drawings, others with various forms of print and print-like forms. Some, like Monica, provided a running commentary, addressed to no one and generally ignored by the others, of their plans and actions. Others wrote silently; Latoya usually laid head on arm and proceeded quietly to compose. Still others, and James was most often in this category, immediately engaged others in conversation about what they should write, how many pieces of paper they could take, or how many staples they could put in one book. James was the self-appointed monitor of writing procedures.

During this time Emily had several roles. She and Sharon, the instructional assistant, were available to children for informal conferences if they needed help or wanted to read their new stories to an adult. On some days, Sharon and Emily each sat at different writing tables to get an idea about how individual groups were functioning and to provide advice as needed. Toward the end of the year, Emily introduced more formal teacher/student conferences, and both solicited and responded to requests for these individual writing conferences.

JoBeth's role was to tape record and take notes on the group interaction during writing time. She concentrated on one of three focal children (James, Latoya, or Monica) each day. Sometimes she would ask questions, request that a child read something to her, or respond to a direct request for assistance; usually she just took observational notes. The children never questioned her role, and after the first day's explanation, were reminding her to turn her tape recorder on, or suggesting that a peer who had finished a story "read it to Dr. Allen."

All of the adults followed the same basic philosophy of assistance: help the children help themselves. Our most common response to a request for help was to ask a teaching question (e.g., "What sound do you hear?" or "What do you remember about the play?") or to redirect the question with a teaching statement (e.g., "Monica knows how to spell 'the'—she can help you" or "Like—l—l—ike.")

After the children finished writing each day, they had several options. They could have a conference with Emily, read their story to a peer, read a library book to themselves, or read a library book to a peer, or an adult if one was available. At Emily's signal for cleanup, everyone returned to the writing table to straighten pencils and crayons, put writing folders away, and clean up any scraps of paper on the table or floor.

Sharing time was next. Some days, the children returned to the whole-class circle to listen to four or five classmates read their compositions and respond to comments and questions from the group. The children actively vied for the honor of being the first in the Author's Chair (Graves & Hansen, 1983). James did more than vie for it; he just sat in it, announcing he was sharing first, even when he knew his chances were slim. On other days, children remained at their writing table to share. James, as well as the others, liked this procedure better because everyone got to share.

Emily structured a collaborative learning environment by her physical arrangement of the room, the elements she included during writing time, and the expectation that children would learn from each other. She facilitated collaborative learning by encouraging the children to go to each other for information and assistance. She believed that children learned well from their peers, especially children like James who had previously learned as part of a community of child learners, communities built in daycare centers and on neighborhood porches (Heath, 1983).

In the next section, we will examine the nature of the collaborative learning enabled by Emily's structure, and how these kindergarten children changed as teachers and learners.

TEACHING/LEARNING DEVELOPMENT

In order to learn how the children taught and learned from each other, we analyzed transcripts from twenty-one writing sessions (January–April), written products (September–June), and interview protocols. JoBeth interviewed the children in May about how they were learning to read and write, who they were helping learn, and who was helping them learn.

The broad categories that emerged early in the data collection period were requesting, teaching, and learning moves. Throughout the study, we elaborated and refined these categories by comparison with new data. The teaching/learning episodes we analyzed were only the ones that transpired during the composing part of writing time; mini-lesson and sharing interactions are not included. We tabulated frequencies of individual moves; more importantly, we looked at moves in relation to each other within sequences to determine teaching/learning patterns. After describing interactional patterns, we compared them with adult/child interactions, and looked at the patterns over time. Our main question concerned how the children developed as teachers and learners.

Teaching/Learning Episodes

We defined instructional episodes as occurring when a child asked for help (a requesting move) or spontaneously offered help (a teaching move). There were 106 instructional episodes, 66 involving children only (like the portion of an episode between James and Monica we related at the beginning of the chapter). Requests for help were usually followed by help in the form of teaching, informing, or confirming; such help, along with spontaneously offered help, constituted teaching moves. We followed the episode as long as two or more children were talking about the initial request or offer, so we could develop a sense of how long episodes were, what responses children were likely to give when certain requests or offers were made, and what written and verbal action might be taken (learning moves).

Requesting moves were the initiating event for most (67 percent) of the instructional episodes. These included direct requests for help (48 percent), such as "How do you spell 'coach'"; implied or perceived requests (16 percent), such as "I don't know what to draw"; requests for information (25 percent), such as "Do you like heart balloons or star balloons?"; requests for confirmation (11 percent), such as "What's this, 'O S'?"

Teaching moves were used most often in response to requests. These moves included telling ("It starts with 'H'"), demonstrating ("I'll make you an 'R'"), and confirming (usually brief, affirmative statements). In a very few instances, children did not confirm (2 percent) or refused to help (5 percent) because they couldn't ("I don't know. I forgot it 'cause I wrote it yesterday") or wouldn't ("I ain't gonna help you").

Sometimes, teaching moves initiated instructional episodes (33 percent). Most initial teaching moves were unsolicited teaching ("A leaf doesn't look like that. A leaf looks like this"). Occasionally, episodes were initiated with a teaching question or statement, as when Kevin wanted Latoya to read what he had written, even though he could read it himself. "What this say, Latoya?" was his teaching question; and later in the sequence he used a teaching statement to prompt, "W-w-world."

Learning moves were the child's response to a teaching move. Learning moves might be positive (41 percent) or negative (31 percent). In other instances, children seemed to ignore the teaching (7 percent) or made a request (21 percent). We should note here that in some cases where children rejected or seemed to ignore teaching, they later incorporated the knowledge, as James did when he made a four-sided house after rejecting Monica's initial (unsolicited) teaching. Positive responses included action (James copied a 'D' on his paper after Kevin showed him how to make one) and accepting statements. James accepted Monica's teaching statement that "[House] doesn't start with a 's'" by emphasizing the beginning of the word as he sounded "House—hu—hu—house." Negative responses were almost always verbal, as when James rejected Monica's unsolicited teaching: "I ain't lookin' at your picture, ... 'cause I don't wanna make no 'E'—E—E—E—E—E!"

Development

Children became better teachers, as well as better learners, over time. We believe they became better teachers in part by emulating the adult models, and in part by the way their peers responded to and thus shaped their teaching moves.

The adult teachers responded to requesting moves with teaching questions or statements twice as frequently as they did with direct teaching. Child teachers responded to peer requesting moves with direct teaching 76 percent of the time. We can see this contrast in the following episode:

Monica [*leafing through* Places to Know *childcraft*]: I'm trying to find the world.

Ivan [*perceiving this as a request for help*]: It's at the end of the pages.

Monica [*rejecting his teaching*]: Uh-uh. Where is the world? ... I'm gonna find the world because I'm gonna copy it. Look at this—this is Egypt! I wonder where the world is—I had it yesterday.

JoBeth: Do you know how to use the index?

By the end of the year, we were beginning to see children using teaching questions and statements, especially when helping each other sound out words. One example of this is in the opening sequence of the chapter, where Monica gives James the letters he needs early in their interaction; by the end of the interaction she is elongating the pronunciation to help James hear the sounds for himself.

Another example shows the power of adult modeling. In Emily's classroom, the children dictate stories as well as write their own. When children have difficulty reading their stories, the adult often reads the story first. James shows his awareness of this procedure in the following exchange, which begins when James presents JoBeth with a story:

JoBeth: Are you going to read it for me?

James: You read it first—I don't know what it says. [*JoBeth reads.*]

James: That's a *good* story. Want me to read it? [*He retells the story.*]

Later that same writing period, James selects a book by his classmate Margaret from the library corner. He orally composes a story to go with her pictures, "reads" it several times, and is quite pleased with himself. JoBeth suggests that he go get Margaret, then asks her if she'd like to read her book.

Margaret: I can't read that.

James: I can! Want me to read it first? I read it, then you can. "The snowman. The snowman melt. Margaret built a snowman and the snowman pop the ground and bust." Now you read!

Margaret: "The snowman. I went outside and built a snowman. When I
built a snowman, I gave him a carrot nose, and rock eyes and some
buttons down his shirt. . . . I went outside and I kissed Frosty goodbye
because I knew he was going to melt. But he melted right after I kissed
him. The end."

From James' skeletal retelling of her story, Margaret was able to tell an
elaborate, well-developed narrative (much more complex than the one she
actually wrote). Neither child seemed bothered by the discrepancies between
their versions. Rather, they adopted the adult/child interaction strategy
modeled frequently for them so that both children experienced success
with Margaret's text. Further, James was a successful teacher, reconnecting
Margaret with her text.

The frequency as well as the length of episodes involving only children
(without adults) increased over time. All but one of the sequences initiated
by a child requesting help of a peer occurred in the second half of the
study. While requests of adults for help remained fairly constant throughout,
requests of peers outnumbered requests of adults two to one by the last
half of the study.

The average length of the peer episodes also increased. In the first
third of the observations, the average number of moves per episode was
2.6; in the final third of the observations, the average was 6.9 moves per
episode. It appears that this increase was due at least in part to child
teachers asking for clarifying information and asking teaching questions or
making teaching statements within episodes; and to learners requesting
additional help and/or confirmation, requests that were seldom ignored,
and thus were useful in extending episodes.

Another area in which teaching/learning episodes seemed to become
more productive over time was unsolicited teaching. Unsolicited teaching
was often emphatically rejected (as in James "I don't wanna make no
'E'—E—E—E—E!"). James especially perceived unsolicited teaching as
insulting, and in this case even accused Monica of making fun of him
because he did not know how to make an "E." Toward the end of the year,
the child teachers began to use their increasingly sophisticated teaching
strategies to extend a sequence initiated by their unsolicited teaching.

We have shown our perceptions and interpretations of how the children
developed as teachers and learners in a collaborative learning environment.
In the next section, we will examine the children's perceptions of themselves
as teachers and learners.

SELF-PERCEPTIONS AS TEACHERS AND LEARNERS

When JoBeth interviewed the children, almost all of them identified other children when asked who was helping them learn to read and learn to write. They also recognized that they helped other children in the class, and their identification of whom they helped tended to correlate with our perceptions. Both Monica and Latoya said they helped James. He agreed, but was quick to add that he also helped them, an assertion they both initially denied in an interactive interview where all three were present. Monica eventually softened and said that James had helped her, but Latoya was steadfastly negative. And indeed, when we reviewed the transcripts, we did not find any instances of James helping Latoya.

The children were also able to verbalize to some extent the nature of the teaching and learning among them, as we can see from the following splicing of several interview transcripts:

JoBeth: Who do you help learn to write?

Monica: James.

JoBeth: And how do you help James?

Monica: I don't know.

JoBeth: What kind of things do you help James with?

Monica: What he's gonna write about. He says what he wants to write and then I sound the word out and then he says thank you.

* * *

JoBeth: Do other children help you [write]?

James: Yeh, they'll help in the other group—they listen to the sound, they do like "s-s." They say the sound and I be listenin' to the sound and I figure out what letter.

For these children, literacy learning is a social activity. In addition to specific literacy skills, they are learning to "do school"—how to use materials, seek information, and use language during and about their activities (Dyson, 1984). Such learning may be most crucial to children who have not had school-like literacy experiences prior to formal schooling, children who are unsuccessful in school almost from the beginning (Heath, 1983). We have constructed a profile of one such learner, James, by examining sequentially every teaching/learning episode in which he participated, identifying his teaching and learning roles, and mapping this against his literacy development. We charted literacy development through James' written products from September through May, including dictations, and through his readings of these products.

JAMES: LEARNING TO LEARN

As a black male in Georgia, James is statistically at high risk for being retained and eventually dropping out before completing high school. His socio-economic and educational background increases the risk that the language and learning competency he brings to school will not match the school's expectations. He lives with his mother and two older sisters in a public housing project about a mile from the school. His mother is unemployed; she and Emily established their relationship when Emily taught James' oldest sister for two years in second grade. At a prekindergarten screening, Ms. Hamm explained that James could be "a handful." Because the Hamms did not have a phone or a car, Emily and Ms. Hamm exchanged notes throughout the year to discuss James' progress and behavior. Both were proud of his progress and frustrated with his behavior.

James' behavior also put him at risk in a school system that values respectful compliance. JoBeth and Emily read a familiar story on his face, especially in his eyes, and hoped that the ending would be different from the one they had come to expect. The easy, contagious grin that showed James' delight in the world and in himself often turned to an angry scowl when he felt threatened or belittled. His eyes sparkled when he knew he was being outrageous or pushing a situation to its limit, a habit he pursued with adults and children alike. But the sparkle could become a fire of volatile anger when challenged.

James had no trouble learning the rules and routines at school. He was very vocal in explaining, at times demanding, the school expectations for adult and child behavior. However, he had trouble shaping his exuberance and desire for attention to conform to the expected norms. His inability to control his behavior led to frequent clashes with teachers throughout the building. Emily kept him near an adult when possible so he could get some of the attention he needed as well as the extra support to keep his behavior in line. We all struggled to help James gain control of his behavior without sacrificing his joyous spirit.

Part of James' difficult adjustment to school expectations may have been because kindergarten was his first organized learning experience. He spent his preschool years playing with other children in the project and watching television. At the beginning of school he was unable to write his name. Although he could recognize only three letters, his math skills and concepts were more developed. He loved listening to stories at school and quickly joined in the refrains of patterned books. He especially enjoyed sharing familiar books, an option he often chose after composing. His book retellings were usually well organized, close to the meaning of the actual print, and often contained elements of the literary style and language of the text.

James developed as a writer in diverse and dramatic ways. His first writing piece was a large head with two legs, with several mock letters and the dictated message, "I was looking at a ghost and I had ranned." He soon was using letters from his name (which his sisters had taught him to write at home, on Emily's request), "reading" from his letter strings, and dictating longer stories. By the time the study began, he was doing some teacher-assisted invented spelling (BC for Pacman, PT for peanut) and attempting to copy letters and occasional words from print around the room. In February, James demonstrated his awareness that what he had written could be read when he explained to JoBeth, "You see how I write Gingerbread man up here?" as he pointed to his text: toragggggann.

His dictated stories continued to show development through the incorporation of narrative devices, coherent story lines, and third-person perspective by the end of the year. A story in February shows some of this development, as well as James' perception of himself:

> This is a table rolling down the street. It got a phone on it. And it got a little tinsy-winsy TV on it. It's rolling down the street. It go crash. It going to crash and crash and crash 'til it get tore up. And I grabbed the little TV out and I bust through and I stopped the table. And that's the end.

March brought an explosion of writing development. James carefully copied parts of the daily story and read it successfully one day. Soon after, he accurately verbalized the names of letters as he wrote a letter string. He made his first attempt at independent invented spelling, "S is M" for "This is me." He began revising his writing by erasing and changing letters. By the end of the year, he was using three-word labels (DRACKR for "the race car"), attempting longer sentences, and once even produced a partially connected story across pages.

James' enthusiasm for writing was always high. He went to his table immediately when writing time was announced, and seemed excited about expressing himself on paper. He usually wrote and drew rapidly, with little attention to detail in his pictures. His style changed, however, when he began copying from the daily story, a lengthy, tedious process that did not seem to frustrate him, and when he was sounding words out, especially if someone was helping him. While he was rather single-minded during these activities, at other times it was rare for a conversation to go on in the group without input from James.

Other than his frequent attempts to monitor other people's behavior, James did not operate as a teacher in his writing group. Perhaps because his writing forms were less sophisticated than forms used by other members in the group, the other children did not request his help often. He did not present himself as a teacher by offering unsolicited teaching as Monica and Latoya did. As the guardian of his own ego, he may not have felt competent to teach others about writing. He did not hesitate to teach when he felt confident, as when he offered to demonstrate karate to Ivan (Emily said NO!) or to provide information about who was "going with" whom, or to assert, with that characteristic gleam in his eye, that ET was not from outer space but in fact lived in South Carolina. The few times he did offer academic help were in situations where he was competent: he helped Monica spell his name twice and offered Margaret help in reading her story after he had experienced success reading it to JoBeth.

James' real growth was as a learner. At the beginning of the study he rarely requested help from adults or children, and he rejected all unsolicited teaching. He hated feeling that anyone was laughing at him, even though he teased and laughed at the others regularly. A typical response to unsolicited teaching was "I'm gonna tell. You pickin at me." A pattern he developed was initially to reject help from a child who offered it, but to ask another child later for the same help, or to incorporate the idea quietly, as if it were his own. Over time, James began to return to the person who offered help and request what he had previously rejected. But it had to be on his terms.

In March, at the same time his writing development exploded, James began requesting help from his peers. Consistent with his need to control situations, he learned how to set up the teaching/learning episode. At the beginning of writing time one day, he announced, "I want to sit beside you, Latoya, 'cause I want you to help me spell something." A few minutes later, he even accepted unsolicited teaching from Latoya related to his spelling. However, soon after that he emphatically rejected her attempt to help him orally compose his story.

For the rest of the study, James used requests to initiate teaching/ learning episodes and to extend episodes. His success at sustaining a teaching/learning relationship with his peers is seen in the increase of the mean number of moves in an episode. There was an average of 5.2 moves in his first seven observations, and 9.9 moves in his last seven observations. The difference may be at least partially accounted for by James' increased use of requests within the sequences. He used none at the beginning of the study (Observations 1−7) and eighteen in the last seven observations.

James' literacy development as well as his development as a learner would not have been as apparent in a classroom where children were not encouraged to learn collaboratively in a literate environment. By the end of the year, James had a wide variety of teachers to choose from. What would have happened to him if he had had only one? What would have happened if he had had a teacher who felt James had to learn to behave before he could learn anything else? Who asked James to sit quietly in a group, turn to the correct page, make the x by the picture that started like "h-h-house"?

Who felt James must form his letters correctly and read at least a few sight words before he could learn to write?

Emily admits that in previous years she was just such a teacher. "If James had been in my classroom another year, his literacy experiences would have been very different. He would not have had the same opportunities to learn from his peers, and I would not have realized how much James knew and was capable of learning. I would have been focusing on his behavior and his ability to work in the phonics workbook. Now I believe that children like James cannot afford to wait until they learn to behave before they learn to read and write."

At the required end-of-year assessment, James was able to identify many letters and a few letter sounds in isolation. He was beginning to get his behavior under control; during the last observation, as things began to get a bit wild at the table, James muttered, "I gotta get out of this place" and left to write by himself on the floor. Due to the variety of learning situations Emily had provided, James was learning how to learn in the large group, in his small group, and even by himself.

We have examined James as a learner, a child who is becoming literate and learning to "do school" (Dyson, 1984). He seems to be less defensive, recognizing that everyone is a teacher *and* a learner. James is learning how to request help, how to sustain a teaching/learning episode, and how to structure his own learning, making use of the people and print in his environment. We believe James' growth occurred because of the environment that Emily created during writing time, which allowed him to build on and expand his language and literacy knowledge among peers who were willing and capable collaborators.

In the final section, we examine policies that often prevent teachers from establishing such environments and children from forming collaborative learning communities.

POLICY ISSUES

Two policy issues are particularly germane to the recommendations we make for the kind of collaboration we have discussed. One is a building-level policy, and might be called the quiet classroom policy. The other is a district-level policy issue and concerns the increasing pressure in our country to "put children through" the reading readiness workbooks and instructional sequences, as well as the preprimers, in kindergarten.

The quiet classroom policy is almost always an unwritten expectation, and not usually even verbalized as a policy. Yet any teacher knows if his or her principal ascribes to the policy. Principals make shaping statements such as, "Your kids must really have been working hard today—I didn't hear a sound as I walked by!" or "She is an excellent teacher—her class is always so well-behaved and hard-working": translation—QUIET. Sometimes they are even more direct, as when one principal visiting kindergarteners during writing time said, "I had to go into my office and shut my door after I was in your classroom this morning. It gave me a stomach ache it was so noisy!" Principals who value child interaction make statements such as, "What a lively discussion I heard as I walked by—they must have really been involved in that topic," or "Your groups are really working well—everyone seemed to be talking about writing when I was in your room this morning."

From these statements, from word-of-mouth between old and new teachers, and from more formal principal-teacher evaluation goals and suggestions, teachers quickly determine the principal's expectations for the learning environment at their school. If the expectation is for quiet classrooms, then we suggest the following strategies for teachers who believe in the efficacy of collaborative learning:

1. Bring the rule out into the open with your principal. Listen to her rationale, then state your own. Provide supporting literature on collaborative learning specific to your grade level including articles on more structured forms, such as cooperative learning and peer teaching.

2. Invite your principal to visit your classroom during a time when you have structured collaborative learning (e.g., writing time). Prepare her for the structure and make suggestions of what to look and listen for. You might even suggest the principal take observational notes, with particular attention to teaching/learning episodes, for your later discussion.

3. Shut your door.

4. Establish the quiet voice as a condition during writing time and help children monitor their own groups. We found an abundance of behavior monitoring, which was often verbally rejected but in fact almost always effective in bringing the peer in line with established rules.

In order to discuss the negative effects of a district-level policy of a "readiness program" in kindergarten, let us contrast a workbook phonics lesson with a collaborative phonics lesson. First, a lesson from the Teacher's Guide for *Getting Ready to Read* (Durr, Hillerich, & Johnson, 1986, p.296–298) on "Associating Sounds with Letters Dd":

Instruction

Point to "d." Say, "You are going to learn about the sound for d." Point to "duck" and ask children to name the picture.

Print the word "duck" on the chalkboard or on paper. Say, "Here is the word 'duck.'" Underline the "d" as you ask, "What letter does 'duck' begin with?" ... (d) "The letter you see at the beginning of 'duck' is 'd.' The sound you hear at the beginning of 'duck' is the sound for 'd.' ... When you see the letter 'd,' think of the sound you hear at the beginning of 'duck.' Then you'll remember the sound for 'd.'

[*Children then decide which of ten plastic objects begins with a 'd,' and can be placed in the 'd' box.*]

Guided Practice

[*The teacher now gives the children pencils, and has them name the two "d"s on the big chart. Then they name and underline a series of pictures beginning with "d" in their workbooks.*]

Ask children to watch while you print small 'd' on the chalkboard or on paper. Say, "Here is small 'd.' Watch while I trace over small 'd'" ... Then point to the first 'd' in Box 1 as you say, "Trace over the dotted lines to make a small 'd' in Box 1. Now trace over the dotted lines to print small 'd' two more times. Then try to print some 'd's' all by yourself on the same line."

[*The lesson concludes with more naming and underlining of pictures. An optional activity is for children to dictate a story about a dinosaur or a doll. An Enrichment Master and an Extra Practice Master are also available.*]

Note that at no time are children making the 'd' sound and writing the letter 'd' simultaneously. Even an elementary concept of word must be violated by "ddd," according to Ferreiro and Teberosky's (1982) finding that children learn very early that a word consists of contrasting letters. In contrast, much of the independent writing we observed was accompanied by the sound, momentarily isolated, or drawn out within the word. Of course children did not hear/write all the sounds in words, or even always write correctly all the sounds they attempted. What they did have, and what is conspicuously missing in this workbook lesson, is the opportunity to reflect on and discuss sound/symbol correspondence. We offer one of several letter/sound discussions as an example:

April 3, 1987

James: T-t-t tall T-te-te [*James repeatedly sounds out "Tall T," frequently voicing the 't' so it sounds like 'd.'*]

James: How you make a 'd'?

Kevin: Want me to make you a 'd'? [*Writes one on scratch paper.*]

James: Uh—I'll do it. [*Copies the 'd' onto his own paper.*] Duh—duh—'w'— 'w.' [*Writes 'M' as he says 'w.'*]

Kevin: That ain't no 'w'—that ain't no 'w'—uhuh—uhuh

Monica: Mr. W is right there. [*Points to wall chart.*]

Latoya: How do you make a 'w'?

Monica: It's like this. [*Loud, indistinguishable argument about 'w.'*]

Monica: It's like this, James, this is how a 'w' goes.

She writes a 'w' on his paper, which greatly disturbs him, and he leaves to tell the teacher. Later, during sharing, he first reads "Mr. D," but on second reading revises to "Tall T." These are both "Alphatime" terms the class has used in letter discussions. Four days later, he uses a 'd' correctly in an assisted spelling of Dr. Allen—"DLN."

In the midst of this dynamic exchange, there is a genuine exploration of some of the puzzles of the English sound/symbol system. 'D' and 'W' sound alike in name; 'T' and 'D' sound alike; and 'W' and 'M' look alike. We believe that through collaborative explorations of the similarities and differences of sounds and letters, children come to a deeper understanding of how language works. The scripted phonics lesson, in contrast, demands only rote memorization. In our opinion, a policy that fills children's days with such curriculum instead of allowing the curriculum to be drawn from the child is not just uneducational, it is anti-educational.

CONCLUSION

The children in Emily's classroom learned interdependence. They did not depend solely on the teacher (dependence) or solely on themselves (independence), but upon each other. They came to view themselves as both teachers and learners. They learned how to ask for help, how to offer it, and how to keep the interaction going. They learned who would teach them besides the adults, as James shows us in the following transcript, the interaction that directly preceded our opening episode:

James: I know who gonna help me [*laughs*].

Ivan: Dr. Allen?

James: No.

Monica: Me?

James: Uh—huh. Come over here, Monica.

Monica: Where you want me to sit?

James: Right here.

In Chapter 4, we maintain our focus on the child, but expand our view to consider other factors that may lead to success for children identified as at risk by their teachers. Candelaria, Elena, Karen, and Freddy, like Anna and James in the preceding chapters, were not predicted to succeed as first-grade readers. In each case, something happened to reduce the risks, something "fortuitous, even haphazard." The profiles of these children show us that there may be very simple things that we can do, as parents and teachers, to help children.

Chapter 4

Making Success a More Common Occurrence for Children at Risk for Failure: Lessons from Hispanic First Graders Learning to Read

Claude N. Goldenberg

IN 1983 I began a year-long study of nine Hispanic kindergartners who appeared headed for trouble in first-grade reading (Goldenberg, 1984). Based on kindergarten teachers' assessments of various "readiness" attributes, it seemed likely that these nine children would be among the ones to have the most difficulty learning to read. They were, in other words, at risk for reading failure, according to kindergarten indicators such as attention, visual and auditory memory, oral comprehension, and beginning knowledge of sounds and letters.

By first grade's end, however, four of the children were doing relatively well in reading (according to school norms), while five were achieving substantially below the school's norms. The question I addressed was why did five of the children do very poorly, while four—with equally dim prospects for first-grade reading success—do well?

The question I began with was practical and immediate, rather than theoretical. Certainly, I was guided by previous research and theory on children's school achievement. As is well known, a number of home, school, and child variables are thought to be causally related to achievement, particularly reading achievement. Previous research has demonstrated relationships between reading achievement and numerous factors: parents' education (Hinckley, Beal, Breglio, Haertel, & Wiley, 1979); reading in the home (Bloom, 1981; Durkin, 1966); parents' academic aspirations and expectations for their children and their general academic orientations (Bloom, 1981; Entwisle, 1977; Hess, Holloway, Price, & Dickson, 1982); frequency and type of teacher's interactions with the child (Bloom, 1981; Cooper & Good, 1983; Rosenshine, 1986; Shipman, 1976); teacher expectations (Cooper & Good, 1983); parent-school contacts (Hemphill & Chandler, 1983); amount of time a child spends reading (Leinhardt, Zigmond, & Cooley, 1981); attention to instruction and reading tasks (Ross, 1976); and motivation (Bloom, 1976).[1]

My goal was not to modify or add to this list. Rather, it was to try to see these factors in action, that is, to see whether they could explain why a subset of the children at risk for reading problems succeeded in first-grade reading, while the rest did not. Such a study, it seemed, might suggest ways in which other children at risk for underachievement could be helped to improve their chances of academic success.

During this year-long study, I learned a great deal about these nine children, why they did well or poorly, what sequence or confluence of events led to their level of reading achievement at year's end. I also learned about the wisdom of W. I. Thomas' dictum that if people define situations as real, they are real in their consequences (Thomas, 1966). What made the difference in the children's end-of-year achievement was not their objective status as determined, for example, by parents' education (which was generally low) or the child's group placement at the beginning or middle of the year. Rather, what was decisive was teachers' and parents' subjective perceptions of the child at each point during the year and the actions or inactions to which these perceptions led.

A corollary to Thomas' dictum also emerged: If teachers and parents perceive a need to act in some way that is out of the ordinary—that is, if they feel the situation demands special or unusual measures—they will act to address the cause of the disturbance; otherwise it will be business as usual, even if children's achievement is sub-par. Ironically, despite the fact that the school's business is academic achievement, sub-par achievement, in and of itself, was usually not sufficient to prompt any unusual action by the teacher, although it did promote actions by parents once parents realized children's achievement was sub-par.

I would also say that in studying these nine children intensively I learned a great deal about how children in general—especially those at risk for failure—succeed or fail in school. The validity of this assertion, of course, depends upon two things: first, the accuracy of my observations and conclusions; second, the extent to which the children I studied share common features with other children in other situations. But the sample I chose was not randomly drawn from a larger population. Rather, I included all kindergarten children at one particular school who satisfied the selection criteria described below; so I cannot claim generalizability. In the final analysis, the reader is left to judge whether the events and situations described here ring true, that is, whether the findings have some degree of generalizability or external validity. Eisner's (1984) notion of "referential adequacy" comes closest to the criterion for validity I am using:

> Given our experience, does this work have anything to say that illuminates what we already know but are not fully aware of? We validate material we read by looking backward into the past as well as by looking forward to the events of the future. (p. 198)

My observations and conversations during the year of the study revealed that parents and teachers had certain views and responses to children's behavior and achievement that influenced their actions—or inactions, as it sometimes turned out. I therefore spent a great deal of time trying to understand teachers' and parents' definitions of each child's situation in the classroom: Was progress in reading adequate or not? If not, why not? Was it because of the child's attitude and effort? How did the teacher perceive, and respond to, this child's classroom behavior?

THE FORTUITY OF SUCCESS IN FIRST-GRADE READING

For purposes of this volume, what is most important about these nine cases, and what I would like to emphasize at the outset, is that any of these nominally "at-risk" children could have been successful, at least with respect to the school's reading norms. From the school's standpoint, the success of four of the children was fortuitous, that is, their achieving at grade level was essentially accidental. Their success in reading was not the product of a special program or intervention or even of a teacher's purposeful attempts to bring children up to grade-level norms; their success was a result of other factors.[2]

Why, then, did some of these at-risk children succeed, while the others failed?

I have found it extremely difficult when presenting or talking about this study's results to come up with a satisfactory generalization, a succinct statement that captures the essence of why four children did relatively well in first-grade reading while five did not. This is, of course, what most people—and the profession as a whole—want to hear, a study's "major findings."

But each case was so different, the relevant factors and key elements so unique, that to this day I do not feel I can accurately sum up what happened without either distorting what *really* happened or else offering a completely banal statement. I am caught between the demands of science— for parsimonious, abstract, and generalizable explanations of phenomena— and the resistance of social life, when very closely observed, to explanations that have widespread applicability to all, or virtually all, individuals. Perhaps this tension was inherent in the study's design: I was not looking for average tendencies or differences between groups; rather, I was trying to understand and construct plausible explanations for each child's success or failure in first-grade reading. I therefore had to examine and analyze each case—each child—on its own terms. This made abstraction and generalization problematical.

I can summarize the findings this way, risking, as I have said, the banality that seems to come with all of my previous attempts at general- ization: Someone—either a teacher or a parent or both—did something somewhat out of the ordinary, something that had an *academic* focus and that eventually led to the child's better-than-expected reading achievement. What this suggested, in turn, was that the other children, who were equally at risk for poor reading achievement, could have been successful as well if comparable actions had been taken. What I will argue is that teachers had at hand, but did not necessarily use, the available means for improving achievement of children at risk for failure.

SUBJECTS AND METHODS

By virtually any educational indicator—test scores, grade retention, referral rates to special education, drop-out rates, educational attainment— Hispanics of Mexican or Central American origins lag behind non- Hispanics in the United States (Arias, 1986; Orfield, 1986). In spite of appreciable gains in Hispanic students' achievement recently, the gap between minority and nonminority students remains large (Congressional Budget Office, 1987). The low, overall achievement status of this group makes it especially urgent that we examine closely and try to understand the reasons for different levels of academic achievement among Hispanic students.

The nine children included in this study were first graders in a low- income, predominantly (80 percent) Hispanic elementary school in southern California. They had no known handicaps, were Spanish dominant, and had low scores on the Kindergarten Student Rating Scale (SRS), a reading readiness questionnaire filled out by kindergarten teachers and known to predict reading achievement in early elementary school (Feshbach, Adelman, & Fuller, 1974, 1977). A low score is defined as being between one-half and one standard deviation below the class mean. The children's scores fell between the sixteenth and thirty-first percentiles of their respective kindergarten classrooms. Thus, although these children were not the very lowest in their classrooms, they were in the bottom third.

Of the thirteen children who met these criteria, the parents of eleven agreed to participate in the study. Two children moved during the year of the study, leaving nine children as subjects.[3]

Six of the nine lived with both parents, while three lived with their mothers only. All fifteen parents were born and educated outside of the United States: ten in Mexico, four in Central America, and one in Puerto Rico. With the exception of two fathers who had gone beyond high school, all other parents had between a second- and sixth-grade education. All parents who worked outside the home were employed in unskilled or semiskilled occupations.

Except for teacher ratings and a small amount of testing, the methodology I employed throughout the study can best be described as direct observation, which Coles (1977), borrowing from Anna Freud, defines as

> a sustained involvement with a person or a family, maintained long enough so that the observer has some basis in experience, in words heard and actions observed, for coming to whatever more general conclusions seem warranted. (p. 559)

Data to explain the different achievement outcomes were gathered from three sources: teacher ratings and interviews, classroom observations of children and teachers, and parent interviews.

Teacher Ratings and Interviews

Around the eighth week of school and again around the sixth month of classes, I conducted open-ended interviews with each first-grade teacher, where I asked for assessments and explanations of children's academic performance, especially in reading. At the first of these interviews, teachers were asked to predict their students' reading success for that year, using a 1–9 scale, with 9 indicating high predicted reading success. Teachers were also asked to explain their predictions about the study children and, to avoid drawing attention to them, about a random selection of other students as well. With the exception of the prediction question, which was highly structured, all interview questions were open-ended.

In addition, throughout the entire year, I frequently spoke with teachers informally. I asked about children's motivation, abilities, comportment, and any other aspect of their classroom functioning that seemed relevant for understanding their progress, or lack of progress, in reading. Most of the information I gathered about teachers' views and assessments of the children came from these intermittent, often brief, and casual exchanges.

Classroom Observations

During classroom observations, I recorded all behaviors (verbal and non-verbal) related to the target child's attention to academic tasks, interest and attention to books or written material, quality and frequency of teacher-child interactions, and teacher's responsiveness to the child. The structure and content of reading instruction were also noted during the observations. Occasionally, and not in any systematic fashion, I took one of the teacher's reading groups and taught or reviewed some material. I generally did not interact with the children in the study, however, unless they approached me. When there was interaction, it was almost always in Spanish.

Observation periods lasted from under ten minutes to almost an hour, the average being approximately thirty to thirty-five minutes. The nine children were observed in first grade from July until March,[4] approximately every two or three weeks. Total first-grade observation time per child was approximately six hours, not including unscheduled observations made when I was in the room waiting to speak with the teacher, observing another child, or for some other matter. I observed during reading time, library time, story time, language arts time, and at miscellaneous times such as roll call, announcements, and daily calendar. I observed children doing independent seatwork, during small-group lessons, when they were with the entire class, and when they had bits of free time.

Parent Interviews

Three home interviews were conducted with each child's parents—in the first, fourth or fifth, and eighth month of classes. Both parents were present for interviews, except in the three cases where the child lived with only the mother. All interviews were conducted in Spanish, although two fathers often answered questions in English. Interviews were semistructured, with mostly open-ended questions. Topics covered were reading in the home; parents' attitude toward school achievement; parents' involvement with child's school learning; general home cognitive environment, as determined by parents' conversing with the child, family outings, television viewing; parents' assessment of the child's interest in reading and child's achievement level; extent and nature of parents' contact with the teacher.

Parents were also asked for demographic and socio-economic information, although they were not asked about family income or immigration status.

Interviews lasted between forty-five minutes and two and a half hours, with an average of approximately ninety minutes each. No mechanical devices were used, either in the home interviews or in the classroom observations.

CHANGE IN ACADEMIC STATUS: KINDERGARTEN TO FIRST GRADE

When the children in this study were nearing the end of kindergarten, they were, according to their teachers, among the lowest in their classes in academic and preacademic skills considered important for learning to read, reflected in their low SRS scores. These were the children who helped make up the low-ability groups; they were among those who progressed most slowly, were least verbal, and about whom kindergarten teachers made such comments in their year-end summaries as "needs to put forth effort," "pretty much borderline," "practically nonverbal," "needs a lot of individual help and repetition of concepts," "having trouble with reading readiness." Their low academic standing, and the generally low expectations kindergarten teachers held out for their first-grade reading success, are shown in Table 4–1. These children were at risk even within a population that is as a whole at risk for school failure (Arias, 1986; Orfield, 1986).

At the end of first grade, however, some of the children's academic status had changed dramatically. As Table 4–2 indicates, a portion of the group was on grade level in reading, having performed well on a word-recognition and decoding test I administered individually to each child in the study.[5]

The key part of the test (part 3) consisted of twenty words taken from the mastery test of the second first-grade preprimer. Four children—one boy and three girls—scored 14/20 (70 percent) or higher on this part (See Table 4–2, column 3). Each child in the unsuccessful group scored 8/20 (40 percent) or lower. All successful readers outscored the unsuccessful ones on parts one and two of the test, comprising sight words and decodable words from the first preprimer (Table 4–2, columns 1 and 2). In three cases (Sylvia, Fernando, and Violeta), the test was discontinued, as children appeared to be at a loss as to how to begin decoding or recognizing words they were given. Before discontinuing, however, the children were shown all the items and asked whether they knew or could read any of the words.

As I will discuss, teacher judgments corroborated the test results.

Table 4–1   **Kindergarten Teachers' Ratings and Predictions.**

	Kindergarten SRS Score[a]	Kindergarten Teacher's Prediction for First-Grade Reading Success[b]
Marta[c]	−.9	−.9
Elena	−.5	−.4
Candelaria	−.7	−.4
Freddy	−.6	−.6
Sylvia	−1.0	.2
Fernando	−.6	−1.3
Violeta	−.8	−.3
Karen	−.9	−1.0
Mario	−.6	−.6
group mean	**−.8**	**−.6**

Source: (Adapted from Goldenberg, 1984)

Note: Ratings and predictions are in standard units (z scores), standardized within class. Classes are constituted randomly, so scores are comparable across classrooms.

[a] Low score on the Kindergarten Student Rating Scale was the basis for including children in the study.

[b] Teachers rated all students on scale of 1−9 (low to high success prediction). Rating was then standardized within classroom. For the entire kindergarten cohort ($n=158$), correlation between SRS and kindergarten teacher's reading success prediction (both standardized) was .84.

[c] All names used are pseudonyms.

NO APPARENT SIMPLE EXPLANATION FOR SUCCESS AND FAILURE IN FIRST-GRADE READING

There was, however, no apparent or simple relationship between first-grade reading achievement and variables or indicators that might be expected to predict end-of-year achievement. Kindergarten SRS scores, kindergarten and first-grade teacher predictions, and third-month scores based on a reading readiness test were virtually identical for the successful and unsuccessful groups (see Table 4−3).

Table 4−2   **Reading Achievement at End of First Grade.**

	End of Year Decoding and Word-Recognition Test: Number Correct		
	Part 1[a] (max=15)	Part 2[b] (max=16)	Part 3[c] (max=20)
Successful Children			
Marta	15	16	14
Elena	15	14	14
Candelaria	15	16	16
Freddy	14	16	16
Unsuccessful Children			
Sylvia	12	8	x[d]
Fernando	x	—	—
Violeta	x	—	—
Karen	11	13	8
Mario	6	12	1

Source: Adapted from Goldenberg, 1984

[a] High frequency sight words from first preprimer (book 3 in series).

[b] De-codable reading words from first preprimer.

[c] De-codable reading words from second preprimer (book 4 in series). Children were considered on grade level according to school norms if they mastered this book's phonics content by the end of first grade.

[d] Test discontinued.

Nor were there discernible relationships between the children's achievement and family socio-economic status, parents' reading habits, or parents' educational aspirations and expectations for their children (see Table 4−4).

In one sense, the absence of clear relationships between such predictors and achievement is not surprising: the sample was very small and subjects came from a fairly restricted achievement range. But although there were essentially no differences between the groups in terms of these variables,

Table 4-3　SRS Scores, Kindergarten and First-Grade Teacher
Prediction of Reading Success, and Mid-Year Test
Results for Successful and Unsuccessful Children.

	Kindergarten SRS Score (z-scores)	Kindergarten Teacher Prediction (z-scores)	First-Grade Reading Teacher Prediction (z-scores)	Third-Month Test: Decoding (max=4; raw scores)	Third-Month Test: Other (max=15; raw scores)
Successful Children					
Marta	-.9	-.9	-1.2	2	13
Elena	-.5	-.4	.5	4	11
Candelaria	-.7	-.4	-.8	0	14
Freddy	-.6	-.6	-1.5	4	14
Group Mean	**-.7**	**-.6**	**-.7**	**2.5**	**13.0**
Unsuccessful Children					
Sylvia	-1.0	.2	.3	4	13
Fernando	-.6	-1.3	-2.1	1	13
Violeta	-.8	-.3	-.6	2	10
Karen	-.9	-1.0	-1.0	2	12
Mario	-.6	-.6	.7	3	13
Group Mean	**-.8**	**-.6**	**-.5**	**2.4**	**12.2**

Source: Adapted from Goldenberg, 1984

there were some very important differences in the children's experiences
regarding their opportunities to learn to read. It was these differences, and
how and why they came about, that explain the differences in reading
achievement. As I have said, in each case someone did something a little
out of the ordinary, something that had an academic focus and that
resulted in children's better-than-expected reading achievement. What is
important is what happened and why. No less important is why nothing
comparable happened in the five unsuccessful cases.

Table 4—4 **Parents' Education, Occupation, Reading Habits, and Educational Aspirations and Expectations for Their Children.**

	Education[a] (highest grade)	Occupation	Reading	Aspirations for Child[b]	Expectations
Successful Children					
Marta	3 or 4/—	watch factory/—	weekly mag from market	at least elementary school	no idea
Elena	2/—	in home	none	would not say	same
Candelaria	6/3	in the home/hotel cleaning, busboy	daily newspaper	professional degree	"lucky if she finishes h.s."
Freddy	6/B.A. + community college in U.S.	in the home/rstrnt, prchsng; inventory; cashier	Bible/paper (Father only)	no idea/beyond college-doctor	no idea/some college, maybe finish
Unsuccessful Children					
Sylvia	2/6	in the home/builds furniture frames	none/paper, library books, Eng. lessons	could not say	no idea/h.s. "at least"
Fernando	6/12 + community college	in the home/ cleans airplanes	paper, newsmagazines, religious books	beyond college: doctor	finish college
Violeta	3/2	food packing/buys and sells misc. items	none/classified ads	finish h.s./lawyer	finish h.s. "at least"
Karen	6/4	in the home/irons at cleaners	Eng. lessons/paper books on history, religion, philosophy	would not say	same
Mario	2/—	in the home/—	none	teacher or doctor	could not predict

Source: Adapted from Goldenberg, 1984 and Goldenberg, 1987
[a] Mother's response, followed by father's, if different. Dash (—) indicates no father in home.
[b] Responses taken from interview #2, December, 1983.

SUCCESS AND FAILURE: THE ROLE OF PARENTS

I will begin with the two successful children whose cases are easiest to explain. (The following discussion draws, in part, from case study material presented in Goldenberg, 1987.)

Elena's and Freddy's parents, although for entirely different reasons, were essentially responsible for their children's first-grade reading success.

In Elena's case, despite a rather high initial rating for her expected reading success (see Table 4–3), the teacher expressed concern about Elena's academic abilities early in the school year.

> She can't retain as well as the others; she can't discriminate some syllables. Her own ability to memorize, to blend [letter sounds] will impede her progress. She won't 'power on' like some others. You can challenge her only until a certain point. I want to set up success for her. I don't want to give her things over her head. She's been easily confused in the past.

In fact, the teacher was so convinced of Elena's tenuous grasp of the beginning reading concepts that despite passing her reading book's mastery test, Elena was moved to a lower group to review the book's concepts before proceeding with the next one.

Elena behaved appropriately, she completed her work, and although her mind seemed to wander occasionally during lessons, she generally paid attention and participated in class. But she seemed hesitant when asked to respond in class, she did not give the quick, firm responses teachers look for as indicators that a child knows a concept well and is ready to proceed. Even at the end of the year, by which time it was clear that Elena was doing satisfactorily in reading, the reading teacher told me she was "good, but slower" than the others in her group. I had noticed this same quality in her responses when I administered the end-of-year test. I noted that she "sounded everything out—knew sounds, but [was] not fluid [in her reading]."

Clearly, if it had only been up to the teacher, Elena would have received limited opportunities to learn new letters and words, since her halting, slow responses suggested she could not, as the teacher put it, "power on." But fortunately for Elena, her mother felt she needed to make certain Elena learned to read. This was so even though the mother had not gone past the second grade, did not read regularly on her own, nor were there magazines, newspapers, or books in the house, except for a Bible and occasional advertisement flyers left in the mailbox or the door.

The mother took it upon herself to teach Elena to read because her daughter had started school very late. Elena had arrived from Guatemala, where she had not attended school, and by the time she began first grade, she was more than seven and a half years old. When I asked the mother in a year-end interview why she had been so active in teaching Elena to read, she told me that she had wanted to see if Elena could move ahead with her reading. "She is older, [and] it's necessary that she become more intelligent. She has already lost one year. She's eight, and she will soon be nine." And, the mother added with some satisfaction, "Now she can read . . . just about anything you put in front of her. By and large, I taught her all the letters."

To teach her daughter to read, Elena's mother had bought Elena and her kindergarten-age brother a set of magnetic plastic letters, and the children played and practiced with these. She also taught Elena using more direct means. She had her copy letters and words, read short sentences, and write words and phrases from dictation. She of course made certain Elena completed any homework from school, but she also gave Elena additional tasks daily, even on weekends and during vacations. Sometimes, the mother said, she got angry at the children for fighting or becoming too loud, and she would make them turn off the television and do some lessons she would devise, usually copying letters or numbers.

Throughout the year, Elena's mother taught Elena words and letters the children had not yet been exposed to in school. The mother also gave Elena extra practice with letters they *were* studying, but which Elena might otherwise have had difficulty remembering.

In none of the other eight cases was there the level of involvement in the child's learning to read as there was in Elena's. Elena's mother's help—the constant daily practice of letters, syllables, and words—probably helped compensate for whatever learning weaknesses the teacher had sensed. In addition, the mother taught Elena new letters, sounds, and words. I tested Elena at different points in the year, and she could read words and syllables her reading group had not yet been taught. When I asked her where she learned to read them, she answered, "My mother teaches me."

In contrast to Elena's case, Freddy's parents did not become actively involved in his learning to read until much later in the year. Through the first week of March, approximately two-thirds of the way into the school year, it appeared certain that Freddy would be one of the unsuccessful children in the study.

Freddy's academic fortunes began to decline almost immediately upon entering first grade. In the third week of classes, Freddy's teacher said he was not doing very well. She said she had to work with him individually, and that even then he often did not "get it too quickly." His major problem, the teacher thought, was his lack of attention. She said his "work habits" were poor, and he needed to play around less and do his work more. Her ratings of his attention and effort and her prediction for his reading success were all extremely low (Table 4–3). A month later, the teacher repeated that Freddy's major problem was his inattention. In addition, she said, the "work is hard for him." She saw him as a child who learns slowly and for whom learning is difficult. She also mentioned his occasional practice of writing backwards as a cause for concern.

Freddy's academic fortunes deteriorated steadily. In October, the teacher felt he did not know the material sufficiently well to advance to the next book (as most of Freddy's group was about to do), and she placed him in a lower group. He also did poorly in the lower group. In January, the teacher told me he was "really struggling," still confusing the first four consonants of the reading curriculum. Around this time, the aide in Freddy's homeroom teacher's class mentioned he was "spacy," and he seemed always to be "on the moon." She said he was sure to end up in a special education class. The teacher commented to me after school one day that he had almost been retained the previous year in kindergarten. It was too bad he had not been, she said: "He would have been perfect for kindergarten this year. As it is, he's not getting any positive reinforcement."

By the beginning of February, Freddy was in the lowest reading group, where he and his group-mates reviewed and practiced letters and syllables they had been practicing since the beginning of school. He was successful in this group, but he was learning very little new material.

The best thing to happen to Freddy that year was his failure, in March, to bring in his reading homework for the third consecutive day. He and several other children had not been bringing in homework, and the teacher instituted a new policy: no homework for three consecutive days, and your parents are called. Freddy was the first victim—or, as it turned out, beneficiary. The teacher, quite angry with him, called Freddy's mother that very day and told her she would suspend Freddy unless the parents came to school immediately for a conference. That afternoon, Freddy's parents went to see the teacher.

The teacher had originally called Freddy's parents because of the boy's failure to bring his homework, but during the conference the teacher told them that Freddy was far behind in his reading achievement and that he would probably be retained in first grade. Freddy's father was extremely angry, the teacher said, and he was pacing up and down the room. He said he would send his wife during the reading hour for the next two weeks to work with Freddy, to make sure he did his lessons, and to help him catch up.

Freddy's mother came in during the reading hour every day for the next two weeks. She also worked with him at home daily. She told me later that he worked on his reading willingly, sometimes wanting to do another workbook page after she said they were through for the day. Within a week, Freddy had finished the reading book he was in, passed the test, and moved to a higher group.

By year's end, Freddy was in the third reading group (of six) from the top. He was one of the successful children in the study, with the second highest score on the word-recognition test I gave. His reading group placement was the highest of all the study children. The teacher said she was very satisfied with his reading achievement. (She did retain him in first grade, however, due to his "general immaturity." Freddy's teacher the following year said she was surprised he had been retained since his reading skills were so good.) None of these outcomes could possibly have been predicted three months earlier, when Freddy was working on reading skills he had been taught six months ago and before his parents were called.

Freddy's parents' account of what had happened at the conference and after it was essentially the same as the teacher's. They felt their intervention had its most direct and important impact on Freddy's motivation and his attention to his lessons. They also thought the mother's help, both at home and at school, had made a big difference. Regardless of the precise *psychological* explanation for Freddy's unexpected success, everyone agreed that the conference constituted a turning point. Ironically, it seemed that Freddy's failure to bring his homework precipitated a chain of events culminating in his first-grade reading success.

In my last interview with Freddy's parents, they expressed dismay that the teacher had waited so long to inform them of their son's poor reading progress. The mother said they had a conference with the teacher some months before. The teacher had said Freddy "was a little low, but she didn't say he could not read nor write. She just said he needed to practice more." Freddy's father agreed: "She didn't say anything about how poorly he was doing. That's what bothers me the most. . . . Why did she wait so long? . . . We would have done something."

The father said Freddy would not have been so low in his reading if the teacher had contacted them earlier. "Maybe," the father said, "it's because there are so many children, and there is not enough help, that they don't bother to call parents." Still, the father said, he could not understand why teachers did not at least contact the parents of children who are obviously low.

One reason teachers do not contact parents of low-achieving children might be that they do not expect low-income minority parents to be able to make much of a difference. There is a sense that these families are so stressed, they are incapable of making their children's educational progress a high priority. Early in the year, the teacher, who had Freddy's sister in her class the year before, told me that she knew the family situation. According to his teacher, Freddy comes from a "pretty chaotic background. There is definitely not a priority list at home. [School is] not a priority now."

The teacher said Freddy's mother tried to sell her a dress the year before, and the teacher interpreted this as evidence of the family's desperate economic predicament, which, she assumed, left little time or energy for worrying about the children's schooling. Moreover, the teacher said, Freddy's natural father had died and the mother had remarried. The mother had told the teacher that Freddy was fidgety and stubborn, and that her new husband was "up the wall" with the situation. The teacher therefore had assumed that no one in the home could help Freddy with his reading. She only called in the parents when she became piqued over Freddy's delinquent homework.

PARENTAL HELP: THE UNTAPPED POTENTIAL

Elena's and Freddy's cases (as well as cases presented below) suggest two important points. First, neither language-minority, low-economic, nor low-education status were obstacles to parents' ability or willingness to help their children learn to read. Despite low educational levels, parents had sufficient literacy skills to help children in the beginning and early reading stages. (Freddy's father *was* unusually well-educated for this population—he had gone to college in his native Guatemala. But it was Freddy's mother, with only a sixth-grade education, who worked with Freddy on his reading lessons.)

Second, in the absence of any unusual circumstances, such as Elena's late entrance into first grade (which of course does not guarantee parental action), parents will not normally take it upon themselves to teach their children to read. Parents implicitly rely on the teacher to tell them how their child is doing. As one father said, if they do not hear anything from the teacher, they are going to assume all is well—or at least well enough. In Freddy's case, the parents did not realize anything was wrong with Freddy's reading achievement until they were informed at the homework conference.

Because reading activities are not common in these homes, there are few opportunities for parents to become aware of their children's progress. And perhaps even more importantly, because parents feel the educational system here is different from the one they know, they are extremely reluctant to interfere. A good illustration is provided by the mother of Violeta, one of the unsuccessful children. Earlier in the year, the teacher had sent a note home asking the parents to help their children learn the consonants in the alphabet. The mother told me she had sat down with Violeta one afternoon and taught her all the consonant names. At the next conference, however, the mother said the teacher had told her that reading was not taught in this manner—children are not taught the letter names. Violeta's mother stopped teaching her daughter altogether, fearing, she said, she would only confuse the girl. The mother said that was how she learned to read, by learning the letter names, but that was not how the school did it here. "It's not the same here, as it is in one's own country," she said with a shrug.

It falls upon the teacher, then, to mobilize the home resources, to inform parents when children's progress is not as good as it should be, and to provide guidance for what parents can do to help a child. As Freddy's father clearly stated, parents want and need to know what they can do to help improve their children's achievement. This is probably true regardless of ethnicity and socio-economic status.

Yet most parents were not given this information. Four of the five parents of the unsuccessful children were under the impression their children's reading progress was at least "satisfactory." I asked about this explicitly in the end-of-year interview with parents: Did they know their children were significantly below grade level in reading?

Mario's mother said his reading teacher (Mario went to another teacher for reading) had told her he was doing well in reading. Sylvia's parents said all the teacher's comments about Sylvia were "positive." Her only problem, the teacher reportedly said, was that she worked too slowly. Karen's father said he was "completely satisfied" with her academic performance in school. Violeta's mother also thought her daughter's progress was good. In fact, at the last parent conference, the mother said, "The teacher told me she was learning to read very well .... I came home very happy."

The only parents who knew their child was not progressing adequately in reading were Fernando's. His mother had been working regularly with him at the beginning of the year in order to improve his progress. But Fernando's teacher, fearing the parents were putting too much pressure on the boy, asked them to stop instructing him at home.

The parents of all the unsuccessful children were capable of reading and of helping their children learn the letters and sounds. But they were either unaware there was a need to help their children, or they did not know what to do to complement the school's efforts to teach the children to read. The parents either were not contacted by teachers, or if they were, teachers failed to address the achievement issues confronting the children.

Karen, one of the unsuccessful children, provides a particularly revealing case because it suggests that parent contact in and of itself is not sufficient. The *substance* of the contact must be such that it prompts parents to act in ways that will help the child academically.

Karen's teacher (who was the same as Freddy's) thought the girl was capable academically—"she's OK, a smart little girl"—but that her behavior was a problem. The teacher told me in the first month of school that Karen had real problems working with others. She was "aggressive and demanding of attention," and she needed "better work habits." Things got worse, and in the second month of school the teacher contacted the parents. "She wouldn't stay still," the teacher told me. "She scratched or hurt other children, she cursed. . . . I wouldn't put up with that behavior."

The parents were called in, and they acted immediately to correct Karen's behavior. (In fact, the teacher told me the father asked why they had not been called earlier.) One day when I was observing, the mother came to school to ask the teacher about Karen's behavior and to request that the teacher send home daily reports. In my final interview with the parents, Karen's father told me that following their meeting with the teacher, he had sat Karen down and told her he wanted her behavior to improve. The change, he told me, snapping his fingers for emphasis, was immediate. The teacher confirmed that Karen's behavior had improved substantially since the conference. Her behavior, attention, and effort continued to get better from that point on, according to the teacher. In the mid-October report card the teacher wrote that Karen "has put forth a great deal of effort in all her subjects. Her work habits have changed and now she is doing very well."

The parents responded to the teacher's definition of what the problem was—Karen's behavior. I later asked the teacher and the parents whether Karen's behavior had been the only topic discussed at the conference, and all said it was. Karen's academic progress had not been addressed, nor did the teacher mention things the parents could do to help Karen in reading that year. The teacher saw Karen's problem as one of comportment, and this is what she communicated to the parents: "I said it [i.e., her behavior] was affecting her academic progress, as is logical."

But while Karen's behavior improved, her reading progress did not, and at year's end she was one of the unsuccessful children. The teacher did not initiate any more parent conferences after the one early in the year. Karen's behavior was completely satisfactory (especially in light of what it had been), and she was sufficiently consistent in bringing her homework (the teacher told me). She was no longer an irritant to the teacher and therefore did not prompt any action by the teacher that might have helped her reading achievement. Yet her reading achievement was poor, even by the teacher's standards. In June the teacher told me Karen was "struggling."

Freddy, as I have discussed, did prompt the teacher to act because of his failure to bring in homework. Fortunately for him, the teacher also told the parents about his poor reading achievement. Not only did he start bringing his homework consistently, his achievement also improved dramatically. In Karen's case, her behavior improved but her academic achievement did not.

PRECIPITATING TEACHER ACTION

I would like to shift the discussion and address more explicitly the question posed by Freddy's and Karen's fathers: Why didn't the teacher contact them sooner? In Karen's case, the question more properly is why didn't the teacher call the parents *at all* regarding Karen's achievement? What accounts for teachers' failure to call parents or otherwise take some other steps to improve the achievement of a child who is not doing well academically? One answer has already been suggested in Freddy's case—the teacher assumed Freddy's family was under so much stress for economic and other reasons that they would be incapable or unwilling to help their son academically. Some unexpected findings suggest another possible explanation.

Contrary to earlier discussion in this chapter, it is not exactly true that there were no differences between the successful and unsuccessful groups of children early in first grade. There was a difference, although it was an unexpected one—the successful children, as a group, had lower teacher ratings of effort and attention to academic tasks. (See Table 4–5.)[6]

All theories of achievement (cf. Haertel, Walberg, & Weinstein, 1983; Ross, 1976) point to a *positive* association between attention and effort and achievement. How can we interpret these contrary and counter-intuitive findings?

The answer seems to be that the extremely low attention and effort ratings (which we find in the case of two successful students, Freddy and Marta) reflected annoying and problematic *academic* behaviors. These problematic behaviors required some sort of response from the teacher, that is, some action that was somewhat out of the ordinary *and* had an academic focus. In Freddy's case, all along the teacher and aide had complained about his lack of attention and his being "spacy." The particular behavior that precipitated teacher action was his failure to bring homework. It seems likely that the teacher's growing irritation over his frequent failure to pay attention and make a sufficient effort reached a climax when he did not bring homework for three successive days, violating, not incidentally, the teacher's newly promulgated homework policy.

In the case of Marta, we see even more clearly how the teacher's perception of extremely poor attention and effort, coupled with the child's bad behavior, prompted action that might otherwise not have been taken. In other words, Marta, as did Freddy and Karen, forced the teacher to act.

Marta was the teacher's most problematic student at the beginning of the year. The teacher said Marta did her work hurriedly, poorly, and carelessly, and that, in general, her attitude toward schoolwork was entirely unacceptable. The teacher also found Marta's behavior obnoxious and intolerable: Marta laughed and played in class, pushed other children, tattled, and acted silly, the teacher said. Marta was the only student whom

Table 4–5 **First-Grade Teacher Ratings of Children's Effort and Attention to Academic Tasks.**

Successful Children	z-score of Rating[a]
Marta	−2.4
Elena	.5
Candelaria	−.5
Freddy	−1.1
Group Mean	**−.9**
Unsuccessful Children	
Sylvia	.7
Fernando	.4
Violeta	.4
Karen	−.3
Mario	−.5
Group Mean	**.1**

Source: Adapted from Goldenberg, 1984

Note: All first-grade teachers rated their children on four items taken from the First-grade Student Rating Scale (Adelman & Feshbach, 1971) that asked about student attention and effort during instruction. Reliability (alpha) of the four-item scale was .92.

[a] Scores are standardized within classroom and indicate child's attention and effort rating relative to first-grade classmates. A negative value means the child is below class mean in attention and effort; a positive value means child is above class mean.

the teacher considered a "behavior problem." Not surprisingly, Marta's teacher gave her the lowest attention and effort ratings of all the children in the study and one of the very lowest in the entire first grade, z-score=2.4.

But it was Marta's attitude toward her schoolwork that the teacher found most aggravating of all. Marta was not trying, the teacher said, "and I don't like it when they don't try." Marta, like many in her low group, was making poor progress in her reading. But unlike her group-mates, she was misbehaving and not making an effort. The teacher felt that her behavior and attitude were at least partly responsible for her poor progress. Several months later, when the teacher was recalling how Marta had been earlier in the year, she said Marta was "like a space girl. [It] kind of made me mad." This anger prompted the teacher to act.

Early in the second month, Marta's teacher kept her after school and told her she needed to improve her behavior and her attitude. She needed to be more careful and neat with her work, the teacher had told her. "I told her," the teacher informed me later that month, "that if she didn't try she wasn't getting anywhere." Several more times during the month, the teacher informed me, she told Marta to "slow down and work more carefully." The teacher said Marta's attitude and behavior improved somewhat, "but not that much." The teacher still did not see Marta in very optimistic terms, as her low rating of Marta's attention and effort indicated. "She'll keep plugging along," the teacher told me, almost resignedly, "[although] I don't think she'll totally bomb out like I thought before."

Since the improvement was only minimal, the teacher contacted Marta's mother for a conference. She told her that Marta still needed to be more careful with her work and more disciplined in her behavior, that Marta needed more practice with the letters and syllables they were learning and that she should work with her daughter at home. As in Karen's case, the mother was called in because of a behavior problem. But unlike Karen's case, where the teacher thought Karen was "smart" and "academically OK," Marta's teacher thought Marta also needed help learning the letters and syllables, and she told the mother this. Karen's teacher made no mention of helping the girl with her reading, assuming this would take care of itself once her behavior was brought under control.

Several weeks later Marta's teacher told me that Marta "had come alive." Marta was "participating, catching on; her handwriting was much improved; she takes more interest and pride in her work." The teacher said she was even thinking of moving Marta up to the next higher group. In my observations, it did seem as if Marta was remembering the *m* sound and how it blended with the vowels, at least more consistently than the others in her low group. But the most important and noticeable change, the teacher told me later, was in Marta's more general attitude and behavior—it had improved dramatically. Three weeks later the teacher moved Marta to a higher group.

From this point until the end of the year, the teacher had almost exclusively positive comments about Marta's progress. In my own observations, I saw Marta become increasingly more task-oriented and, seemingly, more and more self-assured.

In the ensuing months, the teacher sent notes home asking that someone practice with Marta. The teacher told me she thought someone was in fact working with Marta, because "she really knows her syllables very well. ... [She] consistently gets them right." In addition, the teacher told me later in the year, Marta was able to read things the teacher had not yet taught the group. She took this as evidence that someone was practicing at home with Marta.

The teacher was correct; Marta's mother had been practicing with her. One of the things that was most interesting in this case was that of all the children in the study, Marta's prognosis for first-grade reading success was unquestionably the lowest. Not only were her ratings, scores, and predictions the lowest, but in addition, Marta's home environment was the least conducive to reading development. Marta, her two sisters, and her mother lived in a small apartment on a busy street, where the sounds of trucks, radios, televisions, and men hanging out constantly intruded. Her mother was an extremely quiet woman who, according to her own report, rarely conversed with Marta. She generally spoke very little, Marta's older sister told me. After my first interview, I wrote in my notes that the mother seemed practically nonverbal. She had far more difficulty answering my questions than did any other parent I interviewed. She seemed lacking in certain basic information, such as what season of the year it was. She had completed either the third or fourth grade—she could not remember which.

Nonetheless, she apparently responded to the teacher conference. She told me she practiced reading and writing the letters and syllables with Marta, and, as she told me in the final interview, "I tell her to behave." During my second interview with the mother, she said the teacher had told her that Marta was not paying attention. At the third interview, the mother said it seemed that Marta had improved and was now being more attentive. This coincided with what the teacher had told me.

As in Freddy's case, it is impossible to know what precisely was responsible for Marta's success. Was it the teacher's motivational talks? The extra attention she gave Marta (in spite of her extremely low expectations for Marta's reading success)? The mother's help? The mother's admonition that she behave? Whatever the exact explanation (and most likely each of these factors made some contribution), Marta's improvement had its roots in the actions the teacher took in response to the girl's troublesome behavior: The teacher told Marta and her mother that Marta's behavior needed to improve and that she needed to be more careful with her work. She also requested that the mother practice at home with Marta. Marta's behavior and achievement began to improve (although it was the behavior that most concerned the teacher), Marta moved to a higher group, and she steadily improved throughout the year.

This explanation for Marta's success gains plausibility when we contrast Marta's case with that of her first-grade classmate Sylvia. Marta began first grade with the poorest prospects for reading success and ended the year as one of the classroom's best readers. Sylvia's story was exactly the reverse.

TEACHER INACTION: GREAT, BUT UNFULFILLED, EXPECTATIONS

Unlike Marta, Sylvia (who had the same first-grade teacher) had the most promising outlook of the study children. Although her kindergarten SRS score was the lowest of the study children, her kindergarten teacher said Sylvia had made enormous progress by the end of the school year (approximately two months after the teacher had completed the SRS). When asked to predict Sylvia's reading success in first grade, the kindergarten teacher rated her 6, which was slightly above average for her class. She said Sylvia had "caught on at the end," and that by the end of the year she was "by far the highest in the low group."

The first-grade teacher's assessment was consistent with the kindergarten teacher's report. She said Sylvia was a "whippy kid," whose hand was up very frequently during lessons and who generally answered correctly. In ratings of the children's attention and effort during lessons, the teacher rated Sylvia as being among the top third of the class. This was the highest rating given to any of the children in the study (see Table 4–5). The teacher also had relatively high expectations for her success in first-grade reading, the second highest of the children in the study (see Table 4–3). "She'll do very well," the teacher said, confidently. The teacher's expectancy rating placed Sylvia among the top 40 percent in the classroom. Furthermore, Sylvia's score on the reading readiness test I gave in the third month was the second highest of the study children. If any child was to defy his or her at-risk status, and do well in first-grade reading, it seemed certain that Sylvia would.

But she did not; she became one of the unsuccessful readers.

Sylvia had, as teachers say, "poor work habits," meaning she did not finish her class assignments. But in contrast to Marta, who could at times be disruptive, Sylvia was extremely quiet and well-behaved. She just did not finish her work. I knew from my observations that she spent a lot of time watching other children or simply staring off. What she did of her work, however, was neat, and her performance during teacher-directed lessons was good. So Sylvia did not present the teacher with a strong stimulus to act.

But because of her poor work habits and the growing volume of seatwork assigned, Sylvia consistently failed to finish her assignments. "She's really fallen back," the teacher told me in March, and she showed me a stack of Sylvia's unfinished papers. Sylvia's failure to finish her work led the teacher to assume Sylvia was working at her limit. Moving her to a higher group, or otherwise presenting her with more challenging material, was not even an issue in the teacher's mind, she told me, since Sylvia was not even completing the work she was given.

The teacher's initially favorable judgment and high expectations kept her from doing anything to correct the situation. At the beginning of the school year, the teacher said, Sylvia "seemed like she'd pick up quickly, answer readily, you know, be happy, get stars, that sort of thing." When Sylvia's unfinished papers started piling up, "I didn't act on it right away," the teacher said. "I thought she'd pull out of it." And since "she wasn't misbehaving or being disruptive," the teacher said, Sylvia presented the teacher with no pressing need to intervene in some way. Sylvia was very responsible with her homework and her behavior was good, so in contrast to Freddy, Marta, or even Karen, the teacher saw no reason to do anything out of the ordinary.

Several months after the study's completion, I shared with the teacher my "theory" about why Sylvia's reading achievement had been so disappointing. I showed her a preliminary draft of what I had written about Marta and Sylvia. The teacher said I was probably correct. "I think I kind of ignored [Sylvia]," the teacher said, "because I thought she'd be OK by herself." Unfortunately for Sylvia, initial high expectations made the teacher think "she'd be OK" and that "she'd pull out of it." And her good behavior and her consistency in bringing homework simply made it easy for the teacher to fail to take any action that would have changed Sylvia's first-grade reading fortunes.

THE MAINSPRINGS OF TEACHER ACTION: SOME CONCLUDING COMMENTS

Why do teachers act to correct a situation in some instances, but in other cases fail to take needed action? The conclusion I reached while conducting this study is that very often teachers won't act unless a student (or someone else, such as a parent or supervisor) virtually compels them to. Perhaps teachers are no different from anyone else in this regard.

What compels teachers to act? For one thing, bad and disruptive behavior compels action. Not only does bad behavior interfere with the smooth functioning of a classroom, but it is also annoying. It calls attention to itself; it requires the teacher to do something, especially if the class as a whole (as was true of the classes I observed) is generally well-behaved. In these instances, poor behavior stands out and must be dealt with.

Another thing that can compel action is failure to bring homework. Not bringing homework is seen as a sign of irresponsibility, not caring, failing to put forth a minimum of effort. It might also have something to do with the power relations that exist in classrooms—teachers want children to complete and bring in homework, and not doing so can be seen as an act of defiance, of disregard for the teacher's authority, and can make a teacher angry.

Teachers, it seems, take out-of-the-ordinary actions—such as conferring with students or parents and seeking (even demanding) certain changes in behavior—when they become angry, when they find something so annoying or disruptive that they have to do something about it. Unfortunately, poor achievement per se is not sufficiently annoying or disruptive to prompt special action, though it can be extremely frustrating (depending upon how seriously one takes these things). I am not entirely certain why this is so. It may be that there are so many things that demand teachers' attention and energy that we must be selective about what we respond to. And since it is widely assumed that there will be a range of achievement levels, poor achievement in itself will not prompt special action.

In any event, none of the teacher actions discussed above resulted from teachers trying to remedy poor achievement situations. Rather, they stemmed from annoyance or anger over bad behavior or failure to bring homework. Fortunately for some children, such as the Freddys and the Martas, teachers' responses to the annoyances they create contain elements that have beneficial effects on achievement.

TEACHER JUDGMENT AND REAPPRAISAL: THE CASE OF CANDELARIA

The final successful case differs from the other case studies, and, in a sense, is the most difficult to present and analyze. It illustrates a number of points, among them that poor achievement, in itself, seems insufficient to prompt teacher action. In all likelihood, this child would have remained in the lowest reading group and been one of the unsuccessful children had it not been for the presence of an outside observer who suggested to the teacher that she reevaluate her judgment of the child's attention and motivation. In this instance, I renounced my role as an indifferent spectator. I intervened, setting off, I think, a chain of events culminating in this child's better-than-expected achievement.

Two things are of interest: first, the sequence of events my intervention seemed to have triggered; second, the possibilities this case suggests that teachers can empirically test their judgments of children and adjust them accordingly, thereby increasing the chances children will receive the sort of learning opportunities they need.

Candelaria was a shy, quiet, timid little girl; she had large, deep-set, dark eyes that suggested a mournful expression. I observed her to be very motivated and attentive during class time, although she was usually very quiet and hardly ever called attention to herself. She almost always had her eyes glued to the teacher or intent on her book or the chalkboard.

Candelaria's teachers (after the third month of school, she went to a different teacher for reading), however, thought she was unmotivated and inattentive. The teacher's very low prediction for her first-grade reading success was due, the teacher said, to the fact that it was so "hard to keep her engaged all the time." In the third month of school, Candelaria was moved to a lower reading group with the teacher next door. This teacher also found her to be a problematic student, but not in the disruptive sense Karen and Marta had been. The teacher said Candelaria "dreaded" being called on; she felt she was "regressing." By all accounts, Candelaria's reading progress was poor, and it appeared that her first-grade reading achievement would be substantially below grade level.

Based on my observations, I had come to the tentative conclusion that Candelaria was considered inattentive and unmotivated because she was so quiet and timid, and therefore overshadowed by more zealous classmates. She never called out "Teacher!" or "I know!" as did many of the other children. I could see her attentiveness very clearly because I could watch for extended periods. But the evidence was fairly subtle, and it seemed to me that her teacher literally did not see the behaviors that revealed her motivation and enthusiasm. Moreover, when the teacher did call on her to respond, she seemed to freeze—she sat back in her chair, her big dark eyes got bigger and darker. The teacher interpreted this behavior as refusal to participate.

In late January, I decided to share my impressions with Candelaria's reading teacher and see what would happen. I told her I thought Candelaria was actually very motivated, but that her shyness and timidity, in the context of very active reading groups, kept the teacher from noticing it. I suggested the teacher observe Candelaria sometime, not when she was teaching a lesson but when she could observe for several minutes without interruption.

For the next month or so, there was no evidence that the teacher either took my advice to observe Candelaria or revised her judgment about her. We often talked about this or that group and specific children (including Candelaria) within them. While the teacher sometimes mentioned a child whom she thought was doing better or having some trouble, she gave no indication of having reconsidered Candelaria's attention and motivation.

In mid-March, however, the teacher said Candelaria "really seems to be on the ball ... [she] is able to read more proficiently [and] her skills have improved." Candelaria, the teacher said, had been "pretty attentive and wanting to try. ... She's never distracted and she's willing to volunteer."

This of course was a radical departure from what the teacher had previously thought about Candelaria. I elicited from the teacher her version of how this change occurred:

> I just perceived her as, well, because she's not assertive, I assumed she was not motivated. But I realized she's just that kind of kid. ... When you used those words [i.e., motivated and attentive, when referring to Candelaria in our conversation almost two months earlier], I thought, 'Are we talking about the same kid?' But then I watched her and saw that ... yeah [nods for emphasis].

Then she added, "But I reached my own conclusions."

What had happened in the previous two months was that the teacher, through her own observations, tested her assumption that Candelaria was unmotivated and inattentive. The teacher found that Candelaria was much more motivated than she had realized. She then encouraged her to speak out and found that Candelaria was more competent than she had thought. The teacher moved Candelaria to a higher reading group, and she further encouraged her to participate more overtly.

Candelaria was one of the successful children in the study, and the teacher said her reading achievement was "definitely" within the average range for first-grade readers. Moreover, the teacher pointed to her reassessment of Candelaria as a pivotal point:

> As soon as I realized she wasn't ... slow [which had *not* been discussed previously, but which the teacher had assumed] ... and I realized she was just quiet and timid, [I] wanted to know what she knew. And when I realized she had progressed much faster than the others, that's when I put her in the next group up. ... I [had] thought she was very low. I didn't see her as ready to attend. Her maturity level was low. I couldn't ever imagine her doing a lot of the activities she's doing now. I was happily surprised.

There are, of course, several possible explanations for Candelaria's turnaround. As is true for the other successful children, we can only speculate about the exact, psychological reasons for Candelaria's success. Following the teacher's observations of Candelaria (prompted by my suggestion that the child's attention and motivation had been misjudged), Candelaria was encouraged to participate more overtly, the teacher's expectations were raised, and Candelaria was moved to a higher reading group. Participation, high expectations, and higher group placement are all known to be associated with improved achievement; any or all of these may actually explain Candelaria's first-grade reading success.

What was important, however, and what was necessary for teacher encouragement, raised expectations, or placement in a higher group was the teacher's *reassessment* of Candelaria—that is, the change in her judgments about Candelaria's motivation and ability. This is what constituted the turning point academically. Prior to her reassessment, the teacher confessed, she had thought that Candelaria was inattentive, uninterested, and of very low ability. Under these circumstances, achievement expectations would probably have remained low, Candelaria would have remained in the lowest reading group, and she would not have received the encouragement and learning opportunities she needed and from which she eventually benefitted.

Just as important is the fact that the teacher reached her own conclusions based on her own observations: "I watched her," the teacher had told me six weeks after our conversation about Candelaria's attention and motivation. This is what is critical, since it suggests that the teacher was explicitly testing her hypothesis about Candelaria, a hypothesis she eventually discarded. And the teacher was emphatic about who, finally, was responsible for the revised view of Candelaria: she was.

Teachers' judgments about student motivation, ability, or other characteristics tend to be simplified and often only partly accurate (Shavelson, 1983; Shavelson & Stern, 1981). This case suggests that teachers can test their judgments of children empirically and adjust them accordingly.[7] Candelaria's teacher revised the hypothesis and changed her behavior toward Candelaria, encouraging her to participate more overtly. The teacher then discovered Candelaria knew more than she had realized. The teacher altered her judgment about Candelaria's abilities, which in turn led to further encouragement and a move to a higher reading group.

Candelaria's case suggests that regular and systematic observation in the classroom might help teachers avoid reaching simplistic and inaccurate conclusions about students. (See also Strahan, 1983, and Williams & Loertcher, 1986, for further discussion and examples of teachers observing in their own classrooms.) This might be especially important for children who are already at risk for educational underachievement.

CONCLUSION: PROMOTING ACTION
TO HELP CHILDREN AT RISK

To return to my original theme, what these cases illustrate is how fortuitous, even haphazard, some children's school success is: A parent takes it upon herself to teach her daughter to read because the girl started school late. A teacher calls parents in for a conference because the child has violated the homework policy and, incidentally, she tells them he is terribly behind in reading. A teacher confers several times with a child, and then her mother, because she perceives the child's behavior and attitude to be very poor; again, incidentally, she tells the mother to help her daughter with the letters and syllables they are learning. And finally, a teacher reassesses a child's attention, motivation, and ability because an outside observer suggests she take another look.

The fortuity of these children's success suggests we need to re-examine our assumptions about the size of the "inevitable" achievement spread we see in all classrooms. Certainly there are differences among children, and certainly these differences will translate into differences in attainment. But teachers, in particular, need to realize that if some children are not making it, there is an excellent chance that it is because we are not extending ourselves sufficiently to help more students succeed.

If it is true that more children who are at risk could be successful if teachers and parents took the kinds of actions I have described here, the next question is: How can teachers and parents be encouraged to do these sorts of things? That is, how can we make success for children at risk more of a planned, systematic event and less of a fortuitous, haphazard one? This is a topic for another paper and perhaps several other research studies. I will conclude with some brief suggestions.

With respect to parents, the implications seem fairly clear: the interest and the motivation are already there; parents simply must be made aware of how they can help their children and that there is a need for them to do so. This suggests a possible study: What would be the effect on at-risk children's achievement if the teacher informs parents (1) that the child is behind academically, (2) what skills or concepts the child needs help on, and (3) what kinds of activities parents can initiate at home? All three components are necessary, because my guess is that parent contacts, in and of themselves, are not sufficient. They must specifically focus on the child's academic needs and what parents can do to address them.

I do not think that all students will immediately be up to grade level as soon as teachers start calling parents. And, probably, as children go through the grades and as academic tasks become more demanding, poorly educated parents will be less capable of directly helping children learn specific skills in the curriculum. But the essential fact is this: There are not enough hours in the school day to permit teachers to fully address the academic needs of all students. Consequently, other resources must be mobilized, and parents are uniquely suited to this task. My hypothesis is that virtually all parents can help, at some level and in some way, and that virtually all will—provided the teacher contacts them and informs them of the need for their help. And the earlier in a child's school career his or her parents become involved, and that involvement is sustained, the bigger the payoff.

Prompting teacher action along the lines I have suggested—substantive, focused conferences with the parents of underachieving minority children and planned, systematic observation in the classroom—is probably more problematic. Teachers, more than ever before, are under tremendous pressure. Political currents, public opinion, legislative requirements, published test scores, new guidelines and regulations, newly revised or mandated curricula all contribute to the classroom teachers' feeling overwhelmed. In addition, as a matter of course teachers must deal with yard or lunch duty, putting on assemblies, maintaining an attractive physical environment in the room, attending meetings and special events after school hours, and, of course, being responsible for instructing large numbers of children.

If teachers are to initiate and maintain substantive parent contacts or engage in systematic observation in their own classroom, time must be set aside for each of these. While there is much that can be done without major changes in policies, administrative leadership and support can be crucial. Principals can be enormously influential in helping provide the time for such activities and for making them a high priority at their school. Otherwise, the variety of obligations teachers face and the daunting complexity of life in classrooms will continue to make it unlikely that many children receive the attention they need. And the children at risk for failure are among the most likely casualties.

How much of a difference would initiating parent contacts or incorporating regular and systematic observation in the classroom make? These are empirical questions that I think merit empirical investigation. Again, my hypothesis, based on the study I conducted and my own experience as a teacher, is that they would make a significant difference. To my mind, there is little doubt that we can make success for children at risk a more common occurrence than it currently is. The only question is whether we will.

NOTES

[1]Intelligence, or IQ, was not included as a potential factor in this study because its high correlation with the screening instrument used to select the children at risk (Feshbach et al., 1974, 1977) would preclude meaningful variation among study children's IQ.

[2]The definition of first-grade reading "success" I am using here is based on gradewide norms that are below what is actually desirable. As an indication, finishing or nearly finishing the second of three preprimers in first grade was considered being on grade level for the school. According to publisher's norms, however, all three preprimers were to be completed in first grade. The reading coordinator and the teachers made a distinction between the publisher's grade-level designations for the basal texts and what was "realistic for this population."

[3]All study children were learning to read in Spanish, and all references are to their Spanish reading achievement. In accordance with the district's transitional bilingual education program, children learn to read in their native language until they have sufficient English oral skills and Spanish literacy skills to permit a smooth transition to English literacy instruction. This transition usually occurs sometime between the end of the third grade and the fourth grade.

[4]The school operates on a year-round calendar.

[5]Strictly speaking, I am defining success and failure in this study in terms of decoding and word-recognition skills. These skills, of course, represent only a portion of what reading involves. But decoding and word-recognition receive the greatest emphasis in beginning reading instruction at the school, and, consequently, I decided to concentrate on explaining outcomes consonant with the school's own reading program. Such an emphasis does not mean teachers were indifferent to children's acquiring comprehension skills (nor that the two—decoding and comprehension—are unrelated, which is not the case; see Chall, 1983a).

Nor should this study's focus on decoding and word-recognition skills suggest that I assume these to be the necessary first steps in learning to read. This very issue is the subject of an enormous literature (see, for example, Chall, 1983b; Moffett & Wagner, 1983), and I have no intention of entering the fray here. But because the reading instruction program lays greatest emphasis on letter- and word-recognition, and children could not advance until they gained certain proficiency in decoding, this became the achievement outcome of interest.

[6]In the third week of classes, all first-grade teachers rated their children on four items taken from the First-Grade Student Rating Scale (Adelman & Feshbach, 1971) that asked about student attention and effort during instruction. The reliability (alpha) of the four-item scale was .92.

[7]Carrasco (Carrasco, 1979; Carrasco, Vera, & Cazden, 1981) makes a similar point about teachers failing to see important aspects of their students's behavior, then re-evaluating students once they are made aware of children's competencies. But in Carrasco's studies, teachers were shown videotapes of their students behaving in ways the teachers had not seen before. Candelaria's case suggests that teachers can reach more accurate assessments of their children without elaborate technical apparatus.

ACKNOWLEDGMENTS

Revised version of a paper presented at Symposium, "Effective Literacy Experiences for Young Children: Reducing the Risk Factors," International Reading Association Annual Convention, Anaheim, California, May 7, 1987. Deepest thanks to Ronald Gallimore and Ellen Dorfman for their help and advice and to Laura Seidner and Deborah Stipek for their suggestions. Thanks also to volume editors, JoBeth Allen and Jana Mason. The preparation of this paper was made possible by a Spencer Fellowship from the National Academy of Education.

We learned how much difference a teacher can make in the lives of individual children like Candelaria, Elena, Karen and Freddy. The chapters in the following section describe other ways in which teachers make a difference, especially in the literacy curriculum and environments they establish. The first teachers we study are those from The Children's School, serving predominantly black and Hispanic, low-income children in the Bronx. Delisle's detailed description of the environment and curriculum provides a working model for teachers and other curriculum planners.

Learning with Teachers

Chapter 5

The Children's School Project

Robert G. Delisle

THE CHILDREN'S SCHOOL

The Setting

The Children's School Project is a cooperative venture between Lehman College of the City University of New York and Public School District 10, The Bronx. School District 10 is the most populous of the school districts in New York City, with 32,000 elementary and junior high school students housed in thirty-two schools. Of these children, eight thousand are evenly divided between kindergarten, grade one, and grade two. The large kindergarten population is due in part to New York City's instituting all-day kindergartens in 1984.

As a result of this large school enrollment, School District 10 has built annexes, reorganized schools, and rented space for classrooms. One of the spaces that has been rented is in an underutilized school in an adjacent school district. The Children's School is located on two floors of this school. Nine classrooms, an art and a music room, a gym, two lunchrooms, a teachers's room and offices house two hundred and twenty children, twelve teachers and teacher aides, a head teacher, a director, a secretary, and a part-time professor-in-residence.

Classrooms in The Children's School are organized to reflect the philosophy that young children learn from interactions with adults in environments that are structured to promote intellectual and social-emotional growth and independence. All classrooms are set up to facilitate the integration of language activities into the various content areas. Each classroom has the following areas: library, home life, block, listening, writing/dictation, art/craft, manipulative, and science.

The Personnel

Eight classroom teachers, two special education teachers, and a corresponding number of aides have the major responsibility for day-to-day instruction. A music teacher and an art teacher provide the children with daily periods of art or music. A head teacher acts as a resource person for all of the teachers and the director oversees the entire project.

A professor-in-residence is on site two days a week and acts as a resource to the staff and to the director. In addition, the professor-in-residence conducts a course for the staff, as well as a series of workshops for other elementary teachers in the school district.

The Children

The children who attend The Children's School are bused from schools experiencing overcrowding conditions. The children must be at least 4.9 years of age and reside in the school district. The ethnic and racial make-up reflects that of School District 10, which is predominantly Hispanic and black with a recent influx of Asians and East Europeans. The socio-economic levels of the families reflect the lower end of the scale. One hundred percent of the children qualify for Chapter 1, and 50 percent for Chapter 53.

The Environment

The Children's School environment incorporates those features found most conducive in promoting literacy.

1. *Children are surrounded by language and print.* From the very first day that the five-year-olds enter the school they are surrounded by language and print. They are encouraged to engage in language activities and they learn when certain activities are appropriate. Halls and lunchrooms buzz with meaningful chatter; classroom talk is focused on the tasks at hand. Books can be found in all areas of all classrooms and children can find their own books, as well as books and other materials from

their teacher. A "Days of the Week" book is in the library area while a teacher-made "Time" book is in the manipulative area. Literature bulletin boards are found in the lunchroom, and books and stories are in the art and music room. All occasions are seen as language development occasions.

2. *Children are provided with models.* One teacher starts each day by reading to the children. Later in the morning he writes a story on the board and shares his writing process with the children. In the afternoon he sits with a small group in the home life area and, while drinking from a small cup, talks with them about the meal they have just served him. Modeling occurs throughout the day in every interaction that occurs in the class and in the school.

3. *Children are encouraged to value literacy.* Other teachers start the school day with language and print. Sharing time is followed by the first of several story reading sessions. Reading, writing, and language occur first because children know that teachers start the morning with what they consider to be the most important activity. In this school, books, reading, and writing are most important.

4. *Children are provided with occasions to use language and print.* Reading, writing, and speaking are encouraged throughout the school. Language occasions are frequent and realistic. Children role-play "teacher" with a big book in the library area and read to the baby in the home life area. Plans are entered into the "Block Plan Book" and new words and stories are written into the "Book of Block Words" and the "Book of Block Stories" or the "House Stories" book. Children innovate on text or create their own stories and sit in the Author's Chair. Journals are kept and read at home and stories are dictated, published, and circulated from the library. Language and print are used at every occasion.

5. *Children have high expectations set for them.* Tomika sits with her teacher and "pretend-reads" a story. She is praised and encouraged to pretend-read to others until she is ready for the next stage. Charles who writes that "I lk skl" is seen as having mastered many of the elements he will need in order to read and write; he is encouraged to write often. The process of becoming literate is seen as a developmental one, and all the children are seen as performing at a point on a continuum with the ability to proceed to the next point.

6. *Children are empowered.* As a teacher reads the story she hears John say to Linda, "What's a germ?" Ms. Jones nods to the questioner but continues to read. As she does, she hears John say, "I know what a germ is!" Later, when talking about the story, they notice that the author uses many words that sound alike. Ms. Jones could easily have

stopped the reading to give the meaning of the word but she would have taken away from John an opportunity to exercise power over language. She would also have done the same if she had preplanned a lesson on beginning sounds. Power over language is being transferred from teacher to student. Children are being given the lead in letting teachers know when they—the children—are able to use a cueing system independently and when they need the teachers as resources.

7. *Children are trusted.* Darrius left school on the first day in a very bad mood. His mother reported the following day that he was disappointed that he was not yet able to read. For the next few weeks, when left to choose areas, Darrius always went to writing, library, or to the listening corner. At the end of several weeks Darrius was reading. There was no sequence followed nor were skills developed in a manner that might be thought to be logical. The order in this situation was imposed by Darrius in his efforts to learn to read. It was he who set up the timetable for learning to read.

8. *Children are encouraged to risk.* Carlos reads "me and my family" for "me and my friends," and the teacher says, "Oh boys and girls, look at how Carlos read this line. Isn't it interesting he read *family* for *friends.* Sometimes we can do that. Now Carlos, let's try reading it with the other word, the word that is on the page." Carlos knows that the word he substituted was different from the text, but he doesn't feel bad about the substitution. In fact, he has been made to feel good about having made a meaningful substitution and willingly reads the word on the page. Wanda, who is reluctant to write, is asked to illustrate a simple pattern book and then willingly sits in the Illustrator's Chair. After the applause she can't wait to get to the writing table so she can next sit in the Author's Chair.

9. *Children are provided with occasions to see the wholeness of learning.* Tomika reads *Brown Bear, Brown Bear,* picks up the pattern quickly, and is soon reading the book. "Big Circle, Big Circle" soon appears in the art room as well as "Orange Square, Orange Square." Finally, in the manipulative area Tomika finds a matching game using big and little colored shapes curiously like those in books she has previously "read."

10. *Children are exposed to different purposes for reading and writing.* Daniel is asked to find a picture of an otter to see if what the author describes is accurate. He finds this information in a series on animals. William decides he would like to write about bears, but first he must read about them or have someone read to him about them. After reading *Dandelion* the children want to invite Ms. Jones to their class for "tea and taffy!" The children write "Yellow bus, yellow bus" for the children in the adjoining classroom. All activities are seen as having the potential for developing reading, writing, and speaking abilities.

The Curriculum

The Children's School was seen as a unique opportunity to implement a language and literacy curriculum. Working within the existing framework of Lehman College's Early Childhood Program, The Children's School faculty designed and implemented a curriculum that reflected the research about what young children coming to school know about literacy (Ferreiro & Teberosky, 1982; Mason, 1980; Sulzby & Teale, 1985); the stages through which it is thought children might proceed when coming into literacy (Bissex, 1980; Clay, 1975; Dyson, 1982; Ferreiro & Teberosky, 1982; Sulzby, 1985a); and the strategies young children use in the process of becoming literate (Bissex, 1980; Harste, Woodward, & Burke, 1984). Finally, it attempted to reflect what the research says about settings and practices that promote literacy among young children (Bissex, 1980; Clark, 1976; Clay, 1982; Durkin, 1966; Goodman, 1986; Graves, 1983; Holdaway, 1979; Paley, 1981; Taylor, 1983). It is best understood by examining the flow of a day in a kindergarten classroom. (See Figure 5–1.)

The children's day starts with class routines including attendance, weather, and news of the day. Some teachers modify the routine by giving children this time to look at and share books and using the opportunity to observe the book and reading behaviors that exist within their classrooms. Others group their children for sharing and have each group report back to the whole. They observe the levels of oral language development as well as the development of social skills. Still others spend this time singing or doing oral language exercises.

Following opening exercises is the first of two sessions devoted to reading aloud to children. In this first session the teacher uses patterned language big books. The teacher attempts to follow the sequence that parents might use when reading to their children: repeated readings of books; pointing out significant features of print; developing prediction and recognition skills; memorization of text; association of text with page; and association of text with text. The teacher makes observations of the children's behaviors and these observations become the basis for the formation of groups during the remainder of the day.

Next the children are asked to select an area in which they would like to work. As the children work in these areas, the teachers work with small groups, circulate noting the language being used, take dictation, or interact with children around an activity.

Each of the centers is designed to promote facility in a dimension of the language arts. Before going to the block area, children are asked to think and talk about possible constructions. These options are noted in a "Block Plans" book and construction starts. Children then make a visual record for the "Block Book" and a written record for the "Block Stories" book. Or, given particular kinds of structures, stories are written in the

Figure 5–1   **Kindergarten Classroom Schedule**

	Monday	Tuesday	Wednesday	Thursday	Friday
8:00–9:15	ADMINISTRATION				
	SHARING TIME				
9:15–9:45	READING ALOUD Patterned language book is used in a shared (Big Book) book experience. Teacher will also focus on some concept about print as well as doing letter or word work which arises from book.				
9:45–10:30	AREAS Children select areas in which to work. Teacher circulates taking down language. Teacher also works with small groups in reading/writing.				
10:30–11:15	MUSIC			ART	
11:15–12:05	WRITING Teacher demonstrates writing of a story. Children then select areas and the teacher circulates taking down language. Teacher works with small groups in writing/reading.				
12:05–1:00	LUNCH Children sit in small conversation groups with an adult leader.				
1:00–1:30	READING ALOUD Non-patterned books are read. Teacher allows responses, takes vocabulary once or twice a week.				
1:30–2:15	AREAS Children select areas in which to work. Teacher circulates taking down language. Teacher also works with small groups in reading/writing.				
2:15–2:30	DISMISSAL Recapping the day.				

"Bridge Book," the "House Book," or the "Zoo Book." These are then shared with the class.

In the home life area, the teacher places magazines near a rocker and books next to the cradle and the high chair. Paper and pencil are available for list making and paper is on the refrigerator door and near the telephone for note writing. The arts and crafts area has books illustrating different techniques used by illustrators as well as a "Clay Book" for records of what has been made. Blank books are available for spur of the moment sessions, integrating such things as mathematics vocabulary into the center. Children will paint or draw and then either talk or write about what has been done or what is being done. At times they may prepare illustrations or paintings for narratives that have been written by the class or they may recreate part of their favorite book.

Books and stories written for and by children are in the library area, which also includes flannel board stories, activities for the retelling of familiar stories, and games involving familiar story characters. The manipulative area has a variety of easy to difficult puzzles, word/letter games drawn from literature that has been read, individual word boxes for those children who want them, math manipulatives, and a host of other items, all designed to promote growth in thought, language, and literacy.

The listening center has familiar recorded stories; the writing center has examples of written work from the children, the teacher, and from well-known authors. Children go there to copy favorite words, to write stories, by innovating on familiar texts, to write their own stories, to practice penmanship, or to dictate stories to an adult.

After a period of time the children are called together with a song and then go to art, two or three days a week, or to music, two or three days a week. In art, the children engage in age-appropriate activities that often have a language component attached to them or embedded in them. A session using shapes is related to books in the manipulative area in the classroom, whereas "Three Little Kittens" may end up as a game in mathematics. In music, the children spend much time on rhythms and patterns, learning songs and poems that will end up as large charts in their classroom.

Once back in the classroom the teacher writes a story, either on the board or on chart paper, for the children and shares with them the process of composing. At first the story is simple, but with greater proficiency the process becomes more complex. The teacher demonstrates writing and the use of cueing systems needed to begin to write. The children again select areas and the teacher circulates, this time focusing on bringing children to writing.

Lunch for children is an occasion for developing oral language skills. Children sit at tables in groups of six to nine with an adult circulating from table to table, participating in conversations, and occasionally connecting them to events of the day. Lunch is followed by a rest time during which the children may nap, talk quietly at tables, or read.

Following lunch is the second read-aloud session. In this second session a non-patterned language book is read to the children. The teacher waits for responses, allowing children to say what was important to them and what they remembered. Then the teacher shares with them what she likes and dislikes about the books and, especially important, why. On occasion the teacher will ask the class if there are some words that they think they would like to own, words that are particularly interesting to them. A list is generated and made available in the writing area for anyone who would like to use them later on. As the year progresses children generate other lists from read-aloud sessions, such as favorite phrases or names.

Another area selection follows, and then dismissal activities, which usually include a song and a recapping of the many things the children learned during the day. The children then board the bus for the ride home.

The Third Year

The Children's School Project originally conceived as an overflow facility for kindergarten children and as a multifaceted project with potential for bringing about lasting change is now in its third year of operation. No longer a project, it has expanded to three hundred children in eleven classrooms, and has been designated as a school. Over the next two years it will expand into a facility accommodating grades one and two and, in the near future, grades three through six.

The Children's School Project was seen first and foremost as facilitating the design, implementation, and evaluation of curriculum that reflected the state of the knowledge about how young children learn and in particular about how young children come into literacy. Although not evaluated in traditional terms—children's achievement on a test—the curriculum is recognized as a valid one for young children. It has been selected as one of three models for replication by New York City's Project Child (a major effort directed at high-risk students), and several New York City and suburban school districts have started replicating the work done at The Children's School. In addition, large numbers of teachers have initiated replications in their classrooms.

The school was also seen as bridge building between public schools and universities, encouraging cooperative ventures, ventures where knowledge created by teachers, schools, and universities could be mutually validated. Although not fully developed until this third year, two projects have been initiated that hold promise. The Research Associates Project has been set up to allow university persons to explore questions related to literacy development; parallel to this the Teacher Associates Project has been developed. Presently two Research Associates and four Teacher Associates under the guidance of an educational anthropologist are exploring issues related to literacy development.

Finally, The Children's School Project was seen as facilitating the renewal of teachers as well as their enculturation into new ways of viewing young children and into new ways of viewing themselves. In keeping with these goals, teachers were involved during the first two years in working with the professor-in-residence on literacy development; in the third year the teachers have assumed the leadership in curriculum development. They are conducting a series of inservice sessions that deal with developing literacy in the curriculum area of mathematics. They have also developed case studies of children in their classrooms.

POLICY RECOMMENDATIONS

The conditions that promote literacy in young children are abundantly clear from both the research perspective as well as the classroom practice perspective. Although the focus of this paper has been on one aspect of these conditions, the curriculum, it must not be forgotten that this development does not occur solely within the context of the classroom. Rather, it occurs within the larger context of the school and, just as conditions are created for children, so too must conditions be created for teachers.

These conditions must insure that:

1. *Teachers are surrounded by resources that encourage the development of literacy.* These resources must not only take the forms of books and supplies to be used by the teachers and children, they must also take the form of university courses and inservice sessions conducted on and off site.

2. *Teachers are encouraged to see the wholeness of language.* They are asked to observe children and to use these observations to plan curriculum. They are not asked to keep plans in the traditional manner nor are they observed in the traditional manner. Rather, they keep logs of observations and are observed interacting with children in the environment which they have created.

3. *Teachers are encouraged to take risks.* They are urged to explore new curriculum areas and to think about their work and its appropriateness for young children. They are asked to observe their colleagues and to engage in meaningful dialogue around this work.

4. *Teachers are trusted and empowered.* They work to implement the goals that have been agreed upon for the school year and are given the freedom to implement them in their own style, within the school's philosophical and theoretical framework.

5. *Teachers are provided with models.* These models should come from the research, literature from protocols, and from observing all adults in the school interacting with children.

6. *Teachers are encouraged to value literacy.* They are encouraged to redefine literacy to include art and music with occasions provided for discussing observations of children in all areas.

7. *Teachers have high expectations set for them.* Just as the expectations are that kindergarten children will read and write, so too is it expected that teachers will create environments that nurture and encourage all children to learn to read and write.

In Chapter 6, we examine more closely the effects of the kind of developmentally appropriate literacy instruction at The Children's School. The Kindergarten Emergent Literacy Program in San Antonio is based on the same philosophy and incorporates a very similar literacy curriculum. We learn in detail in this chapter how children respond to such a curriculum. We will see how two children, Lan and Bernard, "grow into literacy" in this supportive environment.

Chapter 6

No-Risk Kindergarten Literacy Environments for At-Risk Children

Miriam G. Martinez
Markay Cheyney
Connie McBroom
Ann Hemmeter
William H. Teale

STATISTICS tell us that certain children who walk through the door the first day of kindergarten are at risk for poor achievement in reading and writing as they go through school. To help these children develop as fluent, willing readers and writers is one of the greatest challenges faced by our schools. As Goldenberg (this volume) points out, the process by which an at-risk prediction ends up being a story of successful achievement in school is a complex one, involving a confluence of (1) characteristics of the child himself or herself, (2) the instruction the child receives, and (3) interactions between the school and the home. In this chapter we describe selected aspects of a Kindergarten Emergent Literacy Program, aspects that we have found especially important in our attempts to teach kindergarten children who fit the traditional at-risk description. Our discussion does not pretend to provide *the* solution to the challenge. It focuses mainly on what can occur in the early childhood classroom to maximize the likelihood that the child's initial academic experiences with literacy will set the basis for success in reading and writing. It also addresses to some extent school/home connections that have resulted in stronger programs for at-risk kindergarten children. We agree with Goldenberg: the answer is more complex than what is presented here. However, we do feel that the literacy environment the teacher fosters in the early childhood classroom is of paramount importance in getting children on the road to becoming lifelong readers and writers.

A NO-RISK ENVIRONMENT FOR AT-RISK CHILDREN

The basic contention of this chapter is that in order to give at-risk children the best chance of success in literacy, we must create a no-risk environment in the classroom. A no-risk kindergarten classroom feels somewhat like a positive home environment for literacy learning, and it is intended to function in much the same way. That is to say, the classroom provides a wide variety of literacy experiences for the child in the context of an emotionally supportive environment.

In building the positive emotional climate the teacher accepts the children as they are, attempting to use their existing experiential and language base as the foundation for curriculum. It is a social fact that in industrialized, English-speaking countries today, a disproportionately large number of at-risk children are from ethnic minority and/or low-income backgrounds. This state of affairs provides a particular challenge, for teachers must learn to view linguistic and cultural diversity as differences rather than deficits. By focusing upon what children *do* know and what they *are* able to do, the stage is set for the emotionally supportive climate. The teacher accepts the children's attempts at reading and writing and encourages experimentation and risk taking. Just as a parent is overjoyed at a daughter's or son's first attempts of speaking—even though those attempts are wrong by adult standards—so does the teacher accept and encourage the young child's attempts at literacy, even though many times they too are not conventional. The teacher's encouragement of experimentation with language and acceptance of the children's attempts are especially important because they help promote children's confidence in themselves as readers and writers and their willingness to take chances in attempting to produce or comprehend written language.

In addition to being emotionally supportive, the no-risk environment provides a literacy-rich experience for the children. Just as literacy is part and parcel of a wide range of activities in the home (Heath, 1983; Taylor, 1983; Taylor & Dorsey-Gaines, 1988; Teale, 1986), reading and writing are inextricably bound to the everyday activities in the classroom. Literacy becomes an integral part of the social fabric of the classroom. For instance, written language is used to help organize the classroom so that things run smoothly, it is integrated into children's play, it is experienced daily through activities like storybook reading and the writing center. The classroom provides the children with countless opportunities to: (1) participate with proficient adults in literacy activities, (2) engage independently in reading and writing attempts, and (3) observe reading and writing being demonstrated by the teacher, other adults, or older children. In short, the at-risk child is steeped in a literate environment.

A KINDERGARTEN EMERGENT LITERACY PROGRAM

The no-risk environment is just the type of learning situation that we have attempted to implement in building a Kindergarten Emergent Literacy Program (KELP) in classrooms throughout the greater San Antonio, Texas, area over the past four years. Development of the KELP was spurred by the past decade of research on early childhood reading and writing, which, in taking new perspectives, has provided exciting fresh insights into young children's literacy learning. The term *emergent literacy* (or *emerging literacy*) is now being widely used to describe development during these first years of children's lives (see, for example, Anderson, Hiebert, Scott, & Wilkinson, 1985, or Teale & Sulzby, 1986). Emergent literacy focuses on the period between birth and the time when children read and write conventionally. Emergent literacy regards young children's reading and writing conceptions and behaviors as legitimate aspects of the process of literacy learning and views all children in a literate society like ours as "in the process of becoming" literate long before school entry.

The other major conclusions emanating from an emergent literacy perspective might be summarized as follows:

- Literacy develops out of real-life settings in which reading and writing are used to accomplish goals. Therefore, the functions of literacy are integral to learning to read and write.

- Reading and writing develop concurrently and interrelatedly in young children.

- Young children learn about reading and writing by constructing their knowledge, not by mere imitation of adults or through rote memory.

Attempting to take these conclusions into account in devising classroom practice, we have focused the KELP on providing children with a wide range of functional, holistic, meaningful activities that involve reading or writing in some way. The program stresses informal yet challenging activities rather than formal instruction. The attempt is made to integrate literacy into the fabric of the everyday work and play in the classroom. Group storybook reading, classroom libraries, and opportunities for independent "reading" of familiar books (Teale & Martinez, in press), writing (Martinez & Teale, 1987), and integration of reading and writing into the children's dramatic play form the core activities in the program.

EMERGENT LITERACY AND THE AT-RISK CHILD

In general we have found that the principles and practices inherent in the Kindergarten Emergent Literacy Program are appropriate for the range of children present in the early childhood classroom. However, recent experience with implementing the program in classrooms with large numbers of at-risk children has aided our understanding of special considerations that need to be taken into account when working with such children. In this chapter we focus on the particular characteristics of a kindergarten program that will most effectively support at-risk children's literacy development.

As a general comment, let us point out that successful implementation of an emergent literacy program for at-risk children is related to the general makeup of the class. In particular, we have found that classrooms containing students from a variety of literacy backgrounds seem to require different emphases in experiences than classrooms composed entirely of at-risk children. Whereas some children are willing to write from the first day of school, others may first need different kinds of literacy experiences. This need for varied emphases can be illustrated by briefly describing the programs in two classrooms.

Mrs. C's school is located in an older neighborhood in an urban community. It is a motley neighborhood containing families from different ethnic groups—Hispanic, black, Anglo, and Asian—and from different SES groups. Many of the students in Mrs. C's classroom would be considered at-risk children, including children whose families are below the poverty line, children whose first language is not English, and children whose parents are illiterate. However, in Mrs. C's classroom there were also students who regularly participated in literacy activities at home, many of whom were from mainstream backgrounds. The makeup of the class was important because it enabled Mrs. C from the beginning of the school year to initiate literacy activities with the children. They were invited to listen to stories, to engage in independent emergent readings of stories, to dictate language experience stories, to write at the classroom writing center, and so forth. In Mrs. C's classroom, the children from the literacy-rich backgrounds were never hesitant to engage in any of these activities. Seeing their peers so willingly participate, the at-risk children soon followed their lead. By capitalizing on peer support, Mrs. C was able to begin her emergent literacy program fully from the first day of school.

Mrs. H's classroom stands in contrast to Mrs. C's. The school in which Mrs. H taught was an inner-city school in a black neighborhood. The community was extremely poor, and the children entering kindergarten typically had had comparatively few opportunities to participate in activities mediated by reading or writing, and few of them had been read to regularly at home. Mrs. H's students were reluctant to participate in certain types of emergent reading and writing activities at the beginning of the year. The one type of classroom literacy activity in which they willingly participated was storybook reading. The children appeared to be starved for stories and seemed like they would willingly have listened to Mrs. H read all day long. They participated with Mrs. H in producing dictated experience stories at the beginning of the school year, yet adamantly refused to engage in attempts at writing. It was some six weeks before they began to engage in emergent reading of storybooks and even longer before most developed an interest in writing activities. In fact, many children were not willing to visit the writing center until after Christmas.

In this chapter we describe ways of structuring the reading and writing components of a kindergarten emergent literacy program to foster at-risk children's involvement in both interactive and independent practice activities. We remind the reader who is concerned with applying these ideas that successful implementation requires sensitivity to the students themselves. Activities should not be the heart of teaching; students should. Therefore, the implementation of a kindergarten literacy program will depend greatly upon the literacy backgrounds of the children.

We begin with the reading component of the program, for two reasons. First, in working with at-risk children we have found that if the reading component is carefully organized, it can serve as a framework for many of the children's writing activities. Therefore, our discussion serves as a basis for the subsequent discussion of the writing program. Second, we have found that if children enter school having had few or no opportunities to listen to stories read aloud, the teacher *must* begin the literacy program with storybook readings, and so we begin at this same point.

THE READING COMPONENT

The kindergarten teacher must provide for two major types of reading experiences: storybook readings by the teacher and emergent readings of storybooks by the children. Storybook readings are those all-so-familiar occasions upon which the teacher reads aloud to a group (most frequently the whole class) of children. Emergent readings are attempts by not-yet-literate children to read books that have been read aloud to them.

Storybook Readings

At-risk children must have extensive opportunities to listen to stories. Hence storybook reading forms the core of the KELP reading component. The value of these experiences cannot be overestimated. A host of corre-lational, experimental, and ethnographic studies attest to the important contribution that storybook readings can make to young children's literacy development (e.g., Burroughs, 1972; Cochran-Smith, 1984; Durkin, 1974–75; Feitelson, Kita, & Goldstein, 1986; Heath, 1982; Snow, 1983; Taylor, 1983; Teale & Sulzby, 1987; Wells, 1985). Studies like these indicate that storybook reading experiences positively facilitate a variety of facets of children's literacy orientation: their attitudes toward reading, their knowledge about the form and structure of written language, their understanding of the functions and uses of written language, and their actual reading strategies. Such research underscores the fact that storybook reading is an instructional activity for young children, not merely a fun thing. In summary, we believe that storybook reading plays a special role in the development of literacy in young children. We offer the following three guidelines for making storybook reading an integral part of the classroom experience for at-risk children.

Guideline 1: Provide Maximum Exposure to Books. The traditional storytime, in which a single story is read daily to the class, must certainly be implemented in emergent literacy programs for at-risk children, but we have found that these children seek far more exposure to stories than can be provided with a single daily storybook reading. Instead, they must be virtually saturated with literature through story readings. The time devoted to multiple daily storybook readings can easily be justified, for in a real sense these readings provide the chance for at-risk children to develop knowledge and concepts of print comparable to those of peers who may have been read to since infancy and enter school having participated in hundreds of storybook readings.

Although it is easy to build a rationale for devoting time to multiple storybook readings, the teacher must still contend with the problem of finding time for reading in an already crowded curriculum (especially in a half-day program). We have attempted to solve this problem by integrating children's literature into the content areas, and there are endless ways to do this. *Stone Soup* (Brown, 1947) is an ideal book to be used in a unit on nutrition. What could be a better way to introduce a science lesson on spiders than with Eric Carle's (1984) *The Very Busy Spider*? The concept of cooperation is beautiful illustrated in Leo Lionni's (1968) *Swimmy*. *Caps for Sale* (Slobodkina, 1947) and *Petunia* (Duvoisin, 1950) present opportunities for problem solving. The listing could go on and on, of course, because there is a wealth of children's books that can be used in math, science, social studies, and the language arts. For an extensive discussion of current resources that teachers can use in identifying children's books that support content area lessons see Pillar (1987), and for many good suggestions for how to integrate story reading into various facets of the early childhood curriculum see Coody (1983).

There are additional ways of maximizing children's storybook reading experiences. Classroom libraries can be equipped with listening centers in which both teacher-made and commercially prepared tapes accompany the books in the center. We have found teacher-made tapes especially useful in listening centers because the teacher can personalize the reading more.

Teachers can also forge links with the home to promote more extensive exposure to books. Children can check out books from the classroom library to take home. Ideally a parent or older sibling will read the book to the child. It is possible, of course, that no one in the home can read, in which case the parent can be encouraged to listen to the child's emergent reading of the storybook. In either case, the parent is involved in the story reading experience and so plays a part in promoting the child's literacy development.

It is not uncommon, however, for teachers to receive little support in promoting literacy from parents of at-risk children. One reason why certain children are at risk is because they were not read to during their early years. Volunteer readers in the classroom can extend storybook reading activities in an important way: by lap reading. Lap readings are conducted one-to-one, or one-to-two. Such readings are more intimate than the traditional group story readings and thus have the potential for providing an even richer experience with storybooks. Group storybook readings can be related to the individual child's background and developmental sophistication only to a certain degree; lap readings can be much more finely tuned to a particular child. Thus, we encourage the use of parent or grandparent volunteers (from a neighborhood senior citizen's center, for example) in the classroom, with each volunteer reading to one or two children.

Guideline 2: Provide Children with Exposure to Many Types of Quality Literature. One of the main objectives of the KELP is to expose children to a wide variety of worthy children's literature. Emergent literacy is based on books, all kinds of books—wordless books, rhyme books, fairy tales, fantasies, realistic stories, informational books, alphabet books, counting books, big books. Good stories form the heart of the child's early experience with books. In addition, we should like to draw attention to two types of books that are also important in working with young at-risk children: predictable books and informational books. We systematically include predictable books among the many that are read aloud to students. Predictable books are characterized by their use of natural repetitive (thus, predictable) language patterns and/or are structured according to set patterns. Many of the most popular works of children's literature are predictable, including titles like *The Little Red Hen* (Galdone, 1973), *The Three Billy Goats Gruff* (Galdone, 1973), *Where the Wild Things Are* (Sendak, 1963), and *Over in the Meadow* (Keats, 1971). (For published guides to predictable books see Allen, R.V., 1976; Bridge, 1986; Heald-Taylor, 1987; Rhodes, 1981; Tompkins & McGee, 1983; Tompkins & Webeler, 1983; Weaver, 1988.) The distinctive features of predictable books make them relatively easy for children to reconstruct independently once they have been read aloud to them, and this is especially important for at-risk children because these emergent readings (i.e., the child's attempt to use picture cues in reconstructing a story from memory) facilitate young children's literacy development. Although we strongly advocate the use of predictable books with at-risk children, a word of caution is nonetheless in order. The predictable book is but *one type* that should be included in the literature program. The overarching goal must remain wide exposure to *many types* of children's literature.

Guideline 3: Read Stories Repeatedly. At-risk kindergartners seek repeated readings of stories, and this response is fortunate because the increased familiarity resulting from hearing a story repeatedly enables children more easily to engage in an emergent reading of the story. Not all stories need be read repeatedly, but we do recommend that teachers make repeated readings a *systematic* part of the read-aloud program. To insure that repeated readings are systematically included in the program, we suggest that at least two of the stories read each week be ones that have been read previously. Teachers can invite children to take turns selecting stories for special read-aloud sessions that feature old favorites. Also, the children's response to stories can guide teachers in selecting ones for repeated readings. The desire to introduce children to as many stories as possible is an important goal for the kindergarten; however, it should be balanced with the practice of repeated readings as part of the story reading program.

Emergent Readings

Emergent readings of storybooks are attempts to read familiar storybooks by young children who are not yet conventionally literate. The behaviors exhibited in these readings include labeling or commenting upon individual pictures in the book, monologic storytelling, using a reading intonation to recreate the story almost verbatim, attempts to decode certain words in the book, and reading selected sight words. (See Sulzby, 1985a for a complete description of all the categories of behavior young children exhibit.) As was mentioned earlier, emergent readings contribute directly to young children's literacy development by giving them the opportunity to practice and extend what is learned during read alouds (Holdaway, 1979; Sulzby & Teale, 1987). Children have the chance to reconstruct the vocabulary and syntactic structures of written language. They can practice the fluency and expressive reading of the mature reader. Further, these emergent readings allow children to engage in important reading strategies such as monitoring the meanings they construct and using multiple clues to predict upcoming words. Evidence of such facilitating effects comes from a variety of sources. Parents of early readers have frequently reported that their children spend long periods of time pretend-reading to themselves, to siblings, to pets, or stuffed animals (see, for example, Clark, 1976; Durkin, 1966; Tobin, 1981). Case studies of literacy development in early childhood have described this phenomenon (Baghban, 1984; Bissex, 1980; Haussler, 1982; Hoffman, 1982). Also, Sulzby's (1985a) descriptions of two-, three-, four- and five-year-olds' emergent reading behaviors show them to be developmental in nature.

In working with at-risk children, we try to structure the classroom reading program to maximize the occurrence of these independent reenactments of storybooks. Both the storybook reading program and the classroom library are intimately involved in this attempt. In discussing the read-aloud program, we have mentioned emergent readings several times. This was almost unavoidable because of the natural link that exists between storybook reading and emergent readings—the interactive experience leads naturally to the independent experience.

To take advantage of this link and to make it even stronger, we structure the read-aloud program to foster the occurrence of emergent readings. This is done by including predictable books among the ones read aloud and by reading books repeatedly. However, we have found additional ways of encouraging children to engage in emergent storybook readings, and we will focus on these techniques in this section.

Teachers report varying degrees of success in involving their at-risk students in emergent readings at the beginning of the school year. Teachers in classrooms that contain both at-risk children and children from literacy-rich homes encounter few difficulties. For many children from literacy-rich homes, emergent reading is an activity they have spontaneously engaged in before entering school. We find that when these children model emergent reading, the at-risk children soon follow their lead. The case is different in classrooms comprised exclusively of at-risk children. Under these circumstances, the teacher should consciously organize children's literacy experiences to encourage and support emergent reading behaviors. The teacher must also wait patiently, weeks or even months, until the children are willing to try independently reading or reenacting storybooks.

One of the teacher's most effective tools in promoting emergent readings is the classroom library. Providing children with access to a supply of books that have been read to them enables the children to return to their favorite titles until they are comfortable with them. Morrow and Weinstein's (1982) research provides information useful in designing classroom libraries. They found that children use classroom libraries when they are comfortable places to visit. Libraries should be large enough for five or six children and be carpeted and/or contain pillows or bean bags. In addition, children prefer libraries that offer privacy by being partitioned off from the rest of the room. Classroom libraries should contain a large assortment of books (five to eight per child) of different types. Other desirable features include book related posters, puppets, stuffed animals, flannel boards, and a listening station.

A carefully designed library center draws children to it, but it is also necessary to be concerned with how children use the classroom library and, in particular, how to foster the occurrence of emergent readings. A carefully structured read-aloud program is the most effective means that we have found of encouraging children to engage in emergent reading. Earlier we recommended the use of repeated readings of storybooks, including pre-dictable books. We have found that if the library is stocked with many of the books read aloud to the children, they very naturally select those books for their independent use in the library; these books become special favorites of the children. In libraries containing some fifty books, we have observed children selecting only five or six very familiar books (repeatedly read) over and over, and frequently these books are predictable (Martinez & Teale, 1988).

Teachers can also structure response activities to promote emergent readings of storybooks. Flannel boards are especially useful tools. If the teacher models the use of flannel board figures in presenting stories and then makes the materials available in the library center, along with the accompanying book, children will work alone or in groups repeatedly reen-acting the story. Stories that have relatively few characters, are action oriented, and contain minimal description are especially appropriate for flannel board presentation. Many predictable stories have just these characteristics. In general, children have a great deal of success using the flannel board to reenact folktales such as *The Three Bears*, *The Three Little Pigs*, and *The Gingerbread Boy*. Teachers can also extend invitations to their students to "read" a story to the class. We have observed children engage in a flurry of practice activity in preparation for this event. Teacher-organized creative dramatics activities promote independent reenactments of stories as well. These dramatics activities do not have to be (nor should they initially be) major productions in which children are expected to assume the roles of individual characters and play stories in their entirety. When working with young children, a more appropriate beginning in creative dramatics is the use of synchronized movement, in which a whole class moves together representing the action of a story (or portions of a story) as the teacher reads. For example, as the teacher reads *Caps for Sale* (Slobodkina, 1947), the children can become the monkeys who imitate the peddler. Or for *The Seven Skinny Goats* (Ambrus, 1969), the children can become the goats who dance themselves into a frenzy each time the main character plays his flute. These teacher-led creative dramatics activities frequently spawn student-initiated dramatic reenactments of stories.

THE WRITING COMPONENT

The writing component must offer the child opportunities similar to those afforded in the reading component—opportunities to write with proficient adults and to engage in emergent writing activities. By collaborating with adults in projects requiring writing, children have the opportunity to learn about both the functions and the forms of our writing system. Opportunities to engage in emergent writing enable students to try out (or practice) their concepts about the writing system. As Dyson (1982) has noted, it is through writing that children can become actively involved in "solving the written language puzzle" (p. 829). Writing also enables the reading and writing processes to reinforce each other in learning, a feature that Sulzby (1985b), researching young children's writing and rereading of their own writing, found to be useful in development.

We believe that at-risk kindergartners should be invited to write on the first day of school. The form the writing takes should be the individual child's choice. Scribbling must be as valued as the use of invented or conventional spellings. However, it seems appropriate to repeat our earlier warning: Some at-risk children may exhibit reluctance to write regardless of the teacher's attempts to make writing a risk-free activity. This is especially apt to happen in the classrooms where all the children come to school with limited literacy backgrounds. By no means does this indicate that the teacher should abandon the idea of having the children engage in emergent writing activities. Rather, the teacher must take special care to support the children's emergent writing by involving them in the literacy experiences that provide the foundation they need to function independently. The literature experiences discussed earlier certainly contribute to this foundation. In addition, the teacher, as an expert writer, must frequently provide demonstrations of the uses and functions of the written language. That is to say, the teacher must *be* a writer in the classroom. Finally, the teacher must participate with the children in writing activities.

One type of teacher/child participation activity in our classrooms is the dictated story. The use of dictated experience stories affords the teacher some unique opportunities to promote children's literacy development. By participating in a variety of different kinds of dictated writing activities, children learn about many of the functions of written language. Experience stories offer children the chance to learn about the composing process and develop basic concepts about the writing system. In the next section we discuss ways of structuring the writing program to enhance the effectiveness of this activity.

The Use of Dictated Stories

Experience—all kinds of experience—breeds successful writing. Children's experiences outside of school can serve as the bases for their stories, as can the shared experiences of the class, including those provided vicariously through literature. In fact, in working with at-risk children, we find literature to be an especially powerful springboard into dictation or writing, and in light of at-risk children's enthusiastic responses to storybook readings, this perhaps comes as no surprise.

We frequently use works of children's literature as models for dictated stories. Predictable books are especially effective models in that they provide a structure that supports children's compositions. One teacher used *It Looked Like Spilt Milk* (Shaw, 1947) in this way. The children turned their book into a Halloween story entitled *It Looked Like a Skeleton*. The final product, accompanied by the children's own art work, was a cohesive and imaginative story.

It Looked Like a Skeleton

Sometimes it looked like a witch.
But it wasn't a witch.
Sometimes it looked like a bat.
But it wasn't a bat.
Sometimes it looked like a cat.
But it wasn't a cat.
Sometimes it looked like a ghost.
But it wasn't a ghost.
Sometimes it looked like a piece of trick or treat candy.
But it wasn't a piece of trick or treat candy.
Sometimes it looked like a jack-o-lantern.
But it wasn't a jack-o-lantern.
Sometimes it looked like a skeleton.
But it wasn't a skeleton.
It was just a cloud in the sky on Halloween.

While studying a unit on the five senses, one class read *Brown Bear, Brown Bear* (Martin, 1967) in which the author organizes the text by repeatedly asking a series of animals, "What do you see?" The children employed a similar organizational framework, but they used each other's names and asked the questions, "What can you taste?" The resulting book was entitled *Children, Children, What Can You Taste?* The final version was written on posterboard (cut in the shape of lips, of course), and each refrain was accompanied by magazine pictures of the appropriate food.

Children Children, What Can You Taste?

Tamara Davis, Tamara Davis
What can you taste?
I can taste pancakes,
Sweet with syrup,
Hot with butter.

Felipe Martinez, Felipe Martinez
What can you taste?
I can taste peanuts,
Hard like rocks,
Bumpy when you eat them.

Chris Taylor, Chris Taylor
What can you taste?
I can taste corn,
Sweet and crunchy and buttery.

Lupe Sarabia, Lupe Sarabia
What can you taste?
I can taste chips,
Hard and salty.

Sandy Alexander, Sandy Alexander
What can you taste?
I can taste hamburger
Hard and sweet.

Henry Uribe, Henry Uribe
What can you taste?
I can taste spaghetti with meatballs,
Soft and sweet.

Patty Ramon, Patty Ramon
What can you taste?
I can taste bread,
Soft and good.

Derek Turner, Derek Turner
What can you taste?
I can taste candy,

Tastes like cinnamon toast crunch,
Tastes like sugar,
Tastes hard.

In one class, Eric Carle's *The Very Busy Spider* (1984) served as the basis for several activities, including two group-composing experiences. The book was first used to teach the children what a main character is. The spider in this book is an unusual main character, indeed, for she is completely silent and never deigns to answer any of the questions the animals ask her. Using *The Very Busy Spider* as a springboard, the children composed their own book entitled *Santa and His Friends*. However, it differed from the stimulus book in that Santa, the main character, answered all his friends' questions. In writing the story, the children learned the difference between a statement and a question as they wrote the dialogue between Santa and his friends, and just so the language book would not be repetitious and thus boring, they looked up *ask* and *answer* in a thesaurus and incorporated new vocabulary into the dialogue tags to make them more interesting. Finally, the teacher suggested that they send a copy of the story to Eric Carle. This led to dictating a letter in which the children pointed out how their main character was different from Mr. Carle's.

Many of the stories modeled after children's literature are made into class books, which are placed into the classroom library. Yet another link between the reading and writing components becomes apparent when watching the children use these class books, which are especially popular for emergent readings.

Literature has provided the experiences that feed many of the dictated stories, but direct experiences have been equally important. Whenever possible, opportunities are provided for the children to cook, taste, or touch. Visitors are invited to share information. Animals are brought to class. The children are taken on nature walks on campus and field trips into the community. Teachers also draw on children's out-of-school experiences as the basis for dictation activities. "The News" is one of the most successful activities of this type that we have observed. On Fridays, the teacher who originated this activity involved her children in predicting the weekend news. Each child was asked what she or he would be doing on the weekend and responses were written on chart paper. Then on Mondays, a new chart was completed containing the weekend's news as it actually happened. All the children had news to report on Monday, so student response to the activity was overwhelmingly positive. The children never allowed the teacher to forget The News.

Throughout the chapter we have said that natural links exist between interactions between teacher and students and students' independent activities. Children learn about the written language system by participating with a proficient writer in dictated experience stories or morning message activities. They subsequently practice what they learn in emergent writing activities. Just how rooted emergent writing is in teacher-student interactions became apparent in one classroom during The News activity. The News had always been organized as a dictated experience activity until one day after spring break a child stood up at the beginning of the activity and announced that she would do the news that day, and she did. "So what's your news?" the self-appointed news recorder asked each classmate and then proceeded to write the answers using invented spellings. Six months of participation with the teacher provided this child with the support needed to engage independently in the activity.

Emergent Writing

At-risk children must be invited to write at the beginning of the school year. Some children respond to the invitation immediately, but others may not respond for several months. When the children in the KELP are ready to engage in emergent writing, they are encouraged to write at various times throughout the day. One vehicle for promoting emergent writing is the writing center. Children who express a willingness to write are encouraged to work at the center daily. It is critical to the success of the center that the children view writing as a risk-free activity. Any form of writing a child might use is accepted. These include drawing, scribbling, letter-like forms, and invented spellings, as well as conventional spellings.

The center is stocked with a variety of types of paper, pens, pencils, markers, and crayons. The children rotate through the center in small groups. If possible, an adult is available in the center to work with the children. This adult, who can be the teacher, a parent, or a community volunteer, plays a number of key roles. As a prewriting facilitator, the adult can urge the children to think about their topic before beginning to write. While writing, children may ask the adult for help. The most frequent requests for aid are made by children who want assistance in correctly spelling a word. In response to such requests, teachers generally encourage the children to work out the spelling as best they can in an attempt to urge them to explore the sound/symbol relationships of the language. When the children have finished writing, the adult serves as an audience as the children are asked to read what they've written. After listening to the children read individually, the adult gives them feedback on the content and/or form of their stories. Finally, for children whose writing is not easily read by an adult, the teacher serves as a recorder, writing on a separate sheet of paper what the children say as they read their papers. The sheet is kept in the child's writing folder, which serves as a record of the child's progress during the course of the year.

We realize that the teacher may not always be available to work in the writing center and that finding volunteers is difficult in many communities. Under these circumstances, the writing center is still workable, though expectations related to what can be achieved may have to be scaled back. However, we have found that if the writing center is going to succeed, the teacher must find a way for the children to read their stories to an adult. If this cannot be done immediately after the children write, then it should at least be done during the course of the day on which the children write. Having an audience for one's writing helps to make it a *purposeful* activity, and we have observed that children grow as writers when they view their emergent writing activities as purposeful.

At the writing center the children write on both assigned and free-choice topics, a combination that has been effective. Assigning topics helps insure that children engage in varied kinds of writing. Writing in a variety of genres—lists, stories, invitations, personal letters, and so forth—is important in light of Sulzby's research, which indicates that young children sometimes use different writing strategies for different tasks (Sulzby & Teale, 1985). Letting children self-select topics is equally important because it encourages them to take fuller responsibility for their writing.

Throughout this chapter, we have emphasized the importance for at-risk children of basing the emergent literacy program on children's literature. Many of the assigned topics for children's emergent writing use literature as the stimulus, and we find that for these assignments the children often develop their ideas more fully and sometimes even use more sophisticated writing strategies than for other assignments. The experiences represented in stories frequently touch responsive chords in children and launch them into writing about their own experiences. They are, for example, acutely aware of their likes and dislikes, and so after listening to *The Temper Tantrum Book* (Preston, 1976), children are likely to write prolifically about the things they like and dislike. All children have dreams and secret wishes. After listening to Zolotow's (1965) *Someday* kindergartners are masterful at expressing those dreams in oral and written language. One quiet child who longed to take dancing lessons drew herself performing on a stage and wrote, "Someday I will dance before an audience." Another child wrote, "Someday I'll parachute out of an airplane." Most children have experienced the same kind of day as Alexander did in *Alexander and the Terrible, Horrible, No Good, Very Bad Day* (Viorst, 1972). After listening to this book, Rick drew the picture and wrote the story that appears in Figure 6−1. When asked to read the story, he read:

> One day I cut myself with a knife when I was making a see saw and I then until a few more days later I thinked of using boxes to make a house and then I did. And then I cut my thumb with the windows in the box and it was a horrible, terrible, no good day.

Figure 6−1   **Rick's Story and Picture**

After listening to "Little Bear's Wish" (Minarik, 1957), June used invented spelling to write about what she wished to do (see Figure 6−2). Reading her story, she said:

> I will ride my bike when it is summer. When it is summer I feel like hot. When it is summer I will play outside.

Figure 6−2 **June's Invented Spelling**

Literature can also be used to set up a writing assignment that requires problem solving. The teacher can read up to the point in the story where the problem is fully developed and then invite the children to devise a solution. We have found students respond enthusiastically to this task. Using invented spellings, James devised a means for the peddler in *Caps for Sale* to get his stolen caps back from the monkeys (see Figure 6−3):

> The peddler shaked the tree and the hats fell down. That's all.

Confronted with the same problem, June scribbled a number of solutions (see Figure 6−4):

> He could have climbed the tree and got it or he could have chopped the tree down. He could have digged a big old hole and took it out. He could of shaked the tree.

In the KELP, writing is not viewed as an end unto itself but as a way of getting things done. As such, writing moves beyond the writing center and into many of the activities the children engage in during the day. For example, one class at Thanksgiving toured the school, taking snapshots of all the people who worked in the school and interviewing them about their job-related responsibilities. The children then wrote notes to everyone to thank them for all they did. Finally, the children wrote invitations asking everyone to come by their classroom for a cup of stone soup (yes, literature slipped into this project as well). Writing thank-you notes and invitations are real-world tasks, and the students' responses to such tasks are enthusiastic. Real-world writing occurs in other contexts as well. Students are encouraged to correspond with other children when postal systems are established in the classroom or even the school. When writing materials are placed in dramatic play centers, children incorporate writing into their plays. The waiter in the classroom restaurant makes new menus, takes

Figure 6–3　**James' Story and Picture**

orders, and writes out bills. In the classroom supermarket, workers write logos on plain brown bags and make out labels for cans.

Like the reading program, the writing component of the KELP can also be organized to build links between the home and school. To encourage the children to write at home, one teacher turned a classroom bulletin

Figure 6−4   **June's Scribbled Solutions**

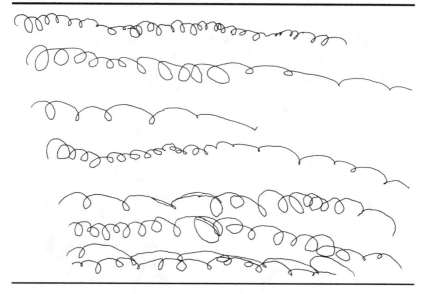

board into a writing board on which the children posted messages they composed at home. The teacher planned to respond to every message that appeared on the board. On the first day three children brought messages from home. The next day five children posted notes on the writing board. Soon fifteen or sixteen notes a day were appearing on the board, and the teacher was hard pressed to find time to respond personally to each one. A second successful project intended to encourage emergent writing at home was the writing suitcase. A small suitcase was stocked with every imaginable type of paper and writing instrument. Each day one child was permitted to take the suitcase home. The children anxiously awaited their turns for the writing suitcase and never failed to return with a suitcase full of stories and notes.

CHILDREN'S GROWTH IN THE KELP

Although we are only now documenting at-risk children's growth as emergent readers in the KELP, we have followed the development of many children as emergent writers by means of their writing folders. The indices of growth exemplified in a class are often quite variable. Progress may be marked by development in a child's understanding of the functions of written language. Other children's growth is most apparent in their use of increasingly sophisticated writing strategies. Yet all the children with whom we have worked have clearly grown as emergent readers and writers during the course of the kindergarten year. To illustrate this growth we include two case studies. We selected these two children because they so clearly appeared to be at-risk children. Given their backgrounds, conventional wisdom would not have predicted that they would make a great deal of progress in kindergarten as readers and writers. Yet when they had the opportunity to work in a no-risk literacy environment, progress is exactly what we observed.

Case Study 1

Lan was born in the United States of Southeast Asian parents. In their homeland his parents had been farmers. They are illiterate in their native language, and after eight years in this country remain illiterate in English. Lan's father now works as a janitor, and his mother is a care giver in her home to several small children. Lan is the youngest of six children. As a kindergartner, he was designated as a special education student and qualified for classes in English as a second language and for language development classes taught by the speech therapist.

The writing center in Lan's class was first established on December 2. Lan's interest in writing was evident from the beginning. Every day he was the first to choose to go to the writing center and was already writing and in some cases ready to read to the teacher what he had written before many of the children were even settled. Because of his curiosity about the writing process and his eagerness to read and write, this child at risk made remarkable progress in the six-month period extending from December through May. We have documented Lan's literacy development through selected writings from his writing folder.

On Lan's first visit to the writing center, he chose to write using a single letter repeatedly (see Figure 6–5). When asked to read his story, Lan did not respond using the intonations of a reader but told about his picture.

> Five turkeys, I've got five turkeys. I've got a lot of turkeys. Flowers and the green thing down there (points to stems) and we color it. We color the turkey and the turkey laughing to get it. And we make a foot and I make a footprint. And we saw a elephant, a turkey, a dog and a alligator and a good fish. And we gave him food. And we saw a flying turkey.

On December 10, Lan combined two different writing strategies—letter-like forms and scribbling (see Figure 6–6). He read this story as follows:

> I like to play with the dog and with the toys, and I like play with the blocks, and I like to put something in my cubby hole. I like to play with the toys. I like to look at the clocks. I like to look at the dominoes, and I like to play.

Figure 6–5   **Lan's Writing (December 2)**

Figure 6–6   **Lan's Writing (December 10)**

By February, Lan was consistently using random-appearing letters in his work at the writing center. In this sample written on February 18, Lan ended his message with a question mark (see Figure 6—7).

In a March writing sample, Lan included environmental print (which was displayed on labels in the classroom) in the midst of his random array of letters. Lan clearly signaled that he knew the difference between conventional spelling and pretend writing by boxing in the words "floor" and "toys". His reading of the story made it apparent that Lan had purposefully selected these two words from the environmental print in the classroom (see Figure 6—8):

> I like to play with Clifford on the floor toys, and Clifford on the box all day long. Me and Crystal play with Clifford, and Nikki and Jessica play on the toys. And we play and we sit down on the black line. And Joe and Nikki play on the floor toys. And we play on the box. And we play every day. And me and Clifford is playing. And we put the date on the back of Clifford and we play with Clifford all night long and we go in and play with Clifford. And we play outside with the Clifford and Clifford eats the food. And we play and bring out food and Clifford eats with us. Me and Clifford walk on the sidewalk.

In April, Lan began to use invented spellings in his story, representing one or two of the sounds he heard within words. While reading his story, Lan pointed to the letters from left to right and sometimes puzzled over the letters on the page as he attempted to reconstruct his message (Figure 6—9):

> I like to play with my mom. And I like to play. And I play with my jump rope.

When Lan reached this point in his development, his enthusiasm for writing seemed almost boundless. He would often stay in the writing center for an hour at a time to help his friends write. As his classmates rehearsed their ideas out loud, as kindergartners so often do, Lan would supply them with the beginning sounds and letters they needed in order to put their thoughts down on paper.

The opportunities afforded Lan in the emergent literacy program stimulated his growth as a reader and writer. Despite indicators that he would be at risk for achievement, Lan gained the foundation that enabled him to get off to the right start in reading and writing.

Case Study 2

Bernard was an inner-city black child. Upon entering kindergarten, he lived with his mother, an older stepbrother, and three younger siblings. The father of the stepbrother had lived with the family but left after

Figure 6–7   Lan's Writing (February 18)

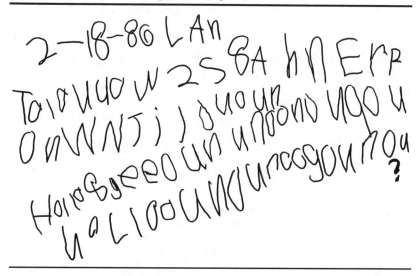

Figure 6–8   Lan's Writing (March 11)

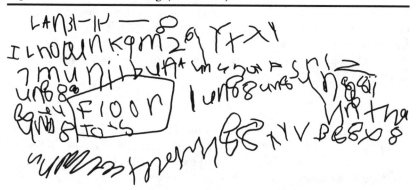

Figure 6–9   Lan's Writing (April 9)

Bernard was born. After that there was no adult male in the home. The family was supported by public assistance.

Bernard came to school with emotional problems. From the time he began school in September until he transferred to another school district in March, Bernard lived underneath a table in the classroom. He called the area under the table his house. When he was pleased with another child, he would invite the child to "come to my house." Bernard typically ventured from his house only when visitors came into the room. In fact, he and the teacher had entered into an agreement that when the principal visited the room, he would sit at a table to make the principal happy. He never stayed in the classroom library to look at books. Instead, he would take books under the table and even invite other students to read with him there.

Bernard's oral language facility was poor. In addition to a small vocabulary, the functions for which he used language were limited. For example, he tended not to express emotions verbally. When he was happy, he would pat the teacher's shoulders; when he was upset, he would throw a tantrum.

During the first few weeks of the school year as the teacher realized the severity of Bernard's emotional problems and his great difficulty in communicating, she tried without success to get the mother to come in for a conference. Finally the teacher went to see the mother at her house. After first trying to throw the teacher out, the mother finally agreed to talk. The mother expressed surprise that Bernard was having problems at school because he was always so quiet at home; the mother did not allow her children to talk at home.

Bernard came to school with few academic skills. He wanted the teacher to read to him all the time, and he always needed to be touching the teacher during storytime. At the same time, Bernard was one of the few children in the class who would write willingly from the beginning of the school year. These two activities—storybook reading and writing—provided the opportunity for Bernard to progress beyond any predictions for academic success based on his personal and home background characteristics. We have only a few of his writing samples available. Nonetheless, they contain a tale worth telling. At the beginning of the school year, Bernard announced that his stepbrother had taught him to write his name. On one piece that he wrote in September, he indicated that the letters Bnb said "Bernard" (see Figure 6–10). When asked to read his story, Bernard read:

I went outside to play.

By February Bernard was using invented spellings in his writing. He also included sight words that he learned from the many chart stories that the class composed throughout the year. He read his February 2 writing

Figure 6−10 **Bernard's Story (September)**

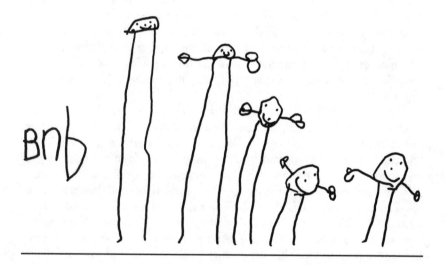

sample as follows (see Figure 6−11):

Mrs. H. went to the store to buy groceries.

In his February 11 story, Bernard again used invented spellings and represented five of the sounds that he heard in the word "window" (see Figure 6−12):

Figure 6–11 Bernard's Story (February 2)

Mrs. H. was sad. She liked to look out the window. She got her hair cut.

The supportive context of the KELP enabled Bernard to make rapid progress as an emergent writer in a period of approximately six months.

Figure 6–12   **Bernard's Story (February 11)**

MRS. H.
WaS SaD
SHE LiKD
OTTnEWiR
D O SHEK6OT
HR HaRKUT

Bernard

CONCLUSIONS

Developmentally Appropriate Literacy Instruction for Young Children

In implementing beginning literacy programs for at-risk children, the challenge is to defy the statistics. The type of program that can meet this challenge and thereby promote the literacy learning of at-risk children is one that takes lessons from positive home environments. In the classroom there are ample opportunities for the children to see others engaged in reading and writing. More importantly, the children themselves participate—both in interaction with literate others and through their own independent explorations—in countless activities that involve reading and writing. These activities stem from a rich experiential base and are integrated into all content areas as well as into the children's play.

Opportunities for at-risk children to experience a wide variety of literacy activities in a risk-free environment serve to build the important base from which further development in learning to read and write proceeds. We need to start at the right place and in the right ways with young, at-risk children. It is significant to remember that literacy learning in its initial phase can be usefully described as proceeding from whole to part. Children first establish an understanding of the functions and uses of literacy. They become aware that literacy is an integral part of accomplishing a wide variety of goals. They also learn to recognize literacy actions and literacy tools like books, lists, pencils, and pens. They even incorporate certain aspects of reading and writing into their play activities and their own attempts to read and write. In short, they understand what reading and writing are about even though they are not yet conventionally literate. With such an orientation, children proceed with the business of learning how to read and write conventionally. Without this orientation, acquiring literacy becomes a more difficult proposition.

We began our discussion by noting that the question we were addressing—how does one best nurture the literacy development of at-risk children—is a complex one. Any attempt to provide a detailed blueprint for a successful emergent literacy program is bound to fail, and the suggestions we have made are not intended as such. Rather, we have attempted to describe what we have observed to be the most appropriate context for children's growth and to provide a basic structure for an emergent literacy program. To serve at-risk children most appropriately, an early childhood program should emphasize participation in functional, meaningful, holistic reading and writing activities. These activities must be built on children's life experiences. Shared literature experiences are especially powerful stimuli for emergent literacy development. When children are permitted to grow as readers and writers in such a context, we believe that at-risk predictions can become stories of achievement.

Policy Issues in Implementing the Kindergarten Emergent Literacy Program

Many readers of this chapter may know something of the state of education in Texas. Over the last few years the wave of educational reform sweeping the country has hit Texas perhaps hardest of all. In 1981 the 67th Texas

Legislature mandated Essential Elements that define the "well-balanced curriculum" at each grade level, kindergarten included. The kindergarten essential elements are divided into the categories of Language Arts, Mathematics, Science, Fine Arts, Health, and Social Studies. The language arts essential elements are rather traditional ones; there are objectives for listening, speaking, reading, and writing. The reading objectives focus on visual and auditory discrimination, letter recognition, letter-sound correspondences, vocabulary, comprehension, and literary appreciation.

We also have statewide competency testing of reading and writing in first grade. The pressure to begin reading instruction in kindergarten has led to a response similar to what Durkin (1987) and Hiebert (1988) have described: traditional reading readiness programs that (1) place heavy emphasis on letter naming and letter-sound matching and (2) introduce children to literacy through workbook exercises rather than through children's literature. In light of these pressures toward a skill-oriented, fragmented program, one may legitimately ask, "How do some teachers manage to implement an emergent literacy curriculum?" It is impossible to answer that question in the space remaining, but we can describe some key factors that have enabled the Kindergarten Emergent Literacy Program to succeed and grow.

First of all, the program has been a cooperative venture between classroom teachers and teacher educators. It has never been mandated from above by administrators or supervisors. Instead, the impetus has come from teachers who wanted to make their classrooms emergent literacy environments or a principal who built a staff of kindergarten and first-grade teachers who teach from an emergent literacy perspective. In several instances where schools have chosen to implement an emergent literacy approach in all of the kindergarten classrooms, the cooperative, or team, concept is also in evidence. In these cases teachers, school administrators, and district supervisory personnel all worked together to implement, evaluate, and modify the curriculum.

Support from peers, from administrators, from teacher educators, or better yet from all three groups, is important to the continued success of an emergent literacy approach. It is easy for a classroom teacher to be worn down if she perceives that she is alone against the rest of her immediate educational world. Teachers who create emergent literacy classrooms may encounter considerable pressure to justify what they are doing because it looks nontraditional. In the face of such pressure it is tempting to take the easy way out and rely on prepackaged, neatly organized, skills programs that are part and parcel of a standardized testing approach to curriculum. We know of one emergent literacy teacher, for example, who worked for three years in a school with a principal who believed that learning centers in a kindergarten classroom were incompatible with the legislation that mandates the essential elements be taught. The teacher found it very difficult to have her ideas treated credibly in the situation. But rather than give in to a worksheet dominated curriculum, she ultimately transferred to another school in which the principal was favorably disposed toward an emergent literacy perspective.

Another source of support is the parents of children in the school. With parent volunteer help in the classroom and parents voicing to the principal and school board members their enthusiasm for the curriculum, one teacher was able to pioneer a Kindergarten Emergent Literacy Program in her school. But she is quick to point out, "It was the parents who saved me." The importance of informing parents and actively building parental support became obvious to us the very first year we implemented the kindergarten program in one school in the San Antonio area. Around mid-year we began to hear indirectly that parents were questioning the methods being used and were unsure of how to interpret the children's work. We responded to the questions to the parents' satisfaction but realized that we had not done our homework at the beginning of the year. That spring we produced a short videotape designed to orient parents to the goals and methods of the program. Since then we have used the tape every fall semester and have found it invaluable in developing parent support. In summary, we cannot stress strongly enough the need for moral and intellectual support when implementing an approach like the one described in this chapter. There are teachers who are the only ones in their buildings creating emergent literacy programs, but they do have support from individuals in the larger educational community.

Another factor that has facilitated implementation of emergent literacy programs is documentation. Samples of students' work and data gathered through observation and informal means like those described by Teale (1988) are emphasized. They have helped assure skeptics that the essential elements are indeed being covered. They also have proven very worthwhile in parent conferences. Writing folders, for example, bring a child's work to life and show what has been learned. Other statistics about the children can be useful. For instance, one teacher documented that not one of the children who has been through her kindergarten emergent literacy classroom in three years has subsequently been retained in first grade. This statistic has not gone unnoticed by building and district administrators. Thus, we encourage teachers and principals to document what they see occurring in the emergent literacy classroom. Good news likes to be spread.

Finally, we offer one last consideration for teachers seeking to implement functional, meaningful, holistic literacy instruction in the early childhood classroom. As one teacher put it, "I spend almost all my day there [in the classroom]. I can't stand to be bored." Emergent literacy classrooms are dynamic places for children and teachers alike. When young children, be they at-risk or gifted children, are permitted to experience and to experiment with the powers and pleasures of written language, exciting things happen. It is a pleasure indeed to see children engaged in becoming literate.

ACKNOWLEDGMENTS

Implementation of The Kindergarten Emergent Literacy Program has been assisted by funding from The University of Texas System Chancellor's Council.

Teachers in both The Children's School and the KELP involve students in shared book reading experiences using Big Books. In Chapter 7, we look in more depth at how the implementation of a shared book experience affects teachers and children. The Head Start classroom described in the following chapter was not a particularly literate environment when the Literacy/Curriculum Connections project was implemented. Dickinson's chapter provides us with the opportunity to study what happens when children are encouraged to fall in love with books.

Chapter 7

Effects of a Shared Reading Program on One Head Start Language and Literacy Environment

David K. Dickinson

> When parents read stories to their children they are creating a safe, warm place for language and literacy learning. The informal discussions that inevitably accompany the story reading help to establish children's understanding about the way in which people communicate ideas through print. Exposed to loving and caring human beings as reading models, children demonstrate an ever-increasing interest in books and stories ... Most important, they begin to view themselves as becoming readers and writers too. (Taylor & Strickland 1986a, p. 506)

The quiet times when parents snuggle with their children sharing the enjoyment of books build connections between children and parents and between children and books. These connections translate into enhanced chances of achieving academic success (Goldfield & Snow, 1984; Wells, 1985). Unfortunately, book reading is not an activity that is integral to all families. While all families in literate cultures make use of print in varied ways, lower income families from a variety of cultural groups such as semi-rural southern blacks (Heath, 1983), and urban Mexican-Americans and

125

blacks in California (Teale, 1986), are less likely than middle-class parents to read books with their children.

Even in families where storybook reading is common, there is variability in how books are read. Parents with low literacy levels are likely to have difficulty engaging children, partly because they must struggle with the task of reading themselves (Edwards, this volume; Heath & Thomas, 1984). Also, there are culturally related differences in parental expectations for child behavior during reading sessions that become more apparent as children get older. Reading sessions with one- and two-year-olds tend to be quite similar, but as children become more verbal, differences in the amount and type of conversations emerge. These differences are related to a complex array of factors, including the child's verbal ability, the type of book being read, the number of times the book has been read, and the number of participants. They also are related to cultural background, which shapes parental beliefs about literacy and influences how parents conceive of their role as "teachers" of literacy. When reading to children, working-class parents tend to limit discussion to factual questions, the kinds of questions they anticipate teachers will ask. In contrast, middle-class parents are more likely to engage children in more open-ended discussions about why events occurred, to elicit children's evaluations of events in the books (Heath, 1983; Ninio, 1980), and to help children make links between everyday experiences and the world of books.

BOOK READING IN SCHOOL SETTINGS

Children also have been shown to benefit from hearing books in school settings. Feiltelson, Kita and Goldstein (1986) found that regular reading to first graders resulted in improved comprehension and language competence. Even more important for the intervention we will describe are results from programs that involve joint reading by teachers and children of enlarged versions of books. A Shared Book Experience program implemented in kindergarten classrooms in South Carolina resulted in improvement on a first-grade readiness test and an increase in placement of children in top reading groups (Brown, Cromer, & Weinberg, 1986). A Shared Reading program was also found to be more effective than a conventional English as a Second Language program for fostering acquisition of English by rural Fijiian elementary school children (Elley & Mangubhai, 1983).

Detailed descriptions of how books were read in these reading intervention programs were not provided, but we know that there are great differences in how book reading is accomplished in preschools and kindergartens (Teale & Martinez, 1986). For example, Dickinson and Keebler (in press) analyzed how three preschool teachers read to the same group of children and found dramatic differences in the amount of discussion encouraged while the book was being read and differences in the content of discussions. Two teachers read interactively, engaging children in discussions while they read. The third performed books, weaving a spell with words that she chose not to break with discussions. The long-term effect of these different approaches to book reading have not been demonstrated. We do know that children need opportunities to reflect on text, learning not only to recall facts, but to speculate about causes using their knowledge of the world. Extrapolation from reading research suggests that an interactive style may encourage children to draw upon their background knowledge and become actively engaged in interpreting text (Au & Jordan, 1981; Hansen, 1981). On the other hand, the intense engagement with story provided by the performance approach might result in deeper appreciation of books, translating into long-term love of books.

ORAL LANGUAGE-LITERACY LINKS

Reading and writing are language-based processes; therefore, programs designed to develop literacy skills of preschool-aged children must strive to facilitate language acquisition (Dickinson, 1987, in press). Oral language development is supported in everyday conversations when adults provide children opportunities to hear their own words and phrases, or equally familiar chunks of language, embedded in sentences that are more complex than those they can produce on their own (Snow, Perlmann, & Nathan, 1987). Occasions when adult comments are contingent upon child comments (i.e., they relate to and extend children's thoughts) boost children's language acquisition (Cross, 1978; Wells, 1985). Language growth also may be facilitated by highly predictable sequences of utterances such as exchanges that may occur during parent-child routines (e.g., bath time) and in verbal games and songs.

Book reading is a time when children can experience both contingency and predictability. For example, when reading a picture book a child might point to a car and and say "car" and the parent might comment, "Yea, that's a red car. It's going to hit the man." Such exchanges that extend meaning by embedding child comments in more complete utterances are common as parents read with children. Even in the absence of such discussions, book reading can help children acquire language by providing them predictable chunks of text. Repeated reading of text can help expand children's language abilities. Children are extremely adept at acquiring language from hearing it in context (Dickinson, 1984; Nagy, Herman, & Anderson, 1985), and they can acquire vocabulary and syntax from hearing the same book read several times (Pappas & Brown, 1987; Snow & Goldfield, 1983). Not surprisingly, repeated reading combined with discussion is an especially potent technique for improving comprehension of books (Yaden, 1988) as well as for improving general language growth.

Although facilitation of vocabulary and syntactic development is important, especially for the child learning English as a second language, not all types of oral language development may be equally important for later reading. Most children reared in English-speaking homes have sufficient control of basic language competencies to cope with the demands of early reading (Wells, 1985). Unfortunately, special language competencies may be required for comprehending the language encountered in books after decoding skills are well established. To comprehend the language in books, especially books that convey information about unfamiliar topics, children need to develop facility interpreting language that lacks the contextual supports provided during face-to-face conversations.

Language can be thought of as lying on a continuum from the contextualized language used between intimates in face-to-face conversations to more decontextualized language such as is used to convey information in textbooks. Decontextualized language is language that successfully copes with three challenges more common to written than oral communication: (1) information is conveyed that is new to the hearer, (2) the message is comprehensible to someone at a distance because its interpretation does not require reliance on gestures, intonation, or facial expression, and (3) background knowledge necessary for the receiver to interpret the message is provided because the sender cannot assume that it is shared.

Skill in interpreting decontextualized language can be facilitated by opportunities to use language for purposes such as discussing past or future experiences and discussing issues about which children are curious. Practice is most likely to occur when adults and children engage in sustained dialogue. Opportunities for such engagement vary across ethnic and racial groups. Heath (1986) traced the frequency with which children from a black mill town, a white mill town, and black and white mainstream families engaged in discourse with an adult for at least five minutes. During the times Heath sampled—when three representative children were between 40 and 48 months old—the mainstream child had 1533 such interactions while each of the mill town children had less than 60 such interactions.

Differences in discourse patterns in the home appear to translate into differential control of decontextualized skills. Lower SES black children have been found to use culturally determined storytelling patterns that can result in extremely artful stories (Gee, in press). Unfortunately, these stories can be difficult for teachers to interpret because they tend to lack information about time and setting that is needed to contextualize them (Michaels, 1981). Low-income children also have been found to have more difficulty comprehending narratives (Dickinson & Snow, 1987) and communicating information (Feagans, 1982) than more economically advantaged children. Acquisition of skill using such language is difficult and may partially explain middle SES children's general success with literacy tasks once they enter elementary school (Snow, 1983). Hearing and discussing books are powerful ways for children to learn to interpret the language of books and may provide occasions when children produce language that is more decontextualized than that used during everyday conversations.

THE LITERACY/CURRICULUM CONNECTIONS PROJECT

Many preschool teachers recognize the importance of book reading and strive to encourage as much interest in books as possible. However, holding the attention of groups of energetic preschoolers is never easy. Sustaining interest in books is particularly challenging when reading to children who come from homes where book reading is not a common experience. These children have not formed strong emotional bonds to books, they are not familiar with routines for listening to and discussing books, and they have limited strategies for interpreting them. Furthermore, many classrooms have children from diverse language backgrounds. How can teachers in settings that include these children provide valuable experiences with books? This is the challenge that the Literacy/Curriculum Connections Project, a project supported by Massachusetts funds for early education, began to grapple with in the fall of 1986.

The Literacy/Curriculum Connections Project attempts to get Head Start children and their teachers excited about books by using the Shared Reading Experience (Holdaway, 1979). At the heart of the project is Holdaway's developmental learning model, which states that learners (children and adults) move through a series of phases as they acquire new skills. Initially they see actions modeled and get excited about acquiring the skill as they are encouraged to join in. Soon they begin to participate and spend considerable time approximating the model with varying degrees of success. Once they have mastered the skill, learners are ready to show off their newly acquired skill.

This model guided the way project staff thought about leading children into literacy and it informed their approach to teacher training. Once a week the staff developer and each teacher had a planning meeting to assess the effectiveness of past books and activities, to discuss what book would be read next, and to plan follow-up activities. Also, especially early in the year, time was spent dealing with questions about how teachers should read to children. This planning process was followed by a trainer coming to the room with a new book. For most of the year the trainer presented the book while the teacher kept a record of the responses of two children being followed by the project. Teachers read on days when the trainer was not present, and late in the year they also began reading when the trainer was present.

The program had four major components. First, there was an infusion of new materials. Most importantly, classrooms were provided books with enlarged print and large colorful pictures and with multiple copies of regular-sized copies of the same books. These books had predictable text, text with rhymes and refrains (see Appendix 1 for an example) that enable children to draw upon their own grasp of linguistic structures, thereby giving them powerful tools for making sense of the text. A listening center with tapes of some of the books was also provided. Second, there was teacher training to introduce techniques for reading the books and leading songs written in large print. Key stylistic elements were dynamic reading by the teacher, pointing to the text with a pointer while reading, encouragement of child participation in the actual reading of the text, and encouragement of child prediction of coming text. Third, teachers were shown how to extend the influence of the books into the broader curriculum by planning follow-up activities that related to the theme of the book. Commonly, the new books were read throughout the week, and on the day the staff developer came, art or occasionally drama activities were planned that extended the children's experiences with the book being featured that week (see Holdaway, 1979, for additional detailed information). Fourth, in early spring a book lending program was initiated to encourage children to read the books at home.

OUR INVESTIGATION

At the same time that the Literacy/Curriculum Connections Project was gearing up to work in preschools, we were planning a study of the uses of literacy in Head Start classrooms. The Head Start staff in a city to be served by the project helped us arrange to observe two classrooms to be included in the project. The research project and the intervention project, thus, were unrelated. This distance allowed teachers to speak freely to us about their feelings about the project, and it allowed us to be objective about the project. Beginning in the early fall we interviewed teachers in these sites, visited classrooms, and videotaped meetings.

This chapter describes what happened in West Village, one of the two sites we observed where the project was being introduced. In East Village, the other implementation site we observed, the classroom was print-oriented before the program began (e.g., children looked at books before the formal start of the school day, both teachers took dictations constantly) and both teachers were extremely enthusiastic about the program at its inception. They read many enlarged texts to the children every day, spent hours of their own time preparing materials, and extended the program throughout the week by preparing follow-up activities to books and creating elaborate displays of children's work. What happened in this site, despite the fact that their group was deemed by many to be an extremely difficult group to control, is inspiring and worthy of its own story. However, the reality of early childhood programs is that teachers are grossly underpaid and rarely have much energy or time to spend doing extensive classroom preparation after work because of child care responsibilities or demands from second jobs. Therefore, I will describe the more modest success of the West Village classroom, because it is a more typical Head Start classroom.

We visited West Village nine times for a total of twelve hours; we conducted formal interviews three times—late October, early March, and early June—and spoke informally with the teachers each time we visited. Videotapes were made of four meetings, two in October prior to the beginning of the literacy project and two after the program was well established, in early March and early June.

The classroom in West Village is located on the ground floor of a building containing subsidized apartments. In the housing project that this program draws upon are many American-born blacks, as well as immigrants from India, Haiti, and Hispanic countries. The room provided half-day care typical of Head Start programs, but many of the parents wanted longer term care. Therefore, there was considerable turnover in the group as parents placed their children into full-day programs, resulting in fluctuations in the total number of children in the room and variations in the overall composition of the group. Roughly half of the eleven to fifteen children's first language was English, with the remaining speaking Haitian French-Creole (four to five children), Indian dialects (three children), or Spanish (one to three children). During the year more young children entered the group; those who entered when others moved to full-day placements generally were those who had recently reached the minimum entry age of 2:10. By the end of the year somewhat less than half the group was old enough to go on to kindergarten.

Information about the children's homes was fragmentary, but the teachers said that they believed the parents kept the children inside nearly all the time because of the dangerous neighborhood. Children were thought to watch considerable television, to spend most of their time with siblings, cousins, or friends, and, with the exception of two or three children, to have little opportunity to hear their parents read to them.

Two teachers worked with the group. The head teacher, Sarah, had taught in this city's Head Start program for several years, and the assistant teacher, Maria, had worked with Sarah for two years. Maria's first language was Spanish. She was extremely self-conscious about her accent, which she felt was most evident when she read aloud. Maria was working toward a certificate in early education, so she was receiving supervision from a local university and was required to introduce some of her own curriculum during meeting times. Both teachers had warm, supportive relationships with the children, who seemed to feel safe and comfortable with them.

CHANGES IN THE LANGUAGE AND LITERACY ENVIRONMENT

The literacy environment changed considerably during the year as a result of the project. First we will describe general patterns of language and literacy use in the course of the day's activities, as exhibited at the beginning of the year. We then focus on meeting time for a more detailed examination of book reading sessions before and after the implementation of the program. Finally, we examine the place of oral language and literacy throughout the day at the end of the year.

Patterns of Language and Literacy Use

Our initial interview and early observations made it clear that facilitation of language and literacy development were not high priorities. Sarah made no mention of literacy-related skills or attitudes when asked to talk about important features of her program. She believed that the primary goal of Head Start is "socialization" of children, especially children from non-English speaking homes. By this she meant getting children acquainted with the routines of school and exposing them to other children from different cultural and linguistic backgrounds. To help acquaint children with school routines, Sarah maintained a consistent schedule and encouraged them to take responsibility for small tasks, such as cleaning up.

The center had a large front room and a smaller back room that adjoined the kitchen and bathroom. The back room had two tables, table toys (construction toys such as Legos), a water table, an easel, and art materials. The larger room included the rug-covered meeting area. On two sides it was enclosed by walls and on the other two sides it was partially screened by shelves housing puppets and blocks. Also in this room was a house area, a library corner, and the children's cubbies.

Children began to arrive about 8:30. They went into the back room where they played with table toys. Maria generally oversaw this activity while Sarah greeted parents or made phone calls. Around 9:00 the teachers told children to clean up, a task generally accomplished quickly with minimal teacher assistance. Children then moved into the meeting area. Meetings were led by one teacher while the other prepared breakfast. Sarah's meetings often lasted thirty to forty minutes; Maria's more often lasted only ten to twenty minutes. After breakfast, which followed morning meeting, there was a forty-five minute activity period during which children freely used the available equipment. Following activity time children went outside in nearly all weather. When the children returned, there was likely to be some teacher-led activity involving cutting, painting, or pasting. Around 11:30 lunch was served. Parents came and picked up children as lunch was ending.

Meeting Time. The content of meetings varied by teacher. Sarah, who led meeting three days a week, nearly always read to children, sang songs, and sometimes talked about some topic of current interest. Maria's meetings generally included songs and some teacher-led activity that involved either physical exercises or used some material she brought to the meeting. She rarely read to children, largely because of her extreme self-consciousness about her accent. Her activities neither made reference to print nor were they designed to support oral language development. For example, in a meeting designed to encourage independence from teacher assistance, she brought in a smock, a pair of pants, and a dress. These were used to show children how to carry out three different actions: zipping, buttoning, and snapping. Throughout the activity, Maria relied on her modeling of the actions to carry most of the information. The objects were presented without being named, and the actions required were shown but not labeled. As children attempted to carry out the actions she generally made no reference to the object or action, instead making general comments such as, "Can you do it, sweet?" and "Nice job." On one occasion when a child had some trouble she did verbally describe the action: "See, you hold it like this and you can pull it up. It's hard." When the child struggled, she added, "Push the zipper in a little bit more." Her most extended monologue of the meeting came at the end when she explained that sometimes there might be a stranger in the room and they wouldn't want to have to ask that person to zip their pants. Finally she revealed the real objective of the lesson: "It's very important to zip up your own pants because I won't do it for you. I'm sorry."

Activity Time. During activity time there was more talk and more opportunity for engagement with print. Children naturally talked to each other and the teachers occasionally engaged children in conversations. Of the two teachers, Maria became more involved, getting down on the floor to play with the children. Sarah sometimes got on the floor, but she tended to observe the group from a chair or attended to managerial tasks (e.g., phone calls, completing forms).

We saw very few teacher-directed activities, but what we did see again indicated little explicit attention to language. For example, late in the year we observed Maria as she was doing a cutting activity. She had magazines and was helping a child cut out pictures. The cutting apparently was being done to help the boy develop fine motor skills, with no broader objectives being pursued. Nothing was going to be done with the pictures after they were cut out (e.g., tell a story, make a collage), and opportunities for discussing pictures were ignored. Verbal interaction consisted only of minimal directions about how to cut: "Look. Open, close, open, close."

Print use during activity times appeared to be minimal. We never saw any children voluntarily approach the library area, a space enclosed on three sides by shelves. It had a table that had markers and paper (sometimes) and two chairs, but no cushions or pillows to encourage sitting on the floor. Maria's supervisor apparently observed the same pattern of avoidance of the area, because she told Maria to try to make it more attractive. In contrast to outside observers' opinions, Sarah maintained that the library corner was used regularly.

Early in the year there was a writing table in the library area. We saw some drawing that had been done with the paper and markers provided on the table, but saw no evidence of attempts at writing. Sarah also made no mention of any writing being done by children. We never observed teachers taking dictations from children and we saw no dictations that were child-initiated, though there was one wall display of children's wishes that evidently grew out of a teacher-led group activity. Finally, children did not integrate writing implements or books into their dramatic play.

Language Throughout the Day. There was little evidence of a conscious effort to encourage children to use oral language during *Table Toys Time*. We did not observe teachers engaging children in extended dialogue, nor did we hear children engage in extended monologues with other children (e.g., constructing narratives about their structures). Teachers never extended children's play with any form of print by taking dictations about the constructions, providing writing implements, or encouraging children to look at books. *Mealtimes* were usually quiet. Teacher-child talk was limited and primarily dealt with procedural (e.g., "do you want more?" "throw that in the trash") or behavioral matters. The most extended conversations during mealtimes and during the table toys time occurred between adults, who talked to each other over the heads of the children. When the children were outside they generally played independently. Teacher-child interaction was limited and generally dealt with safety and organizational matters.

Book Reading

We videotaped book reading sessions, before and after implementation of the project. The videotapes were coded using a scoring scheme adopted from earlier research (Dickinson & Keebler, in press). Categories used were drawn from book reading research and could be applied to child or teacher questions or comments. Several key categories are *Labeling* of pictures or actions (e.g. "what's that?"); *Book Focus*, talk about how books or print works; *Analysis* of characters or events (e.g., "why did he do that?" "why couldn't he hear?"); *Predicting* impending events or text (e.g., "and then what happened?"); linking *Text to Readers* (e.g., "we see fire engines here, too"); and children's *Chiming* together as they read the text with the teacher. (See Appendix 2 for more complete descriptions.) Coding was done of utterance units (units with intonation contours indicating the end of a phrase) directly from the videotapes. Reliability checks of coding of two of the head teacher's meetings revealed 90 percent and 96 percent interrater agreement. We quantified the distribution of comment types for each session by determining the number of comments by children and teacher falling into each category for each session. This number was divided by the total number of child or teacher comments for that story, resulting in proportional scores.

Late October: Before Implementation of the Project. October 21, the first day we videotaped, Sarah selected three small books (approximately 4″ by 8″), each of which had one sentence per page. The first book, *Fire House*, had fourteen pages, and the second and third books, *Animals We Know* and *Tell Me What Time It Is*, each had eight pages. Each book was constructed so that two adjacent pages dealt with the same topic. Only half the pages had text on them, the other half had pictures. Sarah's book choices made one fact immediately apparent—the group was not accustomed to hearing books with much text. Books she chose had very little text, and she did not even read the text of one book, *Animals We Know*. Most of the time devoted to these books was used for discussing them.

In an effort to provide comparability of books in the four rooms in which we were observing, we asked Sarah to read *The Strongest One of All* two days after our first videotaping. We selected this book because it had limited but interesting text (two or three sentences per page), attractive illustrations, and a relatively simple plot. Characteristics of these early reading sessions were identified and are described in following sections.

Discussion Content and Structure. In October, discussions about books had similar structural features, but diverse content. For the four books mentioned earlier, Sarah began by reading the text or pointing to pictures and then asking the children questions. The questions she asked had a focus that was retained throughout the story. For example, when discussing the animal book, Sarah most often had children label animals (*Label* in Table 1), and then asked them what the animal says, and occasionally extended the discussion with additional comments (i.e., *Analysis* of *Event/ Object*).

Sarah: O.K. What's this?

Child: Cow.

Sarah: Right. What does a cow say?

Children: Moo.

Sarah: Good for you. What do we get from cows?

Child: Milk.

Sarah: Good. The farmer milks the cow and sends the milk to the store.

Child: And we buy it.

Sarah: Right.

The other three stories were handled by reading the text, followed by discussions that retained a consistent focus throughout the story. Discussion about *Fire House* and *Tell Me What Time It Is* emphasized connections to children's experiences. Discussion about the fire house book emphasized text-reader connections as Sarah encouraged discussion of children's personal experiences related to fire engines and dealt with associated fears. Such comments accounted for 30 percent of Sarah's comments and 47 percent of the children's comments (see *Text-Reader* links via child *Experiences* in Table 7−1). When reading the book about time, Sarah read the text that described the time of day and queried the children about what they do at that time. Discussion linking books to child experiences accounted for over half the teacher and child comments (see Table 7−1).

These discussions occurred while the book was being read. There was very little discussion about books before they were started and no follow-up discussion. Thus, the book itself provided a time frame as well as the topic for discussion.

Child Participation. An indication of the discussion orientation of Sarah's book reading sessions was her responsiveness to child initiatives (see Table 7−2.) Child attempts to initiate topics related to the text (i.e., not dealing with organizational matters such as being able to see the book) were relatively common, averaging eight per book with a range from four in *Animals We Know* to fourteen in *The Strongest One of All*. Sarah responded to most (84 percent) of these initiatives and sometimes used them as

Table 7-1   **Proportion of Comments by Teacher and Child in Each Content Category During October Story Readings**

Categories[a]	Books Read							
	Fire House		Animals		Time		Strongest	
	T. (n=36)	Child (n=19)	T. (n=26)	Child (n=26)	T. (n=44)	Child (n=34)	T. (n=89)	Child (n=81)
Label/Describe	35	32	31	54	7	3	13	17
Vocabulary				4	4	3		
Moralizing							1	
Book Focus							3	
Recall								
Predicting	3				2		6	
Analysis								
Character							2	4
Event/Object	22	5	31	23	9	9	32	36
Print							1	1
Text/Reader								
Experiences	30	47	15	8	61	76	8	9
Book-to-Book								
Actions				4				
Chiming								
Teacher Request								
Child Chime								
Organization								
Text Break	5	10	15		11		15	16
Minor	3		4				1	
Irrelevant Talk	3	5		11	4	9	17	17

[a] See Appendix 1 for explanation of coding categories.

starting points for discussions. For example, after she read the page in *Fire House* about putting a fire out, a child initiated a topic:

Child: I saw that.

Teacher: You saw them putting out fire with water?

Child: Me too!

Teacher: Yeah. Where?

Child: In a house.

Teacher: I know. The fire engines come here a lot, right?

Child initiatives were rare (two) prior to the story, because Sarah generally began reading without any lead-in discussion.

Table 7—2   **Frequency of Child Attempts and Successes Initiating Topics During Book Reading Sessions**

	Successes Prior to Reading Text	Attempts Prior to Reading Text	Successes As Reading	Attempts As Reading
Fall Books				
Fire House	0	0	7	9
Animals ...	0	0	3	4
What time ...	0	0	4	5
Strongest One ...	2	2	13	14
Spring Books: Enlarged Text				
Brown Bear ...	5	6	13 (2)[a]	13 (2)[a]
To Town ...	2	2	1	1
Yes M'am	0	0	0	2
The Jiqaree	0	0	0	0
Spring Books: Regular-Sized				
March 3rd				
... Wild Things	0	0	0	0
... Night Kitchen	0	0	0	0
June 1st				
... Wild Things	0	0	4	4
... Mother?	0	0	1	4

Note: Attempts not related to organizational matters and not providing direct recall of text.

[a] Attempts not predicting picture coming on the next page.

Pacing. The discussion-oriented nature of book reading in the fall made for slow progress through the books. For the three short books this was no problem, because they had no plot and their language was mundane; they were best used as starting points for discussions. On the other hand, the book we provided, *The Strongest One of All*, had a plot and relatively interesting language. Sarah handled this book as she did the others. After she read the first page, she engaged the children in an extended discussion about experiences falling on the ice (twenty-five teacher and child comments). The net effect of such lengthy discussions was a loss of momentum. Partly as a result of the slow pace and partly because of a homesick child who began crying when Sarah was about half finished, the book was never completed. We left the book and Sarah said that she tried to read it to the group two or three times, but never found it to be very successful.

The pace also was slowed by the fact that, during book discussions and group discussions, Sarah occasionally asked the same question of every child. This questioning style, noted in another preschool serving low-income children (Lubeck, 1985), ensured equality among children, but resulted in a slow-moving, dull discussion.

Organization and Attention. Sarah expended relatively little effort organizing the group to hear the books. In each case she began the book without any preparatory settling of the group. Except for *Fire House*, the first book of the session, at least two or three children were inattentive when each book was started. Attention remained high through *Fire House* and interest in the animal book pulled children into the book, resulting in generally good attention. However, for the two other books, *Tell Me What Time It Is* and *The Strongest One of All*, attention was marginal and deteriorated as the story went on. There were times when two children were talking or three or four were being quietly inattentive (e.g., looking toward the back of the room, watching each other). Sarah eventually became aware of attention problems and occasionally broke from the text to deal with discipline matters. Despite the evidence of limited attentiveness, Sarah provided no explicit rules regarding appropriate behavior; rather, each problem was dealt with as an isolated issue.

Summary and Analysis. Sarah's book reading in the fall was discussion oriented. Books generally were used as starting points for discussions. These discussions began after the first page was read and ended when the text was completed and followed predictable patterns that were suggested by the book. The general tone of book time was informal, being similar in tone, content, and structure to Sarah's group discussions.

The greatest strength of these book sessions was the fact that they provided children opportunities to bring their world knowledge to mind while a book was being read. Children were encouraged to analyze events or objects (e.g., "what do we get from cows?") and to see connections between their experiences and the book (e.g., linking children's experiences with fires to the book). They also benefited from the experience of participating in group discussions that focused on a single topic. Also, children could have some influence on the direction of the conversation; they could feel the power of controlling the topic and have the valuable experience of pursuing a single line of thought.

Book time provided children semantically contingent language when objects and events were labeled and analysis comments extended discussion about them. These discussions were likely of considerable value for the children with minimal English proficiency, but of less value to the proficient language users because of the rather rudimentary words dealt with and the limited range of content covered.

Book Reading After Introduction of the Shared Book Approach

By March the teachers had had many opportunities to observe the trainer reading to children and had practiced reading enlarged textbooks themselves. In early March we videotaped the reading of two enlarged textbooks that were later analyzed, *To Town* and *Brown Bear, Brown Bear What Do You See?*, and two regular-sized books, *Where the Wild Things Are* and *Are You My Mother?* In early June two readings of two more enlarged textbooks were taped that were later analyzed, *Yes M'am* and *The Jigaree*, and readings of two more regular-sized books, *Where the Wild Things Are* and *In the Night Kitchen*.

Discussion Content and Organization. Book reading in the spring was a dramatically different activity from book reading in the fall because unison reading ('*Chiming*' in Tables 7−3 and 7−4) became the dominant form of participation. When reading three of the four enlarged texts, Chiming accounted for approximately three quarters of all child participation. The one book for which this was not true, *Brown Bear, Brown Bear*, had a large number of predicting comments, child attempts to guess what animal would be mentioned on the next page. Similar to children's "reading" of the text, these predictions required memory for the exact pattern of the book, not use of any high level semantic clues, because the ordering of the characters is arbitrary.

Another type of comment that was more common in the spring than in the fall were '*Book Focus*' comments, comments drawing children's attention to the text. This increase occurred because the unison reading was orchestrated by the teacher's pointing to the print and occasionally by her comments about the text. The print-focused reading approach greatly reduced the variety of topics discussed. The greatest variety occurred during the June reading of *Where the Wild Things Are*, the book that included the least unison reading of text. One discussion that resulted in this broader array of category types occurred when Sarah tried to get children to focus on where Max was sitting in order to introduce the word "shoulders":

Teacher: What did Max do?

Child: Jumped on the bed.

Child: Climbed a tree.

Teacher: But what else is he doing?

Child: Climb a tree.

Teacher: He's riding on ... what? What do you call those?

Child: Back.

Table 7-3   **Proportion of Comments by Teacher and Child in Each Content Category During Spring Readings of Enlarged Text Books**

Categories[a]	Books Read							
	Brown Bear		To Town		Yes M'am		Jigaree	
	T. (n=55)	Child (n=85)	T. (n=21)	Child (n=36)	T. (n=5)	Child (n=43)	T. (n=6)	Child (n=20)
Label/Describe	4	7	14	14		5		
Vocabulary								
Moralizing								
Book Focus	2	1	19	6	20			
Recall	4	1				3		5
Predicting	60	58		3				
Analysis								
Character								
Event/Object								
Print								
Text/Reader								
Experiences	2	2						
Book-to-Book	7	7						
Actions								
Chiming								
T. Request	9		43		40		50	
Child Chime		20		72		85		80
Organization								
Text Break	11		5		60	8	50	10
Minor	2		5					
Irrelevant Talk		5	14	6				5

[a] See Appendix 1 for explanation of coding categories.

Child: Shoulders.

Teacher: Shoulders, that's right.

The most interesting discussions that appeared were those that indicated the children were beginning to make connections between different books they had read and their own literacy experiences. The longest prereading discussion observed in the spring occurred prior to the reading of *Brown Bear, Brown Bear* when a child announced that she had the same book at home.

Child: I have Brown Bear.

Teacher: You have books at home?

Table 7–4   **Proportion of Comments by Teacher and Child in Each Content Category During Spring Readings of Regular-Sized Books**

Categories[a]	Books Read							
	W. Things (3/6)		...Mother?		N. Kitchen		W. Things (6/1)	
	T. (n=8)	Child (n=14)	T. (n=7)	Child (n=18)	T. (n=13)	Child (n=27)	T. (n=32)	Child (n=24)
Label/Describe		7		11	8	11	6	4
Vocabulary							6	4
Moralizing							9	4
Book Focus	12							
Recall								
Predicting	12			6			6	8
Analysis								
Character						3		
Event/Object							9	17
Text/Reader								
Experiences					8	4	3	12
Book-to-Book						7		
Actions								
Chiming								
T. Request	12				31		3	
Child Chime		50		78		67		38
Organization								
Text Break	62	29				23	34	4
Minor					15		12	
Irrelevant Talk		14		6	8	11	6	8

[a] See Appendix 1 for explanation of coding categories.

Child: Like this.

Teacher: You have books like this?

Children: [*many begin saying they have this book*] [*Teacher settles children, many of whom are saying that they have that book at home.*]

Child: I have a book about Alice in Wonderland.

Teacher: I read that story when I was a little girl.

Child: I have a book about houses.

Teacher: O.K.

Reference to ownership of books came during the reading of two other books in the spring, but were absent in the fall. These conversations suggest that children were beginning to feel that they belonged to a literate community; children were beginning to see themselves and their friends as readers. The book lending program also contributed to this emerging importance of literacy, because children began to see books as a point of contact between home and school.

Child Participation. The amount of child talk and the relative balance between child and teacher talk was vastly different from that seen in the fall. For all except one book, the June reading of *Where the Wild Things Are*, there was more talk by children than by the teacher (Tables 7−3 and 7−4). The exception resulted from Sarah's attention to minor management problems. Child comments outnumbered teacher comments dramatically (e.g., for *Yes M'am* 5 teacher comments and 43 child comments), because choral reading of the text accounted for much of the child participation later in the year.[1]

The amount of text read by children and the extent to which they read without teacher assistance varied by book. Extreme examples of children taking responsibility for the reading came in March when *Are You My Mother?* was read and in June when the class read *The Jigaree*. Each book was read with almost no teacher assistance. A child who knew the text best read most of it and the others joined in when they reached familiar parts. More typically, the teacher read much of the text and children joined in for the most predictable phrases. The reading of *Yes M'am* illustrates this pattern:

Teacher: Did you feed my pony?

Child: He made a mess? [a genuine question, not from the text]

Children: Yes m'am.

Teacher: Did my pony eat?

Children: Yes m'am.

Teacher: How did he eat?

Children: Glub, glub, glub.

Teacher: How did he eat?

Children: Slop, slop slop.

A result of the shift away from the discussion-oriented reading approach of the fall was a great reduction in the number of child attempts to initiate discussion. There was an average of only 1.25 initiatives for each book with enlarged text and two per book for each regular book. There were few initiatives because, once the group began reading stories, the direction of talk was so clearly set by the text that deviation would disrupt the flow of the reading. The lack of response to the child's question, "He made a mess?" in the above vignette from *Yes M'am*, illustrates the potential for being ignored when attempting to break into a unison reading. Not surprisingly, child initiations were most likely to occur when the unison participation structure was not activated. The story during which the most child initiatives occurred was *Where the Wild Things Are* (4 initiatives), the book that had the least unison reading.

The pattern of spending little time discussing books generally extended to the times before and after books were read. As in the fall, we observed no follow-up discussions. Either the group moved immediately to the reading of another book, to discussion about which book to read next, or they began a different activity. There was somewhat more time for discussions before books were started, but such discussions were not commonplace.

Pacing. As discussion was minimized, the reading assumed a much faster pace and had greater energy than in the fall. Because of the faster pace, more books containing more text were read in a session. Sessions we tape recorded included the reading of nine books in March and five books in June. These were not unusual sessions; in the spring Sarah said that it was common for her to read four or more books in one session.

Organization and Attentiveness. The children were extremely attentive when enlarged text books were being read. At no time during either taping session were any children verbally disruptive, and on only one page in June was more than one child inattentive. Attentiveness to the regular sized books varied with the amount of child participation in reading. Despite the generally greater attentiveness of the group in the spring compared with the fall, there were relatively more times when Sarah broke from the reading and dealt directly with organizational matters. Explicit statements of rules governing behavior during reading time were much more common (e.g., "no toys," "sit on your bottoms"), occurring in nearly all sessions. Apparently as book time came to assume greater importance and became more highly structured, Sarah felt the need to move faster and more forcefully when dealing with management problems.

Summary and Analysis. The Shared Book Experience dramatically increased children's engagement with books and with print in particular. As the books were read, Sarah pointed to print, the group produced the text together and, in contrast to the fall, a considerable number of books were read. Shared Book Experiences resulted in enhanced enjoyment of books and provided children many opportunities to begin constructing concepts about how words map onto print and how books function. Perhaps most importantly, children were given powerful opportunities to experience themselves as readers and to see their friends reading.

However, the cost of this increased pace and heightened focus on print was a decrease in leisurely discussion about text. The decrease in opportunities to discuss books removed the opportunity for teachers to extend children's knowledge about particular words. Also lost were opportunities to discuss links between the text and children's lives and chances to use books as starting points for child-initiated discussions about aspects of stories that confused, excited, or surprised the children.

It is impossible to judge how the changed participation structures might have affected oral language development. The focus on individual words provided by the semantically contingent labeling routines of the fall gave way to exposure to predictable language. The net effect of this trade-off of contingent for predictable language cannot be determined from this study. Nevertheless, it is safe to assume that the more communicatively competent children would have benefited from a more varied diet of language and discussion during the fall as well as in the spring.

Intervention Effects Throughout the Day

The literacy project had its most dramatic impact on meeting times, but it also had effects that spread beyond the morning meeting. It is important to examine these changes in some detail to identify features of programs and teacher behaviors that might be relatively easily altered by introduction of such a program, and to identify other literacy-related aspects of classrooms that are less likely to be affected by such a program.

Meeting Times. In addition to increasing exposure to books, there was increased reliance on print while songs were being sung. Often during meetings that Sarah led, she would sing songs whose words were on display in the meeting area. Children would orient to the words even though Sarah did not get up and point to them.

Activity Time. Activity time also was changed by the literacy program. The listening center, provided by the project, was used to listen to taped versions of project books as well as to Disney books (e.g., *Peter Pan*). Children listened to tapes with rapt attention and some of the more mature girls were even able to stay on the pages that corresponded to what was being read.

Another effect of the project reported by Sarah was a remarkable increase in children's desire to tell stories as they played and while they drew. It was her feeling that there was more such activity than in any group she had worked with previously. Increased interest in narrative may have resulted from the generally high level of interest in books and familiarity with storylines. As she said in March, " . . . these kids, I've got to give them credit. They are really interested in these books, which I really find amazing because some of them are only three, but they're really getting something out of these books." Later in June, despite the fact that the group was somewhat more immature than many she has had, she commented, "I have never worked with kids with the interest in books that these guys have."

Sarah also felt that the children's drawing had improved. If such an effect did occur, it most likely was because of increased artistic activity associated with changes related to the project. In previous years, Sarah had tried to restrict drawing to the smaller room, even though she had found that children tended to avoid that room during activity time. This year she allowed children to spread out and draw on the floor in the larger room, and she gave each child a box of crayons for the first time. The spreading out to work on the floor first occurred during a Thursday follow-up activity. Its success led her to continue the practice, and the increased interest in artwork led to the gift of the crayons.

Teacher-led activities also were affected by the project. Book-related activities most often happened on Thursdays when the trainer was present, but there was also a general increase in the number of teacher-led activities linked to books. For example, one day Sarah spread out all the familiar books and asked children to draw a picture from their favorite book on a large piece of paper (using the same general format as she used on Thursdays). Another example of such a change came before the group went on a field trip to a zoo. Prior to the trip she recorded children's predictions of things they might see. She said that this was a new technique for her. It might have been suggested by the project's emphasis on prediction during story reading.

A final general effect of the project was the fact that it provided Sarah a way to strive to help children acquire English. On several occasions she stated with great conviction that children who had come in with limited English had made great strides. For example, in June she said, "At the time, Denise had only been here for two weeks, hardly spoke a word of English, yet she took *Brown Bear* and read it from cover to cover in perfect English."

She was so convinced that the books were helping children acquire English that she helped Maria overcome her reluctance to read and got her to read regularly with a boy who needed help with his English. It was only in connection with books that Sarah ever mentioned efforts to improve children's oral language.

Language Throughout the Day

Despite the remarkable range of changes that did occur in the room, activities related to literacy, but which were not directly targeted, remained much the same. For example, there was only a limited increase in encouragement of child-generated dictation and no greater effort to model uses of print or encourage children's writing. Perhaps most importantly, there was no change in teacher efforts to support development of children's oral language through informal conversations.

Lending Program

Beginning in mid-March, children were allowed to take one book home at a time. It was checked out by writing the title on a large card. Each child had such a card on which was recorded the book's title, the date when it was taken out, and the date returned. Books were sent home in plastic bags that included a slip on which parents were encouraged to write comments. Each child took at least two books home and a few took four before the end of the year. The response to this lending program was universally positive. Much to Sarah's surprise, most parents wrote something about their child's experience with the books. Sarah said in June, "the parents are so impressed with the kids. . . . Their parents will come in and say, "Do you know that they read this whole book to me?"

In addition to parental pride in their child's success, another indication of the effectiveness of the lending program was revealed by a mother who commented with surprise and pleasure that she could read the books. The program probably was at least partly responsible for the comments by children during meeting times making connections between books read at home and books read in school.

CONCLUSION

A program designed to increase the number of books children hear and to heighten their enjoyment of books can have a major impact on the experiences children have with books throughout the day. Involvement with books occurred in varied social contexts, all of which embedded use of books and print in activities with diverse personal meanings for children. Group times became exuberant yet focused opportunities to enjoy familiar books and songs. Activity times provided occasions to enjoy and reinforce peer bonds by listening with one's friends to tapes of favorite books. The lending program enabled children to share this enjoyment of books and their growing sense of their own competence as readers with their parents.

Some Cautionary Comments

Despite evidence of the benefits of the program, there is continued room for improvement. There were dramatic effects related to the use of books—the focus of the program—but change in teacher behaviors that would help support language development and child interest in writing were minimal. Even in the area of book reading there were some losses that resulted from introduction of the Shared Book approach. These need to be understood because they appear not to be necessary side-effects of this program.

As book time changed from a relaxed, relatively unfocused discussion-oriented time to a highly focused, energetic sharing of books, there was a reduction in the number and variety of opportunities for children and teachers to reflect on stories. In the fall, book time was used primarily to discuss topics related to the book being read. Extended teacher-child exchanges could develop as a result of teacher or child initiatives. The intervention program resulted in a more structured activity that was focused on the text. There were few opportunities to clarify the meanings of stories or to discuss links to children's experiences. Discussion could have occurred after stories were read, but the pacing of the sessions was such that follow-up discussions did not occur. In East Village, the other implementation site that we observed, there was not such a dramatic decrease in time spent discussing books. Thus, the Shared Book approach may tend to reduce discussion time, but the near total elimination that we observed in West Village appears not to be necessary.

The lack of discussion resulted primarily from the structuring of the mode of participation, but it may also have resulted from the nature of the stories. For the most part, the books involved repeated, predictable phrases. The simplicity of the text made it memorable, but did not introduce material that Sarah was likely to feel compelled to clarify. Books with predictable text provided the bulk of the material that Sarah read after the program got started. Her relatively limited range of book selection may have been caused by several factors: she may have believed that the group could not handle more difficult material; she may have selected books that she could see the children enjoyed; or she may simply have used easily available books that she was familiar with. Despite Sarah's pattern of book selection, use of more varied and more complex books was encouraged by Head Start coordinators and by the project. That use of such a range of books was possible is indicated by the fact that at East Village the teachers began the year reading relatively complex material to children (e.g., *Millions of Cats*) who were no more mature than those in the West Village classroom.

The follow-up activity period was when the children could reflect on stories, but these generally occurred only once a week. Given the lack of opportunities for reconstructing their understanding of stories during book time, it would have been useful for children to have follow-up activities related to the books more often. Again, a contrast to East Village is instructive. At that site follow-up activities occurred throughout the week and were quite successful. However, planning for these activities was time consuming and required the cooperation of two teachers, both of whom were totally committed to the program.

Instructional Implications

The following list briefly summarizes central issues that program directors should bear in mind if they consider implementing a Shared Book program.[2]

- Books should be read with great animation[3] and should be read repeatedly.

- The pace of reading generally should be maintained, but some time for discussion should be provided before, after, or during the reading (for brief intervals). Children's questions should be responded to. The amount of time spent on questions should vary over the repeated readings, with a decline once the book is very familiar. Teachers should beware of turning discussions about books into routines in which the same topics are dealt with even though they no longer puzzle or interest the children.

- Children should receive a varied diet of books. Book selection should not be restricted to books with predictable text. Informational books, poetry, and classic children's fiction, and fantasy also should be read.

- Follow-up drama, art, and other language activities should build on vocabulary, plots, and characters experienced in the books. During these activities teachers should be alert for opportunities to make connections between books and children's lives in and out of school.

- Teachers should encourage use of books throughout the day.

- Teachers should see the entire day as providing opportunities for extending children's oral language abilities. Special attention should be given to times when there can be leisurely, extended talk between teachers and individuals (e.g., meal times, relaxed times early in the day).

- Although this paper did not deal with writing, any literacy program should encourage varied kinds of writing by preschool children of all ages.[4]

Policy Implications

- Teachers need time to master use of the technique; on-site assistance is most effective if it can be provided.

- An adequate supply of materials is vital. It should include many big books, regular-sized copies of these books, and listening centers with tapes of the books.[5]

- Children should be allowed to borrow the regular-sized books for short periods of time. Parents should be encouraged to listen to and applaud all their children's efforts.

A Final Word

It should be noted that the project is continuing. Teachers involved last year who are still working in Head Start are still participating. Staff development work is helping them refine their skills, expand their understanding of ways they can foster development of literacy skills across the curriculum, and helping them begin to function independently of the project. With continued growth, some of the initial weaknesses we identified are being dealt with as teachers and project staff reflect on their programs and as teachers become more skilled.

The literacy project that we observed was in its first year of operation at the preschool level. It struggled under the burden of limited funding, it targeted a population at great risk of educational failure, and it was implemented in typical classrooms with underpaid teachers who had no special training prior to the project. Despite these constraints, it achieved a great success: it managed to get Head Start children, their teachers, and their parents excited about books.

APPENDIX 1: BOOK READING CODING

Label/Describe. Naming or describing objects or events shown in pictures. Comments dealing with straightforward labeling of objects or events.

Vocabulary. Talk about word meanings. Direct discussion of meanings as well as provision of additional information about word meaning.

Moralizing. Talk about appropriate behavior, safety, sharing, and fighting.

Book Focus. Talk about how books and print work. Includes basic information about book parts (page, cover) and routine information about book creation (author, title, illustrator). Also covers direct talk about print (e.g., letter names, size of print, picture/print difference).

Recall. Discussion related to recall without particular concern for analysis. Focusing on the literal wording or specific sequencing of text or summarizing actual events.

Predicting. Predictions of coming events not yet pictured.

Analysis. Discussion that examines characters' actions, feelings, or motives and considers connections between events.

1. Characters: Interpreting characters' actions, feelings, or motives.

2. Events-Objects: Considerations of cause and effect; comparisons between pictures or recounted events, or discussion of behavior of objects or animals.

3. Print: Attention to how print works (e.g., directionality, spoken-written linkage).

Text-Reader Links. Linkages between text and children's experiences.

1. Experiences: Links to children's experiences.

2. Book-to-Book: Links from one book to another book, pointing out similarities or differences between books.

3. Actions: Suggests actions to link books to classroom or home such as drawing pictures or taking books home.

Chiming. Choral enjoyment of text either spoken, sung, or chanted.

1. Teacher Request: Explicit or implicit invitation to children to chime in.

2. Children Chime: Child or children join in choral response mode or reading of text. Can occur before teacher begins to read text, during text reading, or after text has been read.

Organization. Comments getting child's attention, reprimanding, requiring proper behavior, etc. These must involve a break from the on-going activity (e.g., reading, discussing text).

Irrelevant Talk. Child comments that have nothing to do with the story or with a teacher's previous question.

APPENDIX 2: EXAMPLES OF TWO PREDICTABLE TEXT BOOKS

To Town

I will go to town on my bulldozer, my big yellow bulldozer.
Brr-rrr, brr-rrr, all the way to town.

I will go to town in my fire engine, my big red fire engine.
Ooooo-aaaaah—Oooooh-aaaaah, all the way to town.

I will go to town in my vintage car, my big green vintage car.
Toot-a-toot, toot-a-toot, all the way to town.

I will go to town in my helicopter, my big blue helicopter.
Choopa-choppa, choppa-choppa, all the way to town.

I will go to town on my motorbike, my big orange motor bike.
Brmmm; brmmm; all the way to town.

I will go to town on my jumping stick, my super silver jumping stick.
Boing, boing, boing, boing, all the way to town.

All the way to town, and then ... all the way back home again.

The Jigaree

I can see a jigaree. It is jumping after me. Jumping here, jumping there, jigarees jump everywhere.

I can see a jigaree. It is dancing after me. Dancing here, dancing there, jigarees dance everywhere.

I can see a jigaree. It is swimming after me. Swimming here, swimming there, jigarees swim everywhere.

I can see a jigaree. It is riding after me. Riding here, riding there, jigarees ride everywhere.

I can see jigaree. It is skating after me. Skating here, skating there, jigarees skate everywhere.

I can see a jigaree. It is climbing after me. Climbing here, climbing there, jigarees climb everywhere.

I can see a jigaree. It is flying after me. Flying here, flying there, jigarees fly everywhere.

Jigaree, jigaree, I will take you ... home with me.

NOTES

[1]Child chiming was counted as a codable utterance (i.e., not direct reading of text) whereas solo reading of the text by the teacher, the only pattern of communicating text in the fall, was not coded.

[2]Those interested in more complete information and much more advice regarding implementation issues should contact the Literacy/Curriculum Connections Project directly. It is headed by Lynn Hall, at 159 Thorndike St., Cambridge School Department, Cambridge, MA 02141.

[3]See Holdaway (1979) for much more advice on use of the books.

[4]For an excellent introduction to introducing writing into preschools get the filmstrip, *Literacy Development in the Preschool*, by Judith Schickedanz, available from Heinemann Educational Books. Also see Loughlin's and Martin's book, *Supporting Literacy*.

[5]Books with enlarged print written especially to have rhythmic, predictable text can be purchased from The Wright Group, 10949 Technology Place, P.O. Box 27780, San Diego, CA 92127, and from Rigby Education, 454 S. Virginia St., Crystal Lake, IL 60014. These publishers sell (rather expensive) sets of enlarged books, regular-sized texts, and audio cassetts. Enlarged versions of old favorites are also now available from Scholastic Books and Milliken. These do not necessarily include predictable text.

ACKNOWLEDGMENTS

I want to thank the Head Start teachers and children who made this study possible, as well as Lynn Hall and other Literacy/Curriculum Connections project members who read and commented on an earlier draft of this paper. I also want to thank students who helped collect and analyze data—Eric Dahms, Patty Crane, Michelle Weene, and Alix Born. This research was supported by a Biomedical Research Award granted to Tufts University.

We move from Big Books to little books. Teachers in rural Illinois Head Start classrooms also implemented a shared book experience, with the emphasis on whole story reading rather than word identification. However, the texts they used were much simpler, and the books themselves could be duplicated easily for ownership and home use. McCormick and Mason draw together several years of interlocking research on the use of these little books at school and at home.

Chapter 8

Fostering Reading for Head Start Children with Little Books

Christine E. McCormick
Jana M. Mason

COULD a low-cost, easy-to-administer intervention foster the development of reading among children attending Head Start? We thought it possible because home-based parent intervention programs have produced moderate academic gains (Bronfenbrenner, 1975; Goodsen & Hess, 1978). Effective programs typically begin in the preschool period and involve parent-child verbal interactions (Lazar & Darlington, 1982; Slaughter, 1983). Thus, an intervention that encourages parent-child book reading during the Head Start or kindergarten year might foster children's later reading in school, for such an intervention could potentially blend a book-focused introduction to literacy with parent-supported talk about literacy events.

A number of concepts about print and reading are acquired prior to entering school as Bissex (1980), Clay (1972), and Ferreiro & Teberosky (1982), among others, have documented. Early aspects of knowledge about reading reflect the family experience of the child, not merely a presence of reading materials in the home (Durkin, 1966). One aspect of early experience is book reading interactions between parents and child. Snow and

Ninio (1986) describe the interactive routines of parent-toddler picture book reading in which the focus is on pictures rather than printed words. Basic rules of literacy are established as parents guide their children in discussions of how to handle books rather than chew or tear them, discussions of the differences between real things and pictures of things, and, as children become more sophisticated in their understanding of how to use books, discussions of story events as separate from experiences in real time. DeLoache and DeMendoza (1987), in their analysis of mother-toddler picture book reading, document a shift in the mothers' verbalizations from that of telling or teaching names of pictured objects to that of introducing additional information once the child knows the names of the pictured objects. Not only do mothers provide more information to the older, more knowledgeable toddler, but they elicit more verbal responses when they sense the child is capable of greater verbal participation.

Another aspect of early experience is the role played by children during parent-child communication. Price, Hess, and Dickson (1981) found the children of mothers who invite child-generated responses through questions, requests, and commands show greater memory for specific content. Preschool children had greater knowledge of letter names in kindergarten and first grade for example, if their mothers asked for specific child responses with questions such as "What's that letter?" and "What's the difference between the two letters?"

Children from families of lower socioeconomic status (SES) are more likely than those from families of higher SES to encounter problems with reading at school (Snow, 1983). There are differences in the amount of support at home for activities related to reading. For example, work by Anderson and Stokes (1984) and Teale (1986b) documented a low incidence of parent-child book-reading activity among working-class and low-income families. Overall, fewer low SES families than middle SES families seem to serve an intermediary role of helping their children learn about print. These children are at greater risk for failure in reading.

We proposed that involving the lower SES family in the child's first attempts at behaving like a reader would help them foster parent-child communication about print and encourage their children to focus on letters, printed words, and story information. It would foster beginning reading success in school.

Our approach to understanding development of early reading concepts and the differences in these skills in relation to family experience uses a stage-model perspective. Mason (1977, 1980) proposed such a model from a year-long study of children in a university preschool, finding three levels of early reading. At each level children were found to use a different set of strategies to identify printed words. Children's early understanding about how to recognize words is the foundation behind our proposal to provide book activities that foster children's early attempts to behave like readers. The following distinctions among the three levels clarify the stage model and provide the rationale for our focus on children who are operating at the first level of reading.

Children at the first level identify words primarily by remembering them in their context (e.g., recognizing STOP when it appears on a road sign) and through unique configurations of letters (e.g., LOOK appears to have 2 eyes in the middle). This primitive process of word learning is likened to looking at and remembering pictures, with each word in each location treated as a different object-like entity. A few words are thereby recognized by sight and remembered within their context. Words important to the child, such as his or her name, are best remembered. Ehri and Wilce (1985) describe similar results and call this level visual-cue word learning. While lessons involving many exposures of words in their meaningful contexts will enable children at this level to recognize some words, they are likely to make wild guesses about words out of context and will have difficulty remembering any but the most familiar words that they are taught.

As children are taught phonics or become acquainted through informal literacy activities with letters and the printed forms of words, by having books and signs and labels read to them, they become aware that letters signal particular sounds, and that these phonetic sounds, particularly those at word beginnings, can be heard in words. Children at this level can use initial letter sounds to spell and read some short words, and they do a credible job of learning and remembering familiar words. Ehri and Wilce (1985) call this level phonetic-cue word learning. Some children reach this level as the result of the informal instruction provided at home or pre-school. That is, parents or preschool teachers may have pointed out the consistency in initial consonant sounds during book reading or sign and label reading and the children may have begun to apply this information in their own attempts at reading and writing. For most children this level matches the typical instruction of kindergarten, such as tasks of identifying initial consonant sounds.

A third level of development occurs when children develop efficient means to recognize a larger number of words. To do this they attend to both letter information and meaning. They begin to hold a more flexible view toward letter-sound relationships, recognize words that have unique patterns, and develop confidence in their knowledge about letter-sound patterns to figure out the pronunciation of regular-patterned words. More-over, they make better use of context in word identification and are able to use strategies such as skipping unknown words and reading ahead in order to recognize words. Children at this level use vowel and consonant infor-mation to decode and spell most regularly formed one-syllable words. This level corresponds to the cipher stage described by Gough, Juel, and Roper-Schneider (1983). This level is typically not reached until the child has begun systematic reading instruction in school, usually first grade.

LINKING EMERGING WORD READING WITH INFORMAL READING ACTIVITY

In the process of delineating the early reading model, Mason (1980) developed a set of little books, which were six to eight pages long with four to five words and a picture on each page, for teachers to use in the preschool study. At the time they were constructed (1974), no commercial materials were available that children could easily use. In New Zealand, Clay (1972) recommended the use of books containing easy-to-see print, a small number of different words (low type count), and useful picture information. Holdaway (1979) described book-reading procedures, called Shared Book Experience, that emphasized class recitation of familiar children's story books containing repetitive, predictable story lines. Mason's approach introducing books was quite similar to the procedure recommended by Holdaway. However, the little books provide a much simpler text, enabling nearly all children to recite the little book texts easily. Moreover, the format of the little books allows them to be duplicated easily, so that the children can take them home and involve parents in the use of the books. In Mason's study (1980) with these little books, even children who were at Level 1 learned to recite and remember the texts, they borrowed them for home use, and they read them to one another during play time. This work suggested that little books could be an effective way to introduce Level 1 reading informally to children who receive limited literacy experiences at home.

A southern Illinois rural community was chosen next to study the impact of the little books on early reading skills because most of the children entering first grade had less knowledge of sign and label words, letter names, and letter sounds than the children two years younger of middle-income families studied earlier by Mason (1977, 1980). In this first training study, Mason and McCormick (1981) introduced preschool children in day care to little books over a two-week period. The more effective procedure, later called Book Recitation, was to read and then reread the text until children could recite it with the teacher. Throughout the reading children were encouraged to comment on the text and read along with the teacher or another child. After ten book reading lessons in which one new book was introduced and one or two favorites reread together, children were given copies of their favorite books to take home and keep. Comparisons determined that the approach that focused on text reading and rereading until children could do it without help was more effective than the approach that attempted to have the children attend to letter sounds and words from texts.

Parents in both groups responded favorably to the gifts of little books and reported that their children used them frequently at home, and were even initiating reading with family members. The parents commented that they hadn't realized their child was interested in trying to read until the child brought home the books. Some also said that the child was behaving like a reader, carrying the books around and showing off an ability to "read."

The follow-up parental interview data suggested that the little books encouraged children to take a more direct role in looking at and trying to read printed information and to engage in verbal interaction with parents about the pictures and print. Videotapes of Head Start children's participation in group book reading sessions, which were collected shortly thereafter (Mason, 1985; Mason, McCormick, & Bhavnagri, 1986), indicated that over the course of several sessions with the little books, children became more able to interact verbally with the teacher. They became more able to express to the teacher metacognitive strategies such as monitoring, planning, and evaluating text information. The analysis suggested again that Book Recitation provided a format for Head Start children to predict and discuss the story line as well as to express confusion or a need for clarification about the printed text. The child's first experiences with text recitation did not focus on letter sounds or word recognition. Rather the discussions more closely resembled the parent/child interactions of picture book reading, only in this case the discussions included references to print as well as story line.

The use of little books was next studied in a home intervention study with another group of rural families from southern Illinois (McCormick & Mason, 1986). Children were tested in the spring before kindergarten as part of the district's prekindergarten screening. Brief tests of letter naming, sign and label reading, spelling, and little book reading were added. Parents were given a packet of three stories and a note explaining how to help their children read the books at home. Virtually all the children were at Level 1 with limited letter-name knowledge and no knowledge of letter sounds or printed words. Two months later the children received another set of three books in the mail, and the following fall a third set of three. September testing compared these twenty-three children with a matched control (based on scores from the Peabody Picture Vocabulary Test). Control children were in the same kindergarten program but had not received any of the book materials. Follow-up testing at the end of kindergarten included tests of sign and label words, letter-name and letter-sound knowledge, recognition of common words, pseudoword reading, and reading two little books.

Results showed that the children who had received little books at home made greater gains in word knowledge, spelling, and book reading, while both groups made equivalent gains in letter names.

The reading progress of the children at the conclusion of first grade was also measured. The six first-grade teachers, who did not know about the earlier study, ranked all the children in their classes in overall reading skill and reported children's placement in reading groups. Higher average rankings occurred for children who had received the little books. Moreover, only 6 percent of the book treatment children were in the lowest reading group, compared to 29 percent of the control group (and 29 percent of all children in the six classrooms). Thus, the treatment made the greatest impact for those children who were likely to get off to a slow start in reading instruction.

Although this study indicated that receiving little books at home was more effective than not receiving books, the effect could have been due to the books or merely to receiving something in the mail. Moreover, test and questionnaire information was not sufficiently detailed to understand the nature of the effect and the sample had a mix of SES levels. Finally, although earlier studies suggested that combining Book Recitation with sending books home was effective, we did not test a combined approach.

The study we present here allowed us to compare what we thought to be an effective low-cost intervention, which was Book Recitation at school and sending the books home over a protracted period of time, with an alternate intervention, Story Discussion at school and sending picture materials home. Thus, children in both groups were given an intervention at school that took the same length of time, and they received the same amount of mail at home. The major difference was that the Book Recitation group saw print and practiced reading it while the Story Recitation group saw pictures and discussed the story ideas. Participants were children of low-income families (incomes under $11,000) attending Head Start. We began the study when children were in Head Start and continued to send materials home in the kindergarten year. We assessed children's reading progress again at the end of first grade.

YEAR 1

Method

All children ($N = 51$) in four Head Start classrooms of a small, midwest city were used as subjects. Forty-nine of the children were Caucasian and two were black. Most were four or five years old with an average age of four years, seven months. In January the children were pretested and parents filled out a questionnaire. The children were pretested individually on measures of letter naming, sign and label identification, and little book reading. The questionnaire addressed children's interest in and knowledge about literacy and parents' support for it. The children were also given the Peabody Picture Vocabulary Test-Revised (PPVT-R) as a measure of receptive vocabulary. Teachers completed a teachability rating on each child (Keogh & Kornblau, 1980). This measure assesses teachers' perceptions of the ideal student and has several subscales, two of which were used in our study: school appropriate behavior and core items for the ideal student. (See Appendix 1 for details regarding these measures.)

The children were assigned to Book Recitation (BR) and Story Discussion (SD) groups by dividing an alphabetized list of the children from each class in half and placing the first half of the lists from two classes and the last half of the lists from the other two classes in the Book Recitation group; the remaining children were placed in the Story Discussion group. The children in the two groups were roughly equivalent on all pretest measures.

Following the pretesting, both groups received ten- to fifteen-minute lessons once a week for six weeks, presented by McCormick, in groups of four to six children who were taken to a room adjacent to the classrooms for each lesson. Each Book Recitation group was introduced to one new book each week. Books were selected from the Pint Size Print series (Mason & McCormick, 1985), an expanded set of the books originally developed by Mason. Each Story Discussion group was introduced to one classic story each week, such as *Three Little Pigs*, *The Three Bears*, and *Little Red Riding Hood*.

McCormick taught Book Recitation by asking children to predict the text topic from the book's cover and encouraging them to discuss their experiences related to the topic. This step helped children become engaged in the text. Next she modeled reading by showing the print and pictures to children and pointing to the words as she read aloud. She then encouraged children to recite the text with her, first as a group and then singly, each saying a portion of the text. Children were allowed to comment or repeat the recitation of a child whose turn it was to respond. The goal was to provide just enough support that children would talk freely about the text or topic and would learn to recite the text. That is why the text was modeled until the children were willing to say it as a group and why they were allowed to insert comments at any time. After reading the new book, children chose and recited as a group one of their favorite books from an earlier lesson. Each week the book introduced for that week was mailed to the child at home. This later proved to be a challenge since at least half of the children moved at least once during each of the three years of the study.

In the Story Discussion groups the story was told by McCormick, so there was no text for the children to see, reading was not modeled, and children did not recite a text. McCormick told the story while showing the book's illustrations, emphasizing what was happening in the pictures. Following the initial presentation, the children were asked individually to retell the story. Each child was shown a picture from the story as a prompt to elicit their comments about the story. Favorite stories were retold in subsequent lessons. Illustrations that had been used during the group presentation were mailed each week to the children at home.

In April the children were posttested on the same measures of letter naming and sign and label identification that they had been given in January. They were also asked to read a little book that had been taught to the Book Recitation group and a little book that was unfamiliar to both groups. For this task they were handed the book, told its name, and asked to read it. Since there were pictures on each page, all the children were able to participate, though of course most merely looked at and labeled the pictures or made up a story. The children were also shown six labeled pictures and asked to "point to where there is something to read" (a task adapted from Ferreiro & Teberosky, 1982 by Peterman & Mason, 1984). A point was assigned for each printed label the child pointed to. Parents responded again to the questionnaire on their literacy support and child's interest and knowledge about literacy, with questions regarding the child's interest in the materials that had been sent home added.

Results

We ran a hierarchical multiple regression analysis to determine which measures could predict the posttest score at the end of the Head Start year. The posttest score was the sum of the standardized scores on the six posttests. Table 8−1 shows that at each step the measure (or combination of measures in Step 2) significantly contributed to the posttest score.

The first step indicates that parents who said they supported reading and writing prior to treatment had a positive influence. Step 2 indicates that children who follow directions, are eager and are able to complete classroom tasks, and are alert and attentive to classroom proceedings have higher reading scores at the end of Head Start. Also influential at Step 2 are the PPVT-R scores and parents' estimates of their child's literacy, indicating the advantage given to children with higher receptive vocabulary and pretreatment interest in reading and writing. Step 3 shows that the early reading pretest makes a small contribution. Step 4 shows that the treatment is effective, above and beyond parents' support for reading, teachability, receptive vocabulary, and incoming knowledge about reading. Children who were provided opportunities in Head Start to recite the text

Table 8–1   Year 1 Regression Analysis Predicting Reading at End of
             Head Start

Step	Variable	Correlation with Posttest	Multiple R	R^2	F value	p
1	Parent literacy support	.40	.40	.16	9.09	.004
2	Sex	−.17				
	Age	−0.1				
	PPVT-R	.43				
	Teachability	.58				
	Parent estimate of child literacy (pre)	.54				
	School-appropriate behavior	.62	.73	.53	6.94	.000
3	Reading pre-test	.60	.77	.59	7.50	.000
4	Treatment	.53	.90	.80	18.35	.000

in little books and use them at home gained more early reading knowledge than did children who listened to and retold stories and had pictures from the stories at home.

Not unexpectedly, the biggest difference between the two groups was on book reading. The Book Recitation group had the largest score advantage on book reading. Nevertheless, all six posttests favored the Book Recitation group (see Table 8–2). Since there were no significant group differences before treatment, these results indicate that Book Recitation effects extended beyond taught stories to new reading materials.

The parent questionnaire given in May repeated questions from January on the child's knowledge of letters and words and interest in reading and indicated small changes in the parents' responses, favoring the Book Recitation group. The "Parent estimate of child literacy" score (see Appendix 1) for the Book Recitation group indicated that these children gained in their interest in and knowledge of letters and words (a pretreatment average of 15, and a posttreatment of 29) while the score for the children in the Story Discussion group did not change (pre and postaverages of 15). Also, children in the Book Recitation group received nearly the same amount of support from parents at both times (pre and postaverages of 16 for the score on "Parent literacy support") while children in the Story Discussion group received less support in May than in January (preaverage of 16 and postaverage of 13).

Additional questions in the May questionnaire asked about parents'

Table 8−2   Means for Pre- and Post-test Subtests, Year 1, and
Effects of Head Start Treatment on Each Subtest

	Highest Possible Score	Book Recitation N=26		Story Discussion N=25		F Value for post-tests	Prob.	Correlation with Treatment
		Pre	Post	Pre	Post			
Picture label	20	10.8	13.1	11.0	11.6	6.52	.01	.27
Label (no picture)	20	1.3	2.2	1.2	1.2	4.08	.05	.24
Letter naming	10	1.9	2.8	2.0	2.7	.07	—	.01
Taught book	13	1.4	11.4	2.0	1.6	244.87	.00	.91
New book	13		4.0		1.6	12.11	.00	.48
Points to print	6		4.2		3.3	.93	—	.19

perceptions of their child's interest in the materials received in the mail and their child's current interest in activities related to literacy. These added questions showed large differences in how often the children used the materials and in their increased interest in print-related activities. This portion of the questionnaire is shown in Figure 8−1. Comparing group responses on questions 1 and 2 with questions 3 and 4 suggests that though both groups were interested in the materials, children in the group receiving the books used the materials more frequently than did children in the group receiving pictures from stories. On the questions of change in interest, the parents of the group receiving little books reported greater child interest in hearing stories, in telling stories, in printing or trying to print, in trying to read, and in naming words in signs and labels than did the parents of the group receiving pictures. The only activity for which the parents of the group receiving pictures reported greater child interest was that of drawing.

YEAR 2

Since we wanted to follow the children's progress with beginning reading skills in school and nearly all of our Head Start children could still be characterized as Level 1 readers, we believed that our little books would continue to be beneficial during the kindergarten year. We did not involve kindergarten teachers in Year 2, except for the assessment of the children's

Figure 8–1   **Percent Responses by Treatment Group to Parent Questionnaire at End of Head Start**

1. Is your child still interested in the pictures or little books which were sent in the mail?

Yes	No
96 (BR)	4 (BR)
95 (SD)	5 (SD)

2. Did your child read or tell you the story when the materials arrived?

Yes	No
91 (BR)	9 (BR)
95 (SD)	5 (SD)

3. Does your child still use the materials?

Yes	No
100 (BR)	0 (BR)
76 (SD)	24 (SD)

4. If yes, how often does the child use the materials:?

every day	2–3 times a week	once a week	once in a while	never
4 (BR)	48 (BR)	26 (BR)	22 (BR)	0 (BR)
10 (SD)	24 (SD)	19 (SD)	19 (SD)	24 (SD)

Please check any changes you have noticed in your child since he or she began receiving the materials in the mail:

BR	SD		
74	52	——	5. more interest in hearing stories
83	67	——	6. more interest in telling stories
30	48	——	7. more interest in drawing
57	29	——	8. more interest in printing or trying to print
70	43	——	9. more interest in trying to read
61	38	——	10. more interest in naming words in street signs or food labels

progress at the end of the school year, because we thought the children could use the books at home without additional introduction at school. Book Recitation children continued to receive little books at home, and Story Recitation children were sent worksheet activities that we supposed that the children would enjoy completing with their parents since they were similar to the kinds of activities often found in children's magazines. Since no school intervention was provided, we called the first group, *Home Book*, and the other, *Home Activity*.

We were able to follow into Year 2 about half of our children from the Head Start year; these were the children who entered a kindergarten class in the same city. A check on the initial pretest scores for these children in Year 2 indicated that the groups were indeed roughly equivalent at the beginning of our study in Year 1. All schools in the city used the Alpha Time (1972) reading readiness program, which teaches initial consonants and medial short vowels through a variety of media including inflatable plastic letter-people with an accompanying descriptive phrase, worksheets based on the letter people, and theme songs for each letter.

Method

Beginning in January of the kindergarten year, the children received six sets of materials in the mail; materials were mailed about three weeks apart. The Home Book group of thirteen children who had been in the Book Recitation group the first year continued to receive our little books in the mail. The Home Activity group of eleven children who had been in the Story Discussion group the first year received worksheet activities that did not emphasize printed letters or words but could be shared with parents. These worksheets included activities such as matching figures, finding hidden pictures, and picture completion.

In May of kindergarten the children were posttested. They were individually given the reading and spelling subtests on the Wide Range Achievement Test (WRAT). The procedures described in the manual were used for administering the spelling and reading subtests on the WRAT, but the scoring procedures were modified to obtain evidence of their knowledge of letter sounds (see Appendix 2). Following administration of the WRAT, each child was asked to read three little books. One book had been taught to the Book Recitation group during the Head Start year (*Time for Bed*), one had not been taught but was mailed during the kindergarten year (*Pick up Toys*), and one story (*Can You Carry?*) was new to both groups.

At the end of the school year the six kindergarten teachers who taught one or more of the children in the study completed a questionnaire estimating their reading skills and predicting their likely success in first grade. Parents completed a short questionnaire on their children's use of the materials received in the mail and interest in reading and printing at home. During the summer following kindergarten, parents of the children in the Home Book group who could be located were interviewed regarding their reaction to the intervention and the child's use of the materials at home. Another accounting of children's academic progress was made at the end of first grade.

Results

The results indicated significant differences between the two groups on nearly every measure (see Table 8–3). Using a simplified six-level version of Sulzby's (1985) levels of story reading, Home Book children's reading

Table 8−3   T Tests on Mean Scores for Home Book and Home
Activity Groups in Year 2

	Points Possible	X Home Book N=13		X Home Activity N=11		t	p
Level of book reading		%		%			
Book from Year 1	6	4.00	67	2.27	38	3.20	<.01
Book from Year 2	6	4.38	73	2.82	47	3.75	<.01
New (transfer) book	6	4.08	68	1.82	30	4.28	<.001
Correct words in reading							
Book from Year 1	13	7.92	61	3.55	27	4.12	<.001
Book from Year 2	21	14.38	68	5.55	26	4.53	<.001
New (transfer) book	11	5.00	45	2.64	24	2.36	<.06
Wide Range Achievement Test							
Letter sounds	27	10.38	38	3.27	12	2.70	<.02
Parental assessment							
of children's knowledge	35	28.17	80	23.20	66	2.52	<.02

attempts of the book taught in Head Start, the one sent home in kindergarten, and the new book were at a higher level than were the same reading attempts by children in the Home Activity group. An average score of 4 by the Home Book group describes the use of a written language-like story while a 2 by the other group describes an embellished labeling of pictures. The number of words correct also differentiated the two groups. The Home Book group scored significantly higher on the two familiar books and on the new books, the difference approached significance (see Table 8−3). All children in both groups printed their first names and nearly all accurately identified the fifteen uppercase letters on the WRAT reading subtest. Letter-sound identification scores from the spelling subtest on the Wide Range Achievement Test indicated that the Home Book group was able to identify significantly more letter sounds than was the Home Activity group. Fifty-five percent of the Home Activity group received a score of 0 for printing letter sounds on the WRAT spelling subtest. In contrast, only 15 percent of the Home Book group received a score of 0 on this measure. Figure 8−2 gives an example from each group of a child's responses to the measures of spelling and book reading. Tested differences were mirrored by parents' assessment of their children's knowledge about literacy. A summary score from questions to parents about their child's knowledge of literacy (how often the child plays school at home, looks at books, asks to be read to, reads or pretend reads, prints or tries to print, and how many printed words the child reads and how many words the child writes) was significantly higher for the Home Book group than for the Home Activity group (last row of Table 8−3).

Figure 8−2   **Examples of Responses from Home Book Group and Home Activity Group**

Test WRAT spelling	Home Book Example (printed response)	Home Activity Example (printed response)
1. "go"	1. O	1. 1
2. "cat"	2. CAT	2. 2
3. "in"	3. EN	3. 3
4. "boy"	4. BE	4. 4
5. "and"	5. AD	5. —
6. "will"	6. WEL	6. —
7. "make"	7. MAG	7. —
8. "him"	8. HEM	8. —
9. "say"	9. SE	9. —
10. "cut"	10. CUT	10. —

(Child told book's title)	(spoken response)	(spoken response)
Time for Bed		
read a story	"read"	"read a book"
brush your teeth	"brush your teeth"	"brushing teeth"
get a hug	"hug"	"no response"
climb in bed	"get in bed"	"television"
nighty night, sleep tight	"go to sleep"	"no response"
Pick Up Toys		
pick up bus	"pick up bus"	"pick up toys again"
pick up bear	"pick up teddy bear"	"pick up toys"
pick up boat	"pick up boat"	"pick up toys"
pick up ball	"pick up ball"	"pick up toys"
pick up bunny	"pick up rabbit"	"pick up toys"
pick up blocks	"pick up blocks"	"pick up toys"
oh oh BOOM	"oh oh boom"	"pick up toys"
Can You Carry		
a cat	"a cat"	"can you carry a hat"
and a cap	"a hat"	"can you carry a cat and a hat"
and a cup	"a cup"	"a cat a hat and a cup"
and a cake	"a cake"	"a cat and a hat and a cup and a cake"
and a clown	"a doll"	"a cat and a hat and a toy and a cup and a cake"
on a cow?	"a cow"	"cat and a toy and a hat and cake and cup"

Figure 8–3   **Percent Responses by Treatment Group (B = Home Book, A = Home Activity) to Parent Questionnaire at End of Kindergarten**

---

1. Did your child use the materials when they arrived?

Yes	No
100 (B)	0 (B)
82 (A)	18 (A)

2. Does your child still use the materials?

Yes	No
100 (B)	0 (B)
45 (A)	55 (A)

3. If yes, how often does your child use the materials?

every day	2–3 times a week	once a week	once in a while
8 (B)	39 (B)	31 (B)	23 (B)
0 (A)	9 (A)	9 (A)	82 (A)

Please check any changes you have noticed since your child began receiving the materials in the mail:

B	A	
70	27	—— 4. more interest in hearing stories
85	27	—— 5. more interest in telling stories
69	73	—— 6. more interest in drawing
69	64	—— 7. more interest in printing or trying to print
92	18	—— 8. more interest in trying to read
69	36	—— 9. more interest in naming words in street signs, store signs, or food labels

10. How often does your child play school?

never	once in a while	once a week	2–3 times a week	every day
	31 (B)	23 (B)	23 (B)	23 (B)
	55 (A)	18 (A)	27 (A)	27 (A)

11. How often does your child look at books?

never	once in a while	once a week	2–3 times a week	every day
			39 (B)	62 (B)
	9 (A)	9 (A)	46 (A)	36 (A)

12. How often does your child ask to be read to?

never	once in a while	once a week	2–3 times a week	every day
	23 (B)	8 (B)	46 (B)	23 (B)
9 (A)	9 (A)	27 (A)	27 (A)	27 (A)

13. How often does your child read or pretend to read books to himself or someone else?

never	once in a while	once a week	2–3 times a week	every day
	8 (B)	15 (B)	46 (B)	31 (B)
	36 (A)	18 (A)	36 (A)	9 (A)

14. How often does your child print or try to print?

never	once in a while	once a week	2-3 times a week	every day
	8 (B)		8 (B)	85 (B)
	18 (A)		46 (A)	36 (A)

15. How many printed words do you think your child can read?

not any	1 or 2	about 5	about 10	more than 15
8 (B)	8 (B)	15 (B)	39 (B)	31 (B)
9 (A)	27 (A)	36 (A)	18 (A)	9 (A)

16. Please list the words your child can read, including signs and labels such as STOP, K-MART, JELLO:

17. How many words does your child write or try to write?

not any	1 or 2	about 5	about 10	more than 15
	15 (B)	15 (B)	15 (B)	54 (B)
9 (A)	46 (A)	27 (A)	18 (A)	

18. Please list the words your child writes:

The parental questionnaire given at the end of kindergarten showed large changes over time for Home Book children's frequency of use of literacy materials, their interest in the materials, and their knowledge about reading and writing. The questionnaire and responses are shown in Figure 8–3. Questions 1–9 repeated the questions from May of Year 1 (Head Start) regarding the child's use of the materials and interest in literacy activities. Questions 10 through 18 had been used in January and May of Year 1.

Comparing group responses of question 1 with questions 2 and 3 suggests that the initial interest in receiving the materials was sustained through Year 2 with books but not with activity sheets. Responses to questions 4–9 suggest that having the books at home fostered an interest in reading and storytelling. Particularly large differences, in favor of the Home Book group, were noted for the questions on increased interest in hearing stories and telling stories (questions 4 and 5) and for the questions on increased interest in trying to read and naming words in signs and labels (questions 8 and 9). In terms of frequency of usage, questions 11, 13, and 14 indicate greater involvement by the Home Book children in literacy activity. Questions 15 and 17 suggest that having the books at home influenced the number of words they could read and print. Note that 70 percent of Home Book children could read and print 10, 15, or more words compared to 18–27 percent of Home Activity children. Open-ended comments from parents on the usefulness of the books also showed that parents perceived quite different reactions from their children. Home Book parents were quite explicit in their descriptions about how the books succeeded in getting children interested in reading and in using them to read aloud, sound out words, reread, figure out word meanings, or teach a younger sibling. Their comments included: (1) "April really enjoys the materials you sent to her. She would like more if you want to send them to her." (2) "He reads the books himself. He's starting to notice the words in different books too." (3) "She enjoyed reading them and read them over and over." (4) "She always enjoyed getting the mail, then reading them, and she's kept all of them and looks at them and also read them to me." (5) "She thinks she can read. With the picture can get the meaning even if some of the words are wrong." Home Activity parents reported: (1) "Yes, they helped Timmy alot." (2) "Yes, he liked getting mail." (3) "Some was helpful. Others were too easy." (4) "Didn't show much interest."

The teachers' predictions of the children's ($N = 24$) likelihood of success with first-grade reading were analyzed using a chi-square test in which the number of children "likely to be retained in kindergarten" or to "experience difficulty" in first-grade reading was compared to the number of children in the categories of "likely to get by" in first-grade reading or to "do well" in first-grade reading. The children in the Home Book group were significantly more likely to do well or get by in first-grade reading (77 percent) than were the children in the Home Activity group (36 percent), according to their teacher's predictions.

During the summer following the kindergarten posttesting, parents from the Home Book group who could be reached were interviewed by McCormick for more in-depth information regarding the use of the books at home. All parents said they were very familiar with the stories the children had received in the mail and indicated that the children had involved the parents in reading the stories, both by reading to them and by asking for help with new stories. The parents viewed the stories as helping their children learn to read. One father even stated that he wished he had stories like these when he was learning to read. Gina's mother (see Figure 8–4), who said the books really boosted her daughter's morale, captured the general sense of enthusiasm for the little books. Excerpts from three of the interviews presented in Figure 8–4 show that the children were reading the stories at home, that parents were aware of their child's success with this reading task, and that materials provided a vehicle for the parents to interact with children.

A subsequent accounting of children in first grade has determined that of nine children from the Home Book group who could be located, three were in high reading groups, three in middle groups, and three in a low group, all going on to second grade. Of eight in the Home Activity group who could be located, one was in a high reading group, one was in a middle reading group, and six were in a low reading group. Of the six in the low reading group, two had been placed in a transition room mid-year and were also receiving Learning Disabilities (LD) tutoring, one was

Figure 8–4　**Excerpts from Interviews with Parents of Home Book Group Children at the Conclusion of Year 2**

Mark

Did Mark use the stories he received in the mail?
　He used them and got to the point where he could read them.
How did Mark use the stories?
　He could read them by himself. He showed 'em off.
How were they helpful?
　Got him interested in reading. Before he liked to listen to stories, but not read. At first he just liked the mail, then he wanted to read them.

Gina

Did Gina use the books she received in the mail?
　Gina used the books a couple of times a week; really helped to have new ones come.
How did she use them?
　She listened while I read. Instead of just listening she actually tried to learn to read. Now she can do the same thing with some library books.
Were they helpful?
　Those books helped immensely. She showed her dad she could read; boosted her morale a whole lot.

Sisto

Did Sisto use the books he received in the mail?
　He loved them; mainly read 'em to himself over and over. Some he needed help.
How did he use them?
　He flipped through them every day for about three weeks after they came in the mail, still has them and uses them once in a while.
Were they helpful?
　Yes. They are a very good idea.

---

receiving LD tutoring while remaining in the regular classroom, and one was retained in first grade. Thus, reading group placement as well as the amount of additional services now differentiated children who in January of their Head Start year had been equivalent.

DISCUSSION

Strong and consistent results supporting use and ownership of our little books converge from three sources: our tests, parents' perceptions on several questionnaires, and teachers' evaluations. Children initially functioning at Level 1 who were given the opportunity to hear and recite texts from little books and then to receive them for an additional year at home were more likely to be effective readers in the first years of school than were children who missed the opportunity to recite books at school and use them at home. Moreover, the effects increased over time despite the elimination of book recitation at school and were generalized beyond little book reading. A greater awareness of letter sounds in words was evident because more children in the Home Book than Home Activity group could spell words phonetically and were reading at Level 2 or 3 by the end of kindergarten. There was also a better understanding of how to read a book. End of kindergarten differences in children's text reading, as measured by Sulzby's emergent reading level and our counts of word reading accuracy, appeared not only for the text the Home Book group had learned to recite in Head Start but also for ones that had not been taught at Head Start. This indicates that sending little books home encourages children to use language that is more similar to written language for their reading attempts.

Parents' assessment of their children's interest in print as well as kindergarten teachers' reports of children's ability and progress show substantial difference between the two groups after the treatment. On into first grade, 67 percent of the Home Book group, but only 25 percent of the Home Activity group, were placed in middle or high reading groups. Furthermore, none of the Home Book children, but half of those in the Home Activity group, had already failed a grade or had been given supplementary reading instruction.

Our conclusions regarding the little books need to be tempered by several considerations. First, although the original samples of children (beginning of Year 1) did not have significantly different scores, receptive vocabulary, parental literacy support, and parent estimate of child literacy were slightly higher for children in the Home Book group. Second, although all children in Year 2 used the same reading readiness program in kindergarten, they were scattered among a number of teachers and we did not measure differences among the teachers in implementation of the program. Third, the number of children in Year 2 of the study was small.

Nonetheless, consistency over time for the children in this study and the similar findings in our earlier work suggest that experience with little books and subsequent availability of the books at home foster reading for Level 1 children. These experiences, provided before and during kindergarten, familiarize children with print and what it means to read. Such an introduction, which is not unlike that provided in literate homes, allows children to benefit from the phonics instruction that many receive in kindergarten and all receive in first grade. We believe the little books provide children with an opportunity to talk about, pretend read, and recite complete, meaningful texts to parents and important other people at home. As they acquire knowledge about how to read these materials, and with parents' help, they reach out for other literacy materials and activities.

Another possible way to explain the effects is to consider that most children do not have a Level 2 understanding of reading until they enter first grade. If children receive instruction that focuses on Level 2 constructs (letter-sound identification) before operating competently at Level 1 (by naming letters, recognizing words and stories by sight, and connecting the print with their oral language and its meaning), they may have insufficient grounding to carry out Level 2 activities successfully. Level 1 activities such as listening, reciting, and reading little books provide an important introduction to analysis of words into letters and sounds and may be an essential introduction for children who enter kindergarten with little book-reading experience. Book recitation and subsequent book use at home provides that introduction, allows children to build information about literacy, and gives a context for making sense of letter-name and letter-sound activities that pervade most kindergarten programs.

CONCLUSION

The results of this study, in conjunction with the earlier studies, support the thesis that children initially at risk for reading can be helped by learning to recite texts and receiving little books at home. The process of change appears through an increased interest in reading and more parental involvement in their child's interest in literacy. Children then try to read, they read and write more often, and they learn more letters, letter sounds, and printed words. We conclude that such a treatment for academically at-risk populations of children can lead to active involvement in literacy and to a more even start in first-grade reading.

What recommendations then do we make from this study? While we are not suggesting that the little books are the only approach to familiarizing Level 1 children with print and what it means to read, we do suggest that they are an exemplary material for Level 1 children. They provide a means for preschool and kindergarten teachers to give more attention to Level 1 skills for those children who need them, that is, for children whose home environments have not encouraged informal experiences with print. Our little books, or similar materials that could be constructed by teachers or adapted from commercial children's books, not only allow for the children to behave like readers but, when sent home, involve the parents in the child's first attempts at reading. These materials can easily be integrated into any preschool or kindergarten curriculum. In this study we introduced the books to the children. However, introducing the books is an easy procedure that any teacher could readily implement. The only caution is that teachers need to recognize that Level 1 readers are learning how to approach and derive meaning from simple texts: emphasis should not be given to sounding out words or to sight-word recognition. Teachers and parents need to appreciate and value story rereading and recitation as a forerunner of letter-sound and word-attack activities. Although many teachers and parents mistakenly assume that letter-sound and word identification are the first skills of beginning reading, our research indicates the added value of activities such as book recitation and home book reading.

POLICY ISSUES

The research presented in this chapter does not imply that policy changes are required in Head Start programs. The curricular changes we recommend, as noted earlier, are fairly easy to implement because of local control of curriculum in both Head Start and school programs for at-risk four- and five-year-olds. What is required is for teachers and administrators of programs to be aware of more holistic approaches for children in the early stages of reading and the value of simple, high-interest texts.

The needs of children from families who do not provide many literacy experiences at home are often greater than those of children from homes providing informal instruction in what it means to read. Materials that help children behave as readers and become active participants in relating printed words to spoken words through assisted reading fit with what we know about how children become successful readers.

A second policy issue concerns parent involvement in Head Start and other early education programs. Getting parents to become involved in home literacy activities with their children is recognized as an important component of such programs. We have shown that children use the little books with their parents in first attempts at reading. Even parents who themselves are not readers find this a nonthreatening activity. Using little books at home might even serve as a common experience leading parents to talk with one another about their children's interest in print. These discussions might suggest other ways for parents to become involved in their children's academic progress.

APPENDIX 1: DESCRIPTION AND SCORING PROCEDURES FOR ASSESSMENTS USED IN YEAR 1

Letter Naming. The child was asked to name 10 uppercase letters: R, P, H, A, F, D, T, M, E, B. The printed letters were presented individually and each correct letter name given by the child received 1 point, resulting in a possible score of 10. (Administered pre and post.)

Sign and Label Identification. The child was first asked to name individually presented black and white line drawings of 10 common signs and labels. The child's response to each picture was scored 0, 1, or 2. One point was given for a response that was a generic description of the item or synonym. Twenty points were possible. (Administered pre and post.)

Sign and Label Print Identification. The child was shown 10 cards, one at a time, which presented only the print form of the signs and labels, and was asked to tell the examiner what the word said. Responses were scored 0−2: 0 given to no or wrong response, 1 point given for part of the printed label or a generic description of the item, and 2 points for the correct word. Twenty points were possible. (Administered pre and post.)

Book Reading. Each child was given a copy of the book, *Stop*, a 6-page, 13-word text in which a word or phrase per page matched an uncluttered illustration, and told that it was a story about a cat at a stop sign. The child was then asked to read or "pretend read" the text to the examiner. The responses were written down verbatim and later scored for word accuracy with 1 point given for each word the child said that matched a printed word on that page, regardless of whether the child was attempting to read. Thirteen points were possible. A second text, *Go*, which was used in the posttesting, contained 13 words. The same procedure was used and 13 points were possible. (*Stop* was administered pre and post; *Go*, post only.)

Printed Word Task. The children were shown 6 pictures, presented one at a time, of familiar objects. A single printed label was beneath each picture. For each picture the child was asked to "Show me where there's something to read." An indication of the print rather than the picture received 1 point. Six points were possible. (Administered post only.)

Parent Questionnaire. Each parent completed a questionnaire that was sent home by the teachers concerning the child's interest in and knowledge of letters and words and the parents' support for activities at home related to reading. Twelve questions concerned the child's interest in and knowledge of letters and words, such as: How many capital letters does your child try to print? Does your child ask to have stories read to him? Does your child try to read a story to you? The questions were scored 0 to 3. Total possible points for the "Parent estimate of child literacy" was 36.

Nine questions concerned parental support for activities related to reading, such as: Does someone read to the child at home? Does your child talk to you about Sesame Street? Responses were scored 0 to 3. Twenty-seven points were possible for the measure of "Parent literacy support." (Administered pre and post.)

Teachability. The teacher completed a rating of 0 (almost never) to 5 (almost always) for 16 descriptive terms designed to measure the child's teachability. Eight descriptors were those selected by teachers at all grade levels to describe the ideally teachable student. The other 8 terms were those items identified by the authors of the scale to measure "school appropriate behavior." Forty points were possible for each scale. (Administered pre only.)

APPENDIX 2: DESCRIPTION AND SCORING PROCEDURE FOR ASSESSMENTS USED IN YEAR 2

Wide Range Achievement Test. Each child was given the spelling and reading subtests according to the directions in the manual, except that all children were asked to attempt to print the first 10 words from the WRAT spelling list. For our analysis we scored the spelling subtest by counting the number of letter sounds correctly printed by the child, for a possible score of 27 for the 10 words. For the reading subtest the child was asked to identify 13 printed upper-case letters, 2 letters in his name, and the printed word list until 8 words were missed.

Book Reading. Each child was asked to read the following three books to the examiner: *Time for Bed, Pick up Toys,* and *Can You Carry?* The child's responses were written down by the examiner and later scored in two ways. The first procedure used a modified version of Sulzby's storyreading levels (Sulzby, 1985) in which 1 point was given for labeling items in the illustration, 2 points were given for a primarily action-governed response, 3 points were given for a primarily oral storytelling response, 4 points were given for a mix of oral storytelling that embellished the phrase on each page of the story, 5 points were given for close approximations of the phrase on each page, and 6 points were given for an accurate reading of the text. Each text was scored in this way. The texts were also scored by counting the number of correct words (except articles) that were given by the child for each page of the text. Using this method 13 points were possible for *Time for Bed,* 21 points were possible for *Pick up Toys,* and 11 points were possible for *Can You Carry?*

Teacher Questionnaire. Each child's kindergarten teacher completed items regarding the child's skill in (1) naming printed letters, (2) producing sounds for printed consonants, (3) recognition of printed words, and printing words. The teacher also indicated the child's interest in reading and interest in printed words. Total possible points for the teacher's assessment of child's skills was 26. A final question asked the teacher to rate the child according to the following categories of readiness for first-grade reading instruction: 1 = retention in kindergarten is recommended, 2 = will probably not do well in first-grade reading, 3 = will probably get by in first-grade reading, and 4 = will probably do well in first-grade reading.

Parent Questionnaire. Parents answered 3 questions on how often materials were used at home, noted any changes in their child's interest in literacy, and then rated their child 0 (never) to 5 (every day) on each of the following 5 questions: How often does your child play school? How often does your child look at books? How often does your child ask to be read to? How often does your child read or pretend to read books to himself or someone else? How often does your child print or try to print? Two questions, how many printed words do you think your child can read and how many words does your child write or try to write, used the categories 1 (not any) to 5 (more than 15). The last question asked for comments about the materials the child had received. The responses to the 7 questions scored 1−5 were used as the score for the Parental Assessment of Children's Knowledge. Total possible score was 35.

ACKNOWLEDGMENTS

The work upon which this publication is based was performed pursuant to Contract No. 400−81−0030 of the National Institute of Education. It does not, however, necessarily reflect the views of this agency. Portions of this manuscript were presented at the annual meeting of the American Educational Research Association in San Francisco, April 1986. A version of this paper also appears as Technical Report No. 388 at the Center for the Study of Reading.

We move from the preschool and kindergarten classrooms to first grade, and to children who have been identified as being at risk for reading failure. In Chapter 9 we learn about a first-grade intervention, Reading Recovery, which has proven effective in New Zealand and now in Ohio. This short-term, one-to-one program incorporates many of the developmentally appropriate reading and writing practices detailed in the preceding chapters. However, the teachers have been specially trained to create an individual curriculum that builds on the child's concepts of literacy, with the goal of returning the child to his or her classroom instruction as soon as possible.

Chapter 9

A Systemic Approach to Reducing the Risk of Reading Failure

Gay Su Pinnell

BY October of his first-grade year, it was already clear that six-year-old Anthony was far behind his classmates in learning to read. He had received extensive phonics instruction, and he knew the alphabet and could represent some sounds with letters, but he paid little attention to print when he actually tried to read a book. Predicting from a strong sense of meaning, Anthony invented text that had little to do with what was actually written on a page. He produced the example of reading behavior shown in Figure 9–1 when tested for eligibility for special help.

When instructed to look at the word or sound it out in classroom reading, Anthony became confused and guessed wildly, losing his sense of language and story. That confusion was generally not noticed because he seldom read stories in class instruction. Instead, he studied words and letters and struggled to complete worksheets. Anthony was confused about reading; he just didn't know what it was all about and instruction was not helping. Meanwhile, he was in the lowest of four reading groups and was falling farther and farther behind.

Anthony is one of many children in primary classrooms who are at risk of failure in reading. It is unlikely that he will catch up with other children

Figure 9–1 Anthony's Reading of *We Like Colors*

In September, Anthony was asked to read a very easy patterned text, *We Like Colors* (Scott, Foresman & Co., 1979). This text was used for testing material because the language was similar to that children were being asked to read in classroom reading groups, although it was somewhat more natural in quality. The tester was instructed to read the first page to the child and then to ask the child to continue reading through the text. The text is printed below, with Anthony's reading indicated above the text for each page.

Page 2

Illustration: Children looking in a store window that displays clothing.

Anthony: (Tester reads to child.)
Text: I like the red coat
I like the purple dress.

Page 3

Illustration: Children looking in a store window that displays clothing, including a red coat, a green sweater, and a purple dress.

Anthony: ✓ See a purple dress
Text: I like the green sweater. \

Page 4

Illustration: Children looking in a store window that displays toys, including a teddy bear, a yellow truck, dolls, a blue wagon, and several other items.

Anthony: ✓ see a toy •
Text: I like the yellow truck.

Page 5

Illustration: Children looking in a store window that displays toys, including a teddy bear, a yellow truck, dolls, a blue wagon, and several other items.

Anthony: the/sc see a bear •
Text: I like the blue wagon.

Page 6

Illustration: Children looking in the window of a candy store with jars of candy and a cash register on top of the counter.

Anthony: ✓ see the machine • • •
Text: I like yellow, purple, green, and blue.

Page 7

Illustration: Children standing outside the window of the candy store, each holding an ice cream cone of a different color.

Anthony: the I the 'ice cream store • •
Text: We like pink and brown and orange too.

Key:

✓ = accurate reading

$\dfrac{\bullet}{\text{text word}}$ = omission

$\dfrac{\text{child's word}}{\text{text word}}$ = substitution

$\dfrac{\text{child's word/SC}}{\text{text word}}$ = self correction

in his class. Longitudinal studies (e.g., Wells, 1985) show that children who make a poor beginning tend to stay behind year after year, not changing their rank in the school group. In spite of a considerable investment of money, time, and commitment to compensatory education, many children remain at risk of failure, especially in reading, an area where large numbers of low-achieving children receive extra help year after year.

Although many questions and issues surround efforts to help at-risk children, most educators as well as the general public are acutely aware that the number of children at risk is increasing (Hodgekinson, 1986). There is general agreement that efforts to help those children become literate are of national concern. Compensatory programs have been considered necessary for children who, because of economic or other conditions, are at a disadvantage in learning to read, but there is some dissatisfaction with current efforts.

First, there is little evidence to indicate that compensatory programs actually result in significantly greater learning that is transferable to classroom work or have long-term benefit to students (see Slavin, 1987). Often, those programs involve instruction that is not connected to the instruction children are receiving in the classroom. Most compensatory programs tend to focus on teaching skills in isolation. Thus, the result is often that the least able children are asked to practice two separate, difficult, and sometimes confusing programs of study. Under those conditions, there is little chance of transferring learning from the supplemental program to the classroom. And, since participation in extra programs means more time spent drilling on skill items, children actually have less time to participate in classroom reading and writing (Allington, 1977, 1980, 1983). The advantages of extra help may not outweigh the disadvantages of conflicting instructional processes and loss of classroom participation.

Additional problems with compensatory programs involve issues of labeling children and professional responsibility. Remedial reading assumes some deficiency on the part of the child; and, since children participate in those programs for at least one year, and often for many years, there is danger that they will become known to themselves and others as poor readers thus lowering expectations for achievement. Related to that problem is the question: Who is responsible for teaching the child to read? As children begin to receive help from reading specialists, there is the danger that classroom teachers may feel less responsibility for achievement in reading. The specialist teacher may look for children's performance in the remedial instructional program but feel little responsibility for children's progress in classroom work. They may even be unaware of the expectations for satisfactory performance, as children continue year after year to require remedial help.

Some programs have been successful in helping children and addressing issues such as those mentioned above; others have had only limited success. We must now learn from our experiences how to create new systems to address current problems. The question is: How can we best use our resources to reduce failure in literacy learning?

One promising answer to that question is to intervene early in the child's school career, before the pattern of failure is firmly established. The concept of early intervention is not a new one; for example, the impact of Project Head Start is well known. It seems that providing an enriched environment and experiences for children helps them to cope better with the later demands of schooling. Of the many special programs designed to give extra help in reading, those that serve younger children have had the most promising results (Anderson, Hiebert, Scott, & Wilkinson, 1985).

Though most children make the breakthrough to literacy during the first years of school, an increasing number are like Anthony—they find it difficult to learn to read and write. Those children quickly fall behind in school, meet failure again and again, and require continuous and expensive extra help for many years; often they never learn to read very well. When a child cannot read, the problem quickly goes beyond reading to include many other school problems. The major goal for these early intervention efforts is to help children before reading failure becomes failure in all areas of the curriculum and the gap is too great to be repaired.

VIEWS OF EARLY INTERVENTION

Although early intervention makes sense to some educators and researchers, traditional views of reading as a maturational concept have raised warnings that children should not be asked to move into reading before they are ready (see Gesell, 1940). Teale and Sulzby (1986) have provided a useful history of views that have influenced reading instruction in the beginning years of schooling. For decades, and even today, popular educational theories influenced teachers to assume that the onset of reading was dependent on the natural process of development.

In the 1950s the view shifted toward the idea that readiness for reading was influenced not only by development but by experience, but we still had the idea that there was a prerequisite group of skills that must be in place before a child could, or should, begin to read. With the idea that readiness could somehow be taught, reading readiness programs became firmly established in first-grade reading instruction and eventually in kindergarten. These programs included activities such as exercises for visual motor coordination and practice on letters and sounds, but seldom involved the child in actual reading or writing. It was believed that those activities would be appropriate later, when the child was "ready."

Research in language acquisition began to present a different view of children's learning. As language learners, children were found to "construct" language actively while learning it. Consistent with this view of child learning, research on literacy learning appeared to confirm that children begin very early, long before entering school, to explore and discover essential concepts related to reading and writing (Bissex, 1980; Brown & Biggs, 1986; Clay, 1982; Harste, Woodward, & Burke, 1984; Sulzby, 1985a; Teale & Sulzby, 1987). Not only do young children know much more than was previously thought about reading and writing, but given plenty of opportunity to read and write for their own purposes, they continue to develop as literacy learners (Clay, 1975; Farr, 1985; Ferreiro & Teberosky, 1982, Y. Goodman, 1984, 1986; Harste, Woodward, & Burke, 1984).

Recently, researchers in early literacy development (see Mason & Allen, 1986; see Teale & Sulzby, 1986) are challenging the readiness notion by suggesting that becoming literate is a natural process that begins long before formal schooling and takes place in very individual ways. When children experience and use reading and writing in real-life settings, they learn more and more about those processes, emerging as readers and writers. Educators now believe that, except in very gross ways, there is no set prerequisite body of skills or a particular level of neurological development necessary before beginning the acquisition of literacy.

Most children enter school with hundreds of experiences in functional reading and writing; others have less opportunity to use written language (see Heath, 1983; Teale, 1986). When children have difficulty, the problem may not be immaturity or the lack of readiness skills. Our usual answer is to have children practice the kinds of exercises designed to instill isolated skills. What children at risk really need is to immerse themselves in the kind of functional, meaningful experiences that good readers and writers learn from (Holdaway, 1986). And those experiences should occur as early as possible.

Clay argues strongly that not only does early intervention make sense but we cannot afford to wait to see whether children will grow into reading or catch on later in school. Clay succinctly describes the results of waiting:

- There is a great gap or deficit to be made up,
- There are consequential deficits in other aspects of education,
- There are consequences for the child's personality and confidence.

An even greater problem is not that the child has *not* learned but that the child *has* learned unproductive responses that have been overpracticed.

The child "has learned; and all that learning stands like a block wall between the remedial teacher and the responses that she is trying to get established" (Clay, 1985, p. 11).

Our recent experience with an early intervention program in literacy confirms the power of providing holistic experiences to children early in their school careers. The program, Reading Recovery, originally developed in New Zealand by Marie M. Clay (1979, 1982, 1985), was the result of extensive and detailed observations of good readers and of good teachers working with children at risk. Reading Recovery is based on the assumption that early, intensive, individual, and quality help has the greatest potential for lasting impact on children's achievement and for reducing the need for continued compensatory services. The program goal is to get many children out of the remedial track by enabling them to develop the kind of self-generating system they need to continue learning without extra help.

Reading Recovery is not a method or a prescribed set of steps for learning. The program is a system intervention with required long-term inservice for teachers and an established network of educational support systems. As such, it is consistent with programs such as the currently recommended (Slavin, 1987) comprehensive programs to improve under-achieving schools. Reading Recovery requires long-term inservice for teachers in order to learn to be sensitive observers of children and to understand and apply the special procedures. Children receive intensive one-to-one daily tutoring that focuses on developing strategies while reading and writing whole texts. Teachers closely observe children and document their reading and writing behavior as well as the contexts from which that behavior emerges.

Reading Recovery successfully avoids some of the problems common to compensatory programs. In this program children spend almost every minute of the thirty-minute lesson reading or writing continuous text; thus, the amount of reading time is greatly increased. The teacher is specially trained to help children become aware of effective strategies while they are behaving as readers and writers. As a result of the approach, children develop independent reading systems that allow them to continue learning on whatever material is offered in classroom instruction. Reading Recovery teachers have as a goal the swift progress of the child toward a status not needing extra help. Designing a program to move low-achieving children to average levels means that teachers must be aware of the level of text difficulty children are required to read in order to be in the mainstream group in the classroom.

Although Reading Recovery is a "pull out" program, it is a temporary one. The program is designed to provide daily help for twelve to twenty weeks. The goal is always to help the child make accelerated progress and to discontinue the program as soon as possible. Releasing the child from the program requires close collaboration between the Reading Recovery teacher and the classroom teacher. Responsibility is not removed from the classroom teacher, who must constantly reassess children's placement in reading materials as they are able to cope with more difficult texts. At the same time, the Reading Recovery teacher's responsibility is clear in this statement from the program guidelines: "There is only one position to take in this case. The programme is not, or has not been, appropriately adapted to the child's needs. It is time to take a close look at possible reasons for this, and colleague comment is what the teacher should seek" (Clay, 1985, p. 81).

Teachers and administrators involved with the Ohio program are addressing aspects of the program that need further development, for example, creating closer ties with parents and other caregivers, re-examining classroom curricula to provide for more time in reading and writing, and improving teacher decision-making skill through continuing contact even after the training year. While those developments are still underway, it is clear that Reading Recovery represents a new direction in the implementation of compensatory education.

The Reading Recovery program had excellent results in New Zealand, where it is now a national program. A successful pilot in a large urban city in Ohio (Huck & Pinnell, 1985) led to the establishment of Reading Recovery as a statewide program in that state; subsequent studies (Lyons, Pinnell, Short, & Young, 1986; Pinnell, Short, Lyons, & Young, 1986) have supported the program's effectiveness. Children in the program, initially the lowest achievers in reading, make accelerated progress and reach satisfactory achievement levels in reading within a short period of time, averaging twelve to fifteen weeks. Further, research indicates that children maintain gains and continue making progress without extra help for at least two years after the withdrawal of individual help (DeFord, Pinnell, Lyons, & Young, 1987).

Three years of experience implementing and investigating the outcomes of this early intervention program have provided researchers with new insights, not only for helping poor readers but for the success or failure of remedial or intervention efforts in general. Reading Recovery is particularly designed for a single purpose—to help first-grade children who are failing in reading. It is obvious that the approach can be used to improve reading success for many young children; but Reading Recovery alone will not answer the problems of low literacy and illiteracy. The program is, however, the most comprehensive and cohesive model that has been thus far attempted, and knowledge we have gained from its implementation can inform the broader efforts that are needed.

First, I will describe the Reading Recovery program as a way of illustrating the comprehensive approach it offers. Then, I will outline a range of problems that must be resolved if we are to be successful in helping young children having difficulty in reading and suggest several specific actions that move toward a more systemic approach to the instruction of young children in reading. These insights are largely drawn from our work in the Reading Recovery program, but find support in the work of others.

READING RECOVERY

Individual Lessons for Children

Reading Recovery provides a second chance in reading for young children who have been identified as failing by the end of their first year of school. In New Zealand, where children enter school on their fifth birthday and begin reading and writing immediately, the time of intervention is at age six. In the Ohio project, children enter Reading Recovery when they are identified as having difficulty learning to read in first grade.

Working with the poorest readers in the class, teachers provide an intensive, one-to-one individually designed lesson for thirty minutes each day. The techniques include the reading of many little books and writing and reading short messages. Teachers use special techniques during the writing part of the lesson to help children develop strategies for hearing sounds in words and for monitoring and checking their own reading. Every day the child is introduced to a new book, which will be read independently the next day. The program continues until the individual child has developed effective strategies for independent learning and can function satisfactorily in the regular classroom without extra help. Then the intervention is discontinued and another child enters the program.

Reading Recovery is based on the assumption that knowledge of reading and writing is acquired through immersion in literacy acts that are meaningful to the child. In the Reading Recovery lesson, the children read natural language stories and write stories that are based in their own language. The integration of reading and writing experiences within the lesson aids the child in building strategies that incorporate language and meaning cues in a unique instructional setting. This situation is in contrast to typical classroom work where most of the reading instruction, at least for the low group, has more to do with fill-in-the-blank, workbook type activities that are not productive for helping children learn to read, write, and understand (Allington, 1983; Anderson, Hiebert, Scott, & Wilkinson, 1985; Durkin, 1981; Graves, 1987; Meek, 1982). In Reading Recovery lessons, children spend almost every minute actually reading and writing stories or their own messages. Detailed studies of lessons provide evidence that Reading Recovery teachers stress meaning cues and reading for comprehension (Lyons, 1987; Short, 1986; Woolsey, 1986). The writing that occurs within the lesson is the writing of stories, not one- or two-word answers. The integrated reading and writing lessons are tailored to meet individual learning needs. The elements of the lesson provide a framework, but the content differs with each child in a way that builds on what the child already knows while emphasizing teaching strategies that facilitate the self-improving system necessary for continued accelerated growth.

Materials

Unlike other programs, Reading Recovery is not dependent on materials. It is not based upon the use of any one set of readers or one method of teaching reading. Instead, it depends on teachers developing a systematic knowledge of the reading-writing process and their ability to help children acquire the strategies involved in bringing meaning to texts. Once teachers are trained to work with children in Reading Recovery, they can effectively select and use a wide range of books and can help children use their own writing to assist in reading. And, they can perform and record their own assessments. No prescribed, step-by-step kits or sets of materials are necessary.

The teacher selects books appropriate to the child's reading level from a list of over 350 books on a gradient of difficulty from one to twenty. The levels represent increasingly more difficult reading material through the end of first-grade reading. In addition to these little books, the child writes in an unlined writing book using marking pens and may write on a chalkboard or other surfaces at the teacher's request.

Staff Development

The uniqueness of Reading Recovery can also be attributed to the teacher education model that seeks to make teachers informed decision makers who are professionals in charge of the educational program of the children they teach. They rely on their knowledge, not a set of packaged materials with written directions. Reading Recovery staff development takes place at two levels:

1. Each teacher training class is taught by a teacher leader who has had special training not only to teach the class but to create the Reading Recovery support system within the school district or region. The teacher training class meets weekly for one academic year. Teacher leaders also maintain continuing contact with previously trained

teachers. They provide inservice education to classroom teachers in kindergarten and the primary grades and they communicate with administrators, parents, and school board members.

2. Teacher leaders receive special training over the period of one year from a university-based team that also provides guidance for evaluation and research. The leader class meets for one full day a week for an academic year. The training of leaders is a cooperative venture by the university, the state agency, and the school districts involved. University teacher leaders provide continuing support and inservice education for leaders in the field. The state agency provides administrative support.

Implementers of Reading Recovery claim that the key factor is staff development. Each teacher and/or leader in training works daily with four children in Reading Recovery lessons. They learn to use diagnostic techniques for selecting children and beginning to work with them; they learn the general outline of procedures for Reading Recovery lessons.

Extensive use is made of a one-way glass during weekly seminar sessions. Each teacher works with a child behind the glass, which has a sound system allowing observers on the other side to both see and hear everything that goes on in the lesson. As each teacher demonstrates, colleagues in the class observe the lesson and carry on a discussion about what they are seeing in the way of reading and writing behaviors and teacher decision making. Following the lessons, the discussion group summarizes their observations for each of the teachers and exchange of information ensues. In this way teachers are led to be careful observers of children's reading and writing; they learn to build a coherent rationale for the decisions they make; and as recommended by Duckworth (1986), they actively engage in the process of scientific inquiry.

Support Systems

Reading Recovery is a system intervention that involves a support system and a monitoring and evaluation process. Teachers in the field are observed by leaders in class sessions and in their own buildings as they work with children. Their records are examined and a random selection process is used to collect records for research purposes. The teacher training is intensive and long-term. After the training year, leaders maintain continuing contact with teachers and continue to monitor children's progress. Teachers meet several times each year for inservice sessions in order to continue the development of critical knowledge and to refine their skills.

Teacher leaders are observed by university staff as they work with individual children, offer assistance to teachers individually, conduct training classes, and work with administrators in their school districts. Site visits are made regularly to each Reading Recovery project. Each year leaders provide a technical report of student progress at the site. Teacher leaders maintain a close relationship with university staff involved in the project. Leaders meet regularly with university staff and attend a special conference each summer. Throughout the process, all involved personnel—university professors, teacher leaders, and teachers—continue to work daily with children.

Implementation of Reading Recovery requires the collaboration of school districts, universities, and state agencies. School administrators at each level must participate and establish a working relationship to facilitate the process. Initial implementation of the program is, admittedly, difficult and requires commitment. Once established, however, the system has a greater chance for achieving success than programs that can simply be purchased and tried out with little effort. The features that make Reading Recovery difficult (for example, the intensive inservice program for teachers and the provision of a teacher leader to provide training and long-term monitoring and support) are the features that also assure that the program will be implemented in a high-quality way. Some specific characteristics of Reading Recovery distinguish it from other programs:

1. It is an early intervention program rather than a remedial program.

2. It provides intensive, high-quality, temporary help rather than long-term compensatory help that continues for several years.

3. Children learn how to be independent because they are taught how to solve reading problems using specific strategies; they learn to orchestrate strategies while attending to the meaning of the text.

4. Children spend almost every minute of time reading and writing stories and messages; they do not spend time on fill-in-the-blank activities or drill on isolated items.

5. Each child is helped to reach an average level for the particular instructional setting (class or school, whichever makes sense programmatically) so that he or she can benefit from the instruction and continue to improve in reading without extra help.

6. Teachers strive for more than improvement; they expect accelerated progress from these initially low-achieving children.

7. Every Reading Recovery lesson has both reading and writing components; there is an emphasis on the interrelatedness of the two processes.

8. It provides a framework of activity; however, within this framework the program is different for every child (for example, no child reads the same sequence of books).

9. Teachers and leaders learn on the job while they participate in a long-term inservice course.

10. Reading Recovery cannot be partially implemented; although some components of the program may be profitably used by individuals, all essential components must be in place before an early intervention program may be considered a Reading Recovery program.

CONFLICTS AND CONCERNS

The success of Reading Recovery confirms the value both of early intervention and of establishing a system approach to assure that innovations are implemented in a high-quality way. At the same time, implementation of the program has led to questions and issues that must be addressed to assure maximum opportunity for all children. It is clear that early intervention alone, even one of high quality, cannot fully accomplish that goal. Four major issues are outlined below.

Curriculum

The traditional lock-step curriculum for literacy learning tends to work against the beneficial effects of compensatory programs. In Reading Recovery, for example, children make accelerated progress in their ability to read more and more difficult texts. If the classroom curriculum requires that they complete every worksheet, read every story, and do every unit test before going on to the next book or story, some children who are initially behind may not have enough time to reach the next level or to complete the first-grade curriculum. This kind of problem is most common when teachers hold the view that teaching children to read means moving slavishly through every exercise in the basal reading system. For children to make accelerated progress, teachers must make judicious decisions about the required reading selections and must place children in reading material based on assessment of their ability rather than movement through a prescribed series of worksheets.

The kind of curriculum that requires children to master one set of skills before practicing another kind of skill may make it difficult for children at risk to display their competence. In that kind of curriculum, learning to read is viewed as acquiring and practicing a series of skills, one after the other. In the Reading Recovery view, learning to read means using many skills simultaneously, orchestrating them in order to construct meaning from print. The Reading Recovery approach allows children to use everything they know every time they read. In contrast, those same children in classroom reading may have few chances to actually read continuous text. They may be struggling to master more abstract items of knowledge, which are seen as prerequisites to reading.

Anthony was eligible for Reading Recovery and participated in daily lessons. He read many "little" books and wrote and read a short message or story every day. Through the writing activity, he learned to notice the details of written language and to hear sounds in words and represent them with letters. Through reading and rereading natural language stories, he learned to read fluently, focusing on the meaning while at the same time attending to the visual information he needed. In several weeks, his reading behavior showed evidence of the kind of strategies good readers use, such as monitoring, self-correcting, and using multiple sources of information. His teacher was pleased to see the reading shown in Figure 9–2.

Anthony had made good progress in his Reading Recovery program. His teacher, who was in her training year, had a conference with Anthony's classroom teacher to discuss his moving to a higher reading group. The classroom teacher was surprised to hear that Anthony could read, since he was still having difficulty in the readiness workbook and consequently had not yet been given a preprimer. After discussion, they agreed that Anthony could be given a chance to participate in both the low and the middle reading groups. Several days later, he was doing well enough to be released from Reading Recovery and became a permanent member of the middle reading group. His reading behavior, as indicated in Figure 9–3, provided evidence of effective reading strategies such as self-correction and use of multiple cues in reading.

These teachers' openness and ability to collaborate created a success story for Anthony. He continued to make progress without Reading Recovery and by the end of the year was in the top reading group in his class. The story could have turned out quite differently had the classroom teacher been unable to work flexibly within the curriculum.

Assessment

Current methods of assessing reading ability and achievement are inappropriate and unreliable for young children, especially those who score at the lower end of the scale (Johnson, 1983, 1984). Yet, popular standardized measures are the most common way to select children for programs and to determine whether or not those programs are successful.

An example of the kinds of problems that may be related to assessment is evident in the Reading Recovery selection procedures. Because Reading Recovery teachers are supported in many districts as an option of Chapter 1, school district personnel comply with guidelines of that program in selecting students; that is, the lowest achievers, as defined by percentile

Figure 9−2   **Anthony's Reading Strategies**

Paul comes to school
in a car.   ✓ ✓ ✓

At school,   ✓ ✓
he walks with a walker.   ✓ ✓ ✓ ✓ R _cane_
                                              ~~walker~~

Paul is in our class, now.   ✓ ✓ ✓ ✓ ✓   ✓

At first,   ✓ ✓
I was shy with him.   ✓ ✓ ✓ ✓ ✓

Then Paul played chasing   ~~There~~ ✓ ~~playing~~ Ⓦ R ✓
with us.   Then   played   T
                                  ✓ ✓

We hopped on one foot   ✓ ~~hop~~ ✓ ✓ ✓ R
to give Paul a chance.   hopped
                              ✓ ~~get~~ IRtse ✓ ✓ ✓
                                  give

He caught me first.   ✓ ✓ ✓ ✓

Paul can go fast   ✓ ✓ ✓   far
with his walker.   ~~fast~~
                              ✓ ✓ ✓

Figure 9–3   **Anthony's Reading Strategies**

2

Once upon a time there was a mean man   ✓ ✓ ✓ ✓ ✓ ✓ ✓ ✓

named Grumble.   Ⓦ ✓ ✓
                                         named

3

One day Grumble saw an elf in the woods. ✓ ✓ ✓ *said is* ✓ ✓R ✓✓✓
                                                 saw

Grumble said, "An elf always has   ✓ ✓ ✓ Ⓦ *a-* ✓
                                                always T

a pot of gold.   ✓ ✓ ✓ ✓

I'll make this elf take   ✓ ✓ ✓ ✓ ✓

me to his pot of gold."   ✓ ✓ ✓ ✓ ✓ ✓

4

Grumble took hold of the elf.   ✓ ✓ ✓ ✓ ✓ ✓

The elf began to jerk this way and   ✓ ✓ ✓ ✓ ✓ *J–R* ✓ ✓✓✓
                                                     jerk

that way.   ✓ ✓

But Grumble didn't let go.   ✓ ✓ ✓ ✓ ✓

5

The elf said, "Let me go! Let me go!"   ✓ ✓ ✓ ✓ ✓✓ ✓✓✓

Grumble said, "Take me to your   ✓ ✓ ✓ ✓ ✓ ✓

pot of gold.   ✓ ✓ ✓

Then I'll let you go."   ✓ ✓ ✓ Ⓦ *checked page 4* ✓ ✓

---

scores on a standardized test, are to be taken into the program first. Reading Recovery, on the other hand, requires a comprehensive set of individually administered measures, which serve both for program selection and for diagnosis. Most students who score low on the diagnostic measures usually are also the lowest scorers on the standardized selection test required by Chapter 1.

Rigid application of rules, however, can cause problems when random guessing may make two or three percentile points difference between students who are actually widely different in knowledge and ability. There may even be some extreme cases. For example, Kathleen, who guessed wildly on the first group administration of a standardized test, scored at the 48th percentile, making her ineligible for Chapter 1 Reading Recovery. The Diagnostic Survey, on the other hand, revealed that she was far behind her classmates in basic concepts about written language and in her ability to read and write. Since her classroom teacher insisted that she needed extra help, the Chapter 1 consultant administered the standardized test again, this time in a controlled situation. Kathleen scored at the 2nd percentile, but it was only by that special effort that she was accepted into the program. There is no need to engage in such an expense of time and resources. For young children, we recommend the use of multiple measures, including qualitative judgment by informed persons such as the Reading Recovery teacher and the classroom teacher.

Teacher Expertise

As a result of inadequate or out-of-date preparation to teach reading, teachers have often relied on materials such as basal systems to create a reading curriculum. School district pressure, as well as teachers' own lack of confidence, increases dependence on such materials. If children do not learn, the inadequacy is seen as the child's ability and/or background rather than any weakness in the instructional program. Reading Recovery requires that teachers take personal responsibility for examining and adapting their instruction so that each child is able to achieve in reading.

Teachers involved in the program are able to meet that challenge because of their special preparation. In the Reading Recovery inservice setting, they critically examine their own responses to children and those of others. Without attaching blame or feeling threatened, they are able to analyze children's behavior and their own so that they can make the most productive moves.

Helping children at risk means taking the education of teachers seriously. Short-term workshops and one-day lectures may help to raise awareness but will not develop the kind of knowledge, skills, and decision-making ability teachers need to increase their effectiveness. We need to create new structures for professional development that combine theoretical knowledge with analysis of practice. The Reading Recovery inservice course offers one example of a high-quality practicum. Others, based on the same principles, could be created.

Home Resources

Sometimes children develop expertise in school but have little opportunity to use that expertise in other environments. Being able to read and write when one wants to and to share that ability with family and friends is a major advantage that is not available to all children.

Holland (1987) conducted a study that involved one year of participation and observation in the homes of selected Reading Recovery children. Her extensive observations and interviews with parents and other caregivers indicated that the family members of at-risk children care deeply about the child's learning to read; however, the family may not have the resources in terms of time, expertise, or money to provide all of the experiences that complement the school curriculum. In training classes, Reading Recovery teachers are not encouraged to describe, judge, or even consider the home situation when planning a child's program because they must accept full responsibility for making the child able to read. They do, however, communicate with parents and where district regulations allow it, they send home little books with children. Holland's study indicated the power of that policy. Those little books, which children could easily read and control themselves, were central to the literacy environment in the homes. Children were not dependent on anyone else to read the books to them; they had a new book every day; they read books to parents, grandparents, aunts, siblings, toys, pets and friends. They read them over and over. They not only became more fluent readers; they influenced their younger brothers and sisters.

Even children who can read very little need to have books at home that they can read; that is especially important for children who may not have caregivers with time to read to them daily. Mason (McCormick & Mason, this volume) achieved very good results by mailing inexpensive sets of reproduced books to preschool children. Our experience in Reading Recovery confirms her findings. All of the low-income children in Holland's (1987) study had grocery store variety books and some library books, but it was important that they have written material that they could manage without adult help. There is a precedent for giving children books in programs such as Reading Is Fundamental; but this help needs to begin very early in the child's life. Providing little books and basic writing materials to preschool and first-grade children would be a relatively easy and inexpensive way to improve literacy opportunities for children at risk.

DEVELOPING LITERACY COMMUNITIES

In a time when resources are limited and the number of children at risk is growing (Hodgekinson, 1988), we cannot afford to engage in piecemeal efforts. It appears that the best use of resources is investment in early intervention programs; but even those should not be fragmented and applied in haphazard ways. An integrated approach is necessary, one which takes into account the total environment in which children live. With coordinated effort we could create a system with components that complement each other and work together to provide children with meaningful literacy experiences in many settings simultaneously. These interacting systems could create the kind of synergistic energy that operates for advantaged children who read and write as a natural part of their daily activities both at school and at home.

There is no reason to expend energy in separated programs when a coordinated system could accomplish so much more. Creating such a system would mean following this general principle: Create maximum opportunities for children to engage in purposeful and enjoyable reading and writing. In practical terms, it would mean simultaneous implementation of recommendations, such as those in the following list, that would have far-reaching effects.

1. Redesign classroom instruction so that less time is spent on isolated drill and more time on reading and writing stories and messages. Beginning immediately in the entry year in New Zealand classrooms, young children engage in reading and writing that is connected with real experiences. They enjoy hearing stories and even before they know the alphabet or are able to decode individual words, they behave as readers through shared (unison) reading of enlarged texts. They read and reread familiar stories and have their own writing books. In a very short time, most of these five-year-olds become readers and writers.

2. Work to get high-quality texts available at low cost. These should be books that children can read themselves as well as those that can be read to them by adults or older siblings. The little books could be copied and collated locally (see McCormick & Mason, this volume); or, they could be the kind of paperbacks that are available from New Zealand (see Richard Owen Publishing for the *Ready to Read* Series and the Wright Company for several other series).

3. Provide early intervention programs for those children who need them. For those children who do not engage with reading after their first year of school, provide high-quality intervention programs with the best and most skillful teachers to undercut the instance of failure before it becomes impossible for the child to catch up. Such programs should involve children in massive amounts of real reading and writing. Reading Recovery provides one model, but others may exist. Much could be accomplished by having school districts, universities, and state agencies collaborate to create such programs.

4. Provide high-quality, long-term inservice to help classroom teachers develop the knowledge and skills they need. Professional development

for teachers is necessary to implement recommendations 2 and 3. Developing a dynamic new curriculum that will help even the most difficult children requires that teachers know about the reading process, as well as how children learn and become literate. They need to be able to translate that knowledge into the decision-making process they use. Through feedback and reflection, they need to become sensitive observers of children's reading and writing behavior as well as more aware of their own behaviors and responses to children.

5. Provide books and other materials to enrich children's homes and enable them to create their own literacy environments. Beginning with preschool children and continuing through the primary school years, city governments or school districts could provide little books, blank paper, and markers or pencils for children who are in the at-risk category. Not only could they control and expand their own experiments with written language; they could help to create a supportive context for literacy development for their younger siblings. Resources allocated for those efforts would be well-spent because they would complement school efforts and make them more successful.

6. Create a policy climate that actively supports the development of literacy in young children. Policy at the building level might involve professional development for building administrators to help them understand how young children learn to be literate; and it might also invoke collaboration among a school staff to create environments that convey the importance of literacy through provision of reading materials, display of children's work and interesting material to read, and through activities that show the value of reading and writing. At the district, state, and national levels, creating an effective policy climate means establishing proactive policies as well as minimizing policies that might get in the way of effective program implementation. For example, as in West Des Moines, Iowa (Henke, 1988), a district or state could establish textbook selection policies that allow teachers to consider and choose the kinds of texts that best support young children's reading. It also might mean allowing teachers to buy more books instead of worksheets or workbooks. District and state assessment policies could provide for the use of multiple measures in assessing the reading ability of young children.

Each of the above recommendations has potential for reducing the risks for children, but each is fraught with frustration when roadblocks arise from the other components. Investment in each component could make all of the others work better. It is time that we really invested to create the world of literacy for children at risk.

ACKNOWLEDGMENTS

Research on Reading Recovery was undertaken with colleagues Diane E. DeFord and Carol A. Lyons at the Ohio State University. Ideas for this paper are also drawn from the proposal for the Early Literacy Research Project (Pinnell, Huck DeFord, & Lyons, 1987), funded by the John D. and Catherine T. MacArthur Foundation and from an earlier document on literacy intervention prepared in collaboration with Charlotte Huck from the Ohio State University and with colleagues from New York University, Angela Jaggar and Bernice Cullinan.

As effective as Reading Recovery has been, Pinnell feels that "early intervention alone, even one of high quality," cannot "assure maximum opportunity for all children." We need to develop literacy communities. In Chapter 10, we gain a clearer understanding of how important the involvement of families can be in establishing community support for literacy development. Communities of Cheyenne Indians and Texas migrant workers became involved as teachers and program planners, and in the process of helping their children, these adults became empowered.

Learning with Families

Education as a Cultural Process: The Interaction Between Community and Classroom in Fostering Learning

Beverly McConnell

CHILDREN'S motivation for learning to read has been shown to be closely related to the function of literacy in the lives of their parents and their culture. Many Jewish homes, for example, have a long tradition of promoting scholarship and literacy because families considered it essential that children acquire the skills they would need as adults to be able to read and understand the Talmud, the body of laws that guide the Jewish way of life.

Most American Indian tribes, on the other hand, did not have a written language, as theirs was an oral tradition in which one generation passed on to the next the religious beliefs and wisdom of their forefathers. In many cases, the Christian missionaries were the ones to develop a written form of the language in order to encourage the indigenous populations to study and read the Bible and be converted to its teachings. From the perspective of the Indian family, the act of learning to read constituted an abandonment of their cultural orientation. As schools were established, staffed mainly by non-Indian teachers who seemed bent on denying the Indian children their own language and culture, the schools were seen as instruments of alienation.

My work for over twenty years has been in the development and evaluation of educational programs among Indian children and the children of Spanish-speaking migrant farm workers. More recently, my work among migrant families has included children of Asian refugees, particularly Laotian families who had been peasant farm workers in their native Laos and have become seasonal farm workers in the United States.

From this perspective, I have come to look upon education as a cultural process. Other authors in this book have stressed how the child-rearing patterns within the family foster or inhibit cognitive development. These, in turn, are shaped to a great extent by the influence of the social, economic, and cultural community in which the families live. There is a question, then, of how far reaching the effects of an educational program can be. How much is it possible to change children's motivation and skills unless the program affects the family as well? How much is it possible for the family to change unless there is some impact on social, economic, and cultural factors or a change in the power, prestige, and status a family enjoys within the community?

The case studies presented in this chapter were programs I was involved with over a period of several years. One was for children of the Northern Cheyenne Indian tribe in southeastern Montana. Another was for Spanish-speaking migrant families in a border area along the Rio Grande river in south Texas. In both communities English was a second language. The adults in the community had very little formal schooling, and most older children dropped out of school long before graduation. The separation between the schools and the majority of families they served seemed very wide.

Despite these conditions, the educational programs for children in both of these communities were strikingly successful. Children learned to read. Test scores soared above national norms. Achievement was significantly greater than for comparison groups. The programs also had a profound impact on the families, the schools, and the communities.

The case studies offered here are examples of the interaction between community and classroom that can help children achieve both the motivation and the skills for successful learning.

THE FOLLOW THROUGH PROGRAM ON THE NORTHERN CHEYENNE RESERVATION

Social and Economic Conditions

The Northern Cheyenne reservation consists of 445,000 acres of mountainous land in southeastern Montana. Among the many Indian reservations in Montana and the Dakotas, it is considered to be the most isolated. The first paved highway was not put through the reservation until 1955, and the tribal headquarters in Lame Deer is over forty miles from the nearest rail or bus line. When the educational program described in this case study was started, there were only 250 non-Indians on the reservation, or about 8 percent of the total population of around 3000 people. The Cheyenne leaders felt this isolation had helped the tribe keep its social structure and values intact.

In the 1970s, the discovery of vast coal reserves on reservation land threatened to bring in a great influx of outsiders eager to develop this energy resource. At the time of my last visit (1974), the Cheyennes were resisting this, feeling that the outside culture would become dominant and that this was too high a price to pay for economic development.

The Northern Cheyennes lived with both poverty and unemployment. The BIA (Bureau of Indian Affairs) reported the per capita income of the Northern Cheyennes in 1971 as $700 per year. In March of 1974, only 67 percent of the available labor force was employed, with nearly a third of these in temporary seasonal jobs. There tended to be an ethnic division of labor on the reservation. Most whites held professional and office jobs and operated businesses—jobs that required headwork; whereas the Indian population tended to work with their hands in a plastic factory or a sawmill started with tribal funds, or in agricultural work.

The Schools

There were three communities on the reservation, each with a different type of school. In Busby, the BIA operated an elementary and a high school which served both day students and boarding students. A 1969 book by Cahn, entitled *Our Brother's Keeper: The Indian in White America*, described Busby school in this way:

> In one school on the Northern Cheyenne Reservation ... there were a dozen suicide attempts in 18 months, among fewer than 200 pupils. (p. 40)

Teddy Risingsun, a resident of Busby who attended the school as a child, gave this description of the school as he knew it:

I remember Busby school and how it used to be because I went there as a child. Everything was like in the military. I was a little boy, and with the other little boys we would get up when the whistle blew, dress when the whistle blew, go out and "police" the grounds picking up any little pieces of paper and things so we would learn to be "responsible." We went to breakfast when the whistle blew, and we stood behind our chairs and couldn't sit down until the whistle blew.

We were punished if we spoke to each other in Cheyenne and we were made to feel ashamed that we were Indians, and ashamed of our family. When I got a chance to go home, I cried that I did not want to go back. But my family said I must go back. So I became deaf. I have been told that it was not a physical deafness, but hysterical deafness. But I could not hear and my family could not send me back to the school. I still, today, have trouble with my hearing sometimes. I think it goes back to what happened to me as a child. The Indian schools have done terrible things to Indian children.

In Lame Deer, the tribal headquarters, land had been leased to the state and a public school was put up for grades one through eight. Driving across a mountain range another twenty-one miles, to Ashland, the third school would be found. This was a parochial school called St. Labre. It also had day and boarding students. There were large old wooden dormitories, some still in use, which were built in the years when all support came from mission funds. In the 1960s, however, one of the priests began to appeal for donations by nationwide subscription, and this was successful, resulting in funds to create a very modern campus of school buildings and a large church, all built from native stone.

In the booklet dedicating their new church, St. Labre described their past relationship to the Indian culture as follows:

[Through] land expansion, Manifest Destiny, ... America emerged from a frontier culture to an industrial society. ... The Indian was unwelcome, unwanted in his own country, had suffered the loss of his land, his culture, his dignity. The Mission of St. Labre kept faith with its dedication to the Indian people, but it was part of its time, a time when western mentality reached out to make the Indian something he wasn't, a western man. Unwittingly the school joined in the depreciation of Indian culture.

By the late 1960s this attitude was changing. The mission's new awareness of Indian culture was evident in the design of their church (built in the shape of a tepee with the figure of Christ represented by a Cheyenne "dog soldier" and the cross made of eagle feathers, which are sacred to the Northern Cheyennes). Despite their awareness of Indian culture, the church clergy retained actual control over all school affairs with a three-member school board, all anglo priests. The five-member school board at Lame Deer had two members who were white and three Indian. The BIA school had no local school board, meaning that five of the eight school board officials on the reservation in 1969 were white. This dominance of the white minority population extended to teaching staff as well. In 1969, in the classrooms, from kindergarten through third grade (the grades affected by the Follow Through program), 79 percent of the teaching staff were white, and 21 percent were Indian.

Key Factors in the Educational Program

The educational program started in 1969 on the Northern Cheyenne reservation was part of a national demonstration program called Follow Through. It was designed to provide a comprehensive educational program for children in kindergarten through third grade. It provided "follow through" for children who had been in Head Start by having similar objectives including extensive parental involvement in the education component, as well as social and health services.

Normally these programs were only funded to public schools, but many Indian reservations protested this because, like the Northern Cheyenne, they had a variety of schools—public, private, parochial, and BIA—on the reservation, and they wanted all to be able to participate. The Indian protest resulted in a key policy decision on the federal level in 1968 that enabled the tribal government, instead of the schools, to apply for the funds and operate the program in all schools on the reservation.

Giving the tribal government control over the grant was, indeed, a key feature of the program: It was the first program for school-age children to be managed by the Indians themselves. The Tribal Council (the governing body of the tribe) delegated the operation of the program to the PAC (Parent Advisory Committee), made up of parents of children served and community members, according to Follow Through guidelines. Unlike most PAC's, which had only an advisory capacity in operating the program, this PAC had the right to hire classroom aides as well as all other program staff, to make policy, and to decide how the money would be spent.

PAC meetings were well attended, as these decisions had considerable social and economic impact. The distances families had to drive to meetings could be as much as forty miles through mountain passes, sometimes in bad weather and often in old and unreliable cars. One PAC member told me that he had more than once walked a distance of fifteen miles in order to attend a meeting. This interest in attending PAC meetings did not happen with other programs funded directly to the schools, in which the parents were only advisory, and parent meetings tended to be either social functions or a time to listen to reports.

The second key feature of the program was the extensive involvement of Indian parents as teaching staff. The University of Kansas model which was chosen for the Northern Cheyenne program required three aides for every classroom, more aides than used in any other model. The sponsor who designed the model required rotation of two of these aide positions so that more of the parents of children in the program could experience it with their children through working as paid aides.

Despite the high level of unemployment on the reservation, it was extremely difficult at first to get parents to take these positions as classroom aides. Teddy Risingsun, a local community coordinator who was charged with recruiting people to fill these jobs, described their attitudes as follows:

> On the reservation, there is open range for cattle. So there is always a cattle guard put in the road leading up to the school to keep the cattle off the school grounds (pipes across the road with spaces in between so a car could pass over, but cattle would put their legs through the open spaces). The Indian people have always felt that the cattle guard applied to them too. It stood as a symbolic barrier separating the community from the school. Children had to go to the school, but the parents couldn't have anything to say about what happened to them there.

For many people, the schools seemed a hostile place. They were afraid of criticism, afraid of failure. Another recruiter said, "The three parents in every classroom were supposed to actually *teach* the children; not just help out with things. At first nobody could get used to this." There had been a scattering of aides used in classrooms before, but they usually assisted with various classroom chores, checked children's work, and helped to maintain order—functions that were not considered teaching.

In this model, the children were taught in small groups and both the teacher and the aides had subject areas to teach. This was against state regulations in Montana, which specified that only a certified teacher could teach "new material," with aides limited to review and tutoring or other types of assistance. This regulation was specifically waived to accommodate Follow Through as a demonstration program.

The aides were quite insecure and likely to quit at the slightest hint of criticism—or at least take two or three days out to think about it before going back to work. Many of them were not accustomed to showing up for work regularly—after all, their experience as unskilled laborers had taught them that one pair of hands could usually be replaced by another pair of hands. The "natural" turnover in aide positions, people quitting because of illness or some other reason, was very high. In one year during my five-year evaluation, the 44 aide positions in the programs were filled by over 140 different individuals. In view of this, the sponsor waived the requirement for planned rotation of aide positions.

But in time, working as teachers began to seem more natural, and there was pride in the progress the children were making. One Follow Through parent described the importance of parents teaching their children:

It used to be that the child got his education from his parents. He learned to ride and hunt. He learned all he needed to know. Then he started to go to white man's schools and all that he learned was from white people. Since this Follow Through program it is again like it used to be. When the child goes to school he learns from his elders, who are teaching now in the classrooms. He learns from his elders, and that is the Indian way.

The third key factor in the educational program was the teaching methods and materials. In order to enable aides without the academic background or prior experience of a professional teacher to be effective, the sponsor who designed this educational program used programmed reading materials based on a phonetic approach. This meant that the materials themselves were sequenced from the less difficult tasks to more difficult, and the teacher did not have to know how to sequence learning steps. Placement and mastery tests were embedded in the curriculum so it was clear where a child needed to begin, and when that child was ready to continue on to the next task.

The most distinctive (and controversial) part of this educational model was encouraging children by giving them specific praise and small tokens for good work or attentive behavior during a teacher-directed learning period. This was followed by a period of time in which the children could select what they wanted to do or play with, and the more tokens earned, the more choices they had. Often, the activities planned for this child-choice time were projects related in some way to the tribal culture—beading, building a teepee, playacting ("hunting for bears," etc.).

For the evaluation, parents and staff were interviewed on the question of whether the methods of the sponsor (e.g., rewarding positive behavior through a token system and the exchange of tokens for preferred activities) fit well with the Indian culture. One Indian teacher who responded that it fit very well with the traditional Indian child-rearing methods had this to say:

Indians have always used praise and a system of rewards to shape the behavior of their children. Years ago, Indian children were awarded feathers, shells, beads, and the like that they could use for adornment. Certain kinds of ornamentation denoted "rank," status, or position within the tribe.

Several staff members who were interviewed felt the system of tokens was misunderstood by visitors to the program as a means to foster competitiveness among children where sharing is more natural. They then explained that the tokens are not given or used competitively; the child's choice of activities is solely dependent on his or her own efforts without regard to the number of tokens any other child has received. It is a Cheyenne cultural pattern to share. In the Cheyenne culture a family honors one member's achievement by a "give away," in which they make gifts, not to the honored person but to other people, and not necessarily on the basis of need. This pattern of behavior was sometimes acted out when children who felt well-off would offer tokens to another child.

For the most part, the attitude of teachers and parents seemed to support the program, feeling that their own school experience had been dominated by fear of teachers and punishment, and that the children in Follow Through showed a much better attitude toward school where teachers used praise, encouragement, and rewards as a method of instruction.

Program Outcomes

Children's Reading Achievement. The Association on American Indian Affairs, Inc. did testing of reading achievement among children on the Northern Cheyenne reservation in 1965. Although the percentages reported in their results included all children in elementary school, not just those in the Follow Through program (K−3), it provides a rough basis for judging the level of reading achievement four years before starting the Follow Through program.

Before Follow Through (1965)

"At Busby 41% suffered a lag of two or more years in reading achievement."

"At Lame Deer over 40% showed reading deficiencies of two years of more."

"At St. Labre 52% needed remedial work in reading."

After Five Years of Follow Through (1974)

"Only 1% of Follow Through students lagged two years behind national norms in reading skills."

"74% of all children in Follow Through scored at or above grade level in reading achievement."

"The average reading score of all third-grade children in Follow Through was 4.8 grade equivalent: almost a full year above the expected grade equivalent score of 3.9."

All children on the reservation were included in the program, so there was no local comparison group. However, the sponsor tested a comparison group of children at other sites, who met eligibility requirements of the Follow Through project. A statistically significant difference was found between reading achievement scores of children in the Northern Cheyenne program and this external comparison group at each grade level. The results showed that in comparing the mean scores by grade level, the comparison group fell further below national norms in reading achievement each year, whereas children on the Northern Cheyenne reservation ended kindergarten exactly at the national norms, and each year thereafter increased the number of months their average score was above national norms.

Decision Making by PAC. The minutes of central PAC meetings were analyzed for the first, third, and fifth year of the evaluation. Excluding personnel actions, this content analysis classified the topics brought up at the meeting as to whether the topic was given discussion only or whether some decision was made or an action taken. The results show the growing confidence of the PAC in its role of policy and decision making:

- 1969–70 Total Topics reported: 40, Decision-making actions: 6 (15%)
- 1971–72 Total topics reported: 33, Decision-making actions: 8 (21%)
- 1973–74 Total topics reported: 39, Decision-making actions: 20 (51%)

Indian-Controlled School Boards. Perhaps the most dramatic outcome of the Follow Through program revolved around the position of community coordinator. This was *not* part of the sponsor's model, but a unique position developed by the Northern Cheyenne. In the sponsor's model, it called for a "community aide," the lowest paying of all aide positions and expected to have the usual duties of the outreach person who worked *for* the school, *among* the parents, checking on absences, taking messages to parents, and helping with out-of-school needs, such as taking children to the doctor.

Since the program was funded to the tribe, the persons hired for this position looked at their role as working *for* the "people," *with* the school—an important difference. Because of the turnover in aide positions, the PAC found that they could not keep up with making all hiring decisions, so they made the first "placement" of aides in each school and left the finding of replacements up to the community coordinator. As the person responsible for finding and keeping instructional aides, the community coordinator quickly became a very key person in the continued functioning of Follow Through.

When the PAC decided to have a central PAC plus a local PAC for each community, the community coordinator became the staff person for the local PAC. This created an organizational structure to carry out community development projects, some of which had nothing to do with the educational program. With these added responsibilities, the pay for this position went up accordingly.

The instructional aides tended to pour out all of their doubts and grievances about the school to the community coordinator, who took on a new role, that of advocate. In one instance, the teachers had assigned the aides all of the responsibility for non-teaching functions such as lunch duty or hall duty. The aides objected to this, and the community coordinator had to negotiate with the school administration to have these responsibilities shared by all members of the teaching team. Later, the pendulum swung the other way with the aides deciding they shouldn't have any of these less desirable duties since they did not work directly for the school (paychecks came from the tribe), and the diplomacy of the coordinator was required once again to restore the concept of equal responsibility.

Probably the most impressive accomplishment of a "community coordinator" was in Busby, the site of the BIA boarding school.

In 1970 encouragement of local control of Indian schools became the official policy goal of the U.S. government. President Nixon announced this policy with these words:

> One of the saddest aspects of Indian life in the United States is the low quality of Indian education. ... the average educational level for all Indians under Federal supervision is less than six school years. ... Again, at least a part of the problem stems from the fact that the Federal Government is trying to do for Indians what many Indians could do better for themselves.

The BIA, to implement this policy, was authorized to negotiate with any Indian community in which tribal members voted by referendum to take local control of a BIA school. The community would then elect a local school board that could negotiate a contract with the BIA for continued federal funds to run the school. Continued support for the school was guaranteed by treaty rights; the level of support was open to negotiation. Teddy Risingsun, who was the community coordinator at Busby, wanted his community to vote for local control.

On the face of it, it would seem logical that the turnover of BIA schools to the local community would be so advantageous to the Indian community that there would be a great rush to gain local control. This has not been the case.

One obstacle is that employees of schools operated by the BIA have civil service status, with its generous retirement provisions and other fringe benefits. Once a school is under local control, it ceases to be a government employer and employees are not under civil service. When a vote to seek local control is being considered, it is common for a rumor to be started telling those eligible to vote that if the community votes in favor of local control, the entire teaching staff will have to leave in order to protect their civil service status. Actually, the BIA allows employees who were working at the time the transfer was made to retain their civil service status as long as they stay in that job. However, accurate information may not be widely circulated, and many Indians who feel a friendship with teachers are likely to vote against local control out of the mistaken belief that current employees would be hurt or forced to leave.

Another factor deterring people from local control was the fear that taking this step toward local control would encourage the government later to back off from its responsibilities for continuous funding. They were afraid of the policy of termination under which the U.S. government paid several tribes a one-time-only settlement that terminated all legal obligations to these tribes. This process utterly destroyed several tribes to which it was applied. As there is no tax base for Indian schools, the Indians recognized their dependence on federal funds and were fearful to take any step that they thought might lead the government to deny them future funds.

Indian leaders had grown skeptical of offers by the federal government since, in the past, they had seen offers retracted on the grounds that the Indians were not yet "ready." Hoping to avoid this charge, the Tribal Council appointed a local school board, of which Teddy Risingsun was chairman, and they met for an entire year studying matters they felt a school board needed to know, such as accreditation and school budgets. Also during that year of preparation for the vote on local control, an intensive effort was made to involve the community—visiting in homes, talking to families, and bringing parents into the school at least once a month for some type of activity.

After a year of building support for local control, the referendum vote was taken in 1970 and the result was overwhelmingly in favor of local control. The results of the referendum were sent to the BIA, but the response was disappointing: the status of BIA schools was "frozen," temporarily at least, and no contract schools would be permitted until certain decisions were made and rules worked out.

The community and Teddy Risingsun continued to fight for local control. As part of this fight they joined with four other Indian tribes and formed an organization called the Coalition of Indian Controlled School Boards. This organization, which started with only five members, grew in three years to 169 members, with a considerable impact at the national level on the forward movement for Indian control of schools serving Indian children.

By the Spring of 1972 the BIA declared a willingness to negotiate once more, and the school board members went to Washington to negotiate. Teddy Risingsun described that negotiation as follows:

> When we were sitting there in Washington, D.C., talking to the very important people at the BIA about getting a contract and taking over our school, I told them "In the past, the school has always been run by outsiders. They come, and they go, and always they know that after a time they *will* go. It will not be a concern of theirs any more what happens to the community. But I am not going to go away.

"In Busby, I have a little house. And last year I planted a tree in the back yard of my house. And when I am old, I expect to sit in the shade of that tree. I expect to have my grandchildren around me and to live to watch the children of Busby grow up and see what they can do with the education they got in Busby School.

"That is why I know that I will work very hard to make Busby a good school. And that is why I think the school will be better off when it is in the hands of the Indian people of Busby."

Until he made this speech there had been much discussion as to whether the local board was "ready" to take responsibility for Busby school. Evidently the speech was persuasive, and a contract was negotiated. A Pow Wow was called in June of 1972 on the grounds of Busby school. An official of the BIA stood on a platform and presented a symbolic key, thereby turning over control of Busby school to the community and its elected school board. Teddy Risingsun, who as a boy had developed a psychological deafness to escape the oppression of Busby school, accepted the key, on behalf of the school board, the Tribal Council, and the people of the Northern Cheyenne.

The mission school followed suit. The school was reorganized as a community school with a seven-member elected school board. When Follow Through started in 1969, there were two school boards, with eight members of whom three were Indian. In 1974 there were three school boards, with seventeen members, all Indian. Indian control of Indian education on the Northern Cheyenne reservation was a realized dream.[1]

MIGRANT CHILDREN IN THE RIO GRANDE VALLEY OF SOUTH TEXAS

In south Texas, a small town called La Grulla is located just two miles from the Rio Grande river that marks the Mexican border. A dusty little town of unpaved streets in 1970, it was the original site for an educational program for the children of migrant farm workers started in that year. The program served children from preschool (ages three and four) through third grade. Having helped to develop the program, I have also been following for eighteen years the progress of children, preschool through grade three, who have participated in it.

Two follow-up studies have been done on this program, which are described under the heading of program outcomes. The third follow-up study, now in progress, is looking not only at what has happened to the children but at what has happened to the parents—particularly those who worked in the program. This dual focus reflects the recognition by those who live in the area that the program changed the lives of whole families, indeed of the community itself. The program seems particularly appropriate, therefore, as a case study of the interaction between the community and the classroom in different cultural settings.

The Social and Economic Conditions

La Grulla is the Spanish name for a migratory bird, now extinct. Like the bird, the people who lived in La Grulla were mostly migrants. A busy place in the winter months, La Grulla resembled a ghost town in the summer, with houses boarded up and nearly all except the old and the sick away in the north working as migrant farm workers. Even the elected mayor of the town went north each year to pick tomatoes.

Poverty and debt were a way of life for the families of the town. Unemployment during the winter months at that time affected 80–90 percent of the population. Most households were two-parent families, making them ineligible for most forms of welfare. They could, however, get credit—at a high interest rate—from some local stores. They could also get a loan from the bank to see them through the winter months of unemployment, provided they could get a crew leader to countersign the loan. Crew leaders were willing to do this, because they could get the backing of one of the large agricultural businesses, such as Green Giant Co. or Del Monte. One crew leader told me that in some years, by March he would have countersigned over two hundred thousand dollars worth of loans.

As a condition of countersigning the loan, the crew leader required the family to sign up all members of the family, including older children, to be part of his crew. This meant that they must take the work that he arranged for as many weeks as he arranged (growers were anxious to keep workers there to the end of the crop because workers' earnings went down at the tail end of harvest and many left if they were free to do so). The crew leader usually arranged housing in the north, and sometimes transportation. For all of these services, the family agreed to pay him a commission, on his terms.

When the crew went north, the crew leader collected the wages, which meant that he could pay back the loan and his commissions before any of the earnings were passed on to the family. Usually it took half the season to pay off the debt from the previous winter before the family had any money to spend. In the remainder of the season, they were never able to save enough to get through the coming winter, so by mid-winter they would have run out of money and need a loan again. (In 1988 this pattern has largely been broken, but this was the way of life for migrant families when the IBI program was started.)

In La Grulla, the median level of education completed by migrant parents before dropping out of school was fifth grade. All could speak

Spanish, and some a little English. Most were U.S. citizens and had gone to schools in the United States. They had learned to read in English and most felt they could read English better than Spanish, but without knowing enough English to understand what they read, they never became fully literate in either language.

There was, in any event, nothing to read. No one in La Grulla subscribed to a daily paper and few had books or magazines in their homes. Certainly they did not carry books with them as essential luggage for the six or seven months of the year they lived on the road often in one- or two-room migrant temporary housing.

The Schools

La Grulla was one community of many that were part of the Rio Grande City Consolidated Independent School District. The county seat and largest town within the school district was Rio Grande City, and most of the families who held political power or had financial resources were generally found to reside there. It was a widely held belief that the quality of the schools followed the money, and that the best teachers and any new programs or resources were most likely to end up in the schools in Rio Grande City. On the other end of the power scale was La Grulla, which had a reputation of being the local "Siberia"—a place of exile to which a teacher who was out of favor could be sent for punishment. Certainly a disproportionate number of teachers who had only "provisional" certificates were teaching in La Grulla schools.

The schools in La Grulla went up to eighth grade, after which it was necessary for children to ride a bus into Rio Grande City for high school. It was difficult to get students to stay in school beyond eighth grade. Marriages were very common at thirteen and fourteen. Rafael Guerra, the principal of the junior high school and later the Texas director for IBI (Individualized Bilingual Instruction), described the problem of talking children into continuing their education:

> They only needed to look around them and they could see there weren't any jobs except working in the fields. I remember last year we held a sort of beauty contest for the girls to pick out one to be Miss La Grulla. There were twelve girls competing. Out of these twelve girls, nine had actually gone on to high school. But the only ones who had jobs were the three who had dropped out of school. They were earning money for going to school in a program that was designed to help dropouts.
>
> The same is true for the boys. I was a migrant so I know how it is. By the time a boy is thirteen or fourteen years old, he can make pretty good money working in the fields. They know they are supposed to go to the school until they are sixteen, but a wonderful thing happens every year when they drive

north. They are thirteen when they leave Texas, but by the time they get to Washington they are sixteen already.

What they earn helps out the family. They have a little money to spend. They feel competitive with the other boys. If your friends are making good money working, it is hard to say I think it is more important to go to school. You don't want to be different.

Key Factors in the Educational Program

The original IBI program was jointly funded by the Office of Migrant Head Start and the Office of Bilingual Education in Washington, D.C. It was planned as a demonstration bilingual program, with many special features particularly designed to meet unique needs of migrant children. One of these features was a two-state operation—the original sites were in Texas and in Washington state—in communities at opposite ends of a migrant stream. (The grantee happened to be in Washington state.) For clarity of description, most of this case study will deal with the Texas site.[2]

It is an unusual situation for a school district to be operating a program outside of its geographic boundaries. From necessity, part of the program design was to have actual program administration carried out at the program sites, except for the oversight of a program manager responsible to the grantee school district who made sure all fiscal and administrative requirements were met.

In any program for a poverty population, the decisions of key importance to the participants are who will get the jobs and who will get the services. From the first, the parents had a deciding voice in these and other policy matters. The parents organization (the PAC) was not simply advisory—they served on the personnel committee and set policy, screened candidates for program staff, and the personnel choices they made were never overturned by the grantee agency. The eligibility for children to be served followed general program guidelines for bilingual and migrant program, but priorities within those guidelines were decisions made by the local parent group, which included staff members.

A key factor in the functioning of the educational program, therefore, was an unusual degree of program control by parents. In Texas, having an out-of-state grantee meant that the program was out of the reach of local politics—it couldn't be taken away from La Grulla and given to more favored schools. Likewise, the crew leaders could not take it over—though one of them tried. Rebuffed in his attempt to dictate who should be hired and which children served, one crew leader threatened to boycott any family in which someone agreed to take a teaching job in the program—no one in that family could be on his crew or get jobs or housing when the families moved north. The program manager, who lived in Washington state, contacted Green Giant Co., who employed this crew leader, and got them to instruct the crew leader to back off and leave the program alone. From the first, therefore, the families looked upon the program as evidence of a change in their relative power in the community.

Getting a job in the program meant having a salary twelve months a year (when the center in Texas closed because families had moved north, the teachers moved too and were employed in programs in the north for part of the year). It was the culture of Hispanic families to help one another through hard times. This meant that one salary was likely to mean that more than one family could make it through the winter months without going to the crew leader to countersign a note from the bank. The families still continued to migrate, but if they went north without signing on with a crew leader, they could choose their own employers and leave or move on when they wanted to. Most importantly, they did not have to sign up all members of the family, and many began to leave behind their teenage children, having them stay with someone in Texas so they could finish school and receive credit for a full semester's work. Before this change, it was almost impossible for a migrant child to accumulate the credits needed for graduation.

When the Texas PAC first began making personnel policies, they decided that priority should be given in hiring based on family need—who needed the job most. Later, the PAC listened to the arguments of the Texas site director, Rafael Guerra (the one who related the story of the Miss La Grulla contest). If children were going to be encouraged to stay in school, he told them, there needed to be rewards for education, jobs open to them because they had stayed in school and graduated. The PAC then changed its policy and gave priority to applicants who had finished high school or passed their GED. This was a significant change in attitudes toward education. For the first time, educational achievement and literacy began to be relevant to migrant families living in La Grulla.

A second key factor in the educational program was the program design, which called for all teaching to be done by migrant adults (paraprofessionals). Certified staff were hired, but their job title was "trainer" and their responsibility was to supervise and train a group of bilingual paraprofessional teachers. They did not work directly with the children. Each trainer worked with about ten paraprofessional teachers, who in turn each had groups of eight children, so in this way each bilingual certified person (there is a shortage) could actually oversee the educational progress of around eighty children.

Migrant adults hired for the program were all familiar with the role of aides in the schools, who worked around children wiping up tables after lunch, ran ditto sheets, and did other tasks that were not considered teaching. In this educational program they were not aides, they were the

teachers, and this took some getting used to. Rafael Guerra related their
changing attitudes in this way:

> The first year we got some little pins for each of them that said "Teacher,"
> and their name. They were a little embarrassed to wear the pins, as if people
> would think they didn't have the right to call themselves teachers. After a few
> months, they didn't feel embarrassed anymore. They could see how much the
> children were learning, and they knew they were teachers. Being teachers
> made them start to feel differently about themselves.

The change from field work, paid by piecework, to a teaching job paid
by a salary involved many changes. Paid holidays were a wonderful new
experience. On the other hand, some teachers had second thoughts about
their salaries when the field work opened up. Most of them could have
earned more in the fields than they did in the classroom, but the project
couldn't afford to lose the training it had invested in teachers by turnover,
so a rule was made that any teacher who left the job to go to work in the
fields could not come back. The director counseled with teachers every
year as they made this decision. A teaching job meant a year-long, higher
income in the long run, but a lower income in the short run. How much
was this change in decision making—to look at long-term benefits—trans-
lated into family interaction patterns that affected children's views toward
education and their own future? This is something we may learn from the
follow-up study now in progress.

A third key factor that shaped the educational program was the widely
held view by people in Washington, D.C., who funded the program as an
"interesting experiment," that it wouldn't work. They felt that hiring
migrant adults to teach would probably result in a lot of babysitting for
kids, but not provide anything of educational value. From the first, therefore,
a very close monitoring system was set up to keep track of children's
educational progress and migrant teachers' acquisition of effective teaching
skills. If an instructional strategy was not working, it was thrown out.

In the first year, the program experimented with two types of training—
one group of teachers had three months of preservice training before they
took responsibility for a group of children and another started teaching
from the first week. The preservice training model was thrown out, when it
became very clear that the teachers who already had a group of children
depending on their teaching got a lot more out of the training, and could
apply it much better, than those who were still waiting to take on actual
teaching responsibilities. After this, all training was inservice training.

It was also found that talking about what to do was less effective than
demonstrating what to do—that is, teachers could observe and then model
very good teaching skills that they could not have explained in words. The
training was set up with modeling as a key step.

The project found that paraprofessionals moving into teaching needed lots of reassurance. Training schedules were therefore set up (and monitored) to make sure every teacher was observed regularly and while teaching different subject areas. The trainer recorded specific teaching interactions so that when it came time to discuss the observation with the teacher it would be possible to describe a great many things the teacher had done right. If there were things that needed changing, a trainer never made more than two suggestions at a time, so it wouldn't be overwhelming.

Because the program was for migrants, it had to be adapted to the fact that children would be entering and leaving the program throughout the year and so allow for individual progress rather than progress as a group. For school-age children, the same programmed reading series used on the Northern Cheyenne reservation was selected because it could be individualized. For the preschool children, the project developed its own materials, in both Spanish and English, to teach children the basic skills of sound/symbol correspondence and blending needed to begin in the programmed workbooks. When the programmed reading materials came out in Spanish, the project adopted these materials as well and literacy skills were developed in both languages.

These curriculum materials were taught through teacher-directed, small learning groups for short periods of time. At the preschool level, the teacher-directed learning periods were alternated with equal periods of time given to child-choice activities in an all-day program.

The process of describing activities or equipment the child might choose to play with and having the child verbalize a choice produced a meaningful conversational exchange several times a day. The informal learning time provided a different learning mode. This was the time when children could choose to listen to stories, to act out a story, or to play games that involved recognizing sight words or matching letters. It was also a time for playing with blocks, art materials, large muscle activity, etc. But whatever the activity, the teachers were involved and interacting with the children, which made these child-choice periods very productive for language development. This informal learning time included many activities that related to the children's daily lives and culture (cooking, dancing, preparing fiestas, etc.).

Weekly progress reports, prepared by teachers for every child, included descriptions of the activities related to cultural learning, as well as the child's final placement that week in the learning sequence for each subject area. The program had a sequence of learning tasks from preschool through third grade for oral language development in English and Spanish, for math, and for reading in English and Spanish. If the tracking of students through the weekly teacher reports showed that certain children were not making progress, the trainer was notified so he or she could work with the teacher to provide supplemental instruction or whatever was needed.

The prophecy when the program started that it "could not work" with migrant adults as the teaching staff resulted in this weekly monitoring of every aspect of the program. In 1973 it was the first bilingual program in the United States to be nationally validated because it had incontrovertible evidence that it was effective.

Program Outcomes

Children who have entered the IBI program over the years have averaged English reading scores below the tenth percentile on national norms. After attending the IBI program for only half a year—100 days—the increase in reading skills was enough to be statistically significant. It continued to increase with each added period of attendance and after three years in the program, IBI children averaged English reading scores at the national norm. This finding was replicated over three different two-year periods of project operation, indicating that it was a stable program result and not the result of a particular group of very able teachers or children.

Analysis was done to see whether the children who stayed in the program for longer periods of time were selectively different from those who dropped out. One method of doing this was to classify all children as being of relatively low, medium, or high ability on the basis of their vocabulary pretests in Spanish, their primary language. Comparing the proportion of children of high, low, or medium ability among children who stayed in the program for a number of years as compared to those who did not, there was essentially no difference. The children who stayed in the program were no more likely than those who did not to come from a high ability grouping. This meant that selective attrition was not taking place, which could have accounted for the higher scores achieved by children after two and three years in the program.

Follow-up studies comparing achievement test scores of children who had been in the IBI program with children from a comparison group in a nearby community were carried out through sixth grade, and then through eighth grade. These showed that children from the IBI program were still significantly superior to the comparison group in English vocabulary and English reading and spelling several years after they had left the IBI program.

Possibly the most interesting evidence of program effectiveness came about ten years after the IBI program had started. District-wide testing was done as usual in the Rio Grande City Consolidated Independent School District. The results showed that La Grulla elementary school children had higher academic scores than any other school in the district. Impressed with this achievement, the principal at La Grulla was promoted to being an elementary school principal in the county seat, Rio Grande City. He was gracious enough not to accept much credit for this turnaround in children's academic achievement. He said he felt it was due primarily to the change in the children and in the attitude toward education of all the families who had been part of the IBI program in La Grulla.

POLICY ISSUES

These case studies have presented evidence of educational change that involved the recruitment of teachers from ethnic and language-minority groups. There are many sociocultural reasons that suggest themselves as to why this resulted in improved academic performance. For one, it minimized cultural shock for the child. School is enough different from the home environment as to cause some shock. However, if the teacher in the school is more like the adults at home there is less shock than if the child encounters someone of different ethnicity using an unfamiliar language and different manner of relating to other people, insofar as these patterns are culturally determined.

It may be that cultural identity with the teacher increases the child's sense of worth. It may be that when the teacher comes from the same ethnic background as the children it increases the probability of contact between home and school, which may reinforce academic learning. If the child can communicate successfully in the school setting, because the teacher uses the mother tongue, it establishes a "habit" of success.

How do these factors weigh alongside the impact of a particular curriculum and teaching methods in determining the success of children learning to read? It is difficult to believe that the dramatic success of the educational programs described in these case studies could be explained without some acknowledgement of the impact of sociocultural factors.

This raises a number of policy issues. One concerns the present trend to improve education through increasing the academic credentials needed by beginning teachers. In my own state of Washington, a timetable has been set after which it will be necessary to obtain a master's degree before being considered qualified to teach. One wonders at the weight being given to strictly academic preparation. Consider the impact if an alternate program had been instituted on the Northern Cheyenne reservation, in which all funds were put into upgrading the academic qualifications of staff. Had the same money been spent to enable the schools to hire non-Indian teachers, all of whom had an MA or a Phd, instead of employing Indian instructional aides and community workers, would the results reported in this case study have been achieved? This escalation of academic credentials for certification seems likely to me to be counterproductive in that it will further decrease the supply of minority teachers.

Another policy issue involved is how to structure the use of minority paraprofessionals to utilize their language capability and their rapport with minority children to maximum advantage, without undermining the professional standards protected by certification, and sometimes by union contracts. In both the case studies related here, this issue came up and someone had to make a determination that this was an allowed educational practice, even waiving certain administrative requirements. In these case studies, however, the curriculum materials were selected to make up for lack of background by teaching staff and extensive training was provided, as well as close supervision. Would the results have been the same had the emphasis been on use of paraprofessional staff without these conditions?

This issue of how to develop an appropriate role for minority paraprofessionals needs serious consideration, because the gap between the numbers of at-risk children in our schools who are minority and limited English speakers is growing at a much faster rate than the supply of certified minority teachers. In some distant tomorrow there may be enough minority teachers, but a child cannot wait for tomorrow. What happens to the child is today.

NOTES

[1] For a more complete report, see ERIC publication ED 134 377 (1975).

[2] For a more complete description of the program and discussion of many more features than can be dealt with in this chapter, the reader is referred to *Long Term Effects of Bilingual Education*, published in 1980. See ERIC publication ED 206 203.

The Follow Through programs in Montana and Texas, like all Follow Through, Head Start, and Chapter 1 programs, have a strong parent involvement component. McConnell showed us what can happen when parent involvement becomes parent ownership. In Chapter 11, we get to know five parents, Head Start mothers who also want very much to become active participants in their children's education. Edwards worked with the mothers to help them learn the book reading interactions typical in literate home environments.

Supporting Lower SES Mothers' Attempts to Provide Scaffolding for Book Reading

Patricia A. Edwards

"READERS are made, not born. No one comes into the world already disposed for or against words in print" (Chambers, 1973, p. 16). Bruner (1975) observed that parent-child exchanges are the focal point for the start of learning; they provide the roots of literacy. Parents who read to their children provide their youngsters with those first models of literacy. Pflaum (1986) suggested that "the interaction with small children over home materials and storybooks is the medium through which notions about literacy are learned" (p. 121). Altwerger, Diehl-Faxon, and Dockstader-Anderson (1985) reported that in read-aloud events between parents and children, "Parents naturally expand, extend and clarify their children's language, while maintaining the focus of language interactions on meaning" (p. 476). Mahoney and Wilcox (1985) concluded, "If a child comes from a reading family where books are a shared source of pleasure, he or she will have an understanding of the language of the literary world and respond to the use of books in a classroom as a natural expansion of pleasant home experiences" (p. ix). King (1980) also concluded that in a home where reading is a high-priority activity a child develops certain expectations about print. He comes to know the pleasures that await him between the covers of a book. He hears the language of books, which will differ in varying degrees from the language he hears spoken. He learns to listen to continuous language related by a logical sequence or the unfolding of the plot of a story. He learns that you can find the answers to questions in books. He becomes acquainted with some of the features of books; how to handle them and follow a line of print. He is exposed to visual symbols, both nonverbal in picture reading and verbal in learning to recognize some words and letters. He encounters new words and new uses of words. He learns to appreciate the different effects that are created by sound patterns and rhythms. The exposure to many acceptable models of expressing ideas develops an awareness of different forms of expression and language patterns. Listening to stories provides him with models which consciously or unconsciously he may adopt into his own speech and his imagination may be stirred. In time [the child] develops a mental set toward literacy (p. 47−48).

While it is well documented that storybook reading is an important literacy event, it appears that some "[lower SES] parents are not sufficiently aware of their impact on their child's reading" (Pflaum, 1986, p. 10). Over the last few years, there has been a proliferation of research on early reading interactions, but one limitation is that almost all of the research focuses on mainstream middle-class parents and children. The few studies on parent-child book reading interactions in low-income families have shown that low SES parents seldom ask questions or elicit words from their children (Heath & Thomas, 1984; Ninio, 1980), do not view their young children as appropriate conversational partners (Heath, 1982a, 1982b), and do not tend to adjust their language to their child's level of understanding (Snow & Ninio, 1986). Ninio (1980) found that lower SES mothers used significantly fewer object names and action words and asked very few questions. Middle SES mothers, on the other hand, were more adept at using questions that elicited talk from the child. According to Farron (1982), middle SES mothers engaged their children in elaborate verbal dialogues. Snow and Ninio (1986) reported that poor black mothers did not seem to adjust their language to their children's actions as did more advantaged black parents. Instead, poor mothers repeated their own speech. McCormick and Mason (1986) revealed that lower SES parents did not foster or support acquisition of prereading skills to the same degree as parents at higher SES levels.

The most extensive body of research describing parent-child book reading interactions in lower SES black families is the research reported by Heath and her colleagues (Heath, 1982a, 1982b, 1986; Heath, Branscombe & Thomas, 1985; Heath & Thomas, 1984). Her research has demonstrated that parent-child interaction patterns in Trackton, a lower SES black community, were different from those found in Roadville, a lower SES white community, and Maintown, a middle SES white and black community. In Trackton, parents did not see young preschoolers as appropriate conversational partners, and occasions in which they engaged these children in sustained talk were rare. Although talk was directed to young children in Trackton, this talk was seldom simplified and children were often expected to understand large spurts of speech. Heath found similar behavior patterns of interaction between a black teenage mother and her preschool child (Heath & Thomas, 1984). This mother seldom asked her preschooler questions such as, "What is this?" or interpreted any of his self-initiated utterances as labels of objects.

Heath found that Trackton children were encouraged to make narratives as conversation, but only after adults opened narrative episodes by questioning children (Heath, 1986). However, before children could answer question(s) posed by the adults in these interactions, either individual adults or adults in dialogue answered the question. According to Heath, "This adult-question-and-answer routine provides preschoolers with the basic components of a narrative, which preschoolers reiterate through performance after the adults have hesitated or fully stopped their question-and-answer routines" (p. 166). She further pointed out that "requests for 'sticking to the story' or telling 'what happened' [are] inappropriate during a telling [of a narrative]. Questions asked about particulars of the story, assessments of how actors played their roles, or 'what would have happened if . . .?' [do] not occur" (p. 168). "Thus, Trackton children learn to use common experiences in their narratives, but they [are] not asked to explain how they [vary] either the genre form or the content from an expected organizational schema or a predicted sequence of events, requests that are made by teachers" (p. 168).

Heath (1983) also found that questions Trackton children heard at home were different from the questions teachers asked at school. As a result, Trackton children had a difficult time responding and/or answering questions asked by teachers at school. Even though Trackton parents accepted children's stories and talked about children's experiences, they were less likely to relate these experiences to books or other literate events.

Despite the fact that research suggests that lower SES mothers and especially most black lower SES mothers have difficulty sharing books with their young children, few investigators have recommended strategies for encouraging those mothers who lack the necessary skills to engage in book reading interactions with their children. Yet there are several models for building successful book reading interactions that can be inferred from the research (Flood, 1977; Resnick et al., 1987; Roser & Martinez, 1985; Shanahan & Hogen, 1983). Even though most of these models are derived from middle SES populations, much can be learned from these parent-child interactions to enhance the literacy development of low SES families.

For instance, Pflaum (1986) has outlined several literacy exchange settings and listed examples of how discussions with children might occur in these settings. She noted that the examples may serve as a way to model literacy exchanges to parents. A sample of these literacy exchanges and examples are listed below:

Literacy Exchange	Example
Specific answers to child	Provide the child with just the information asked for; on occasion, relate it to previous knowledge.
Book experiences	Provide the child with daily storybook experiences.
Exchanges during storybook reading	Read through stories and be able to stop and ask questions.
Questions during reading	Ask the child to name, expand, predict, talk about the setting, discuss concepts, and talk about overall meaning.
Talk about print	1. Focus on the significance of print. 2. Discuss the print and picture.
Talk about words	1. Show words. 2. Identify a few words.
Words in stories	Point out one or two important words to well-known stories, signs, etc.
Spacing and sequencing	Point out spaces, sequencing ideas, and word sequences.

(pp. 121–122)

The purpose of the present study was to extend research concerning the interactive behavior between lower SES black parent-child dyads during story reading and children's responses to these readings. The present investigation focused on the interactions between five lower SES black mothers and their preschool children during story reading. A major purpose was to describe the five mothers' development of successful book reading behaviors and to provide some explanations as to why some of the mothers had difficulty developing successful behaviors. One mother, Flora, who moved from using few to many effective behaviors, is described in more detail.

METHODOLOGY

Background of Book Reading Project

During the fall of 1985, I volunteered to serve as a parent consultant for a local Head Start Center in a rural community located in north Louisiana. I met with families once a month for one-and-a-half hour sessions over a period of nine months. The Head Start director and I informed the parents that each month I would focus on how they could become better prepared to support their children's education both at the Head Start Center and later in the public school setting. Realizing many of the problems lower SES children have in kindergarten and first grade, I proposed a book reading project and explained to all of the Head Start families that parents need to support their children's reading. Several parents then volunteered for a project that would help them interact with their children during book reading.

Subjects

Five black lower SES mothers were randomly selected (except for Betty, who was urged by the Head Start director to participate) from a total of eighteen mothers who volunteered to participate in the study. From information gathered in a structured interview with each mother, I found that none of these mothers had previously engaged in book reading interactions with their preschool children. All of the participating mothers were single. Two mothers had finished high school and three had not completed high school.

Materials

A set of little books, developed by Mason & McCormick (1985), as well as fifteen commercial picture storybooks and ten wordless picture books were used in the book reading sessions. Most of the picture storybooks were pattern books or predictable books. Even though most of these mothers had not read to their young children, nor had their mothers read to them when they were young children, I felt it necessary to include stories that involved characters and concepts that should be familiar to all preschoolers. For Flora, the most capable reader of the five mothers, I included some more difficult texts (e.g., *Jumanji* [Van Allsburg, 1981]; *Why Mosquitoes Buzz in People's Ears* [Aardema, 1975]; *Tom Tit Tot* [Jacobs, 1965]).

Procedures for Initial Parent-Child Book Reading Session

The book reading sessions were held at the local Head Start Center. The mothers made appointments to meet with me individually. At the initial book reading session, I tried to make the mothers feel comfortable. Then, I instructed the mothers to select a book they thought they could read with little difficulty. Three of the mothers selected *Over in the Meadow* (Keats, 1972), one selected *Great Day for Up* (Dr. Seuss, 1974), and the teenage mother selected *Time for Bed*, one of the little books (Mason & McCormick,

1985). After the mothers had made their selections, I simply asked them to read the book to their preschool child as I observed and videotaped the book reading. I told the mothers I was making the videotapes so we could view them together and discuss ways to improve these book reading interactions. Videotapes of the book reading sessions were collected over a period of eight weeks.

Description of a Typical Book Reading Session

Before each mother engaged in a book reading interaction with her preschooler, I asked her to tell me what had happened since the last session or what she had done to reinforce what she had learned about book reading. It should be noted here that while I discussed with each mother the previous week's book reading practices and/or attempts, her child was not present. The child usually played with other children in a classroom near the meeting room assigned to me by the Head Start director. After the child was settled and the mother felt relaxed, I began my inquiry into her previous week's book reading practices and/or attempts. These discussions usually lasted from five to ten minutes, and the mothers usually commented that they had attempted to talk more to their child, that they had pointed out words in the environment, discussed TV commercials like Coca-Cola or McDonald's, bought books from the grocery or drug store.

I then provided positive feedback and encouragement for whatever they said they had done or did not do. For example, I would say "Keep up the good work," and "You are on the right track," or "You are making progress, this is how you can do it better." This part of the book reading session was critical for these mothers. They seemed to need constant reinforcement and moral support, especially since they were nervous about being taped each week.

Before bringing the children back to the meeting room, I tried to be sensitive to the mother's feelings about reading and tried to make sure that they felt comfortable and relaxed. Except in the case of Betty, the mothers usually seemed relaxed after our discussions, or what I call my pep talks with them, prior to their book reading interactions with their children. Before the children returned to the room, the mothers selected a book and previewed it. Oftentimes, the mother would ask me to pronounce words or ask for suggestions of how to phrase certain parts of the story. In several instances, we participated in a dialogue similar to a directed reading lesson. I would pronounce words and discuss what they meant, or I would explain something about the story. Then the mother would read the story to her child while I videotaped the session.

The average book reading session lasted from thirty-five to forty-five minutes. At the conclusion of the session, I replayed the videotape so that the mother and I could analyze the behaviors they had employed. The children returned to a nearby classroom before the replay session, which usually lasted for an additional twenty-five to thirty-five minutes. The mother and I watched the videotape and counted the number of times she asked questions or the number of comments she made before, during, and after reading. I encouraged the mother to increase the frequency of these behaviors.

As a way of organizing my comments and suggestions, I used a checklist similar to the one developed by Resnick et al. (1987) in all of my interactions with the mothers.[1] The checklist allowed us to see progress toward acquiring effective book reading skills. Before I made my comments and suggestions to the mothers I would say, "Tell me what good behaviors you used in this session? What behaviors do you feel you could improve on?" This allowed the mothers to initiate the discussion. Then I would interject my comments and suggestions. I pinpointed at least one behavior that was effective and at least one behavior the mother needed to learn. Some of the effective behavior comments I made to the mothers included statements like, "You allowed your child to hold the book, turn the pages, and explore the book," but most importantly, "You guided your child's attention to the book, maintained physical contact with your child through-out the book reading session, and commented positively about your child's participation."

After I informed the mothers of the effective behaviors I had observed, I would say, "Although you incorporated a number of effective behaviors in this session, there are still a few behaviors that I would like for you to improve on or include in our next session." My comments usually included such suggestions as, "Vary your voice more the next time, make noises and motions in order to make the story more interesting, describe pictures, ask more questions, and comment on the book's content." I would demonstrate these behaviors and read to their children as the mothers watched. As a general rule of thumb, I tried to focus my comments each time on the mothers' progress toward developing their children's knowledge of questions, book reading, print awareness, and oral and written language. In particular, the mothers were encouraged over the eight sessions to ask higher level questions. Initially, they only asked knowledge-level questions. Over the eight-week period the following interactions were suggested:

- using strategies to maintain child's attention
- responding to child's comments
- relating the text to life experiences and life to text experiences
- answering children's questions and relating text to children's own personal experiences

- initiating discussion, recounting parts of a story, sharing personal reactions, and encouraging children to respond similarly

It should be noted that I interacted with the mothers in other settings besides the Head Start Center. I lived in the same community, so I took them to lunch and to the library and even called them on the telephone just to chat. The mothers considered me to be their friend and respected the fact that I was a black researcher interested in helping them better prepare their children for a more successful school experience. From comments made to me by the Head Start director and the five participating mothers, I believe that these personal interactions greatly enhanced my relationship and credibility with the mothers during the book reading sessions.

DESCRIPTION OF THE FIVE MOTHERS' DEVELOPMENT OF SUCCESSFUL BOOK READING BEHAVIORS

Initial Book Reading Behaviors of the Five Mothers

Betty, age thirty-one, had a difficult time reading to her four-year-old son. She exhibited the characteristics of a beginning reader herself. She strug-gled to pronounce every word in the story. Her attention to the text was so intense that she spent little time involving her son in the story. Even though Betty did not talk about the pictures in the book, ask questions about the text, or explain the story to her son, he appeared interested in the story and most especially in the pictures.

Cindy, a teenage mother of two (a son, two years old, and a daughter, three years old) dropped out of school at the age of fourteen. At the time of the taping, Cindy was eighteen years old. She appeared interested in wanting to read to her young daughter but insisted on selecting a book that was "simple, so I can read it." Consequently, she chose *Time for Bed*.[2] Even this book was difficult for her. Cindy appeared embarrassed and constantly looked for me for prompts. For example, Cindy wanted to know whether she should show her child the pictures in the book or not. When I replied "Yes," she began pointing to pictures in the text and talking about them. At one point, Cindy said to her daughter, "The way you climb into bed at home, LaQuiece," relating the experiences in the story to herself and to her daughter's own personal experiences with going to bed.

Janis, age twenty-five, did a fairly good job reading to her young daughter. Even though Janis incorrectly pronounced a few words, she read with expression and was able to use the appropriate voice intonations at the right times. Her three-year-old daughter was interested in the story, but the mother rarely paused to focus the child's attention on specific sections of the text. At one point she said, "See the picture." However, this comment was made near the end of the story. One of Janis's last comments before ending the story was simply the statement, "End of the story."

Sylvia, age twenty-eight, insisted on involving both her three- and four-year-old sons in the book reading sessions. Neither child was able to fully enjoy the story or pay attention to the text because the mother was constantly moving the book from one child to the other. At one point, the three-year-old boy began pulling on the book and raising up in his chair to see the text. At times Sylvia read with expression, but she had difficulty pronouncing a number of words in the story. She hurriedly read the story and rarely did she focus her language and/or comments on a level appropriate for her two young sons to understand the story.

Even though Flora, age twenty-nine, had not been previously involved in book reading interactions with her four-year-old daughter, she proved to be the most capable of the five mothers at engaging in such interactions. Flora was like a child in a toy store. She appeared amazed and excited, almost as if she were a child enjoying a story for the first time. Flora was so involved in the reading of the story *Great Day for Up*, by Dr. Seuss, that she paid little attention to her daughter. She seemed to be reading the story for her own personal enjoyment. Even though her daughter was sitting beside her and constantly peeking in the book to see what her mother was so excited about, Flora never stopped reading to ask questions or involve her daughter. She did not look at her child during the initial book reading session nor did she pause for her preschooler to respond to the text. She did not provide feedback, label or describe pictures, or relate the story to her and her daughter's personal experiences. Figure 11−1 is a transcript of Flora's initial book reading interaction with her young daughter and Figure 11−2 is a checklist highlighting Flora's initial book reading behavior.

Reactions of the Mothers to the Book Reading Sessions

The five mothers differed in their reactions to the interactive book reading sessions and conferences. Betty's inability to read aloud with confidence caused her to view the book reading sessions negatively. She exhibited behaviors similar to a remedial student's frustration and eventual rejection and/or dislike of reading. Figure 11−3 is a transcript of a verbal interaction between Betty and me. Betty appeared defensive during the session. It is unfortunate, but not surprising, that after her second session, she began missing her appointments with me and eventually dropped out of the study. Even though the Head Start director, her child's teacher, and I called and encouraged her to continue, she chose not to do so.

Figure 11–1   **Transcript of a Taped Reading Session, Recorded October 3, 1985**

Flora's reading of the text *Great Day For Up*	Flora talking about text	Tamara's responses
	My name is Flora Lee and this is my daughter Tamara. This afternoon I'm going to read *Great Day For Up* by Dr. Seuss.	Looks at the book cover.
Up! Up! The sun is getting up. Up! Ear number one. Ear number two.		Stares.
The sun gets up. So up with you! Up! Up! Great day, today! Great for up!		
Up, heads! Up, whiskers! Tails!		Smiles.
You Frogs! You butterflies!		
Up! Up! You! Open up your eyes! You worms!		
Up! Girls and women! Boys and men!		Peeks over her mother's shoulder.
Up, whales! Up, snails! Up, rooster Hen!		Smiles.
Great day For up feet Lefts and rights.		
And up! Up! Baseballs! Footballs! Kites!		
Great day to sing up on a wire.		Looks startled.
Up! Voices! Louder! Higher!		
Up stairs! Up ladders! Up on stilts!		
Great day for Up Mt. Dill-ma-dilts.		
Everybody's doing Ups! on bikes . . . and tree . . . buttercups.		
Up! Up! Waiters! Alligators!		

continued

Figure 11–1 *continued*

Flora's reading of the text *Great Day For Up*	Flora talking about text	Tamara's responses
Up, Folks! Up in elevators!		Peeks over Flora's shoulder.
Up! Up giraffes! Great day for seals!		
Great day for up on ferris wheels!		"I rode on a ferris wheel before at the fair."
[Flora ignores child's comment and continues to read.]		
Up! Up! Up! Fill up the air.		Child looks and smiles.
Up, Flags! Balloon! Up! Everywhere.		
Wake every person, Pig and pup, till everyone on Earth. is up!		Child looks.
Up! Up! Up! Great day for up!		
Except for me. Please go away No up. I'm sleeping in today.		Child smiles and asks her mother to let her look at the book.

While Betty did, in fact, agree to participate in the book reading project, it was not without serious coaching from the Head Start director and her child's teacher. They both felt that John (Betty's son) had severely limited language skills for a four-year-old. After talking with Betty, both the director and teacher felt Betty rarely talked to John. They were not sure if Betty listened or heard what John had to say. For instance, Betty remarked that "John does not have a problem talking; I understand what he is saying." Yet the Head Start director and his teacher did not understand him. Another important point that should be noted here is that the director, the teacher, and I (all black) all had difficulty understanding Betty's speech. This problem may have contributed to her apparent defensive and insecure feelings about her own inability to communicate effectively.

Since I was aware of both Betty's and John's language difficulties, I made a concerted effort to work with Betty and her young son. However, I feel that Betty's resistance in cooperating might have arisen from her resentment of outside pressures to participate. She, in fact, probably had not made up her own mind to participate. Perhaps as Pflaum (1986) notes, Betty was not "sufficiently aware of [her] impact on [her son's] reading"

Figure 11-2   Flora's Initial Book Reading Behavior, October 3, 1985

---

1. Mother's Body Management
_____ Sits opposite child.
_____ Places child on lap.
_____ Partially encircles child.
_____ Completely encircles child.
_____ Lies alongside child.
__X__ Sits adjacent to child.
_____ Maintains physical contact.

2. Mother's Management of Book
_____ Previews book.
_____ Allows child to hold book.
_____ Allows child to turn pages.
_____ Permits child to explore book.
_____ Guides child's attention to book.
_____ Points to pictures/words.
_____ Asks child questions.
_____ Links items in text to child's life.
__X__ Varies voice.
_____ Emphasizes syllables.
_____ Acts [makes noises, motions].
_____ Comments on book's content.
_____ Refers to reading as joint enterprise.
_____ Ends reading episode when child loses interest.
_____ Continues to read after child loses interest.
_____ Resists child turning pages.
__X__ Becomes absorbed by book and ignores child.

3. Mother's Language Proficiency
_____ Uses multiple word sentences.
_____ Uses multiple grammatical modes.
_____ Labels pictures.
_____ Describes pictures.
_____ Repeats child's vocalization.
_____ Corrects child's vocalization.
_____ Elaborates child's vocalization.
_____ Gives words to child's vocalization.

4. Mother's Attention to Affect
_____ Pauses for child's response.
_____ Inspects child's face.
_____ Praises child.
_____ Comments positively about child's participation.
_____ Gives spoken affirmation.
_____ Makes approving gesture.
_____ Reprimands child.
_____ Comments negatively about child's participation.

Source: Adapted from "Mothers Reading to Infants: A New Observational Tool," M.B. Resnick, et al. 1987, *The Reading Teacher*, 40, no. 9, pp. 888-895.

Questions I asked Betty and comments I made to her about the story Hi, Cat!	Betty's responses to my questions and comments	Betty asking questions	My responses to Betty's questions
Betty, why did you choose the book, Hi, Cat!	Because I liked the pictures and it was about a little black boy.		
Betty, before you begin reading the story, are there any words you would like for me to pronounce?	Yes.		
What words would you like for me to pronounce?			
Please point them out to me. Betty pointed to the words "reflection," "croaked", "giggled," and "delicious."			
Betty I am going to break the words down into syllables and I want you to repeat the word after me. I will pronounce each word very slowly for you, ok? re.flec.tion reflection	Ok.		
Repeat after me.	re.flec.tion reflection		
Do you know what that word means?	Yes		
What?	It means . . . You tell me.	What does reflection mean?	It means the production of an image given back by a reflecting surface, such as a mirror.
Let's go on to the next word croak.ed croaked			
What does croaked mean?	I don't know.		Croaked means to speak in a hoarse voice or to make a deep harsh sound almost as if you have a frog in your throat.
	Betty smiles.		

Figure 11–3 *Continued*

Questions I asked Betty and comments I made to her about the story *Hi, Cat!*	Betty's responses to my questions and comments	Betty asking questions	My responses to Betty's questions
When you get to that word [croaked] you will have to speak in a deep hoarse voice.	Betty smiles again and says "I don't know whether I can do that or not."		
You can. The next word is gig.gled giggled. What does giggled mean?	I'll try. It means to laugh.		
Very good, Betty.	Betty smiles and says "at least I got one right so far."		
You are going to be ok. The last word is de.li.cious delicious. What does that word mean?	It means good, tasty . . . very good food . . .		
Good. –	I got another one right.		
Yes you did.			
Betty, are there parts of the story that you would like for me to read for you, before you begin reading to John?	Yes.		
What section do you want me to read? Show me.		Would you read this section for me?	Ok. "Why, gran'pa," Peter said. "It's good to see you." "Hello, my children," Archie croaked. "Hi, gran'pa!" Susy giggled.
Is there another section you would like for me to read?	No. I think I'm ready to read.		
Ok.			

(p. 10). Furthermore, she did not appear ready to assume the responsibility for helping him with reading at the time she was asked to participate in the study.

Cindy attended six book reading sessions. She became less embarrassed and began to ask her child questions, describe pictures, link items in the text to her daughter's life, and comment on the book's content. After reading all of the little books developed by Mason and McCormick (1985), Cindy became more confident and began selecting more difficult books to read to her young daughter.

Janis participated for the entire eight-week period. Initially, she rarely interacted verbally with her three-year-old daughter during the book reading sessions. She rarely pointed to pictures in the story or used questions that elicited talk from her daughter. Over the course of the eight-week period, Janis started to guide her daughter's attention to the book and to elaborate on her daughter's comments and questions. Most importantly, she started to ask more specific questions throughout the entire book reading session instead of waiting to ask her daughter a few sporadic questions near the end of the session.

Sylvia also participated for the entire eight-week period. She, like Janis, did not initially involve her two sons in an elaborate verbal exchange during the book reading sessions. She tended to read the story hurriedly, which prevented her sons from engaging in an effective book reading interaction with her. Over the course of the eight weeks, Sylvia did learn to slow down. She learned to ask specific questions about the text, point to pictures as well as label and describe them, and, to a limited degree, she learned to elaborate on her sons' comments and questions.

If given continued support, encouragement, and a longer period of time, I feel that both Janis and Sylvia could have acquired more effective interactive book reading styles. Even so, they and the other three participating mothers were sharing what they learned in their one-to-one sessions with me with other Head Start mothers. For example, I overheard one mother say, "Make sure he pays attention. Stop when he gets tired. Give positive comments when he responds well to your questions. Talk about pictures or ask your child what he thinks about the text."

Focused Description of Flora and Her Preschool Daughter Tamara

Flora, the fifth mother, was able to move from using few to using many behaviors described as effective by Heath and others. Initially, Flora clearly lacked a set of understandings and responses appropriate to her daughter's level. Flora asked questions that her daughter could not answer and followed with the demand that her daughter answer. For example, she would ask,

"What do you think of this book?" "What do you think, Tamara?" "Pay attention!" "I asked you 'What do you think?'" Flora shook and spanked Tamara for not responding when she asked her a question. Flora was also unwilling to end the story when Tamara refused to answer the questions. Flora felt compelled to complete the story and did not pay close attention to her daughter's reactions during the book reading interaction.

In the session conducted on November 4, 1985, Flora chose not to read but rather to ask a series of questions about the story *Why Mosquitoes Buzz in People's Ears* (Aardema, 1975). Figure 11−4 is the transcript of this session, which was one of Flora's most difficult sessions with Tamara. During this session, Flora reprimanded Tamara several times and had to force her to respond to her questions. Figure 11−5 is a checklist of the book reading behaviors Flora exhibited during this November 4th session.

Explanation of Flora's Negative Interaction with Tamara

In the fourth book reading session with Tamara, which took place on November 4, Flora's behavior warrants further clarification and amplification. I feel that there are a number of plausible explanations for the negative interaction. After the October 3 session, which was Flora's initial book reading session, Flora and I viewed the videotape and discovered that she had only employed three of the behaviors listed on Resnick's et al. (1987) checklist. She sat adjacent to Tamara, varied her voice, and became so absorbed by the book that she completely ignored Tamara. We both agreed that she had read *Great Day for Up* by Dr. Seuss for her own personal enjoyment. I pointed out to her that I was extremely pleased she had varied her voice, but there were several other behaviors she could incorporate in her interactions with Tamara. For example, she should pause for her child to respond to the text, provide positive reinforcement or feedback, and label or describe the pictures in the text. In subsequent sessions, Flora attempted with moderate success to incorporate my suggestions for improvement.

In the book reading session prior to the November 4 session, Flora informed me that she felt as if she had a handle on what she should be trying to accomplish in her interactions with Tamara. I was pleased with her new-found realization. She asked me to let her take home *Why Mosquitoes Buzz in People's Ears* (Aardema, 1975) because she wanted to read it in her next session with Tamara. She felt by taking the book home she would have time to preview it and become familiar with the language and the parts she should emphasize. Flora told me that the November 4 session would be her "best session" with Tamara, and she reiterated that point on November 4 in her discussion with me, prior to the book reading session. She felt confident and relaxed and informed me that she

Flora's reading of *Why Mosquitoes Buzz in People's Ears*	Flora talking about text	Tamara's Responses
	Today, Tamara and I are going to talk about the book *Why Mosquitoes Buzz in People's Ears*. She is going to read the story by looking at the pictures. She will talk to me about what's going on in the pictures and answer questions that I will ask her about the pictures.	Tamara looks at her mother.
	Tamara can you tell me the name of the book?	Tamara is frowning and squirming in her seat. She does not answer her mother's question.
	What is the title of the book talking about? Tell me something about the book? You are suppose to be talking to me, ok? Talk to me. Read to me. Tell me about it Tamara, ok?	Tamara is silent with her head hung down.
	Now look at the pictures *Why Mosquitoes Buzz in People's Ears*. Tell me again? What's the title of the book? What's the title of the book? [Flora points to the title of the book and slowly says again, *Why Mosquitoes Buzz in People's Ears*.] That's a pretty nice story. Tell me about	Tamara is silent. When Flora persists, Tamara begins to pout and eventually cry.
	it. Now you are suppose to talk to me about the story Tamara. Now I want you to tell me about the title of the book, Tamara. (Flora points to the title again.) Say it for me. (Flora says again *Why Mosquitoes Buzz in People's Ears*.) Say that. Ok, let's look at the pictures. Now tell me about the story.	Tamara is still silent and refuses to answer.
	Tell me about the story. What is that?	Tamara refuses to answer.
	(Flora asks me to stop the tape for a minute.)	
	Talk to me about the story, Tamara. Come on. I want to hear what you know about this story. Come on.	Tamara still remains silent.

continued

Figure 11-4 *Continued*

Flora's reading of *Why Mosquitoes Buzz in People's Ears*	Flora talking about text	Tamara's Responses
	You can do that later. Come on.	Tamara is playing with the bows in her hair.
	Sit up. Sit up.	Tamara slumps down in her chair and turns her back to her mother.
	Tell me about the book. Come on. (Flora is still coaxing Tamara to tell her the title of the book.)	Tamara remains silent.
	See you are doing this because you don't want to do it. But you are going to do it.	Tamara turns around to face Flora while she reprimands her.
	Tamara, I am losing patience with you. You are beginning to act stubborn and I am not going to put up with it. You are going to read this story. Do you hear me?	Tamara looks at Flora as if to say "I still won't answer, you just watch me."
	Tamara, you are not a baby. You are a big girl. (Flora spanks Tamara.) Did you understand what I said. I am simply not going to put up with this behavior, Tamara	Tamara cries.
	Stand up! (Flora shakes and spanks Tamara again.) Did you understand what I said. I'm not putting up with it. Stop it right now. I refuse to let you dictate this session.	Tamara does not say a word. She stands up and receives her spanking. Then she cries, sits down, and stares.
	No! Every time we start a session, you get worse and worse. Now, let's look at the book! Can you tell me about the book?	Tamara finally looks at the book.
	I can't hear you. Ok. Tell me about the book.	"Ok."
	Can you tell me about the picture? Look at that.	"Yes." Tamara looks at the picture.
	Now tell me the name of the book?	*"Mosquitoes Buzz in People's Ears."*
	That's the title of it. That's right.	Child smiles slightly.
	Now why don't you look at the pictures and tell me the story. Ok?	

continued

Figure 11—4   *Continued*

Flora's reading of *Why Mosquitoes Buzz in People's Ears*	Flora talking about text	Tamara's Responses
	What happened? Tell me about. Tell me anything you see in the pictures.	Child is silent.
	What do you see there?	"Mosquitoes."
	Name the animals in the story? Are you ready to work?	Bows her head in agreement.
	What is the mosquito doing?	"Buzzing in people's ears."
	Now, name the animals in the story.	"Iguana, snakes, bird, rabbit, monkey, crow, owl, lion."
	Very good. What are the animals doing?	"Talking to each other."
	How does an iguana look?	"Like a snake, lizard."
	We are going to talk about how each of the animals look, ok?	Tamara bows her head in agreement.

had really worked with Tamara during the past week. She also shared with me that Tamara's teacher and the Head Start director were pleased that she had volunteered to participate in the project. Tamara's teacher had noticed that she rarely talked in class or responded to her questions, and she felt that the book reading project would help Tamara become more responsive. During the past week, Flora felt that she had made progress with Tamara.

The November 4 session began. Flora had high expectations for herself as well as Tamara in this session and things were not turning out the way she had hoped. Flora wanted so much to show me that she had indeed learned some effective book reading behaviors, but Tamara was not cooperating. At first Flora was extremely patient. Her voice tone was not harsh, and she did not display the forcefulness she had in earlier sessions. She smiled, patted Tamara on the shoulder, and she even said "Come on, you can do it, the way we did it at home." "Show me that you are a big girl." Despite Flora's positive coaching, Tamara refused to cooperate. Flora felt embarrassed, let down, betrayed, and even hurt that Tamara was acting this way. She really wanted to do well in this session. Flora felt that she was ready, but failed to recognize that Tamara was not. Flora's patience began to wane and she said, "Tamara, I am losing patience with you. You

Figure 11-5 Flora's Progress Toward the Development of Successful Book Reading Behaviors, November 4, 1985

1. Mother's Body Management

_____ Sits opposite child.
_____ Places child on lap.
_____ Partially encircles child.
_____ Completely encircles child.
_____ Lies alongside child.
__X__ Sits adjacent to child.
_____ Maintains physical contact.

2. Mother's Management of Book

__X__ Previews book.
_____ Allows child to hold book.
_____ Allows child to turn pages.
_____ Permits child to explore book.
_____ Guides child's attention to book.
__X__ Points to pictures/words.
__X__ Asks child questions.
_____ Links items in text to child's life.
__X__ Varies voice.
_____ Emphasizes syllables.
__X__ Acts [makes noises, motions].
__X__ Comments on book's content.
_____ Refers to reading as joint enterprise.
_____ Ends reading episode when child loses interest.
_____ Continues to read after child loses interest.
_____ Resists child turning pages.
_____ Becomes absorbed by book and ignores child.

3. Mother's Language Proficiency

_____ Uses multiple word sentences.
_____ Uses multiple grammatical modes.
__X__ Labels pictures.
__X__ Describes pictures.
_____ Repeats child's vocalization.
_____ Corrects child's vocalization.
_____ Elaborates child's vocalization.
_____ Gives words to child's vocalization.

4. Mother's Attention to Affect

_____ Pauses for child's response.
_____ Inspects child's face.
_____ Praises child.
_____ Comments positively about child's participation.
_____ Gives spoken affirmation.
_____ Makes approving gesture.
__X__ Reprimands child.
__X__ Comments negatively about child's participation.

Source: Adapted from "Mothers Reading to Infants: A New Observational Tool," M.B. Resnick, 1987, _The Reading Teacher_, _40_, no. 9, pp. 888–895.

are beginning to act stubborn, and I am not going to put up with it. You are going to read this book. Do you hear me?" Then Flora spanked Tamara. Tamara cried, but Flora did not end the session and reprimanded her two more times. Flora was determined that this little four-year-old girl was not going to overpower her. In fact, Tamara had already done so.

Since Flora had informed me in our discussion that she had everything under control, I brought Tamara to the room, turned on the camera, and left Flora and Tamara in the room by themselves. Therefore, I did not become aware of the events that happened between Flora and Tamara until I replayed the videotape and discussed it with Flora. I noticed when Tamara left the room that she was calm, but I could tell she had been crying. Flora was visibly upset with herself as well as Tamara. She said "What can I do? Tamara is so stubborn. I know she knew the answers to the questions that I asked her, but she simply would not answer them. I do not know what I am going to do."

I comforted Flora. I told her, "I know you tried hard and I am proud of you for doing so. By no means do I want you to think that I do not have confidence in your sincerity about the project and your willingness to learn more effective book reading behaviors." Flora felt better, and I then asked if she wanted to engage in a dialogue about this session and she said, "Yes." First, I told Flora that the next time Tamara is unwilling to participate, "Please do not force her to do so, and please try not to spank her." I also told her that she should "end the session if it comes down to having to spank Tamara." We certainly did not want to communicate to Tamara that reading was negative; instead we wanted Tamara to view book reading as a positive experience and something that she should look forward to. Additionally, I told Flora to learn to relax with Tamara and that her sessions with her daughter should be fun not drudgery. Even though this was Flora's most difficult session, she moved from using only one positive behavior (varying her voice) on October 3 to using six positive behaviors in the November 4 session. Flora previewed the book, commented on the book's content, varied her voice, made noises and motions, asked questions, and pointed to pictures/words. In the four sessions that followed, I recognized growth in Flora's development toward acquiring successful book reading behaviors. What was most gratifying was the fact that neither Flora nor Tamara cried again.

Initially, Tamara repeatedly gazed at her mother as if to monitor her mother's reactions to her answers. She used rising intonation in her answers as if asking, "Is this right?" Her responses to locative questions were nonverbal, she simply pointed to a pictured object. Even though Flora asked several questions that were difficult to understand, she did ask several questions that Tamara did, in fact, understand but chose not to answer. Tamara's apparent stubbornness persisted for approximately three sessions. It was unclear as to why she simply refused to participate verbally in the sessions, and why she responded with hostility when Flora tried to involve her. There may be some plausible explanations for Tamara's initial stubbornness. For example, when Flora used force, it must have frightened Tamara and caused her to resist her mother's attempts to involve her. Tamara's shyness, as noted by her teacher, may have been another reason for her unwillingness to respond in this strange setting. Flora's attempt to force her may have prompted her to withdraw totally from the reading interaction with her mother. There ensued a battle of wills between Flora and Tamara, with Flora attempting to force Tamara to participate and Tamara rebelling against Flora's efforts to coerce her. Perhaps this was Tamara's way of saying, "Mama, I'm not ready yet. Please give me a little more time and try to be more patient with me."

With my support and encouragement, Flora began asking questions, responding more positively to her daughter's answers and comments, looking at her daughter more often during the book reading sessions, relating the story experiences to their personal experiences, and, most importantly, relaxing and enjoying the time that she and her daughter shared in these book reading sessions. From these sessions, both mother and child developed a repertoire of successful strategies. Figure 11–6 is a checklist of the book reading skills Flora developed over the eight-week period.

Over the course of the eight book reading sessions, the frequency of Tamara's gaze monitoring of her mother and questioning tone shown earlier declined significantly. Later, she began to participate in verbal and nonverbal interactions. She learned to be a more active participant in the book reading sessions. Although she never asked questions, she learned to answer questions. In particular, her answers became more specific and focused.

At the beginning of the study, Tamara's book responses resembled those of a two-year-old. Tamara seemed unable (or unwilling) to identify and name actions in pictures or participate in a verbal dialogue with her mother. She tended either to hunch her shoulders or nod her head in response to her mother's questions. She appeared totally despondent and her feelings were depicted in her facial expressions and body language.

Tamara's apparent unwillingness to cooperate might be attributed to the fact that she had not been previously engaged in book reading interactions and now, at age four, her mother was expecting her to participate actively in such interactions. Tamara might not have been ready for such an intensive interaction, and Flora's eagerness to engage Tamara might have overwhelmed her. For example, Flora's initial questions were similar to those used by the parents of mature four-year-olds, and Tamara seemed unable to participate successfully at this level. She remained silent and did not ask or answer any questions. However, Flora's acquisition of successful

1. Mother's Body Management

_____ Sits opposite child.
_____ Places child on lap.
_____ Partially encircles child.
_____ Completely encircles child.
_____ Lies alongside child.
_X_ Sits adjacent to child.
_X_ Maintains physical contact.

2. Mother's Management of Book

_X_ Previews book.
_X_ Allows child to hold book.
_____ Allows child to turn pages.
_X_ Permits child to explore book.
_X_ Guides child's attention to book.
_X_ Points to pictures/words.
_X_ Asks child questions.
_____ Links items in text to child's life.
_X_ Varies voice.
_____ Emphasizes syllables.
_X_ Acts [makes noises, motions].
_X_ Comments on book's content.
_____ Refers to reading as joint enterprise.
_____ Ends reading episode when child loses interest.
_____ Continues to read after child loses interest.
_____ Resists child turning pages.
_____ Becomes absorbed by book and ignores child.

3. Mother's Language Proficiency

_____ Uses multiple word sentences.
_____ Uses multiple grammatical modes.
_X_ Labels pictures.
_X_ Describes pictures.
_X_ Repeats child's vocalization.
_____ Corrects child's vocalization.
_X_ Elaborates child's vocalization.
_____ Gives words to child's vocalization.

4. Mother's Attention to Affect

_X_ Pauses for child's response.
_X_ Inspects child's face.
_X_ Praises child.
_X_ Comments positively about child's participation.
_____ Gives spoken affirmation.
_X_ Makes approving gesture.
_____ Reprimands child.
_____ Comments negatively about child's participation.

Source: Adapted from "Mothers Reading to Infants: A New Observational Tool," M.B.
Resnick, 1987, *The Reading Teacher*, *40*, no. 9, pp. 888–895.

book reading techniques enabled Tamara to succeed so that she became increasingly able to respond within Flora's maternal scaffolding. Figure 11−7 is a transcript of a successful book reading interaction between Flora and Tamara.

DISCUSSION

An important question is why Flora was able to acquire these successful book reading behaviors to a degree that the other four mothers were not. First of all, Flora was more willing to change, and she was the best reader of the five mothers. Consequently, over the eight-week period I was able to spend concentrated time helping her gain skills to employ in book reading interactions with her young child. Moreover, Flora came to recognize the importance of reading to her preschooler and assisting in her young daughter's understanding of the text. Dunn (1981) noted the importance of parental motivation and belief in children's achievement. He pointed out that children of parents who felt that it was their job to teach children letter and number skills performed more highly on letter naming and number measures than those whose parents did not view these skills to be their responsibility.

While the other four mothers exhibited interest and motivation and acquired some knowledge about book reading, they did not read fluently themselves. As a result, I spent a significant amount of time not only providing information to them about parent-child book reading but also helping to increase their personal literacy skills so they could read to their children. For Betty, Cindy, Sylvia and Janis, I had to pronounce words and discuss what they meant and explain something about the story before they could successfully engage in a book reading interaction with their young children. My interactions with these four mothers were quite different from my interactions with Flora, who could read all of the books. I had to model for these mothers the type of scaffolding they needed to provide for their children during story reading; Flora could try out techniques by discussing them with me.

I do not want to communicate the message that all lower SES mothers cannot read, but I do want to point out that it is a harsh reality that some lower SES mothers do in fact have difficulty reading. Betty was one of those mothers. Betty's development of successful book reading skills would have taken longer, but I would not write off a mother like Betty. I would recommend picture books or wordless picture books for mothers like Betty. Perhaps, in her efforts to hide from me her inability to read well, Betty chose books she in fact could not read. After all, I asked the mothers to select books that they, themselves, felt they could read. Betty obviously

Figure 11−7   **Transcript of a Taped Reading Session,**
              Recorded November 20, 1985

Flora's reading of text *Over in the Meadow*	Flora talking about text	Tamara's responses
	It is important that you talk Tamara. Make sure you respond when I ask you a question.	The child is looking at her mother as she is telling her that she must talk when she asks her questions.
	We are going to read a story. The title of the story, Tamara, is *Over in the Meadow*.	
	Now, as you can see on the front of the book—look at the front and there it is, a meadow. You have plants all around and it is something that is going, that is going to happen in the meadow. Let's look and see.	The child looks at the cover of the book as her mother is talking. She is smiling, because her mother is smiling.
		Child looks.
	Ok?	Child looks again.
Over in the Meadow in the sand in the sun lived an old mother turtle. Dig said the mother. I dig said the One. So we dug all day in the sand in the sun.		
	Look at the turtle.	Child looks.
	Can't you see the mother turtle?	"Yes."
	Ok.	
	And her baby turtle?	Child looks.
	Look at the little turtle.	Child looks again.
	Mama and the turtle they were playing. You see that?	Child looks.
	Where are the turtles? Do you know where the turtles are? They are digging in what?	"In the sand."
	In the sand. That's right.	
Over in the Meadow where the stream runs blue, lives an old mother fish and little fishes Two.		

continued

Figure 11−7 *Continued*

Flora's reading of text *Over in the Meadow*	Flora talking about text	Tamara's responses
	Look at that! Do you know who that was? Who do you think that was? Fish.	Child looks. "Fish."
	Mother Fish and how many baby fishes? Two.	"Two."
	Very good listening, ok? I like the way you are listening.	Child nods. Child smiles.
Over in the Meadow in a hole in the tree lived a mother blue bird and her little birdies Three. Sing said the mother. We sing said the Three. So they sang and they were glad in the hole in the tree.		
	How many little birds were there? How many did I say? There were how many? Count them. Want to count them? How many babies?	"Four?" Child is silent. "One, two . . . One, two, three. Three."
	Three baby birds. Very good. And where were they? Where were the babies? In where? Where was the hole? Where was the hole? Where is there? In what? They are living up in a what? A hole in a tree. Ok. Let's go on.	Child smiles. Child is silent. "In the hole. Hole." "Hole. Right there. Hole." "In the tree." Child smiles. Child waits to go on.

wanted to impress me. Unlike Cindy, Betty chose difficult books and was unsuccessful, and that may be one of the reasons she felt compelled to drop out of the study. Though I suggested to her that she try easier books and perhaps she would be more successful, she refused to continue.

Cindy, like Betty, had some difficulty reading, but she chose to start with the little books developed by Mason and McCormick (1985). Cindy wanted to realize success, and the little books provided her with that opportunity. Cindy was also encouraged by me and the Head Start director to go back to school and get her GED. I feel that Cindy's interaction with her young daughter helped her realize the importance of being literate.

Even though Janis and Sylvia read more easily than Betty and Cindy, they needed my assistance with some words and sought my advice on how to phrase certain parts of stories they selected to read to their children. A significant amount of the time I spent with Janis involved showing her how to increase her verbal interactions with her daughter and ways she could explore books. The time I spent with Sylvia was mostly focused on getting her to slow down and on showing her how to pause, how to ask/answer questions, and how to make comments about the text. Because the time spent during sessions prior to book reading focused so heavily on the mothers' literacy development and an understanding of how they should participate in book reading interactions with their children, it was difficult to see the implementation of these 'new skills' due to the brevity of the study.

CONCLUSIONS AND RECOMMENDATIONS

Although we should develop programs at school to help lower SES children make a smooth transition from home to school, Teale (1987) questioned whether the "classroom storybook reading experience [can] substitute for the more intimate one-to-one (or one-to-two or three) interactions typical of the home" (p. 64). Morrow (1988; 1987) is an advocate of classroom storybook reading for children who come to school not having been read to, but she too recognizes the importance of the home and recommends the need to "continuously inform parents about the importance of reading to their children" (Morrow, 1987, p. 82). I argue that to simply inform parents about the importance of reading to their children is not sufficient. This study suggests that we must go beyond *telling* lower SES parents to help their children with reading. We must show them how to participate in parent-child book reading and support their attempts to do; we must help them become confident readers simultaneously. At the same time, we must not assume that lower SES parents cannot acquire the necessary skills to engage in successful book reading interactions with their children. To make such an assumption only reinforces the self-fulfilling prophecy that lower SES parents are incapable of helping their children.

One of the most important results of this study was that these five mothers participated in a literacy event they had not been engaged in previously. While I have no way of knowing whether they will continue to read to their children, I do know at least that they were introduced to a new literacy event (sharing books with their children). Even though some of the mothers showed more progress than others, I feel that they all could have acquired more interactive book reading strategies had I had a longer period of time to spend with them.

The growth in Flora's and her young daughter's ability to interact during parent-child book reading raises the question of why children like this preschooler do not quickly master this activity in the school setting. Two factors may account for the difference. First, parent-child communication provides a much more intensive apprenticeship than can be found in the one-to-many interactions in school settings. Even when a child receives individualized attention from a teacher, such contact is not sufficiently frequent or lengthy to achieve the fine-tuning that a parent can give. Morrow (1988) admits that "one-to-one readings in school can be time-consuming" and suggests that "asking aides, volunteers, and other children to read to youngsters could be helpful" (p. 105). While this approach is helpful, it is not sufficient. Research comparing mothers and teachers engaging in the same dyadic task with children has shown that mothers and teachers act differently, the mothers acting to provide maximum assistance for children's success, the teachers working for maximum independence on the part of the children (Edwards, 1988a). In institutional interactions, a child is unlikely to achieve the level of understanding or develop the participation strategies made possible in the parental tutorial.

Due to the limited number of studies in this particular area of emergent literacy, more information is needed about the book reading behaviors of lower income families. Also, we need more information about the potential for encouraging and supporting mothers to engage in book reading interactions with their young children. Teale (1986b) noted that "we are still in a period in which the area of emergent literacy is lacking in coherence," and he warns that "descriptive research of this nature is very labor-intensive, and longitudinal study of storybook reading is even more so" (p. 199). However, additional insights into lower SES home environments and these children's literacy development are essential.

Models like the ones described in this study may work for some parents. Regardless of the strategy selected, the poignant message emerging from this study is that the time has come for teachers to shift from *telling* to *showing* lower SES parents how to read with their children. Presently, I am involved in a year-long research project aimed at showing instead of telling lower SES mothers (both black and white) how to read effectively with their children. Videotapes developed by kindergarten and first-grade teachers, the parents, themselves, and myself comprise the training materials. I plan to spend school year 1988–89 studying the development and progress of these mothers toward acquiring the necessary skills to interact with their young children effectively during storybook reading (Edwards, 1988b). Even though I feel my approach to answering some critical questions about parent-child book reading in lower SES populations is valid, I recognize that there are a number of other strategies that teachers can employ. Teachers as well as administrators need to select the most appropriate combination of strategies that would best meet the needs of their parent-child population.

NOTES

[1]It should be noted here that the Resnick et al. instrument was used in my retrospective analysis of the data and served as an excellent way for me to highlight for the reader specific book reading behaviors each mother had acquired.

[2]The text of *Time for Bed* is as follows: "read a story, brush your teeth, get a hug, climb in bed, nighty-night sleep tight." For each phrase there is a corresponding picture on the page.

Chapter after chapter has emphasized the importance of the home-school connection. In Edwards' chapter, we saw parents trying to learn more about school expectations. In Chapter 12, we are urged as educators to try to learn more about family and community expectations and literacy sets. We can do this by asking parents to share their children's and their own literacy experiences, by spending time in the communities in which their children live, and by creating literacy opportunities for personal identity and participation in community life— maintaining and strengthening children's connections with their families and communities.

Chapter 12

Learning from Families: Implications for Educators and Policy

Denny Taylor
Dorothy S. Strickland

INTRODUCTION

What makes families work is the irrational involvement of a parent and a child. Some might call this love but it is also commitment. It is the whatever-happens-I-will-love-you that empowers families and enables children to survive. In the research studies (Taylor, 1983; Taylor & Dorsey-Gaines, 1988; Taylor and Strickland, 1986; Taylor, in progress) of *functioning families* (see Hansen, 1981; Schlesinger, 1982) that form the basis for this chapter, irrational involvement, love, and commitment come together as parents create a firm foundation for their children's lives. And yet, it is evident from these long-term studies that love and commitment are not always enough to counter the societal risks that endanger children and jeopardize families. The shifting patterns in social, political, and economic support for families creates an uncertain climate that makes it impossible for some parents and difficult for others to provide healthy environments in which children can grow up to live enjoyable and productive lives.

251

In recent years much attention has been given in the research literature to the interrelationships between the social and academic lives of young children (Bissex, 1980, 1984; Bloome, 1983; Clark, 1984; Fahs, 1987; Ferreiro, 1984; Gilmore & Glatthorn, 1982; Goldenberg, 1987; Grannis, 1987a, 1987b, 1987c; Green, Weade & Graham, in press; Heath, 1983; Kifer, 1977; McDermott, 1976; Strickland & Taylor, 1988; Taylor, 1983; Taylor & Dorsey-Gaines, 1988; Taylor & Strickland, 1986a, 1986b). Many of these researchers have focused on language and literacy as social processes that cannot be separated from the social development of young children. The implications of these studies leave us in little doubt that many of the societal risks that impact upon the lives of young children can become academic risks that increase in severity as children progress through school.

In this chapter we will explore some of the ways in which the changing patterns of the social organization of everyday life affect the literacy learning opportunities of children both at home and at school. But first we will provide a context for this discussion by describing ways in which families can be regarded as educational institutions, where parents and children educate one another. We will explore (1) the moment-to-moment uses of literacy, (2) the deliberate uses of literacy that can occur in family settings, (3) the multiple meanings of any literacy event that occurs in family settings, and (4) the dynamics of shared and solitary literacy experiences. In this way we will establish a framework that supports the notion that language and literacy are social processes that cannot be separated from the social development of young children.

We will then examine the impact of stress upon the literacy learning opportunities of children both at home and at school. We will discuss briefly (1) how rituals, routines, and the use of time and space influence the literate learning opportunities of individual children, (2) how critical incidents can impede or constrain their literacy learning opportunities, and (3) how critical incidents can enhance their literacy learning opportunities.

Throughout this chapter, as we focus upon parents and children as members of families that are educational institutions, we will be continually addressing the question of how our interpretations can be used by educators to inform policy and to improve educational practices. What can teachers and administrators learn from ethnographic studies of families and literacy? How can they become better informed about the family lives of their students? How can they make use of this information to structure curriculum, to support home-school relations, and to improve the quality of family life? These questions are deliberately embedded in the text so that our ethnographic descriptions, questions, and interpretive explanations are closely connected and conveniently juxtaposed.

FAMILIES AS EDUCATIONAL INSTITUTIONS IN WHICH PARENTS AND CHILDREN EDUCATE ONE ANOTHER

In families, parents and children learn from one another—a mother learns to read storybooks with each new child and each child learns to share books with his father as well as his mother (Taylor & Strickland, 1986). Parents and children have their own personal styles and agendas that influence the ways in which they live together and educate one another. Undoubtedly, "the interplay of the individual biographies and educative styles of the parents becomes the dominant factor in shaping the literate experiences of the children within the home. And yet, from the very beginning, the children are active and reactive in the sharing of literate experiences with their parents" (Taylor, 1983, p. 23).

Moment-to-Moment Literacy Experiences of Parents and Children

Many (perhaps most) of the literate experiences that occur at home take place as parents and children go about their daily lives. Many of the types and uses of literacy that have been found in family settings are literacy "events" that pass by unnoticed as print is used to fulfill some purpose of everyday life. For example, families use written messages to communicate with one another. In *Family Literacy* (Taylor, 1983) the tale is told of Dan Dawson being called away on a business trip after Jessie, his wife, had left for work. Dan left her a note on the kitchen table that stated where he was going and how long he would be away. Tacked on the bottom of the note was the postscript, "I've found my underwear." The purpose of the note was to communicate vital information. Jessie needed to know about the trip. The postscript was a personal note, a reminder of a shared experience.

It is in such ways that messages are written in many families as parents and children try to keep on top of their busy schedules and maintain family relationships. From the study of families in which there is not a parent at home on a full-time basis (Taylor, 1988c) it is difficult to imagine how families cope with the stresses and strains of their day-to-day lives without schedules and written notes. This position is graphically confirmed in the Shay Avenue Study, *Growing Up Literate* (Taylor & Dorsey-Gaines, 1988), which focuses upon black inner-city families living below the poverty level. This study provides further insights into the moment-to-moment print involvement that is typical of so many American families, while at the same time it confirms that there is no social, cultural, or racial monopoly on the types of literacy used in our society. Expanding upon the types and uses of

Table 12−1   **Types and Uses of Reading—Categories Described in the Shay Avenue Study***

Categories	Types & Uses of Reading	Examples
Instrumental	Reading to gain information for meeting practical needs, dealing with public agencies and scheduling daily life.	Directions on toys, watches, and radios sold in the street or bought in stores; labels, addresses in address books; telephone numbers in address books & written on old envelopes or scraps of paper; notes left on refrigerator; applications for food stamps, AFDC, WICS; applications for Housing Assistance Payments Program; letter of default for nonpayment of rent; hospital bracelet worn to show need of assistance; job applications; notices of graduations; cutting out coupons from the paper and saving coupons included in packages to use when food shopping.
Social Interactional	Reading to gain information pertinent to building and maintaining social relationships.	Letters from friends and children away for the summer; letters received from prisoners, some of whom one has never met, others one has visited, many of whom are serving life sentences; greeting cards; newspaper features notices of local events, births and deaths.
News-related	Reading to gain information about third parties or distant events, or reading to gain information about local, state, and national events.	Newspaper items; news magazines; flyers; news items about local politics; news items about present governor and the candidates in state primaries.
Confirmational	Reading to check or confirm facts or beliefs, often from archival materials stored and retrieved only on special occasions.	Birth certificates; social security cards; school report cards; honor roll cards; personal attendance records for work; letter of recommendation; children's letters, poems, and drawings; newspaper cuttings (e.g., a cartoon box with the heading "Graffiti" and the message, "The cost of failure is greater than the price of success".

continued

Table 12−1 *continued*

Categories	Types & Uses of Reading	Examples
Recreational	Reading during leisure time or in planning for recreational events.	Reading local and national newspapers; magazines (*Time, Newsweek, Ebony, Essence, Jet, Black Enterprise*); books; poetry (written by friends or cut from the newspaper); clues to crossword puzzles and conundrums; comics and cartoons.
Critical/Educational	Reading to fulfill educational requirements of school and college courses. Reading to increase one's ability to consider and/or discuss political social, aesthetic, or religious knowledge. Reading to educate oneself.	Textbooks and papers, real estate, paralegal and insurance, also general courses in sociology and psychology; reading *Time, Newsweek, Black Enterprise*; reading stories (occasionally) to small books on criminal law; researching individual cases; literature to help with one's own political and social situation—"Trust in Renting" "A Guide to the Rights and Responsibilities of Residential Tenants and Landlords."

*Categories adapted from "Ways with Words" by Shirley Brice Heath.

reading and writing identified by Heath (1983), the examples of literacy in Tables 12−1—12−4 were collected from the families in the Shay Avenue study.

The families used print to fulfill requirements for assistance, to build and maintain social relationships, and to create a socio-historical context for their everyday lives. Much went by unnoticed. On many occasions the act of reading or writing was not the focus of attention, the print had no intrinsic value, the "message" was embedded in some other event, useful within the context in which it was written or read but otherwise appearing to be of little importance (see also Teale, 1986).

The Deliberate Uses of Literacy in Family Settings

Perhaps the most obvious example of the deliberate uses of literacy in family settings is family storybook reading (Taylor and Strickland, 1986a). This does not mean that parents deliberately set out to teach their children to read (in our experience most do not). It does mean that in many families a conscious decision is made to share books and that storybook reading

Table 12−2   **Types and Uses of Reading—Categories Emerging from the Shay Avenue Neighborhood Study**

Categories	Types & Uses of Reading	Examples
Socio-Historical	Reading to explore one's personal identity and the social, political, and economic circumstances of one's everyday life. Conserving writings to be re-read and cherished that create a permanent record of the family's life history.	Autobiographical writings; writing of names of family members in the family bible; saving the first writings of one's children, poems they have written, pictures that they have drawn; birthday cards and love letters.
Financial	Reading to consider (and sometimes to make changes to) the economic circumstances of one's everyday life. Reading to fulfill practical (financial) needs of everyday life.	Keeping an eye on the economy with the view to establishing a small silk-screening business; reading reports of the stock market, prices of cars and appliances; reading apartment ads paying particular attention to prices; reading forms that include statements about one's financial status; reading "money-off' coupons; reading prices in supermarkets and on other products.
Environmental	Reading the print in the environment.	Signs on store fronts and businesses; road signs; billboards; teeshirts and bubble gum wrappers.

"becomes a part of everyday life, with rituals and routines that seem to fit the needs and interests of individual family members" (Taylor and Strickland, 1986a, p. 19). Books *energize* the experiences that families share (Taylor, in press), and as this sharing takes place an interest grows in the printed words that stories contain. Important language and literacy lessons take place, and although many parents are adamant that they are not teaching reading per se, most parents with whom we have spoken appear to believe that storybook reading helps to prepare their children for learning to read and write in school.

Many of the deliberate uses of literacy found in family settings occur when moment-to-moment uses of literacy are in some way lifted out of context to become specific events that are the focus of attention. Clearly the designation of an event as one thing or the other is an interpretive construction. Nevertheless, such constructions are helpful to us as we try to understand the types and uses of literacy in family settings. In *Growing Up Literate* (Taylor & Dorsey-Gaines, 1988), Ieshea spoke of the notes that

Table 12−3   Types and Uses of Writing—Categories Described in the Shay Avenue Study*

Categories	Types & Uses of Writing	Examples
Reinforcement or substitute for oral message	Writing used when direct oral communication was not possible or a written message was needed for legal purposes.	Messages written to children and other family members; letters written to teachers (regarding homework, immunization etc.); letter requesting a copy of high school record.
Social Interactional	Writing to establish, build, and maintain social relationships. Writing to negotiate family responsibilities.	Letters to family members and friends, letters to prisoners; letters to children ("I Love You" letters, "clean up your room" letters); thank you letters; greeting cards; writing and drawing with young children; helping with homework assignments.
Memory Aids	Writing to serve as a memory aid for both the writer and others.	Writing of college schedules (dates, classes, instructors, assignments); bathroom schedule for potty training; recipes; monthly planner (appointments and information to be remembered); list of post-natal exercises; list of friends to attend baby shower; menu for Thanksgiving dinner; notes on refrigerator; notes on dates of menstrual cycle; lists of books read and books to read.
Financial	Writing to record numerals and to write out amounts and purposes of expenditures, and for signatures.	Writing weekly and monthly budgets; working out financial payments; filling out forms that require statements on financial status; signatures on checks.
Expository	Tasks (occasionally) brought home from work, often from educational institutions.	College and school papers; writings on criminal law.
	Writing in connected prose to summarize generalizations and back-up specifics for other people.	Statement to children regarding the running of the household.
	Writer envisions or "knows" audience and writes to the addressee.	Autobiographical writings.

*Categories adapted from "Ways with Words" by Shirley Brice Heath.

Table 12-4   **Types and Uses of Writing—Categories Emerging from the Shay Avenue Neighborhood Study**

Categories	Types & Uses of Writing	Examples
Instrumental	Writing to meet practical needs and manage/organize everyday life; writing to gain access to social institution or helping agency.	Writing schedules; keeping calendars and appointments; planning a Thanksgiving dinner; keeping telephone and address books; signing name on "visitors pass" to gain access to school application for day care; school forms; summer programs; health check-up forms; hospital forms; instrumental filling in form of Existing Housing Assistance Payments Program.
Autobiographical	Writing to understand oneself; to record one's life history; to share life with others.	Letters written to oneself in difficult times; keeping a journal; writing names of family members, circling them and writing "my family"; writing names of new babies.
Recreational	Writing during leisure time for the enjoyment of the activity.	Crossword puzzles; conundrums; doodling; writing letters.
Creative	Writing as a means of self-expression.	Writing poetry; painting with children, experimenting with the size, shape and color of letters and the configuration of letters in words; writing names of family members in different forms of script; playing with the configurations of letters in the names.
Educational	Writing to fulfill college assignments. Writing to educate oneself.	Practicing shorthand; typing to increase speed and accuracy; writing drafts and final copies of term papers; writing out notes pertaining to criminal law; writing out lines from books read and poems from books read; writing down poetry that someone has recited.
Work-Related	Writing pertaining to employment or self-employment.	Bringing home work from a realtor and insurance agency; preparing lettering for silk-screening (names and signs on tee-shirts); sign making.
Environmental	Writing in public places for others to read.	Designing and painting signs for store fronts and businesses.

she left for her children to tell them that she would not be home. Quick notes were jotted down as she hurried through a busy day; other notes were more deliberately written. For example, great care and attention was paid to the letters that Ieshea wrote in response to situations that arose as her children progressed through school. Drafts were made and a dictionary used. One such note reads as follows:

> Dear Ms. ———— ,
>
> Thank you for your note regarding Teko's failure to complete his homework assignments. Except for one occasion when he told me that he had left his book in class, I was under the impression that he was completing his homework* [see insertion below]. I do not want, nor expect, Teko to be excluded from doing any mandatory school assignments. Furthermore, I cannot conceive of him having told you that he couldn't complete his assignment because he was not home in the evening. Teko is in the house *every* evening before dark, which provides him with ample time to do his homework before his ["his" crossed out] bedtime.
>
> Your note seemed to have been directed towards me in the form of a reprimand for preventing my son from doing his homework. Needless to say, I resent the implication.* (p. 156)

When Ieshea talked about the note she said that the last two sentences were an insert, but she added that she did not think that she had actually included them in the letter that she eventually sent to school. Another draft that she had kept was of a letter to the school nurse in response to a letter questioning Ieshea about the shots Danny was supposed to have received before attending school. Ieshea explained that her son had all of his shots and that the letter had made her angry. She said, "I was so mad at her I didn't know what to do! So I would write and rewrite it." Thus we can say that Ieshea deliberately wrote and that the language of her letter ("I strongly object to the manner in which you have acted relative to the inforcement of the provisional entry clause") was carefully constructed. Writing enabled her to deal with her anger as well as helping her to create an image of herself as a highly articulate and educated woman.

Building upon the types and uses of literacy defined by Heath (1983), we can say that there are times when reading and writing are deliberate acts, when the text becomes as important as the message that it contains. Clearly, such a position is possible in all of the categories presented in the tables on pages 254–258.

The Multiple Meanings of Any Literacy Event That Occurs in Family Settings

In focusing on literacy events in family settings, an openness of meaning is essential. At any one time multiple interpretations are possible, and possibilities for different interpretations are created over time. If we look first at the literacy event as it occurs, we find that for each of the participants the occasion (unless literacy is a solitary endeavor) is socially constructed and personally interpreted through the interplay of the family members' individual biographies and educative styles. In *Creating Family Story* (Taylor, 1986), a mother shares *Chester Cricket's Pigeon Ride* with her three children (Matthew, who is two, Sarah, five, and Jessica, seven). Together they create personal and family meaning for the occasion. Much of the talk is logically relevant to the story, but at one point in the story Matthew puts a marble in his mouth and will not take it out. In this potentially critical real-life situation, the family must use language effectively. An analysis of their reactions to the problem shows that their talk is multi-functional (Taylor, in press). It is instrumental, regulatory, interactional, personal, imaginative, heuristic, and informative:

> Cullen and Sarah talk to Matthew while Jessica holds her breath as she anxiously waits for the marble to be retrieved from Matthew's mouth. Immediately we can speak of the language used by Cullen and Sarah as instrumental and regulatory. Both mother and daughter are working to persuade Matthew to give them the marble, and in this way they are attempting to control his behavior. Sarah, 5, is a sophisticated persuader. "I'll give you a piggy," she croons. We could speak of their talk as interactional, for Sarah and Cullen work cooperatively as they encourage Matthew to give them the marble. "Let Sarah show you how a marble will roll," Cullen says to Matthew. Then Sarah demonstrates.
>
> Expressions of individuality and personality are clearly visible in the family talk. Cullen's patience and Sarah's willingness to help are plain to see, while Jessica's quiet concern is easily recognizable in the way she sucks in her breath. Then it is Jessica who brings the family back to the story as she reads to them from the book. This is the role that Jessica has played several times during the reading of the story, she keeps them "on track." On one occasion Jessica said, "Now keep going," bringing her mom back to the book.

As the event takes place, each family member is active and reactive in attempting to get Matthew to take the marble out of his mouth. Looking from the outside in we can see that it is not the same occasion for the individual children participating in the event. Matthew listens as Sarah persuades, Jessica watches and is ready to bring her family back to the book when the marble is retrieved, while their mother eventually decides that the marble must be removed even if it has to be taken without Matthew's consent. Thus, we can say that multiple meanings are constructed in and around any literacy event, and that moment-to-moment occasions are sometimes embedded in the activity that lead to further interpretation and social construction. At the time of the occurrence the event is dynamic, creative, and constantly evolving. Each family member participates in personal ways that lead to individual interpretations of what is happening.

Over time these interpretations change. Old events are seen through subsequent events. In *Growing Up Literate* (Taylor & Dorsey-Gaines, 1988, p. 154), the example is given of Jerry reading cases in criminal law while he was in prison. He read and took notes to check facts about the law in archival material, so we can say that his reading was *confirmational*; it was also *social-interactional*, as he read to help his fellow prisoners with their particular cases. Jerry's reading was undoubtedly *critical/educational*, as he increased his understanding of the law and his ability to discuss the cases that he studied. In another sense, his reading was *instrumental* in that he was trying to help some of the other prisoners. Eventually the books that Jerry read and the notes that he made became *autobiographical* and *socio-historical*. They contained memories of another time and place that were seen by him through his subsequent experience.

The Dynamics of Shared and Solitary Literacy Experiences

Moment-to-moment and deliberate uses of literacy can change over time. They can also be social events as well as solitary endeavors. In *Family Literacy* (Taylor, 1983), a description of one literacy event serves to illustrate how all these dynamics come into play. On a search for print with Karen, a mother participating in the study, some of Debbie's (four years and ten months) writing was found (see Figure 12–1). The first line was easy to make out, 'The chick and t." Karen said she thought it should say, "The Chick and the Duck," as she was sure Debbie was copying the title of a book they had just read. She then decided that the second line was probably the dedication, "To Libby," and the third line was the beginning of the text, "A duck." The impetus for Debbie to copy the title and dedication of this book grew from a shared experience of reading with her mother and sister. Karen deliberately chose to read stories with her children (although it should be emphasized that her intention was not to teach them to read), but there were many occasions when she just picked up a book to

Figure 12–1   **Debbie's Writing**

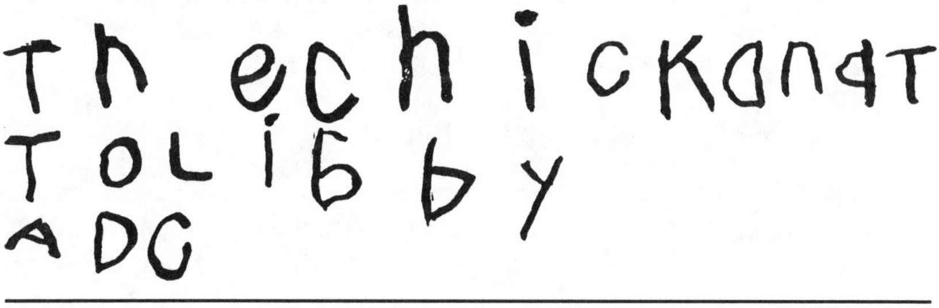

fill an odd moment or to calm a troubled child. Whether this book was one read in passing or one deliberately chosen for bedtime reading is not known. However, we do know that Debbie chose to use the book in a solitary moment to copy the dedication at a time when she had become increasingly interested in practicing how to write. At that time, she was interested in the writing—what it looked like and how it was made.

Alternatively, solitary occasions can become shared endeavors. A book is read and later a story is told. A form is filled in and then its contents discussed. Sometimes solitary events take place in the company of friends. A newspaper is silently read in a busy room. A comment is made, a news item is shared, and reading the newspaper becomes a social event. In *Growing Up Literate* (Taylor & Dorsey-Gaines, 1988), an account is given of the ways in which Pauline, a young mother, read newspapers with her family and friends. There were always many local and national papers in Pauline's apartment. Sometimes on Sundays there were five copies of the same paper as everyone bought his or her own. Reading together and sharing opinions and views on articles read was a frequent pastime. Someone would read an article, comment to whoever might be listening, and listen to the response that usually followed.

> On one occasion Pauline, Trisha, and Trisha's boyfriend Jack were in one of the bedrooms trying to keep cool from the shallow breeze that traveled the narrow passageway between the house in which they lived and the one next door. The three young people were sitting and lying across the bed, taking full advantage of the cool air that came in through the window. There was a newspaper on the bed, and from time to time each of them picked it up and read. Talking and reading, they enjoyed a respite from the heat. It was the day that Alexander Haig resigned as Secretary of State. Pauline said she wondered who would be the next Secretary of State and commented on statements she had read about the political situation. Cora [Pauline's mother] came into the bedroom as this conversation took place, and she commented that Reagan wasn't interested in the poor. She said that it was bad that Reagan had cut so many of the subsidies that go into services for children, and the conversation reached a local level as the family talked about the recent cutting of the playground program that had existed for several years previously. By then, Jack was reading again. The talk about the political and local situation ended as Cora told Jack, who was wearing shorts, that he had better not go into the diner where she worked, as the waitresses would be caressing his legs. Jack laughed and went on reading (p. 133–34).

Implications for Educational Policy

Solitary and shared, deliberate and momentary, social-interactional, news-related, and recreational, literacy is a complex, multi-dimensional phenomenon that can be described and appraised. In family settings literacy can be teased apart and examined but we can never account for it with numbers or tests. Within families, learning tends to be natural and purposeful, with parents and children engaged in meaning making. They try to make sense of the world in which they live. Their understandings are historically located in the lives they live together. New meanings are made from old. When children join the community of learners at school their learning experiences change. The complex orchestration of literacy events that many children have become accustomed to at home are reduced in school to lifeless activities, devoid of meaning and accomplished for no other purpose than to be checked as correct or incorrect. This literate disparity, which exists in the lives of so many children, is illustrated in the following examples of one child's writing. In his first-grade classroom Patrick was not expected to copy the dictation exercises from the chalkboard. His teacher said that he could not do the task. However, his parents insisted that he be given the opportunity to try and so he produced texts similar to the one that follows (Figure 12−2):

> Tab is a sad cat.
> Tab has a pal.
> His pal is Mac.
> Mac is a rat.

There is little to say about Patrick's school writing. It is not authentic. It is meaningless. Of course, it is not meant to be a personal piece of writing. Many of Patrick's letters were rewritten in red, as a major concern was that he could not form his letters appropriately for a first-grade child. Occasionally, the students wrote stories with lead sentences given to them by their teacher, but much of their writing was in the form of workbook pages, dittos, and dictation exercises. At the time that Patrick wrote about Tab at school he wrote the following story out of school (Figure 12−3):

> I like to climb mountains. It is scary. I am climbing Whiteface tomorrow. I fell down the mountain today. I fell in the lake. I was mad. Just like the frog. Then the frog climbed the mountain. He fell too. We are mad. We got out. The puppy fell too. The puppy growled. We were all mad, even the puppy was mad.

This personal narrative opens with a topic sentence and proceeds to develop the opening idea in terms of his intentions, his experiences, and his feelings. It is logical and presents an orderly progression of ideas. It is clear from this story that Patrick understands how stories are put down on paper. He uses the full page, he has spaces between the words, and he has begun to revise. His spelling is moving from invented to standard in a very normal progression. Use of initial consonants is almost totally standard. His substitution of *kl* for *cl* is one of the remaining inventions, which is a

Figure 12-2   **Patrick's In-School Writing**

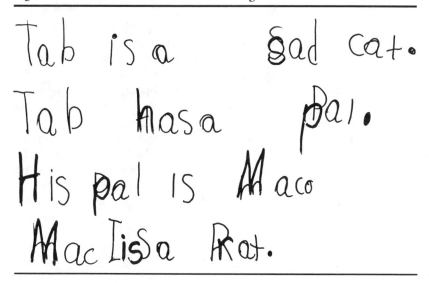

Tab is a   sad cat.
Tab has a   pal.
His pal is Mac
Mac is a Rat.

high level substitution and a common approximation found in the writing of young children. There are a significant number of vowels, used correctly, and some frequently used words have been written in standard spelling. What is particularly interesting about Patrick's story is that he has incorporated many elements from other stories that he has written and from stories that he has read. For example, "Just like the frog" is a reference to an earlier story in which a frog fell down a mountain, and "the puppy" is from a story that he had read. Patrick had asked about the spelling of puppy, and when he wrote the story presented above he remembered how to spell the word.

Unfortunately for Patrick, and for so many other children like him, his school work is judged by his ability to reproduce texts and not by his ability to create them. Patrick is now in second grade and his stories have become imaginatively inventive and occasionally quite remarkable (Taylor, 1988b). However, his stories are not recognized in school as an important "indicator" of his academic development, and he has been referred to the child study team for coding as a child with a language-based learning disability.

If the interpretations of family literacy that are presented here are accepted by educators and policy makers, then the implications for curriculum and instruction in schools can be stated as follows:

1. *Reading and writing instruction begins with the children that we teach.* We need to ask ourselves:
    a. What does this child know about language?
    b. How does this child construct language?

Figure 12–3 Patrick's Out-of-School Writing

1 I lik to Klma
mountai ns It is.
skare I amklimeh rw
whiteface tmro
I fel don the
moun ta inStodog
I fel in the lak I wg
mad jusl like the fog
then the fog Kim th
moun ta in hefel
to we are mad.

2 we got oot the
puppy fel to the pupp,
growled we were
ol mad erin the pug
wus mad

   c. How can I create authentic, meaningful literacy experiences for this child that will build upon and expand upon the types and uses of literacy that are already a part of her everyday life?

2. *Reading and writing instruction begins with the families of the children that we teach.* To construct answers to the questions that we have asked about each of the children we must know something of their families. We need to ask parents
   a. to tell us about their children,
   b. to share with us their children's drawings and writings,
   c. to talk with us about their own literacy experiences.

3. *Reading and writing instruction begins with the place in which the children that we teach live.* To understand the types and uses of literacy that are a part of everyday life we must become accustomed to the community in which the children spend their everyday lives.
   a. We need to spend time in the community by ourselves and with the children.
   b. During these visits we need to collect examples of the types and uses of literacy that we find in the community and bring them into the school.
   c. We need to bring members of the community into the school to participate in literacy events that are jointly constructed to expand upon what the children know about reading and writing in and out of school.

4. *Reading and writing instruction builds upon, expands, modifies, and creates new meanings of the types and uses of literacy that the children will need in their everyday lives.* We need to create school environments that build upon the lives of the children that we teach. Literacy instruction should confirm what individual children already know, build upon their own self-image, and empower them to participate in reading and writing activities that have direct relevance to their everyday lives. Literacy should *enable* children
   a. to meet their practical needs in everyday life,
   b. to build and maintain social relationships,
   c. to gain information about local and national events,
   d. to explore their own identities and the personal circumstances of their everyday lives.

If we as educators and policy makers can create school environments in which literacy makes sense, we will create genuine opportunities for children to *use* literacy in meaningful ways. Much of their learning will be historically located, some learning experiences will occur moment-to-moment at the margins of awareness, and others will be specifically located within the structure and form of the print that is constructed when written or read.

IMPACT OF STRESS UPON THE LITERATE LEARNING OPPORTUNITIES OF CHILDREN AT HOME AND AT SCHOOL

There is no doubt that some educators and policy makers will continue to believe that teaching "the basics" of reading and writing as a set of discrete, decontextualized skills will enable children to become literate. For these educators, the arguments that we have presented for shared literacy experiences that build upon the events in children's everyday lives will be negated. But there are other compelling reasons to create environments for children that pay attention to their lives in out-of-school settings. In a recent *Boston Globe* article (Wyman, 1987) on stress in "top suburban high schools," the statement is made that the students in these schools are contending with stressful environments both at home and at school that were unheard of ten years ago. "Kids in crisis" are described as suffering from frustration, anxiety, and depression. High levels of stress at school are often compounded by high levels of stress at home. The *Globe* cites one senior who spoke of the six or seven parents who had died during the previous year. The senior said that two of them had committed suicide. One counselor interviewed talked of problems ranging from "benign neglect to abuse and abandonment."

In a study of the impact of school stress on early adolescents in an urban junior high school, Grannis (1987a, b, & c) revealed that the question of control over stressor events was critical. Although students varied considerably in the ways that they tried to deal with the stress in their lives, they were all very alert to the events in school that they found personally stressful. The students participating in the study spoke of such incidents as the disruption of class work, physical assaults on themselves and their possessions, and the general disorganization in their school as highly stressful. Some students were found to cope better than others. Some students were so incapacitated by the stress in their lives that they were left back or they dropped out of school. Grannis reports that "even the adults in the environment felt that the things that happened there were beyond their control" (p. 19). He argues convincingly that the adults' inabilities to cope with the stress in their environment had a profoundly negative effect upon the children's own coping abilities.

We are all accustomed to stress in our lives. Learning to cope with stress is a natural part of growing up, and we continue coping throughout our adult lives until the ways that we cope with stress become a part of our growing old. But when stress becomes so acute that we cannot overcome the difficulties that we face, then our ability to cope breaks down, our lives become disrupted. We are overwhelmed and unable to maintain the rituals and routines of our daily lives.

In talking about the stress that parents and children experience in functioning families, a mother asked her sixth-grade daughter what she found most stressful in her daily life. The daughter wrote the following list:

1. Kids telling other kids untrue things about me.
2. Losing my two best friends.
3. People writing notes about me.
4. Not being accepted for who I am
5. Accused of being boring because I don't french kiss.
6. Not being able to be myself without someone saying something
7. The family being under so much stress
8. Getting recent bad grades on two tests.

The child who wrote the list is unhappy in school but continues to cope with the situation. Unfortunately, not all children are capable of such fortitude. For many children in daycare and school settings, the stress can be so acute that it interferes with their ability to participate socially and/or academically within the school community (Elkind, 1981, 1987; Honig, 1986a, 1986b). The lives of children become fractured and their ability to cope becomes dysfunctional.

In our own experience as researchers and educators, we have become increasingly concerned about the high levels of stress both at home and at school. Our observations suggest to us that one area of critical concern is the diminishing amounts of time that families have to spend together. Within this context it is important to note that in each of the families participating in *Family Literacy* (Taylor, 1983) and *Growing Up Literate* (Taylor & Dorsey-Gaines, 1988) there was usually a mother at home with the children. Mothers worked part-time and fitted their employment around their children's schedules. When this was not possible, their jobs were no longer considered as a viable option. In *Growing Up Literate*, when Ieshea became pregnant with Jarasad, she gave up her position as a college secretary and became a welfare recipient. Ieshea did not return to work until she felt that Sarita, Jarasad's younger sister, was ready for daycare. Sarita was three years of age when Ieshea began to look for another job. Undoubtedly, there are families in which single parents or both parents work and stress is kept to a minimum and children thrive. But we would be deceiving ourselves if we did not acknowledge that in many families children suffer for lack of a primary caretaker at home. In these families the opportunities for children to learn in family settings are diminished. The moment-to-moment, margins-of-awareness experiences (including literacy experiences) of children are being concentrated, reduced, and sometimes shattered by the changing patterns of family life in American society.

If we return to the interpretative explanations of family literacy described in the first section of this chapter, and we then consider the impact of changing social realities on the coping strategies of children, parents, and teachers in school, it is not difficult to imagine the problems that can arise when the interrelationships between the education and socialization of children break down at home and at school. As educators and policy makers, we must confront our inability to change the ways in which society behaves. Families will continue to lead stressful lives, and schools will remain stressful environments for many children. However, if we ignore the role that literacy plays in contributing to or detracting from high-stress situations, we lose a valuable opportunity for enabling children to learn to cope with the difficulties they face in their lives. Small changes are possible if we come to understand some of the complex ways in which literacy is inherently a part of our everyday lives.

How Rituals and Routines, Use of Time and Space Influence Literate Learning Opportunities

In recent years the notion of quality time has become widely accepted as an alternate approach to the parenting of young children. If parents cannot spend long periods of time with their children then they are encouraged to make every minute count. Family rituals and routines and the use of time and space have been radically changing to accommodate the working life-styles of family members. Encouraging parents to spend time with their children playing games, reading stories, and going on trips is undoubtedly good advice, but such specific activities cannot replace the moment-to-moment learning that takes place when time is not at such a premium and parents and children can just *be* together. Going to the supermarket and helping a parent shop may not be considered quality time, and yet the opportunities for talk (instrumental, regulatory, interactional, personal, imaginative, heuristic, and informative) and for reading (instrumental, confirmational, financial, and environmental) are extraordinary. When the groceries are hurriedly bought on the way to pick up children from after-school care, an opportunity is lost for them to participate in an essential (families-have-to-eat) family event. Of course, missing the opportunity to go grocery shopping is not such a dreadful calamity, but if other similar activities are also excluded from children's rituals and routines, then it seems fair to state that their opportunities to *use* literacy to accomplish some of the tasks of daily living will diminish.

However, not all the effects of changing family life-styles are negative. If we explore this situation from an alternative perspective, we can add another dimension to the effects of changing family patterns on the literate learning opportunities of children. Tentative interpretations of the data collected in the study of families in which there is not a parent at home on a full time basis (Taylor, 1988c) suggests that literacy becomes a key element in the ability of some families to juggle all of the schedules, rituals and routines, and time constraints that are a part of their daily lives. Communicating through print becomes one of the ways in which families learn to cope. School schedules and after-school activities are juggled with parents' work schedules and late meetings.

One family participating in the study gave the list of rules shown in Figure 12–4 to the children at the beginning of summer vacation. All of the information that was written down was also shared verbally with the children. The mother explained, "By the end of the first week of the summer vacation we were all going crazy. The summer presented a whole new routine that was not defined by school. No one knew the rules to make the family run smoothly and we had only two months. By putting them down on paper, when there was a question I could say, 'There are the rules. Take a look at them.' Our situation is the reverse of what exists when a mother is at home. When you're raised in a family where the mother is at home there is no need to put them up, but you need them when she goes back to work. Here, the rules were posted because the mother was at home for the summer and there was a new lack of structure."

How Critical Incidents Can Impede or Constrain Literate Learning Opportunities

Living on a limited amount of money requires careful planning. Telephones are sometimes disconnected and the electricity shut off. These events, which can be described as literacy events in that they are experienced through the bills and notices that are mailed to the family, critically affect the family's ability to cope with daily living. It is difficult to read a story with a child in a cold apartment. The socialization and education of children is disrupted by the catastrophic events that their parents must endure. Parents do not always survive. Sometimes children do not survive (see Taylor & Dorsey-Gaines, 1988). However hard parents try to take care of their children, their love is not always enough. Ieshea was unable to help Danny overcome the difficulties that he faced in trying to cope with both his everyday life and his school experiences. Ironically, the beating of Danny by his teacher was the outcome of a literacy event. Ieshea explained what happened:

> I asked him [Danny's teacher], "Mr. ———, can I ask you what happened in here today?" So he said, "Yes. We were doing a writing assignment— starting a writing assignment," and he said, "Danny wrote 'Seventh Grade' on the paper, on the heading of his paper, and I told Danny to put 'Grade Seven.'" And he said, "Danny wanted to know what was the difference, that technically they meant the same thing, so if he had wrote 'Seventh Grade' why did he have to change it? Why did he have to put 'Grade Seven'? And

Figure 12−4   List of Summer Rules Typed by Mother

mmmmmmmmmmmmmmmmmmmmmmmmmmmmmmmmmmmmmmmmmmmmmmmmmmmmmmmmmmmmmmmmmmmmmmmmmmmmmmmmmmm

SUMMER RULES FOR EASIER LIVING, 1987

mmmmmmmmmmmmmmmmmmmmmmmmmmmmmmmmmmmmmmmmmmmmmmmmmmmmmmmmmmmmmmmmmmmmmmmmmmmmmmmmmmm

REMEMBER: Rules are not made to be broken, but they certainly can
be discussed or negotiated! Don't wait until the last
minute to do so, however!

1) Check in at home at noon either to a) find out when lunch will be
ready or   b) make yourself a sandwich or whatever else
you would like that is available

2) Be home by 6:00 for dinner!

3) Be ready to head upstairs by 9:00 unless there are special requests
or circumstances arranged for in advance, such as a night-
time outside game, a special TV program, a baseball game, etc.

4) Leave a note to tell me where you are if I am not at home to be told
in person

5) If you want to watch daytime TV, earn the minutes to do so by reading

6) Plan to mow the lawn (boys) on alternate weekends. Sign your name on
the calendar after the job is done.

These are the BASIC RULES. If you can't follow them, especially #1 and #2,
be prepared to pay the penalty.   The penalty is what will be most effective
for the specific person who can't follow the rules.

POINTS TO PONDER: (not really "rules," as such, but nice things to remember)

1) SMILE once in a while at the people around you. It will drive them crazy
wondering what you're up to! (It will also make Mom feel appre-
ciated)

2) Do something NICE for someone in the family who least expects it. It
make them appreciate you!   You never know when it will pay off!

3) Say "thanks" to people in the family when it's appropriate. It shows that
you do care.

4) If you see something that needs doing, do it. Why not?

that's when he went into the explanation about if he gave Danny a parable, like if someone has five pennies and they're at a parking meter and have to put in a nickel, they can't use the five pennies; then he wanted it to say "Grade Seven" and not "Seventh Grade." So I guess at that point he said that Danny became aggravated or angry or exasperated or whatever and he flung the sheet of paper, and the teacher said the sheet of paper hit him and he said that's when he hit Danny.

But still I'm under the assumption that he just, er, snatched him or, you know, I thought it was one lick, you know. . . . So we left, and after we got all the way down to the first floor, and, er, Danny says, "Momma he didn't just hit me, he beat me with the stick." So I looked at Danny. I said, "He did what?" He said, "He beat me with—" I said, "What kind of stick?" So he said, you know, the pointer that you go to the chalkboard with. He said, "He beat me with the stick that—you know—the pointer." And he said, um, "I have whips all over my body." He said, "Because when he was beating me, after the stick broke I walked out of the class and I went down to the office, and the principal took me to the nurse's office." And then Danny gave me, um, um, a sheet of paper from the nurse and it, um, said "Reddened marks on his shoulder, his upper arm, his thigh, and his legs," you know (Taylor & Dorsey-Gaines, 1988, p. 117).

Following this incident Danny was observed in his classroom by the child study team. In a subsequent conversation, a member of the team explained the findings of their evaluation by stating that "'because of his attitude on the days that we worked with him, he might not have been putting forth his best effort'" (p. 120). Essentially his literate learning opportunities were impeded or constrained by what was happening to him both in his classroom and in his everyday life (Taylor & Dorsey-Gaines, 1988). His mother, Ieshea, was deeply concerned about her son Danny. She did what she could to help him, but her own life circumstances were so desperate that she had difficulty coping. There were times that she went hungry so that her children could eat. And although she lived a literate life, her own plans to finish college, to be liberated by literacy, were abandoned.

How Critical Incidents Can Enhance Literate Learning Opportunities

Families use literacy to gain control in difficult moments and to express their feelings when critical incidents occur in their lives. Sometimes when we are upset we write it down. Bonnie was seven years and seven months when she left the following letter for her mother:

> Dear Mommie,
>
>   I really love you. Yes I do.
> You care for me. And I know
> why you tell me to have
> gum only every other day
> I know it all. It is for my
> own good. So I don't get
> cavities you are the mother
> I want for ever
> and ever.   Love Bonnie
>   xxxx ooooooO
>   xxxx ooooooO
>   xxxx
>   I love you

When Bonnie's mother talked about the note (Taylor, 1983, p. 35) she explained that she had been "feeling down" that morning, and Bonnie had known that she was unhappy. She thought Bonnie had written the note because she wanted her mother to know how much she loved her.

A final example comes from the study of families in which there is not a parent at home on a full-time basis (Taylor, 1988c). It is a letter written by an eight-year-old Korean girl who was adopted and became a member of a biracial American family. The letter was written when the child's grandmother was dying. In talking about the letter the child's mother commented that written communication is sometimes safer when emotions are too overwhelming for us to say how we feel.

> My Grandmother is special to me because she doesn't yell she explains. She taught card games. She always has time for us. When each of us came she accepted us as a member of the family right away. She also met each one of us at the airport.
>
> Omni is the name we gave to her when my brother came from Korea. It sound like Halmunee which means Grandmother in Korean. And I will never forget the day I went with her on my birthday. I was turning 8 years old. She went with me shopping. We bought stickers and construction paper and things like that. Omni went with me out to dinner. That was a great day. The thing that made it so special was that it was just Omni and me.
>
> Right now Omni has cancer but she still tries to be the same old Omni. We pray for her every night. Each of us do the best we can to help her. We have been successful so far sort of.
>
> Omni has been so kind to us that I wrote this poem to her last birthday. It is called "Love". People feel that way about Omni too. My godmothers who brought me to America made a song called "Omni" that we love to sing to her.

> > Each Time I feel loved and safe
> > I think of you Omni
> > I feel your hand holding mine
> > Stay near me my Omni
> > Show me the way to live each day
> > Making you proud of me
> > I want you to see
> > Your life in me
> > I love you so
> > > Omni

At a fundamental level, parents and children use literacy to cope with the stress in their lives. There are times when literacy empowers them as they make an attempt to gain some control over the stressful events that occur in their lives. They may not be successful, but they are actively engaged in the struggle. It is in this way that families sometimes use literacy as a means of self-expression, to gain emotional and spiritual comfort, and to make personal statements about themselves and about the society in which they live.

Implications for Educational Policy

Without exaggeration, there is a tremendous need for our society to reassess the ways in which young children are taught to read and write. From early infancy, children of *all* socio-economic levels, ethnic backgrounds, and in all¹ geographic regions of the country are being enrolled in child care programs. In addition, many public schools have initiated programs for four-year-olds, and full or extended day kindergartens are becoming increasingly common. Virtually all of these programs claim to have an educational component of some sort, and without hesitation we can state that there are children in *every segment of our society* who are being "schooled" almost from birth. There is a trend away from the informal, relaxed, and unhurried socialization previously associated with these preschool years, and there is a move toward more rigid programs based upon elementary school instruction, which are being inappropriately applied and used in early childhood settings (see Elkind, 1987). Thus, stress in school has increased at a time when many families face stress levels at home that have become unmanageable. By ignoring the fundamental role that literacy plays in family life, we contribute to the stress that children experience. At home, literacy is used in one way, and at school it is taught in another. A socially relevant academic curriculum could be established that would begin on the first day that a child is placed in care outside the home, and it could be extended through the child's elementary school years and on through high school. The implications for curriculum and instruction can be stated as follows:

1. *Reading and writing instruction enables children to gain their own personal configurations of literacy.* We need to ask ourselves:
   - How can we create opportunities for children to use literacy as a means of self-expression and personal identity?
   - How can we create school environments that enable children to contribute to the everyday life of the classroom community through their own individual interpretations of literacy?
   - When children are immersed in real life events (e.g. the birth of a brother or sister or the participation in a new after-school childcare arrangement), how can we use literacy to help them to gain some control of their everyday lives?
   - How can we share in and show our respect for the individual configurations of literacy that children in our classrooms bring with them when they come to school?

2. *Reading and writing instruction enables children to develop shared configurations of literacy.* We need to ask ourselves:
   - How can we create classrooms in which teachers and children

collaborate through literacy to achieve some genuine function of community life in schools?

- How can we create apprenticeship opportunities for children to work with parents, teachers, and administrators in genuine situations in which they can learn of the types and uses of literacy that are inherent within their school community?
- How can we use these shared learning opportunities to enable children to gain some appreciation of the ways in which they can use literacy to work with their peers?

3. *Reading and writing instruction enables children to understand the inherent role of literacy in American society.* We need to ask ourselves:

- How can we ensure that children are active participants in literate communities and aware of the importance of their own participation?
- How can we ensure that individual children are comfortable with the ways in which literacy functions in our everyday lives so that they can truly participate as members of society with all the rights, privileges, and responsibilities that this position implies?
- How can we empower children to "keep on learning" about the increasingly complex ways that literacy is used within families, schools, and society?

4. *Children benefit when we establish literacy in the social and cultural contexts of their everyday lives.* We need to ask ourselves:

- How can we ensure that we do not divorce children from their literate heritage?
- How can we create a continuum for children that links their personal situations with the historical contexts of their everyday lives?
- How can we expand upon children's awareness of other members of their society?
- How can we provide opportunities for children to gain a sense of how the experiences of all ethnic groups in American society are intrinsically a part of their own cultural identity?

Again, the questions that we ask focus upon making sense of children's everyday lives, making their experiences meaningful, and recognizing that literacy is intrinsically a part of their early participation in American society. We cannot replace family life with classroom experiences, but we *can* recognize the legitimacy of children's social existence and use it as a basis for curriculum and instruction. Children are at risk when meaning is lost in the expensive rigmarole of artificial reading and writing activities. There is no doubt in our minds that children are disenfranchised when excluded from genuine literacy learning.

We cannot parody literacy learning. It is important for us to keep in mind that the world as we know it does not exist except through our individual and shared experiences. Harste and Woodward (in press) state it this way:

> If we view education as a process by which we mediate our world for purposes of exploration and expansion, then literacy is one dimension of that exploration. We do not have direct access to our world (all that hits our eyes are impulses of light); we create sign systems such as written language, oral language, art, music, mathematics, dance, and the like. These systems are fictions, constructs of our imagination, but they allow us to explore our world. It is with them that we mediate our world and in so doing fundamentally alter it as we explore it. (p. 51)

We would expand upon this statement by adding that we also view education as a means of survival, and that literacy can become a life and death issue. In our knowledge-based schools where meaning is often missing from instruction, students sometimes lose a sense of purpose, and in everyday life they find themselves a part of harmful situations that they are powerless to change.

Although literacy is treated as some cultural list that everybody should know (Hirsch, 1987), students fail. We fail, and our failure has a cumulative effect (see Lippmann, 1922). For the child who is retained in first grade because of a lack of phonic skill or some other inadequacy will become the dropout in eighth grade who we knew would never make it through the system. If we abandon the meanings of the signs and symbols in our everyday lives, we exclude children from actively becoming all that, in our imaginations, we know they can humanly be.

We believe that many children already know this deep inside themselves. When a junior in high school says that she has learned nothing in the past six years and she can see no purpose to living, she is telling us that she understands her own worthless state within the system that is supposed to be educating her. The irony of this situation is that the feelings of worthlessness that the student has expressed reflect our own impotent state, for if we empower students to learn then we empower ourselves to teach. Education should not have to be suffered as a tedious exercise, but instead should be regarded as a meaningful opportunity that enables students to grow in the imagination of their own social lives, to accept the challenge of changing social realities, and to grow up as active participants in their families, their communities, and the society to which they belong.

What we may learn from home/school studies discussed in the preceding chapter is that minority children may have culturally determined purposes, styles, and needs as learners. In Chapter 13, Washington builds on this point, and implicitly on the work of McConnell, in her argument that if we treat all disadvantaged children alike, we ignore education as a cultural process. This may be one reason for the school achievement gap that still exists between white and black children.

Literacy Learning for All Children

Reducing the Risks to Young Black Learners: An Examination of Race and Educational Policy

Valora Washington

EDUCATIONAL progress is a particularly important measure of social justice to blacks in the United States. The black community has a long-standing faith in education as a primary means to support upward mobility. This faith has been nurtured in spite of, or perhaps because of, the necessary struggle to attain equal educational opportunities, a struggle that is ongoing (Peterson, 1985).

A well-documented characteristic of the black community of the United States has been high educational aspirations for children. This is a characteristic with historical continuity; both slave and emancipated blacks held a strong desire for literacy and a willingness to endure the hardships necessary to attain it (Bullock, 1970; Owens, 1976).

Yet, the risks of educational failure for young black children remain high:

- While the enrollment of black children in school has increased dramatically since 1850, black children are enrolled in academic or college preparatory programs about 20 percent less often than whites, and in vocational programs about 38 percent more often than whites.

- Black children made significant gains in reading and math in the 1970s, but the achievement gap remains.

- Compared to white children, black children are three times more likely to be placed in an educable mentally retarded class.

- Black children are twice as likely to be suspended from school or to suffer corporal punishment (see Washington & LaPoint, 1988).

The failure of U.S. education to promote success among black children has required a focus on equity issues throughout much of the history of black education. Although both equity and quality are important American values, and schools in this nation are expected to reflect both, different historical periods have tended to emphasize one value over the other. While blacks' quest for equity is rooted in the desire for quality education, the secure establishment of access to educational opportunities has, by necessity, preceded those concerns. Importantly, recent tensions between equity and quality have tended to have strong racial overtones; these tensions also reflect various emphases on whether the corrective action should focus on educational processes (such as school desegregation) or on the expected results of educational experiences (such as reading or math achievement scores).

The unique history of the black population in this country has meant that the attempted resolutions of these tensions have been subject to federal and state policy. Black education has been intertwined with the history of slavery, reconstruction, segregation, "Great Society" programs, and recent restructuring of federal-state systems.

Despite the strong relationships between public policy and efforts to decrease—or increase—the risks to young black learners, few scholars have addressed specifically the link between the social indicators about black children and educational policy. In this chapter I argue that, in critical ways, the advent of educational policy itself can be traced to early efforts to link educational research to the experiences of poor black children. However, despite the prevalent presentation of statistics about black children in policy contexts, the real needs and interests of black children are often obscured. Given this paradox—the focus on black children in the scholarly arena dealing with educational policy and the obscurity of black children in educational policy—I speculate upon future ties between education and policy that might reduce the risks for young black learners.

THE CONTRIBUTIONS OF BLACK CHILDREN TO THE LINK BETWEEN EDUCATION AND PUBLIC POLICY

Three areas of research illustrate the importance of studies on black children in shaping issues related to educational risk among young children: intelligence testing and assessment; preschool development and education, as illustrated by Project Head Start; and improvements in elementary and secondary education fostered by compensatory education programs.

Intelligence Testing and Assessment

During the 1960s, a great deal of research was devoted to the perceptual, cognitive, and linguistic processes of poor black children. These researchers generally concluded that black children were deficient partly as a result of inadequate parenting and that these deficits were reflected in poor school performance and low scores on intelligence or achievement tests.

The presumed link between race and intelligence has been debated for centuries as succeeding generations of Social Darwinists, eugenicists, behavioral geneticists, and other social scientists examine the controversy. The major studies and reports on the genetic-inheritance paradigm are essentially race-comparative studies of black and white children (see Coleman et al., 1966; Herrnstein, 1971; Jensen, 1969; Kamin, 1974; Shuey, 1966). Indeed, intelligence testing in the United States has been, since its earliest days, intertwined with antiequalitarian doctrines based largely on interpretations of research involving black populations (Weinberg, 1977).

Laosa (1985) asserts that the history of U.S. social policies toward children is closely intertwined with the history of intelligence testing. Arguments about "innate" racial differences were used to rationalize many policies, including the passage of racist immigration laws, school segregation, and ability grouping in educational institutions. Further, allegations resulting from racial bias in intelligence tests have formed the bases of a series of policy actions by the judicial, legislative, and executive branches of government, as well as by professional associations. Paradoxically, Alfred Binet, the developer of the first intelligence test in 1905, contended that intellectual attainment could be modified by environmental factors, yet these tests have served to maintain and support inequality in educational opportunity.

Preschool Development and Education

Extrapolating from environmentalist ideas about the role of experience in the development of intellect, educators began to link black children's low IQ and achievement test scores to the lack of intellectual stimulation in their homes. Based partly on the ideas of educational researchers, federal policy in the 1960s and 1970s sought to alleviate the intellectual and social risks of the poor through a variety of parent and child improvement programs such as Head Start (Mitchell, 1982).

Project Head Start, *the* major federal child development program, is a comprehensive effort to provide health, educational, and social services to preschool children and their families. The project has always served disproportionately large numbers of black children: about 42 percent of Head Start children are black and about two-thirds of the children are members of ethnic minority groups.

Consequently, Head Start/preschool intervention research and public policy have a particularly strong relationship to black children. Not surprisingly, issues of cultural diversity surfaced in the early days of Head Start and other intervention programs. For example, the desegregation requirements for Head Start grant eligibility provoked some initial resentment of Head Start programs in several southern states. Despite parent and community enthusiasm for the goals of Head Start, the program has been criticized for the ethnic composition of its staffing patterns, particularly in supervisory positions. Head Start has also been charged with promulgating a deficit view of black children, their families, and communities (see Washington & Oyemade, 1987).

It should be noted that although the major studies and reports of preschool intervention effectiveness have made extensive use of black children as subjects, these studies have considerably less representation and visibility of black scholars (see Cole & Washington, 1986).

Compensatory Education

Several compensatory education programs were designed in the 1960s to reduce educational failure. In 1965 the Elementary and Secondary School Act was passed and Project Head Start was initiated. The Coleman Report (Coleman et al., 1966) appeared in 1966; Sesame Street began in 1969; and 1969/1970 marked the largest wave of court-ordered desegregation in the South. Today, approximately 40 percent of the U.S. Department of Education budget is allocated to provide direct services for disadvantaged elementary and secondary school children (The William T. Grant Foundation Commission, 1987). The major programs are Project Follow Through and Chapter 1 of the Education Consolidation and Improvement Act. About 29 percent of Chapter 1 students are black and 16 percent are

Hispanic (Riddle, 1986). Data on improved reading and math achievement of blacks suggest that Chapter 1 is effective (see Jones, 1983; for a contrary view see Jensen, 1985). Characteristics of high-achieving compensatory education programs include administrative support of academically oriented teaching, monitoring of instructional effectiveness, and a constellation of teaching factors referred to as direct instruction (see, for examples, *Phi Delta Kappa* April, 1982 and April, 1985).

Preschool intervention programs like Head Start have enjoyed widespread popularity and have probably reduced the risks to young black learners, but they have not brought about equal educational opportunity (Slaughter, 1982). By the mid-1970s there was growing cynicism about the marriage of research and educational policy: the school performance of black children had not changed dramatically, critics were questioning programs conceived for minorities by the white majority, and theories of social inequality challenged the deficit assumptions of most social programs. Jensen (1969), on the other hand, concluded that the programs had failed because blacks are not only culturally deprived but are genetically inferior.

Many academics disputed genetic differences theories, but persistent poverty and racial disparities fueled the growing conviction that something even more basic than cultural deprivation was "wrong" with black people. It was widely asserted that additional compensatory education was called for, that is, early intervention tailored to limited intellectual capacities and employing the rote learning strategies for which blacks were said to be better suited. So, for different reasons, educators and the federal government supported additional remedial programs with the expectation that they would change what was thought of as black learning styles (Mitchell, 1982).

Yet, compensatory education programs have consistently been the object of much criticism and analysis. For example, in a poignant essay, Jacquelyn Mitchell (1982) describes her experiences as a teacher in a compensatory preschool program and as a graduate student and researcher. She found the compensatory program to be "patronizing" and to have an "implicit denigration of the milieu of black culture."

Further, the assessment procedures used to determine a child's need for compensatory education often have been viewed as racially biased contributors to improper classification and labelling of black children (Laosa, 1985). The consequences, according to some observers, are reflected in the facts: a black child is more than three times as likely to be classified as educable mentally retarded and twice as likely to be classified as trainable mentally retarded or seriously emotionally disturbed (Children's Defense Fund, 1985).

Carl Bereiter (1985) observes that for two decades, continual acrimony has characterized the debate about the explanations for educational disadvantage. He notes that much of the sensitivity on this topic results from the demographic focus on students, usually by race. While "things are much calmer on the educational disadvantage front today," Bereiter notes that the issues are being avoided, not resolved.

The two primary retreats from the issues are: (1) the movement toward individual, rather than categorical, diagnosis and prescription and (2) the movement toward nonspecific compensatory education based on empirical generalizations about what is required to improve instruction for historically low-achieving groups. In the latter view, the educationally-at-risk are not defined conceptually but are simply those children who have traditionally been regarded as suitable candidates for it.

THE OBSCURITY OF BLACK CHILDREN IN EDUCATIONAL POLICY

Bereiter's (1985) view that issues of educational disadvantage are being avoided rather than resolved may also reflect the normative state for black children vis-a-vis educational policy. Whereas studies of black children have had a tremendous impact on educational policy, this may be peculiar to the field or historical period.

Media, scholarly, and legislative accounts on the status of children typically present a mass of race-comparative information, which creates an initial impression that special attention is being given to black/minority children. Yet this attention often fades beyond the headlines. Indeed, the needs and interests of black children are often obscured in two ways: (1) by the emphasis on economic deprivation as opposed to race and racism in the formulation of education policy and (2) by the implementation of educational policy in ways that undermine the cultural styles of black learners.

Race and Racism in Educational Policy

Compensatory education policy has generally been based on the premise that remedial assistance to children identified by economic variables would reduce educational risk. However, in addition to economic deprivations, a substantial number of the educationally disadvantaged must also confront the well-documented reality of institutional racism in schools. Educational policy has not circumvented this additional barrier to self-sufficiency. Indeed, by focusing primarily on economic deprivations, educational policy fails to (1) consider the historical salience of race vis-a-vis social class in assessing educational risks for young black learners and (2) respond directly to the demographic characteristics of compensatory education recipients.

Race and Social Class. Both educational research and policy have promulgated a poverty-centered approach as it relates to black learners. This approach to educational policy development and analysis fails to consider that Afro-Americans have a peculiar history in the United States that may provide insight into the causes and consequences of and cures for their educational status. Such an historical perspective highlights the particular nature of race consciousness that has been normative in American life.

Almost from the beginning of the black experience in the United States, there were explicit rules and regulations governing the conduct of and opportunities available to black children. These rules—later codified as "Black Codes" or Jim Crow laws in the South—universally and categorically restricted educational opportunity and increased the risk of failure (Washington, 1985).

Just as explicit attention to race limited educational access and opportunity, overt attention to race has been used to attack discrimination. Examples of this latter approach are the Freedman's Bureau and affirmative action policies. It is invidious discrimination that should be eliminated, not necessarily race-conscious efforts or distinctions for positive or remedial purposes.

Nonetheless, a color-blind approach to policy development has predominated. A major assumption of this approach is that the problems of black learners can be solved in the same way as the problems of impoverished whites. This approach has led to educational policy solutions indifferent to the fact that both poverty and educational failure among blacks often result from political, instructional, and economic systems that condone and foster institutional racism.

Although poverty does shape the context for many black children who are at risk, it is not necessarily the only or the predominant influence. By ignoring ethnic-specific experiences, educational policy implicitly opts for the "cultural equivalent" perspective, which reduces differences to social class variations (Allen, W.R., 1976). This is, in many ways, similar to the "cultural deviant" perspective that, although acknowledging unique traits of black learners, sees differences as deviant, pathological, and dysfunctional.

Demographic Characteristics of Compensatory Education Recipients. The continuing salience of race is graphically illustrated in a review of the demographic characteristics of children who are identified as being at risk for educational failure. Young black children are overrepresented in federally sponsored compensatory programs: over one-fourth of Chapter 1 children and almost half of Head Start children are black. Further, significant racial disparities in educational progress have been demonstrated for a long time in terms of reading and math achievement, school completion rates, the relationship between education and income, and numerous other measures (Washington & LaPoint, 1988).

In fact, negative public opinion about public schools may result, in part, from the rapid growth of children who are deemed at risk in them and the emerging demographic profile of urban public schools. For example, one can examine school enrollment trends in the nation's twenty-five largest school districts: in 1950, one in ten students in these school systems was a minority child; in 1960 it was one in three; in 1970, it was one in two (Ornstein, 1982). Today, minorities constitute the majority of school enrollments in twenty-three out of twenty-five of the nation's largest cities (McNett, 1983). These demographic shifts in the public school population have direct bearing on the education of black children.

Ironically, though increases in the child population should heighten public attention to the needs of children at risk, the changing complexion of children may limit public action for children as a result of racism. Indeed, demographic and ecological changes hold the potential for polarization and conflict based on age, ethnicity, family status, and social class.

Age and Ethnicity. The white population is growing older while the minority population is much younger. Since the older generation will be mostly white, and the younger generation mostly ethnic minorities, the potential for increased conflict in priorities (e.g., school lunches vs. retirement income) seems obvious (McNett, 1983).

Family Status. Demographic projections create a probability that the "childless haves" will be called upon to pay for the education of the "fertile have-nots." The category of households that has increased most rapidly since 1980 has been nonfamily. About 64 percent of all households today do not have children, compared to 54 percent fifteen years ago (Feistritzer, 1985).

Social Class. Among people who do have children there are growing class disparities, regardless of race (Darity & Myers, 1984). The number of highly educated, high-income parents is growing, and many of these parents are sending their children to private schools. Indeed, more black middle-class parents are sending their children to private schools (Slaughter & Schneider, 1986). Unless this trend stops, children in public schools, by and large, will be the offspring of single, uneducated, low-income minority parents, who are producing the most children today, proportionately (Feistritzer, 1985).

These three demographic trends—age, family status, and social class— suggest that careful analysis of assistance to children at risk must respond directly to issues of race and racism. These trends underscore the importance of specifically considering the application of federal programs to the needs of young black learners. Black children are significantly affected by educational policy and therefore particularly vulnerable to budget cuts and changes in federal-state relationships.

Cultural Diversity and Policy Implementation

In addition to its failure to address race and racism, social policy obscures the interests and needs of black children in the policy implementation process. The expressed goal of educational policy—to promote measurable progress—can be undermined by educators or legislators who fail to acknowledge and eliminate the racism inherent in curriculum, textbooks, and instructional strategies. That is, equal educational opportunity programs have focused on changing individual children who were expected to accommodate to the schools, rather than adapting to the needs of the children and their communities.

Policy positions that emphasize resocialization of the child in school (e.g., see Hess & Shipman, 1967) have been criticized (Baratz & Baratz, 1970; Tulkin, 1972). This focus on the individual or family as the cause of educational failure, coupled with the establishment of norms for adaptive behavior outside of black communities, is viewed as insensitive at best and more likely as racist (Ogbu, 1981).

It has been demonstrated clearly that the home environment influences the development of literacy skills that are implicated in many of the standard measures of reading achievement (Hess & Holloway, 1985). Yet, many authors (e.g., Hale, 1982; Jones, 1972; Rist, 1973) reject the notion that black families simply mediate and reflect societal values rather than actively filter and protect their children from perceived threats to the children's images of themselves as learners and as people.

A major barrier to the identification of successful black learners, as well as to providing assistance to more marginal students, has been identified as cultural differences in cognitive style. In the past few years black researchers and theorists have highlighted this concept as one that offers exceptional promise for understanding and changing racial disparities in academic performance.

In a widely reviewed book, *Black Children: Their Roots, Culture, and Learning Style*, Janice Hale compiles an array of data to support the view that black children have distinct ways of perceiving, organizing, processing, and using information. This Afrocentric learning style reflects the retention of elements from the African experience in the context of black American history and environments. Research (e.g., Fry & Coe, 1980; Jones, 1981) supports Hale's view that cognitive-style influence is an important variable in the low school achievement of the black learner. To this extent, educational institutions must take a large share of responsibility for the underachievement of black students (also see Ulibarri, 1982).

The divergence between black communities and educational institutions can be characterized along six dimensions: sex role expectations, language, service orientations, reference group orientations, achievement expectations, and problem origination. The child-learner is thrust into the center of this divergence. As both of these systems exert profound pressure on the child-learner, conflicts often emerge in the child's affective and cognitive development or functioning (see Table 13–1).

Black Education: A Critical Link to Policy

Research on the education of black children has had an enormous impact on the link between the field and social policy. The most public and controversial issues in education—intelligence testing, preschool programs, and compensatory education—have strong racial overtones. Research on black child populations has played a distinct and valuable role in shaping these issues.

LINKING RESEARCH, POLICY, AND PRACTICE TO REDUCE RISKS FOR BLACK LEARNERS

In a previous era, research, policy, and educational practice linked together to effectively reduce barriers to social and educational equality, as in the *Brown vs. the Board of Education of Topeka, Kansas* decision and the evolution of Project Head Start. Today, despite media attention on data that reveals that black children are particularly affected by educational policy, the specific needs and interests of black children are obscured by the poverty-centered approach, which favors social class distinctions. This color-blind approach has not been as productive for black children as explicit attention to their status may be.

Addressing the issues of educational risk among black children is an essential task of our time—an imperative task for all Americans, not just black parents or black scholars. The significance of this statement is underscored by many factors, including the demographic shifts expected in the population over the next two decades. In the next decade there will be a dramatic increase in the number of children in the United States, a larger proportion of whom will be black or other ethnic minorities, and poor. Clearly America is becoming more diverse, not more homogeneous. Consequently, black children represent an underdeveloped resource that will become increasingly important to the nation's economic, military, and political strength (Washington & LaPoint, 1988).

Educators, policymakers, and researchers must work with black communities and share responsibility for developing innovative educational

Table 13−1   **Areas of Divergence Between Ethnic Communities and Educational Institutions**

Area	Ethnic Communities	Educational Institutions
Sex Role	Patriarchal/equalitarian	Modified Patriarchal
Language	Dialect/different	Standard
Service Orientation	Communal	Individual
Reference Group Orientation	Self, others	Self
Achievement Expectations	High	Low
Problem Origination	Enclave culture perception; systemic social forces	Personal; family; reference group

Source: "Teaching and Counseling the Black Child: A Systemic Analysis for the 1980's" by Valora Washington and Courtland C. Lee, 1981. *Journal of Nonwhite Concerns in Personnel and Guidance*, *9*, 60−67.

philosophies and methods that will address the specific needs of black children. In the years ahead our nation will face choices that will either harden or diffuse ethnic and class disparities in educational institutions and, as a consequence, in society.

As we approach the twenty-first century the opportunities for black children will be widely divergent. Those children in families that are highly skilled or well-educated may see an unlimited future and prosperity. On the other hand, children of poor, single, or adolescent parents are likely to become increasingly alienated and distant from mainstream American life. Family ties between the black poor and middle class suggest possibilities for research and educational policy and practice that should be investigated. These natural alliances, if buoyed by social support, may provide opportunities for both preventing educational failure and for ameliorating the impact of changing social conditions.

The Importance of Black Educators and Scholars

Productive efforts to reduce educational risks for black learners necessitates the active participation of black scholars. Legislators, researchers, and teachers who have not experienced and, in some cases, not exposed themselves to a contextual framework to understand cultural diversity are ill-prepared to weigh ethnicity, as compared to social class, as one important evaluative criteria in their work.

In this regard, the growing problem of attracting and retaining minority teacher candidates is a serious concern, particularly given data on the significance of the race of the teacher (Washington, 1982). All teachers, regardless of their race or class background, must be held responsible for understanding variables tied to student performance. Although education studies now give more emphasis to the cultural, ecological, social, and interdisciplinary contexts of learning, applications of this knowledge to the classroom do not necessarily reflect these recent findings. Consequently, deficit views of black pupils continue to play an influential role in teachers' interpretations of their behavior and development.

Researchers and educators have the potential to contribute a great deal to the discussion of educational failure and success for black children. The generation of understanding and knowledge about black learners at risk that can effectively dispel myths, promote understanding, indicate policy alternatives, and stimulate advances to general instruction is a challenge that should not go unmet.

The Importance of Parent Involvement

The severe shortage of pertinent research information and of minority group teachers heightens the necessity to involve parents in the education of their children. The effectiveness of parent involvement in schools has been illustrated in predominately black schools with notable records of achievement, where the parents and the surrounding community are involved and supportive (Comer, 1986; Sowell, 1970). Further, Louis Rubin (1980) notes that without parent collaboration it is impossible to coordinate the teachings of home and school.

The effects of social class on school achievement are alterable through parent involvement. Encouragement and discussion of leisure-reading, informed parent-child conversations, and parental expressions of interest in the child's academic and personal progress were among the variables in the successful programs.

There are indications that parents desire closer participation in the education of their children, and that traditional measures like income or occupation do not determine parent/child interactions (Sowell, 1981). Education is foremost on the minds of black parents. There are reports showing that blacks received more parental encouragement in their education than whites. Several studies found that black parents had higher educational aspirations for their children, especially females, than did whites. Higher proportions of students at private black colleges cited parental desire as a reason for attending college than did students from all (private and public) four-year colleges. For blacks, education may represent more an internalization of a general cultural value, as evidenced by the high level of black aspirations despite the low correlation between educational aspiration and occupational expectation (see Washington & LaPoint, 1988).

These findings provide further argument for social policies that facilitate parent involvement in educational institutions. For example, the recently strengthened provisions for parent involvement in Chapter 1 compensatory education programs offer guidelines as to the types of activities with which parents can become involved. These new regulations require schools participating in Chapter 1 to involve parents and to prepare written policies on parent involvement. No particular means for involving parents is required, but recommendations in the regulations for meeting the requirement include activities such as informing parents of the child's eligibility in a timely manner; establishing conferences on the child's progress; providing parent-training in at-home reinforcement techniques; providing timely information on Chapter 1 issues; establishing parent advisory committees; facilitating participation by parents in school activities; and consulting with parents on program design (see *CDF Reports*, July 1986).

With a focus on the quality of schooling that black children receive, many black parents have responded by promoting effective schools whether desegregated or not, by reducing calls for school desegregation, and by sending their children to private schools. These behaviors appear to be increasing disparities among blacks.

PROSPECTS FOR THE TWENTY-FIRST CENTURY: EXCELLENCE WITHOUT EXCUSE

Vincent Franklin (1980) concludes that neither community control nor court-ordered desegregation has done much to improve the education of minority children. One consequence of this is that increasing numbers of black parents are making choices to remove their children from public schools if they can afford to do so. Raspberry (1985) points out that many black parents thought going to school with whites would be a panacea for racial, social, and educational equity. Today, however, many black parents have retreated from school integration or racial balance as a remedy to educational underachievement (Irvine & Irvine, 1980).

It is obvious that racial equality in schooling does not involve desegregation alone, but economic reform and magnet schools programs as well as legal enforcement. Reducing the risks to young black learners must occur on multiple fronts.

One may wonder whether it is a mere coincidence that while growing majorities of black and Hispanic children attend urban schools there is mounting public dissatisfaction with educational institutions and the corollary demands for tuition tax credits and educational vouchers. Whereas educational policy has heretofore attempted to resolve equity issues, it may become increasingly difficult to tax the affluent of any race to support the education of nonaffluent children.

The educational needs and demographic shifts in the American population have the potential to generate renewed interest and excitement about public education. Public attention to education brings the possibility of expanding financial support. Parents with moderate and high incomes have demonstrated a willingness to invest in the education of their children; an appropriate increase in the share of public resources must be allocated for programs that serve the poor, such as Head Start. Decades of research have demonstrated that educational interventions can yield impressive long-term benefits for poor children (Berrueta-Clement, Schweinhart, Barnett, Epstein, & Weikart, 1984; Cole & Washington, 1986).

Education, however, must be viewed more broadly than it has heretofore. It is imperative that all children are prepared to live, work, and play in a multicultural environment (Washington & Woolever, 1979). The expanding proportion of black children challenges educators to maximize the cognitive and social skills of children in ways compatible with cultural diversity.

Clearly, neither parents nor education professionals have reached consensus positions on important issues in black education. It is the responsibility of educators, however, to more clearly specify policy alternatives, devise criteria for analyzing these alternatives, and provide concise analysis of the institutional, political, instructional, and economic factors involved. Further, we must be willing to advance a clear statement about the current status of black learners. Indeed, there is a persistent need to anticipate, adapt to, and influence social forces that shape the context for schooling.

Washington has presented a strong case for reassessing our educational approach for poor black learners. But how can we, at a policy level, make sure that we are meeting the needs of these learners in "ways compatible with their cultural diversity"? In Chapter 14, Mitchell synthesizes this and other policy issues raised by chapter authors. He proposes a policy agenda that considers children within their unique macrosystems. The multifaced approach he proposes would encourage school self-study, broaden teacher professionalism, and rebuild the social network infrastructure.

Emergent Literacy and the Transformation of Schools, Families, and Communities: A Policy Agenda

Brad Mitchell

INTRODUCTION

How many children can America afford to lose? During the baby boom years (1945–1970), the plight of low-income and/or minority children and youth was considered a significant but not critical issue. Employers were in a position to hire the most employable young women and men from a large potential labor pool (*Youth and America's Future*, 1988). Under such circumstances, unfortunately, the captains of business and industry could choose to ignore the vast majority of disadvantaged children and youth. Historically, politicians and business leaders have tended to support policies that either enhance the economic value of children or decrease the cost of caring for children. Richard Nixon's attempts to dismantle Lyndon Johnson's Great Society programs partially grew out of the notion that early intervention strategies such as Head Start were too costly and failed to reap immediate economic gains (Condry & Lazar, 1982). The political lesson learned from President Nixon's 1971 veto of the Equal Opportunities Amendments is that a sense of social justice is fine as long as it is wedded with tangible and immediate economic benefits.

The decade of the 1970s saw children under five become the population age group with the highest percentage in poverty, jumping from 16 to 24 percent. Many policymakers of this era viewed impoverished children and youth as a high-cost "dependency" problem (Coleman, 1987) rather than as a "resource" for economic and social revitalization (Heath & McLaughlin, 1987). Today, more and more business, government, community, and education leaders view the salvation of at-risk children and youth as critically important to the nation's economic prosperity and national security. There is a growing concern that America is "creating a permanent underclass of young people" (Committee for Economic Development, 1987). Employers no longer have the luxury of skimming off the most employable young people from a burgeoning labor pool. Far fewer teenagers and young adults are entering the labor market and a much larger proportion come from poor and/or minority groups that traditionally have had only a limited chance to succeed (*Youth and America's Future*, 1988). Moreover, there is a growing population of disconnected youth who are not in school, not at work, and not in touch with the blessings of a good society.

The numbers of disconnected youth can be measured by what is known as the inactivity rate, that is, the number of people aged sixteen through nineteen who are not in school, the military, or employed relative to their age group (Betsey, Hollister, & Papageorgiou, 1985). In 1983 the inactivity rate for white male teens was 17.8 percent as compared to 8.3 percent in 1978. For white female teens it rose from 17.8 percent to 24.2 percent during the same time period. The inactivity rate for black teens is even more distressing. For black males the rate jumped from 17 to 34 percent and for black females the rate increased from 34 to 48 percent between 1978 and 1983. Essentially, 3.44 million American youth spent at least some of 1983 disconnected from school, work, or the military (Betsey et al., 1985). It is no wonder America's domestic policy agenda is full of concerns about the costs and economic value associated with at-risk children and youth.

A SEAMLESS FLOW OF CONCERNS

Much of the renewed attention on society's disconnected children and youth relates to a widespread belief that the country is experiencing a literacy gap. Like the Soviet-American missile gap, symbolized by the launching of Sputnik, there is a pervasive anxiety in today's information age that the nation lacks the literacy capacity to meet the demands of a highly competitive postindustrial economy. The list of perceived literacy deficits is lengthy. A potpourri of scholars, politicians, and business leaders have lamented the nation's vulnerability in terms of assumed shortcomings in cultural literacy, civic literacy, functional literacy, economic literacy, scientific literacy, technological literacy, social literacy, global literacy, computer literacy, and moral literacy. Yet, as the various authors in this book have discussed, emergent literacy forms the crucible upon which all subsequent literacy learning evolves. The failure to nurture oral and written language attitudes and skills early in a child's life exacts a heavy price on the child, on his or her family, and on society. William Teale's chapter on the Kindergarten Emergent Literacy Program demonstrates how some children are placed at risk by schools and teachers that view linguistic and cultural diversity as a deficit rather than a resource. The chapter by Taylor and Strickland highlights how repetitive decoding and workbook exercises often disconnect children from meaningful literacy events to which they have become accustomed at home. Claude Goldenberg's chapter highlights how teachers and parents often do not realize the array of resources and opportunities at their disposal to help unsuccessful children become successful. Gay Pinnell's chapter persuasively chronicles how early literacy deficiencies relate to academic problems across the curriculum as the at-risk student encounters each new level of schooling.

We know that dropouts disproportionately tend to lack strong literacy skills and attitudes (Carbo, 1987). We know that longitudinal studies (Pinnell, this volume) clearly show that children who start off poorly in school tend to stay behind year after year. We also know that technological and scientific advances are demanding even higher levels of literacy. Yet we continue to view the literacy function of schools as largely a matter of transmitting a definitive set of finite oral and written language skills to all students. We are nowhere near the wholesale implementation of Teale's no-risk classrooms, which provide "... a wide variety of literacy experiences for the child in the context of an emotionally supportive environment." Nor are we close to Taylor and Strickland's call for curricular, instructional, and governance policies that help schools work with families to make home and school more nurturant places to be. Clearly, a critical and systemic look at literacy practices and policies is essential to the transformation of schools and schooling.

Fortunately, there is a strong signal on the political radar screens of state and national policymakers that the transformation of schools is inextricably tied to the transformation of families and communities. This shift in strategy in the educational reform policy agenda is exemplified by the following quote from the *Children in Need* report of the Committee for Economic Development:

> We believe that reform strategies for the educationally disadvantaged that focus on the school system alone will continue to fail these "children in need."

We have learned from experience that effective strategies reaching beyond the traditional boundaries of schooling and providing early and sustained intervention in the lives of disadvantaged children can break this vicious cycle of disaffection and despair (quoted in *Education Week*, September 9, 1987, p. 42).

Of course, disadvantaged children (i.e., low income and/or minority children) are not the only ones considered at risk. Children and youth are at risk whenever their support systems break down or they become disconnected from their support systems. The need to look at the conditions of all children, their families, and the schools they attend has never been more compelling. Rather than noting that a given child is a member of a minority group or from a single-parent household, educators and policy makers need to look at the whole context of the child's life. We must be willing to: (1) consider what aspects of the school and home might be contributing to placing the child at risk, (2) respond to the child as a total human being, and (3) work with parents, community members, and organizations outside the bounds of the school. For such a transformation to take place, the structure, curriculum, and instructional practices of the whole school, not just those of isolated projects or after-school programs, have to be reconsidered (Cuban, 1987; Forum of Educational Organizational Leaders, 1987; MDC, Inc., 1985).

Moreover, relationships with other child-oriented agencies and institutions, including parents, have to be reconceptualized. Tinkering with isolated pieces of the educational system is inadequate. What is needed instead is a critical reexamination of the "functions of educating, nurturing, and supporting that are required to develop competent adults in light of the institutional resources available" (Heath & McLaughlin, 1987, p. 579). Perhaps a good place to start is to reassess the status of home, community, and school in the cultivation of the emergent literacy of at-risk children.

HOME: MORE PRESSURES, LESS SUPPORTS

Demographers simultaneously provide snapshots of what a society is and what a society is becoming. The media bombard us with demographic trends and projections: the yuppies (young urban professionals) and boomers (folks born between 1945 and 1960) are on the decline while tweeners (yuppies born to blue collar parents) and Dinks (dual income households with no kids) are on the rise. All the nifty labels tend to gloss over one stark reality: The American family has undergone a profound transformation in the last twenty years. Consider just a few items from a large list of demographic facts about the American family:

- One of twelve households can be characterized as traditional (two parents, one employed outside the home).

- One of five families with children under eighteen are single-parent, female-headed homes.

- 64 percent of all married women who have school-age children are employed outside the home (Bronfenbrenner, 1986).

- 50 percent of married mothers with preschool children and 46 percent of married mothers with children under three work outside the home (Bronfenbrenner, 1986).

- 53 percent of all mothers in single-parent households with children under age three work outside the home (Bronfenbrenner, 1986).

- 69 percent of all mothers in single-parent households with school-age children work outside the home (Bronfenbrenner, 1986).

Perhaps two acronyms need to be added to the demographer's lexicon: Dips (dual income parents) and Disks (dual income households with stressed kids). We have reliable indicators on how many Dips there are in America, but we uncomfortably scratch our heads when the subject of Disks comes up. Like floppy computer disks, kids from dual income households often are treated as "user friendly" software that can be housed and programmed in a variety of settings. The concept of primary care provider has taken on new meaning as witnessed by the phenomenal growth in both after-school, latch-key programs and preschool/early child care programs over the past decade.

Tensions between work and family life often can become internalized and lead to stress-related behaviors in children and youth (e.g., insecurity and alienation). Bronfenbrenner (1986) notes:

> It is all too easy for family life in the U.S. to become hectic and stressful, as both parents try to coordinate the disparate demands of family and jobs in a world in which everyone has to be transported at least twice a day in a variety of directions. Under these circumstances, meal preparation, child care, shopping and cleaning—the most basic tasks in a family—become major challenges. Dealing with these challenges may sometimes take precedence over the family's equally important child-rearing, educational, and nurturing roles. But that is not the main danger. What threatens the well-being of children and young people the most is that the external havoc can become internal, first for parents and then for children. (p. 432)

As pressures on the American family mount, traditional support systems seem to be eroding. Parents are relying less and less on grandparents, aunts, and uncles to help raise the kids. More and more churches are offering child care programs, yet many of the children in these programs come from noncongregational families. Parks and recreation centers find tough competition for the attention of child and family from video game parlors, shopping malls, and video tape rental shops. Close knit neighborhoods populated with people from all age groups have given way to age-

segregated, highly transient housing developments. Children and youth
grow more dependent on their peers for support and challenge as parents
increasingly shift attention and energy to matters outside the home.

As family support systems weaken, literacy-based links across home,
community, and school become jeopardized (Taylor & Strickland, this
volume). Virtually every chapter in this book operates off the premise that
all children must be exposed to school and nonschool environments rich
with oral and print language because "literacy is an intensely social phenomenon" (Dickinson, this volume). The chapter by Taylor and Strickland
highlights the negative impact changing social realities (e.g., single-parent
and dual income households) have on the "moment to moment uses of
literacy in family settings." McCormick and Mason's work with Head Start
children on fostering reading is founded on the notion that using predictable
books in school and having them at home encourages children to read and
talk with their parents about books. Beverly McConnell's chapter on teaching in semiliterate communities emphasizes the need for strong bonds
between parents and community in the nurturance of emergent literacy.
Gay Pinnell's chapter concludes by calling for coordinated efforts that
provide children with meaningful literacy experiences in numerous settings.

The creation of such literacy communities will require a strong social
support infrastructure for families and schools. Political predispositions
about the nature and scope of the American educational system need to be
critically re-examined. The worlds of work and school need to be more
tightly aligned. Teachers and school administrators must learn how to
simultaneously honor and enhance the literacy heritage of a diverse array of
families. Policies and support systems must be developed to reduce family
stresses and to encourage more parental participation in the life of the
school.

What is the effect of policy on children and families? In early autumn
1987, President Reagan signed an executive order requiring that all federal
policies be assessed for their impact on family "well-being" (*Education
Week*, September 16, 1987). The order directs all federal agencies to judge
their policies against several criteria, including their potential to enhance or
erode family stability; marital commitment; and the authority of parents to
educate, nurture, and supervise their children. Federal agencies must
provide a rationale for any policy that might have a "significant potential
negative impact" on the family. Moreover, every federal agency must
certify to the Office of Management and Budget that it has assessed the
negative and positive effects of policy proposals.

President Reagan's executive order on family well-being may, in some
cases, exacerbate the pressures on some families, especially if some policies
are judged exclusively on political and/or ideological preferences. For
example, student financial aid policies might be reassessed under the

auspices of the executive order by a conservative administration interested in reducing the federal role in higher education. Significant cuts in student aid could restrict access even further to low- and middle-income youth. Middle-class families face the economic reality of being able to have "one major illness, one retirement plan, or send one child to college" (Hodgkinson, 1986, p. 272).

Fortunately, the family-impact executive order represents a new way of developing federal policy related to the well-being of the family. Although vulnerable to ideological manipulation, it provides a better way of looking at how public policy influences home, community, and school bonds, especially in terms of quality-of-life issues for at-risk children and youth. Perhaps educational policy makers should adopt a literacy impact mentality as they develop policies on curriculum, instruction, home-school relations, accountability, and assessment.

COMMUNITY: ACCESS TO SOCIAL CAPITAL

Strong and stable families do not guarantee the effective nurturance of emergent literacy. Broad and deep access to "social capital" also is needed. Social capital refers to "the norms, the social networks, and the relationships between adults and children that are of value for the child's growing up" (Coleman, 1987, p. 36). Coleman provides an example of family-generated social capital that focuses on literacy development:

> A school district where children purchase textbooks recently found that some Asian families were purchasing two. Investigation led to the discovery that one book was for the mother, to enable her to better help her child succeed in school. The mother, uneducated, had little human capital, but her intense concern with her child's school performance, and her willingness to devote effort to aiding that, shows a high level of social capital in the family (1987, p. 36).

The family can produce a social capital, but so can community organizations such as the YMCA and YWCA, soccer leagues, city symphonies, ballet companies, the PTA, Scout troops, swim clubs, art museums, and libraries. Positive and extensive adult-child interactions across the community can promote many forms of literacy, including civic, moral, and functional. Access to an abundance of social capital can provide children and youth with the kinds of literacy, attitudes, motivations, and conception of self that they need to succeed in schools and as adults. Unfortunately, there is a nagging worry that American society faces a growing social capital deficit. Numerous reasons are cited for the erosion in social capital— narcissistic individualism, growth in dual income households, loosely-knit neighborhoods, excessive reliance on television, and the creation of new childrearing institutions isolated from home, work, and community (e.g, for-profit daycare centers).

How does America's stock of social capital stack up against other postindustrial societies? Not well, if one looks at social indicator data such as teenage pregnancy rates, divorce rates, poverty levels, and substance abuse measures. For example:

• America has the highest rate of teenage pregnancy of any industrialized nation—twice the rate of England, the second highest.

• The U.S. divorce rate is the highest in the world—nearly double that of the second-ranked country, Sweden.

• America is the only industrialized nation in which roughly one-fourth of all infants and preschool children live in families with incomes below the poverty line.

• The U.S. has the highest incidence of alcohol and drug abuse among adolescents of any nation in the world. (Bronfenbrenner, 1986, p. 434).

Coleman perceives the loss of social capital, inside and outside the family, as an inevitable outcome of the transformation of the home and the community in American society.

> In effect, raising children once took place informally, as a by-product of other activities, in social institutions—the household, the extended family, and neighborhood-based organizations—that were held in place by these activities. As the locus of the other activities has changed, the institutions have crumbled, and the by-product, childrearing, has crumbled along with them. The institutions that have replaced them (the offices and factories that have replaced households or neighborhoods as workplaces, the shopping malls and catalogs that have replaced neighborhood stores as places to shop, the cocktail parties and rock concerts that have replaced gatherings of extended families as leisure settings) are inhospitable to the relations between adults and children that constitute social capital for the children's growth (Coleman, 1987, p. 37).

Communities with inaccessible and/or impoverished supplies of social capital place all children at risk; however, the lack of community-based social capital particularly hurts children from families with limited social capital themselves. Moreover, these children are likely to be the least literate. It is in these families where successful cultivation of emergent literacy is critical to future educational and economic wellbeing. Patricia Edwards' research on parent-child interactions in the literacy development of low-income families is particularly relevant for families and communities facing social capital deficits. William Teale's Kindergarten Emergent Literacy Program (KELP) also attempts to overcome the erosion of social capital by promoting productive home-school interactions. Claude Goldenberg suggests that it is up to the teacher to mobilize home resources, to inform parents when progress is not good, and to guide parental involvement in the child's literacy development. Finally, the Reading Recovery Program described in Gay Pinnell's chapter represents a systemic and strategic way to enhance social capital investment in early literacy learning.

In a way, literacy development in young at-risk learners has little to do with educational policies governing school organization, curriculum, personnel, and finances. Instead, success in literacy learning for *all* children rests fundamentally on public policies that shape the nature, role, function, and interrelationship of home, community, and school. Put simply, access and availability of social capital provide the prime determinants of how and how well literacy learning is achieved. Literacy learning is the critical conduit in the transmission of social capital. Common and competent literacy is a prerequisite of productive relationships between people, communities, corporations, countries, generations, governments, religions, neighborhoods, families, and technologies. Comprehensive and sustained attention to emergent literacy will promote the kinds of attitudes, effort, and conception of self that at-risk children need to help rebuild the nation's social capital.

SCHOOL: A TURBULENT EPICENTER

Over the past quarter century, the school has come to represent society's first line response to untidy transformations in home and community. Need to reduce racial discrimination in the community? Desegregate the schools. Need to get a handle on the substance abuse problem? Add a couple of courses in the middle and high schools. More mothers entering the labor market? Tag on latchkey programs to the school day. Yuppie parents want to give Junior a head start on social status and economic prosperity? Offer more enrichment programs. The nation is losing its economic competitiveness? Exhort excellence in the classroom.

The excellence-in-education movement of the early and mid-1980s firmly established the schools as the epicenter for economic and social transformation in America. In the early part of the decade, the focus was on the nature and quality of secondary education (e.g., U.S. Department of Education, 1983; Carnegie Foundation, 1983). After a brief dalliance on the state of higher education (e.g., U.S. Department of Education, 1984; Carnegie Foundation, 1987) and the state of elementary education (e.g., U.S. Department of Education, 1986), the attention of reformers shifted to the nature, importance, and quality of preschool education (e.g., Committee for Economic Development, 1985, 1987). By early 1988, the reform rhetoric had moved away from sporadic critiques of various levels of schooling and centered on a growing population of students considered critical to the nation's economic and social well-being—at-risk children and youth.

There is little safety and comfort in the center of an earthquake. The school is in the strongest and weakest position to develop and nurture linkages across home, work, and community. It is strong in the sense that it has been given the responsibility to guide children and youth from the secluded confines of the home to the responsibilities, freedoms, opportunities, and constraints of productive citizenship in a democracy. It is weak in the sense that it is widely considered a governmentally provided service that does not need much direct investment from home or work. In a consumer concious society, we tend to look at schools as one of many goods and services we *purchase* in our daily transactions.

The transformation of the household and the community demands substantial restructuring of schools. Schools must change as families and neighborhoods change. Currently, business leaders are the choirmasters calling for change in schools and schooling. David Kearns, chairman and chief executive officer of Xerox, laid down the gauntlet in an October 1987 speech at the Economic Club of Detroit:

> Public education has put this country at a terrible competitive disadvantage. The American workforce is running out of qualified people. If current demographic and economic trends continue, American business will have to hire a million new workers a year who can't read, write, or count. Teaching them how, and absorbing the lost productivity while they're learning, will cost industry $25 billion a year for as long as it takes. And nobody I know knows how long that will be. Teaching new workers basic skills is doing the school's product recall work for them—and frankly, I resent it.

Mr. Kearns' plea did not fall on deaf ears. Less than one month after the Economic Club speech, the Council of Chief State School Officers (CSSO) endorsed a policy statement to guarantee a high-quality precollegiate education to those students deemed least likely to finish high school. David Hornbeck, outgoing president of the Chief State School Officers, described the policy statement as a "basic understanding" that major structural transformations are needed in schools. The CSSO plan proposes that schools and school systems provide parents and students with eleven "guarantees":

1. An education program of the quality available to students who attend schools with high graduation rates. This core academic program should be supplemented with needed services that are integrated with the regular program.

2. Enrollment in a school that demonstrates substantial and sustained student progress.

3. Enrollment in a school with an appropriately certified staff whose members receive continual professional development.

4. Enrollment in a school with systematically designed and delivered instruction of demonstrable effectiveness and with adequate and up-to-date learning technologies and materials of proven value.

5. Enrollment in a school with safe and functional facilities.

6. A parent and early childhood development program beginning ideally for children by age 3, but no later than age 4.

7. A written guide for teaching and learning for each student, prepared with and approved by the student and his or her parents.

8. A program to allow families to participate as partners in their children's learning both at home and at school.

9. Effective health and social services.

10. Information that would help identify at-risk students and report on school conditions and performance. The information must be sufficient to let one know whether the above guarantees are being met.

11. Procedures that enable students, their parents, or their representatives to ensure that these guarantees are met (*Education Week*, November 18, 1987, p. 17).

The at-risk children and youth issue is complicated, and it will not go away with quick fixes and verbal guarantees. Essentially, a lasting and effective response to demographic and economic imperatives is to reconceptualize and restructure home, community, and school ties. Schools and the professionals who work in them need positive support and encouragement to critically examine policies, programs, and practices related to at-risk student populations. The eighth, tenth, and eleventh guarantees provide an impetus for such self-exploration. However, it is the sixth, eighth, and eleventh guarantees that provide the best hope for bold revisions in literacy policies and practices. At the heart of these four espoused guarantees is the belief that children and families do not intentionally place themselves at risk; school systems endanger students when they uniformly, arbitrarily, and dogmatically impose an inflexible literacy curriculum and an unrealistic timetable for success (Taylor & Strickland, Allen & Carr, Pinnell, and Goldenberg, this volume). The authors of this book share some assumptions about literacy learning that fit nicely with the sixth, eighth, tenth, and eleventh guarantees expressed in the CSSO November 1987 policy statement:

• Children enter school with various language competencies and literary heritage. The child will learn if the school builds on these competencies and heritage.

- Educators have a better chance of fostering literacy learning if they develop a holistic viewpoint about each child. Professional educators learn by (1) formulating an understanding of the child's community and family, and (2) observing, systematically and over time, how each child makes sense of the world, especially through the use of oral and written language.

Claude Goldenberg's chapter provides the most detailed description of how these two assumptions can guide a teacher's ability to foster literacy learning. Goldenberg essentially argues that the "socio-cognitive web" of student, home, and teacher provides the social capital needed to help the unsuccessful child become successful. New techniques, new curriculum, new resources, new categorical aid, new pull-out programs—all are doomed, according to Goldenberg, unless the socio-cognitive web is tightly joined. Basically, Goldenberg's chapter centers on one key question: What compels the teacher or school system to act when literacy learning is not maximized? The system answers the question with a policy; the individual teacher's response is often based on a belief. Remember that little Freddy was saved from being terminally at risk because the system would not tolerate the violation of a homework policy. Doe-eyed Marta was rescued from a life of illiteracy due to the teacher's belief that she could be motivated to higher levels of performance.

Policy is a mountebank if it relies on serendipity to succeed. Teacher beliefs are morally reprehensible if they do not allow each child access to the curricular and instructional resources they need to succeed. Neither good policy nor compassionate teacher beliefs can "guarantee" a child's literacy future; however, both are necessary conditions for success. The secret is to develop policies that support and encourage appropriate teacher beliefs (e.g., understanding family literacy is critical to literacy development of the child; a quiet classroom is not necessarily a productive nor desired educational outcome; early intensive intervention efforts can reduce reading failure over the long term).

Genuine transformation begins when home, community, and school systems converge around a shared understanding of extant political, social, and economic realities and collaboratively strive to overcome their natural predisposition to extend and perpetuate themselves without changing. In other words, self-interest must give way to collective interest if we are ever to experience a social capital surplus in this country. The new politics of school transformation might productively begin in the area of literacy policy.

LITERACY POLICY: NEW POLITICS, NEW AGENDA

Historically, public policy attention on children usually has been a by-product of concern over the economic status of adults. As the ultimate voteless constituency, children lack the political power to directly change the quality of their own lives. Much policy action comes indirectly to children (e.g., welfare, health care, education) through adult-oriented institutions and services. In fact, there are some educational historians who suggest that the passage of state compulsory attendance laws at the turn of the century was due to the lobbying efforts of teachers and school administrators as a means to guarantee job security and expand the public school system (Tyack, 1976).

Today, the efficacy of the public school system is, once again, under intense scrutiny. The passionate criticisms of Xerox executives do not go unnoticed in our political economy. A postindustrial economy demands quality workers and well-paid consumers in order to flourish. More and more policy makers are exploring the three Ds of school transformation—deregulation, devolution, and decredentialling. Expanded parental choice in the form of voucher plans and tuition tax credits is a popular notion among those who seek deregulation of public schools. Increased monitoring and expanded intervention at the state level prompts those who desire the devolution of the federal role in education. More flexibility and the injection of new blood are benefits often cited by those interested in decredentialling the way we train, select, and retain teachers, administrators, and professional support personnel.

One can soon get lost in the salvos and retorts of special interests involved somehow or another in the education of our children. The business community wants higher profits through more productive workers and more economically prosperous consumers. Colleges of education want to stay in business. State departments of education want to expand and legitimate their functions. Legislators and governors want to be re-elected. Graying baby boomers are reaching the zenith of their earning power and worry more about at-risk retirement than at-risk children and youth. Teacher and administrator associations want more say over the organization and control of schools. Parents want schools that simultaneously can provide their children cheap custodial care, strong character development, productive civic sensibilities, and employability. Students want to connect up to schools where meaningful, real, and whole learning experiences are provided. The politics of education has never been more enthralling and more exasperating.

Literacy learning represents virtually the only policy topic in educational politics that interests all the special interests. The transmission of the culture depends on it. RIF (Reading Is Fundamental) logic has given way to LIFE logic (Literacy is Fostered Early). America cannot afford to lose any more children. The nation's burgeoning social capital deficit demands that we quit separating our individual and collective lives. Enlightened collective interest must replace self-interest as the dominant orientation in the politics of education. New political alliances need to be forged that include blacks, Hispanics, child advocate groups, child service providers, educators, and business leaders.

Literacy policies that reduce the risks for young learners reduce the risks for all of us. The time has come to develop a new literacy policy agenda. The agenda must be sensitive to how literacy policies interface with people. Reading and writing are intimate human experiences even when they are designed to be communicated to thousands or millions of people. Literacy learning cannot be mandated through prepackaged curriculum and rigid forms of assessment produced by distal policy agents. Policy makers interested in emergent literacy need to view children and families "as subjects—active human beings whose field of endeavor is structured by their own symbolic systems, their conceptions of world, self, and community, their memories of the past, perceptions of the present, and hopes for the future. Treating people as carbon copies of oneself without taking the trouble to enter their cultural environment, or—worse still—treating them as instrumentalities for, or hindrances to, the realization of a preconceived plan, is a formula for policy failure" (Scheffler, 1984, p. 155).

Unfortunately, there are clear signs on the horizon that the logic of policy failure is winning the day as the literacy policy agenda for the 1990s emerges. In mid-1987, U.S. Secretary of Education William J. Bennett recommended adoption of legislation to revamp the country's largest and most extensive governmentally sponsored educational testing program, the National Assessment of Educational Progress (NAEP). The proposal called for an expansion in the number of students tested from 70,000 to 700,000 and the disaggregation of national data for accurate and comprehensive state-by-state comparisons. The rationale for the proposed changes in NAEP rested on two arguments: (1) comparative state-by-state assessments of educational performance would gauge more precisely where and which schools are failing; and (2) schools would be made more accountable by giving better information to legislators, educators, and parents.

Few people would disagree with the notion that policy judgment is enhanced whenever more information is available. However, the proposed changes in the format of the NAEP go far beyond the "better information, better decision" dictum. It is assumed that more national testing of student achievement and literacy levels will pinpoint the problems of American education with more clarity and better accuracy. However, as many observers of the excellence-in-education reform movement have pointed out (Cross, 1987; Scheffler, 1984; Shor, 1986), real and pervasive reform will transpire only when educators, policy makers, and researchers collaboratively embark on a critical inquiry of schools and society. Expanded NAEP testing will not directly confront the nation's social capital deficit, nor will it reduce the pressures on the American family. In fact, more testing mandates might increase stress levels in many American households.

Despite considerable opposition, the Georgia State Board of Education in early 1988 enacted a policy to make Georgia the first in the nation to require all school districts to use standardized test scores as a primary factor in deciding whether a kindergartner is promoted to the first grade. The ninety-minute examination assesses sound and visual recognition as well as simple number concepts. The rationale for the early assessment policy is based on a belief that early identification will get "needy" students more efficiently and effectively "into the process of remediation" (*Education Week*, 1988, p. 15). Moreover, it is assumed that a better measure is needed to determine a kindergartner's ability to do subsequent academic work. Unfortunately, most notions of readiness and remediation fail to adequately address potentially negative consequences, such as mislabeling young children as slow learners, discriminating against low-income and/or minority children who disproportionately lack emergent literacy skills, and ignoring the likelihood of unpredictable results whenever standardized tests are used on young children who tend to be unschooled and erratic test-takers.

Instead of building such structural impediments to emergent literacy, perhaps policy might be refocused around three strategic issues: (1) encouraging school-based self-exploration, (2) broadening notions of teacher professionalism, and (3) rebuilding social network infrastructure.

Self-Exploration

What are the scope, impact, consequences, strengths, and weaknesses of existing literacy policies and programs for young learners? When solutions to emergent literacy problems are not evident, it is better to gain a deeper understanding of the situation, since inappropriate solutions will be, at best, wasteful, and, at worse, counterproductive. State legislators and/or state departments of education could offer incentive grants for some schools to voluntarily engage in in-depth self-exploration of how their literacy policies, practices, and programs affect young at-risk learners (see Appendix for a fuller example of a school self-study). The process of self-exploration could focus on questions such as:

- What is happening in the classroom that impedes or enhances emergent literacy among at-risk students?

- What school policies are beneficial/harmful for literacy learning among at-risk students?
- What school district, state, and federal policies impede or enhance emergent literacy among at-risk students?

Policy-supported incentives for self-exploration would encourage schools to conduct authentic self-study without threat of reprisal. Moreover, it would help teachers become more informed about the family life of their at-risk students (Taylor & Strickland, this volume), as well as better identify available resources in the system for the literacy needs of at-risk students (Goldenberg, this volume).

Teacher Professionalism

Most educational reform movements come down to one issue: Who controls education? Usually, a wide array of actors stake out squatter's rights for the authority to determine the form of education most suitable for children and youth—federal and state governments, local communities, parents, business leaders, and educational leaders to name just a few. The current excellence-in-education reform movement seems to be coming down to those who call for greater choice in education (e.g., business leaders) and those who seek more professional control over education (e.g., teacher unions). State legislatures ultimately will determine which policy choice will win out. At this point, both expanded choice and teacher professionalism are being advanced (see Carnegie Task Force, 1986) as the reforms that will provide parents more assurances about the nature and quality of education their children receive. Career ladder plans, professional standards boards, and graduate-level, preservice teacher education programs are being touted as the bedrock reforms if teaching is to become a true profession. A literacy policy agenda needs to fit tightly with policies related to teacher professionalism. The beliefs, predispositions, talents, and skills of tomorrow's teachers will grow out of today's policy decisions about teacher professionalism.

Why can't most career ladder plans require master teachers to provide leadership in the development of tighter literacy-based bonds between home and school? Why can't national and state professional standards boards require all teachers to demonstrate substantial competence in fostering literacy learning in all their students? Why can't graduate-level pre-service teacher education programs provide experiential training in home-school relations, ethnographic observation, and family counseling?

Advocates of emergent literacy programs, such as the Reading Recovery Program at Ohio State University (Pinnell, this volume), will miss out on a golden political opportunity if they fail to press such questions to policy makers. The transformation of the teaching profession will require different and ultimately more productive forms of governance and accountability for public schools that enable teachers to practice professionally in the interests of students while preserving democratic traditions (Darling-Hammond & Berry, 1987). A literacy policy agenda eventually will have to recognize a restructured teaching profession, so why not wed the two agendas early on?

Social Network Infrastructure

Can formal and informal literacy support systems be developed across home, community, and school that do not now exist in sufficient strength? In the late 1960s, Mildred Smith (Bronfenbrenner, 1986) developed a program to improve academic performance among low-income minority pupils by bolstering the social network infrastructure of the community. The project

> involved approximately 1,000 children from low income families, most of them black, attending public elementary schools. The principal strategy employed for enhancing children's school performance was including the child's signifi-cant others—the parent and the teacher—as partners, not competitors, in the child's learning process. Parents mobilized other parents to become involved in the school. Parents were urged to provide supports for their children while teachers' inservice sessions focused on the influence of environmental factors in children's classroom behavior and performance. Essentially, support systems were established for all participants in the program (Bronfenbrenner & Weiss, 1983, p. 404).

Literacy learning was a vital part of Mildred Smith's experimental program. Young learners were given tags to wear at home that said: "May I read to you?" (Bronfenbrenner, 1986). Working parents talked to classrooms about the importance of literacy in their work lives. Students in the high school business classes typed and duplicated teaching materials (e.g., pre-dictable books), enabling teachers to work more directly with children and promoting home-school literacy-based linkages.

The story of Mildred Smith's experimental efforts provides a com-pelling rationale for thinking about how schools relate to the home, the workplace, and the community. A great expenditure of new resources is not a necessary prerequisite to the establishment of emergent literacy programs. The socio-cognitive web contains plenty of resources for transformation. Some educational policies might need to be amended in terms of how we organize and run schools (e.g., using high school business classes to produce and disseminate little books that young learners can take home to share with the family). However, some private sector policies will need to be pursued if the home-school partnership is to really blossom. For example, local businesses could facilitate the participation of their employees in the life of local schools by adopting policies on alternative work arrangements (e.g., flextime, job sharing, flexible leave, and alternative work schedules). If businesses wanted to be really innovative they could offer volunteer literacy-leave programs where employees are given released time to work with children, families, and schools in the cultivation of emergent literacy. Such a program might be especially appropriate for businesses involved in computers and other forms of information technology.

The needs are apparent. The policy possibilities are endless. Community-based literacy development will become more and more a reality when advocates present a compelling and comprehensible case. This book represents a good start. We need proactive, interrelated strategies on policy issues related to school-based self-exploration, teacher professionalism, and social network infrastructure. We can reduce the risks for young learners if we are willing to undertake such a bold new literacy agenda.

APPENDIX: EXAMPLE OF A SCHOOL SELF-STUDY

To conduct a self-study, a school could free a group of teachers, administrators, and support staff from some of their existing responsibilities to identify the relationship between the school, its at-risk students, the students' homes, and the larger community. The self-study group could:

1. Identify a sample of students considered to be potentially at risk and interview them and their parents about in-school and out-of-school literacy experiences.

2. Follow ("shadow") a sample of at-risk students during and after the school day to learn directly about school and after-school literacy experiences.

3. Interview reading teachers about the factors they perceive inhibit or enhance their effectiveness with at-risk students.

4. Collect information about the daily operations of the school to identify how particular school policies and practices may be affecting at-risk students differently from those not at risk. Some practices to consider could include
   - the assignment of students to teachers;
   - the placement of students in academic groups or tracks;
   - the opportunities for extracurricular activities;
   - the expectations regarding parental involvement in homework assignments;
   - the procedures for going on field trips or for participating in special functions;
   - the expectations regarding social interactions (e.g., cultural norms for politeness, for participation in discussions, for appropriate adult-child interactions);
   - the quality of instruction (e.g., clarity of lesson objectives, clarity of instructions to students, amount of time spent in interacting with students, amount of time preparing to teach students, etc.); and

- the nature of the adult-student interactions (e.g., how many adults interact with a given student on a daily basis? Does any adult know that student well?).

5. Review the written policies of the school to see if they might be affecting at-risk students differently from those not considered to be at risk. Some policies to consider might include
   - rules regarding absences and tardiness,
   - eligibility for special programs and privileges,
   - rules regarding suspensions and expulsions,
   - graduation requirements,
   - testing policies, and
   - procedures for placing students in particular classes.

6. Identify the various literacy-based programs within the school and review the participation of a sample of at-risk students.

7. Identify how the school links with the family. Relevant questions might include:
   - Are the contacts primarily in the school?
   - Do teachers, administrators, counselors get to know parents in the home setting?
   - Do parents of at-risk students feel comfortable in the school or with school personnel?
   - Do school personnel feel comfortable with parents?
   - Do parents receive positive feedback about students?
   - Is the literacy heritage of the family understood?

8. Identify how the school links with other agencies in the community, especially those who foster literacy learning.

The school self-study model emerges from the policy research work of Robert Donmoyer, Nancy Zajano, and Brad Mitchell at The Ohio State University.

The school self-study model in the preceding chapter provides us, as educators, a place to start building local policy. But just as children and teachers and parents do not operate as isolated systems, neither does educational policy stop at the school district boundary line. There are county, state, and national educational policies that affect and may be affected by local policy. What can we do to influence policy at these levels? Edelman tells us in her call for action.

Chapter 15

What Can We Do?
Marian Wright Edelman

THIS is not time for despair, handwringing, or bystanding. This is the time for committed action. Although there are no quick, simple, or easy answers to many of the social and economic problems described in this book, there are a number of steps each of us can take to begin the hard but necessary task of providing a floor of decency under every American child and family.

Step one is recognizing that it is up to you and me to protect our young and needy. The politicians and the experts will not do it unless informed and organized citizen action demands it. Americans need to dig deep within ourselves and commit to a greater personal tithing of time, energy, and resources to help the needy young and old. If, as a nation, we decided to tithe 10 percent of our planned increases in military budget authority, we could provide an additional $30.5 billion for children's programs over the next five years. All of us—rich, middle class, and poor—need to pull our proportionate weight in making America great. And if we don't have money to tithe, we can tithe our time and commitment. We can tutor some of the children who need help and find countless ways to become the hands and feet and voices of compassion in the personal and political arenas, as so many Americans already are doing.

Step two is undertaking large-scale, but carefully targeted, public education and organizing efforts to build a strong constituency for preventive investment in children and families. Child advocates must increase dramatically the number of Americans, particularly those in decision-making and decision-swaying positions, who know what is happening to American children and the consequences for the children, their community, and the nation.

Step three is defining the most important things children need, the policies and strategies required to meet those needs, and likely opposition and allies. We must resist quick-fix, cosmetic, and politically attractive but inadequate solutions to complex social problems.

Step four is documenting, highlighting, and educating the public and policy makers about a range of successful programs for children and the cost-effectiveness of specific preventive investments in the young. The American public is willing to support programs that make a difference in improving children's lives. A 1986 Louis Harris poll showed a majority of citizens felt our national government was not investing enough in children. A more recent Daniel Yankelovich poll also showed that a majority of Americans of all ages and income groups thought our government was not doing enough for poor children. Child advocates must build on this positive public opinion by disseminating information on programs that work, by setting clear priorities, and by lobbying systematically for their adoption. We have such a strong case to make for increasing investment in children and families that we should not miss an opportunity to spread the word. Head Start works: it helps keep children at grade level and helps prevent more costly education placement and teen pregnancy. But four out of five children who need it are not receiving it. Chapter 1 has a positive effect on raising basic skill levels among disadvantaged children, yet half of those eligible are excluded from the program. What is the rationale for not doubling Chapter 1 as soon as possible to reach all eligible children?

Step five is working to reverse the spending priorities that have favored the haves at the expense of the have-nots. We must stop our national government from actively promoting housing policies that leave children out in the cold (about 30 percent of the homeless population, estimated at 1 to 2 million, are members of families with children); nutritional policies that leave them unfed (budget cuts have excluded 2 million children from the school lunch program); health care policies that leave them more likely than adults to be among the 35 million Americans uninsured; and welfare policies that leave them destitute (1.5 million children have lost some or all AFDC benefits since 1980, and thirty-two states provide benefits that are less than half of the federal poverty line). Three million American children have fallen into poverty since 1979 and 9 million Americans have lost their health insurance.

Step six is knowing how our elected officials have voted on issues important to children and poor families so we can lobby them to do better.

More of us must become strong and persistent proponents of targeted investment in children—in the Congress, in our states, counties, cities, and towns. Children are totally dependent on adult caring and help. They don't vote, lobby, make campaign contributions, or write editorials. Without the organized voice of child advocates, caring adults outside the political process, and thoughtful leaders within the political process, children's needs will be neglected and trampled upon to their and the nation's loss.

Each year CDF publishes a nonpartisan rating of key votes affecting poor children, youths, and families cast by your representatives and senators. We hope you will pay attention to how your congressional delegation is treating children. Regular visits with members at home or in Washington, frequent letters (in care of the U. S. Senate, Washington, D. C. 20510 or the U. S. House of Representatives, Washington, D. C. 20515), and timely telephone calls to home offices or to Washington (202–224–3121) are critically important.

Step seven is broadening the politics of change and the constituency that politicians, policy makers, and citizens see as at risk. We must redefine the face of poverty in the public mind and make clear that it is not just black and Hispanic children and families or those on welfare who are suffering, albeit disproportionately, today. The majority of the deprived are white. The majority of the poor are working and not on welfare.

Nor is it just the 13 million officially poor children and 20 million parents, elders, and others whose survival needs the nation must attend. Equal effort must be made to bolster millions of additional families who are struggling to keep families and homes together despite problems that threaten their capacity to protect their children adequately. Child care, housing, health care, and higher education costs leave these families constantly struggling to stay a step ahead of poverty. Many Americans are just one serious illness away from financial disaster, one plant closing away from welfare and eviction, and one drought away from farm foreclosure. This body of Americans is now legion.

We must constantly work to identify the common threads of self-interest between poor and middle-class children and families, as well as with other constituencies. Indeed, young families seeking to form and stabilize, middle-aged and elderly Americans dependent on a productive work force, private employers dependent on trained workers and consumers with purchasing power, taxpayers concerned about dependency and the high costs of trying to solve problems that could have been prevented, all need to be shown how self-interest converges with investing in the poorest of our children.

Step eight is starting now to make children, families, and the poor of all ages a major part of the presidential and other election debates, both national and local. We need to ask all candidates about their specific policies designed to strengthen children and families and their visions for lifting the weak as well as cultivating the strong. Will they speak out strongly for children? Will they act positively and systematically for children? If we want the nation to place children first, it will take enormous effort.

Step nine is anticipating and identifying the key barriers to achieving a secure and decent future for our children, developing strategies to go around and over the barriers, and, when necessary, to knock them down. The budget will be the most frequently heard political excuse for neglecting children. Our response is fourfold: (1) children did not cause the deficit and hurting them more will not cure it; (2) children and their families have sacrificed proportionately more than any other group, $10 billion per year; (3) investing in children now saves money later—to fail to prevent sickness, malnutrition, and early childhood deprivation is to perpetuate the very dependency cycle and high remediation costs so many currently decry; (4) investing in children is feasible—we know how to do it and how to achieve positive results for relatively modest investment, as has been shown throughout this book.

Careless rhetoric and analysis and single solutions that misstate the problems of the poor and needed remedies are a second barrier. Too often the poor are lumped together in an underclass, which leads too many to blame the victim; conclude that nothing can be done; or to seek uniform answers, rather than a range of specific remedies that various groups of the poor may need at a particular time.

Step ten is mounting effective advocacy. Be prepared. Do your home-work. Think through your options. Have your fallback position ready. Know your opposition and how to get around or defeat it. Know your allies. Take nothing for granted. Pay attention to details. Check all your bases as many times as needed until you have won your goal. Then follow through. A law partner said of Grenville Clark, one of America's great citizens and advocates, that he "proposed like a scientist and hung on like a leech." Effective child advocates must do likewise.

Be specific: Stay away from generalities and offer a menu of specific things that people of varying skills and values will be able and willing to undertake. We must not expect people to simply be "for children" or seek to convert them to our view of the world. Rather, offer specific ways they can act within their own capacities and beliefs. Put yourself in the place of those you need to influence and pitch your appeal to them in ways that they can hear and be moved to act within their ambit of authority. Seek the common ground.

Be efficient: Don't waste your time and other people's time. Don't get on a treadmill of endless meetings. Think hard about your goal and how to get there in the most efficient way.

Be persistent: Children will get exactly what we are strong and persuas-ive enough to insist that they get.

Be positive: It is so easy to wallow in problems and to tear down and be against everything. It is much harder to offer constructive alternatives to problems. Ultimately, what we are for matters a lot more than what we are against.

Be confident and faithful to our cause: Protecting children is a mission second to none in national importance. We are testing once again the viability of the American experiment for the least of the least. Franklin Roosevelt thought the "test of our progress is not whether we add to the abundance of those who have much. It is whether we provide enough for those who have little."

Be courageous: It will take a long time to build a world fit for children, but we must begin at home. Reinhold Niebuhr reminded us of that: "Nothing that is worth doing can be achieved in our lifetime; therefore we must be saved by hope."

ACKNOWLEDGMENTS

This chapter has been excerpted with permission from the Foreword of *A Children's Defense Budget* by Marian Wright Edelman.

References

Aardema, V. (1975). *Why mosquitoes buzz in people's ears.* New York: Dial Press.

Adelman, H. (1978). Predicting psycho-educational problems in childhood. *Behavioral Disorders, 3,* 148−159.

Adelman, H., & Feshbach, S. (1971). Predicting reading failure: Beyond the readiness model. *Exceptional Children, 37,* 349−354.

Allen, J. (1989). Literacy development in whole language kindergartens. In J. Mason (Ed.), *Reading/writing connections: An instructional priority in elementary schools.* Boston: Allyn & Bacon.

Allen, J., & Rubin, D. (in press). Cross-cultural factors affecting initial acquisition of literacy among children and adults. In S.R. Yussen, & M.C. Smith (Eds.), *Reading across the life span.* New York: Springer-Verlag.

Allen, R.V. (1976). *Language experiences in communication.* Boston, MA: Houghton Mifflin.

Allen, W.R. (1976). The search for applicable theories of black family life. *Journal of Marriage and the Family, 40,* 117−129.

Allington, R.L. (1977). If they don't read much how they ever gonna get good? *Journal of Reading, 21,* 57−61.

Allington, R.L. (1980). Poor readers don't get to read much in reading groups. *Language Arts, 57,* 872−876.

Allington, R.L. (1983). The reading instruction provided readers of differing ability. *Elementary School Journal, 83,* 255−265.

Allington, R., Boxer, N., Broikou, K., Gaskins, R., King, S., McGill-Franzen, A., & Stuetzel, H. (1987, December 3). *Strategic instructional issues in remedial reading.* Symposium presented at the National Reading Conference, St. Petersburg, FL.

Allsburg, C.V. (1981). *Jumanji.* New York: Houghton Mifflin.

Alpha time. (1972). Plainview, NY: New Dimension in Education.

Altwerger, A., Diehl-Faxon, J., & Dockstader-Anderson, K. (1985). Read-aloud events as meaning construction. *Language Arts, 62,* 476−484.

Ambrus, Y.G. (1969). *The seven skinny goats.* New York: Harcourt, Brace & World.

Anderson, A., & Stokes, S. (1984). Social and institutional influences on the development and practice of literacy. In H. Goelman, A. Oberg, & F. Smith (Eds.), *Awakening to literacy*. Portsmouth, NH: Heinemann.

Anderson, R.A., Hiebert, E.H., Scott, J.A., & Wilkinson, I.A.G. (1985). *Becoming a nation of readers: The report of the Commission on Reading*. Washington, DC: The National Institute of Education.

Arias, M.B. (1986). The context of education for Hispanic students: An overview. *American Journal of Education, 95*, 26–57.

Au, K.H., & Jordan, C. (1981). Teaching reading to Hawaiian children: Finding a culturally appropriate solution. In H.T. Trueba, G.P. Guthrie, & K.H. Au (Eds), *Culture and the bilingual classroom* (pp. 139–152). Rowley, MA: Newbury House.

Avery, C. (1987). Traci: A learning-disabled child in a writing-process classroom. In G.L. Bissex & R.H. Bullock (Eds.), *Seeing for ourselves: Case-study research by teachers of writing*. Portsmouth, NH: Heinemann.

Baghban, M.J.M. (1984). *Our daughter learns to read and write: A case study from birth to three*. Newark, DE: International Reading Association.

Baratz, S.S., & Baratz, J.C. (1970). Early childhood intervention: The social science base of institutional racism. *Harvard Educational Review, 40*, 29–50.

Bereiter, C. (1985). The changing face of educational disadvantagement. *Phi Delta Kappan, 66*, 538–541.

Berrueta-Clement, J.R., Schweinhart, L.H., Barnett, W.S., Epstein, A.S., & Weikart, D.P. (1984). *Changed lives: The effects of the Perry Preschool Program on youths through age 19*. Ypsilanti, MI: The High/Scope Educational Research Foundation.

Betsey, C.L., Hollister, R.G., & Papageorgiou, M. (Eds.). (1985). *Youth employment and training programs: The YEDPA years*. National Research Council. Washington, DC: National Academy Press.

Bissex, G.L. (1980). *GYNS AT WRK: A child learns to write and read*. Cambridge, MA: Harvard University Press.

Bissex, G.L. (1984). The child as teacher. In H. Goelman, A. Oberg, & F. Smith (Eds.), *Awakening to literacy*. Portsmouth, NH: Heinemann.

Blom, G., Jansen, M., & Allerup, P. (1976). A cross-national study of factors related to reading achievement and reading disability. In J. Merritt (Ed.), *New horizons in reading* (pp. 479–493). Newark, DE: International Reading Association.

Bloom, B. (1976). *Human characteristics and school learning*. New York: McGraw-Hill.

Bloom, B. (1981). *All our children learning*. New York: McGraw-Hill.

Bloome, D. (1983). Reading as a social process. In B. Hutson (Ed.), *Advances in reading: Language research* (Vol. 11). Greenwich, CT: JAI Press.

Bond, G.C. (1981). Social economic status and educational achievement: A review article. *Anthropology & Education Quarterly, 12*(4), 227–257.

Boyer, E.L. (1987). Early schooling and the nation's future. *Educational Leadership*, *44*(6), 4–6.

Bridge, C. (1986). Predictable books for beginning readers and writers. In M.R. Sampson (Ed.), *The pursuit of literacy: Early reading and writing* (pp. 81–96). Dubuque, IA: Kendall/Hunt.

Bronfenbrenner, U. (1970). *The two worlds of childhood*. New York: Russell Sage Foundation.

Bronfenbrenner, U. (1975). Is early intervention effective? In U. Bronfenbrenner (Ed.), *Influences on human development* (2nd ed.). Hinsdale, IL: Dryden.

Bronfenbrenner, U. (1979). *The ecology of human development*. Cambridge, MA: Harvard University Press.

Bronfenbrenner, U. (1986). Alienation and the four worlds of childhood. *Phi Delta Kappan*, *67*(6), 431–435.

Bronfenbrenner, U., & Weiss, H. (1983). Beyond policies without people: An ecological perspective on child and family policy. In E.F. Zigler, S.L. Kagan, & E. Klugman (Eds.), *Children, families and government: Perspective on American social policy*. New York: Cambridge University Press.

Brophy, W.A. & Aberle, S.D., (Eds.). (1966). *The Indian: America's unfinished business* (p. 140). Report of the Commission on the Rights, Liberties and Responsibilities of the American Indian. Norman, OK: University of Oklahoma Press.

Brown V. Board of Education of Topeka, Kansas, 345 U.S. 977 (1953.)

Brown, D.L., & Biggs, L.D. (1986). Young children's concepts of print. In M.R. Sampson (Ed.), *The pursuit of literacy: Early reading and writing* (pp. 49–55). Dubuque, IA: Kendall/Hunt.

Brown, M. (1947). *Stone soup*. New York: Scribner.

Brown, M. (1961). *Once a mouse*. New York: Scribner.

Brown, R. (1987). Literacy and accountability. *The Journal of State Government*, *60*(2), 68–72.

Brown, M.H., Cromer, P.S., & Weinberg, S.H. (1986). Shared book experiences in kindergarten: Helping children come to literacy. *Early Childhood Research Quarterly*, *1*, 397–406.

Bruner, J. (1975). The ontogenesis of speech acts. *Journal of Child Language*, *3*, 1–19.

Bullock, H.A. (1970). *A history of Negro education in the South from 1619 to the present*. New York: Praeger.

Burroughs, M. (1972). *The stimulation of verbal behavior in culturally disadvantaged three-year-olds*. Unpublished doctoral dissertation, Michigan State University.

Cahn, E.S. (Ed.). (1969). *Our brother's keeper: The Indian in white America*. New York: Community Press.

Calkins, L. (1983). *Lessons from a child*. Portsmouth, NH: Heinemann.

Calkins, L. (1986). *The art of teaching writing*. Portsmouth, NH: Heinemann.

Carbo, M. (1987). Reading styles research: What works isn't always phonics. *Phi Delta Kappan, 68*(6), 430–435.

Carle, E. (1984). *The very busy spider*. New York: Scholastic Books.

Carnegie Foundation for the Advancement of Teaching. (1983). *High school: A report on secondary education in America*. New York: Harper & Row.

Carnegie Foundation for the Advancement of Teaching. (1987). *College: The undergraduate experience in America*. New York: Harper & Row.

Carnegie Task Force on Teaching as a Profession. (1986). *A nation prepared: Teachers for the 21st century*. Washington, DC: Carnegie Forum on Education and the Economy.

Carrasco, R. (April, 1979). *Expanded awareness of student performance: A case study in applied ethnographic monitoring in a bilingual classroom* (Sociolinguistic Working Paper No. 60). Austin, TX: Southwest Educational Developmental Laboratory.

Carrasco, R., Vera, A., Cazden, C. (1981). Aspects of bilingual students' communicative competence in the classroom: A case study. In R. Duran (Ed.), *Latino language and communicative behavior* (pp. 237–250). Norwood, NJ: Ablex.

Chall, J. (1983a). *Stages of reading development*. New York: McGraw-Hill.

Chall, J. (1983b). *Learning to read: The great debate* (rev. ed.). New York: McGraw-Hill.

Chall, J., & Snow, C.E. (1988). School influences on the reading development of low-income children. *Harvard Educational Letter, 4*(1), 1–4.

Chall, J., Heron, E., & Hilferty, A. (1987). Adult literacy: New and enduring problems. *Phi Delta Kappan, 69*(3), 190–96.

Chambers, A. (1973). *Introducing books to children*. London, England: Heinemann.

Children's Defense Fund. (1985). *Black and white children in America: Key facts*. Washington, DC: Author.

Children's Defense Fund. (1987). *A children's defense budget: FY 1988. An analysis of our nation's investment in children*. Washington, DC: Author.

Clark, M. (1976). *Young fluent readers*. Portsmouth, NH: Heinemann.

Clark, M. (1984). Literacy at home and at school: Insights from a study of young fluent readers. In H. Goelman, A. Oberg, & F. Smith (Eds.), *Awakening to literacy*. Portsmouth, NH: Heinemann.

Clay, M.M. (1975). *What did I write?* Portsmouth, N.H: Heinemann.

Clay, M.M. (1979). *Reading: The patterning of complex behavior* (2nd ed.). Portsmouth, NH: Heinemann.

Clay, M.M. (1982). *Observing young readers*. Portsmouth, NH: Heinemann.

Clay, M.M. (1985). *The early detection of reading difficulties* (3rd ed.). Portsmouth, NH: Heinemann.

Clay, M.M. (1987). Implementing reading recovery: Systemic adaptations to an educational innovation. *New Zealand Journal of Educational Studies, 22*, 35–58.

Cochran-Smith, M. (1984). *The making of a reader*. Norwood, NJ: Ablex.

Cole, O.J., & Washington, V. (1986). A critical analysis of the effects of Head Start on minority children. *Journal of Negro Education, 55,* 91–106.

Coleman, J. (1987). Families and schools. *Educational Researcher, 16*(6), 32–38.

Coleman, J.S., Campbell, E.Q., Hobson, C.J., McPartland, J., Mood, A.M., Weinfeld, F., & York, R.L. (1966). *Equality of educational opportunity.* Washington, DC: Government Printing Office.

Coles, R. (1977). *Privileged ones: Volume V of children of crisis.* Boston: Little, Brown.

Comer, J.P. (1986). Parent participation in the schools. *Phi Delta Kappan, 67,* 442–446.

Comer, J.P. (1987). New Haven's school-community connection. *Educational Leadership, 44*(6), 13–16.

Committee for Economic Development. (1985). *Investing in our children: Business and the public schools.* A research statement by the Research and Policy Committee. New York: Author.

Committee for Economic Development. (1987). *Children in need: Investment strategies for the educationally disadvantaged.* A statement by the research and policy committee. New York: Author.

Condry, S.M., & Lazar, I. (1982, May). American values and social policy for children. *Annals, AAPSS,* pp. 21–31.

Congressional Budget Office (1987, August). *Educational achievement: Explanations and implications of recent trends.* Washington, DC: Congress of the United States.

Coody, B. (1983). *Using literature with young children* (3rd ed.). Dubuque, IA: William C. Brown.

Cooper, H., & Good, T. (1983). *Pygmalion grows up: Studies in the expectation communication process.* New York: Longman.

Cross, P. (1987). The adventures of education in wonderland: Implementing education reform. *Phi Delta Kappan, 68*(7), 496–502.

Cross, T. (1978). Motherese: Its association with the rate of syntactic acquisition in young children. In N. Waterson & C. Snow (Eds.), *The development of communication* (pp. 199–216). London, England: Wiley.

Cuban, L. (1987). *Schooling the at-risk child: Lessons for policymakers and practitioners.* Presentation made at NCREL Conference, Chicago, IL.

Darity, W.A., & Myers, S.L. (1984). Public policy and the condition of black family life. *The Review of Black Political Economy,* pp. 164–187.

Darling-Hammond, L., & Berry, B. (1987). *The evolution of teacher policy.* Santa Monica, CA: RAND Corporation.

DeFord, D.D., Pinnell, G.S., Lyons, C.A., & Young, P. (1987). *Follow-up studies of the reading recovery program* (Technical Report). Columbus; The Ohio State University.

DeLoache, J., & DeMendoza, O. (1987). Joint picturebook interactions of mothers and one-year-old children. *British Journal of Developmental Psychology, 5,* 111–123.

Dickinson, D.K. (1984). First impressions: Children's knowledge of words gained from a single exposure. *Applied Linguistics, 5,* 359–373.

Dickinson, D.K. (1987). Oral language, literacy skills and response to literature. In J. Squire (Ed.), *The dynamics of language learning: Research in the language arts* (pp. 147–183). Urbana, IL: National Council of Teachers of English.

Dickinson, D.K. (in press). Enjoying language with young children: Long-term effects of facilitating oral language development. In M. Frank (Ed.), Facilitating children's language: Handbook for child-related professionals. *Journal of Children in Contemporary Society.* New York; Haworth.

Dickinson, D.K., & Keebler, R. (in press). Variation in preschool teachers' styles of reading books. *Discourse Processes.*

Dickinson, D.K., & Snow, C.E. (1987). Interrelationships among prereading and oral language skills in kindergarteners from two social classes. *Early Childhood Research Quarterly, 1,* 1–26.

Dr. Seuss. (1974). *Great day for up.* New York: Random House.

Duckworth, E. (1986). Teaching as research. *Harvard Educational Review, 56,* 481–495.

Dunn, N.E. (1981). Children's achievement at school entry age as function of mother's and father's teaching sets. *Elementary School Journal, 81,* 245–253.

Durkin, D. (1966). *Children who read early.* New York: Teacher's College Press.

Durkin, D. (1970). What does research say about the time to begin reading instruction? *Journal of Educational Research, 64,* 521–556.

Durkin, D. (1974–75). A six year study of children who learned to read in school at the age of four. *Reading Research Quarterly, 10,* 9–61.

Durkin, D. (1984). Poor black children who are successful readers: An investigation. *Urban Education, 19*(1), 53–76.

Durkin, D. (1987). A classroom-observation study of reading instruction in kindergarten. *Early Childhood Research Quarterly, 2,* 275–300.

Durr, W., Hillerich, R., & Johnson, T. (1986). *Getting ready to read.* Boston: Houghton Mifflin.

Duvoisin, R. (1950). *Petunia.* New York: Knopf.

Dyson, A.H. (1982). Reading, writing, and language: Young children solving the written language puzzle. *Language Arts, 59,* 829–839.

Dyson, A.H. (1984). Learning to write/learning to do school: Emergent writers' interpretations of school literacy tasks. *Research in the Teaching of English, 18*(3), 233–261.

Dyson, A.H. (1987). *Unintentional helping in the primary grades: Writing in the children's world* (Technical Report No. 2). Berkeley: University of California, Center for the Study of Writing.

Education Week. (1987, September 9). Excerpts from the C.E.D.'s new report, "Children in Need." Washington, DC: Editorial Projects in Education, p. 42.

Education Week. (1987, September 16). Family "well-being" to be new criterion in federal policies. Washington, DC: Editorial Projects in Education, p. 19.

Education Week. (1987, November 18). Chiefs urge that states "guarantee" school quality for those "at risk." Washington, DC: Editorial Projects in Education, p. 17.

Education Week. (1988, March 2). Georgia to test kindergartners for promotion. Washington, DC: Editorial Projects in Education, p. 15.

Edwards, P.A. (1988a). *Lower SES mothers learning to share books with their children: Improving literacy learning at home.* Unpublished manuscript.

Edwards, P.A. (1988b). *Modeling effective book reading behaviors for lower SES parents.* Unpublished manuscript.

Ehri, L., & Wilce, L. (1985). Movement into reading: Is the first stage of printed word learning visual or phonetic? *Reading Research Quarterly, 20,* 163–179.

Eisner, E. (1984). Passionate portraits of schools. *Harvard Educational Review, 54,* 195–200.

Elkind, D. (1981). *The hurried child: Growing up too fast and too soon.* Reading, MA: Addison-Wesley.

Elkind, D. (1987). *Miseducation: Preschoolers at risk.* New York: Knopf.

Elley, W.B., & Mangubhai, R. (1983). The impact of reading on second language learning. *Reading Research Quarterly, 29,* 53–67.

Entwisle, D. (1977). A sociologist looks at reading. In W. Otto, C. Peters, & N. Peters (Eds.), *Reading problems: A multidisciplinary approach* (pp. 74–88). Reading, MA: Addison-Wesley.

Epstein, J.L., and Becker, H.J. (1982). Teacher practices of parent involvement: Problems and possibilities. *Elementary School Journal, 83,* 103–113.

Fahs, M.E. (1987). *Coping with in-school stress: Correlations among perceptions of stress, coping styles, personal attributes and academic achievement of inner-city junior high school students.* Unpublished doctoral dissertation, New York University.

Farr, M. (Ed.), (1985). *Advances in writing research* (Vol. 1). *Children's early writing development.* Norwood, NJ: Ablex.

Farran, D.C. (1982). Mother-child interaction, language development, and the school performance of poverty children. In L. Feagans & D.C. Farran (Eds.), *The language of children reared in poverty.* New York: Academic Press.

Feagans, L. (1982). The development and importance of narrative for school adaption. In L. Feagans & D. Farran (Eds.), *The language of children reared in poverty* (pp. 95–116). New York: Academic Press.

Feistritzer, C.E. (1985, July 16). A new baby boomlet hits the schools. *The Washington Post,* C1.

Feitelson, D., Kita, B., & Goldstein, Z. (1986). Effects of listening to series stories on first graders' comprehension and use of language. *Research in the Teaching of English, 20,* 339–356.

Ferreiro, E. (1984). The underlying logic of literacy development. In H. Goelman, A. Oberg, & F. Smith (Eds.), *Awakening to literacy*. Portsmouth, NH: Heinemann.

Ferreiro, E., & Teberosky, A. (1982). *Literacy before schooling*. Portsmouth, NH: Heinemann.

Feshbach, S., Adelman, H., & Fuller, W. (1974). Early identification of children with high risk of reading failure. *Journal of Learning Disabilities, 7*, 639–644.

Feshbach, S., Adelman, H., & Fuller, W. (1977). Prediction of reading and related academic problems. *Journal of Educational Psychology, 69*, 299–308.

Flood, J. (1977). Parental styles in reading episodes with young children. *The Reading Teacher, 30*, 864–867.

Forum of Educational Organizational Leaders. (1987, June 24). Meeting the needs of children and youth at risk of school failure: The national imperative. *School Board News*, p. 8.

Franklin, V.P. (1980). Public school desegregation and minority social advancement. In L. Rubin (Ed.), *Critical issues in educational policy: An administrator's overview* (pp. 282–290). Boston: Allyn and Bacon.

Friedman, S.C. (1986, September 11). Death in park: Difficult questions for parents. *New York Times*.

Fry, P.S., & Coe, K.J. (1980). Achievement performance of internally and externally oriented black and white high school students under conditions of competition and cooperation expectancies. *British Journal of Educational Psychology, 50*, 162–167.

Galdone, P. (1973). *The little red hen*. Boston: Houghton Mifflin.

Galdone, P. (1973). *The three billy goats gruff*. New York: Clarion.

Galdone, P. (1975). *The gingerbread boy*. New York: Seabury.

Gambrell, L.B. (1986). Reading in the primary grades: How often, how long? In M.R. Sampson (Ed.), *The pursuit of literacy: Early reading and writing* (pp. 102–108). Dubuque, IA: Kendall/Hunt.

Gee, J.P. (in press). Two styles of narrative construction and their linguistic and educational implications. *Discourse Processes*.

Gesell, A. (1940). *The first five years of life*. New York: Harper & Bros.

Gilmore, P., & Glatthorn, A.A. (1982). *Children in and out of school: Ethnography and education*. New York: Harcourt Brace Jovanovich.

Goldenberg, C. (1984). *Roads to reading: Studies of Hispanic first graders at risk for reading failure*. Unpublished doctoral dissertation, Graduate School of Education, University of California, Los Angeles.

Goldenberg, C. (1987). Low-income Hispanic parents' contributions to their first-grade children's word-recognition skills. *Anthropology and Education Quarterly, 18*, 149–179.

Goldfield, B.A., & Snow, C.E. (1984). Reading books with children: The mechanics of parental influence on children's reading achievement. In J. Flood (Ed.),

Understanding reading comprehension (pp. 221–256). Newark, DE: International Reading Association.

Goodman, K., Meredith, R., & Smith, E.B. (1986). *Language and thinking* (2nd ed.). New York: Richard Owen Publishing.

Goodman, Y. (1980). The roots of literacy. In M.P. Douglass (Ed.), *Claremont reading conference forty-fourth yearbook.* Claremont, CA: Claremont Graduate School.

Goodman, Y.M. (1984). The development of initial literacy. In H. Goelman, A. Oberg, & F. Smith (Eds.), *Awakening to literacy.* Portsmouth, NH: Heinemann.

Goodman, Y.M. (1986). Children coming to know literacy. In W.H. Teale & E. Sulzby (Eds.), *Emergent literacy: Writing and reading* (p. 1–4). Norwood, NJ: Ablex.

Goodsen, B., & Hess, R. (1978). The effects of parent training programs on child performance and parent behavior. In B. Brown (Ed.), *Found: Long term gains from early intervention.* Boulder, Co: Westview.

Gough, P., Juel, C., & Roper-Schneider, D. (1983). Code and cipher: A two-stage conception of initial reading acquisition. In J. Niles, & L. Harris (Eds.), *Searches for meaning in reading/language processing and instruction.* Thirty-second yearbook of the National Reading Conference. New York: Ashton Scholastic.

Grannis, J.C. (1987a). *Young adolescents' stress in school, self-reported distress, and academic achievement: A longitudinal study in an urban middle school.* Paper presented at the Annual Meeting of the American Educational Research Association. New Orleans, LA.

Grannis, J.C. (1987b). *Early adolescents' stress in school, distress, and locus of control.* Paper presented at the American Psychological Association Annual Meeting. New Orleans, LA.

Grannis, J.C. (1987c). *The moderation of stress in the lives of students in an urban intermediate school.* Draft material from the final report to the William T. Grant Foundation.

Grant, L., & Rothenberg, J. (1986). The social enhancement of ability differences: Teacher-student interactions in first-and second-grade reading groups. *The Elementary School Journal,* 87(1), 30–49.

Graves, D. (1983). *Writing: Children and teachers at work.* Portsmouth, NH: Heinemann.

Graves, D., & Hansen, J. (1983). The authors chair. *Language Arts,* 60(2), 176–183.

Greene, J., Weade, R., & Graham, K. (in press). Lesson construction and student participation: A sociolinguistic analysis. In J.L. Green & J.O. Harker (Eds.), *Multiple perspective analysis of classroom discourse.* Norwood, NJ: Ablex.

Gustafson, L., & McConnell, B. (1975). *Northern Cheyenne Follow Through program: Serving children on the northern Cheyenne reservation in southeastern Montana* (No. 3). Evaluative Studies of Indian Education Programs (ED 136 377).

Haertel, G., Walberg, H., & Weinstein, T. (1983). Psychological models of educational performance: A theoretical synthesis of constructs. *Review of Educational Research, 53,* 75–92.

Hale, J.E. (1982). *Black children: Their roots, culture, and learning styles.* Provo, UT: Brigham Young Press.

Hanse, J. (1981). Living with normal families. *Family Process, 20*(1), 58–75.

Hansen, J. (1981). An inferential comprehension strategy for use with primary grade children. *Reading Teacher, 37,* 116–121.

Hansen, J. (1987). *When writers read.* Portsmouth, NH: Heinemann.

Harste, J.C., & Woodward, V. (in press). Fostering needed change: New policy guidelines for your family literacy program. In D.S. Strickland and L.M. Morrow (Eds.), *Emerging literacy: Young children learn to read and write.* Newark, DE: International Reading Association.

Harste, J.C., Woodward, V.A., & Burke, C.L. (1984). *Language stories and literacy lessons.* Portsmouth, NH: Heinemann.

Hasan, R. (in press). Reading picture reading: Invisible instruction at home and in school. *Linguistics and Education: An International Research Journal.*

Haussler, M.M. (1982). *Transitions into literacy: A psycholinguistic analysis of beginning reading in kindergarten and first grade children.* Unpublished doctoral dissertation, University of Arizona.

Heald-Taylor, G. (1987). How to use predictable books for K-2 language arts instruction. *The Reading Teacher, 40,* 656–663.

Heath, S.B. (1980). The functions and uses of literacy. *Journal of Communication, 30,* 123–133.

Heath, S.B. (1982a). Questioning at home and at school: A comparative study. In G. Spindler (Ed.), *Doing ethnography of schooling: Education anthropology in action* (pp. 102–129). New York: Holt, Rinehart & Winston.

Heath, S.B. (1982b). What no bedtime story means: Narrative skills at home and school. *Language in Society, 11,* 49–76.

Heath, S.B. (1983). *Ways with words: Language, life and work in communities and classrooms.* New York: Cambridge University Press.

Heath, S.B. (1986). Separating "Things of the imagination" from life: Learning to read and write. In W.H. Teale & E. Sulzby (Eds.), *Emergent literacy: Writing and reading* (pp. 156–172). Norwood, NJ: Ablex.

Heath, S.B. (1987). A lot of talk about nothing. In D. Goswami and P.R. Stillman (Eds.), *Reclaiming the classroom.* Portsmouth, NH: Boynton/Cook, 39–48.

Heath, S.B., & McLaughlin, (1987). A child resource policy: Moving beyond dependence on school and family. *Phi Delta Kappan, 68*(8), 576–580.

Heath, S.B., & Thomas, C. (1984). The achievement of preschool literacy for mother and child. In H. Goelman, A. Oberg, & F. Smith (Eds.), *Awakening to literacy* (pp. 51–72). Portsmouth, NH: Heinemann.

Heath, S.B., Branscombe, A., & Thomas, C. (1985). The book as narrative prop in language acquisition. In B. Scheiffelin & P. Gilmore (Eds.), *The acquisition of literacy: Ethnographic perspectives*. Norwood, NJ: Ablex.

Hemphill, L., & Chandler, J. (1983). *The importance of home-school contacts for school achievement*. Paper presented at the annual meeting of the American Educational Research Association, Montreal, Canada.

Henke, L. (1988). Beyond basal reading: A district's commitment to change. *The New Advocate, 1*, 42–51.

Herrnstein, R. (1971). IQ. *Atlantic Monthly*, pp. 43–64.

Hess, R., & Holloway, S. (1985). Family and school as educational institutions. In R. Parke (Ed.), *Review of child development research* (Vol. 7, pp. 179–222). Chicago: University of Chicago Press.

Hess, R.D., & Shipman, V.C. (1967). Cognitive elements in maternal behavior. In J.P. Hill (Ed.), *Minnesota symposium on child psychology: Vol. 1* (pp. 57–81). Minneapolis: University of Minnesota Press.

Hess, R., Holloway, S., Price, G., & Dickson, W. (1982). Family environments and acquisition of reading skills: Toward a more precise analysis. In L. Laosa and I. Sigel (Eds.), *Families as learning environments for children* (pp. 87–113). New York: Plenum.

Hiebert, E.H. (1988). The role of literacy experiences in programs for four- and five-year-olds. *Elementary School Journal*, November.

Hinckley, R., Beal, R., Breglio, V., Haertel, E., & Wiley, D. (1979). *Student home environment, educational achievement and compensatory education* (Tech. Rep. #4 from the Study of the Sustaining Effects of Compensatory Education on Basic Skills). Santa Ana, CA: Decima Research.

Hirsch, E.D. (1987). *Cultural literacy: What every American needs to know*. Boston, MA: Houghton Mifflin.

Hodgekinson, H.L. (1986). Reform? Higher education? Don't be absurd! *Phi Delta Kappan, 68*(4), 271–274.

Hodgekinson, H.L. (1988). The right schools for the right kids. *Educational Leadership, 45*, 10–14.

Hoffman, S.J. (1982). *Preschool reading related behaviors: A parent diary*. Unpublished doctoral dissertation, University of Pennsylvania.

Holdaway, D. (1979). *The foundations of literacy*. Portsmouth, NH: Heinemann.

Holdaway, D. (1986). The structure of natural learning as a basis for literacy instruction. In M.R. Sampson (Ed.), *The pursuit of literacy: Early reading and writing*. Dubuque, IA: Kendall/Hunt.

Holland, K. (1987). *The impact of the reading recovery program on parents and home literacy contexts*. Unpublished doctoral dissertation, The Ohio State University, Columbus.

Honig, (1986a, May). Stress and coping in children: Part 1, *Young Children*, pp. 50–63.

Honig, (1986b, July). Stress and coping in children: Part 2. *Young Children*, pp. 47–59.

Hornsby, D., Sukarna, D., & Perry, J. (1986). *Read on: A conference approach to reading*. Cammeray, Sydney, Australia: Horwitz Grahame Books.

Huck, C.S., & Pinnell, G.S. (1985). *The reading recovery project in Columbus, Ohio: Pilot year, 1984–1985* (Technical Report). Columbus: The Ohio State University.

Irvine, J.J., & Irvine, R.W. (1980). A reassessment of racial balance remedies II. *Phi Delta Kappan, 62*, 180–181.

Jacobs, J. (1965). *Tom tit tot*. New York: Scribner.

Jensen, A.R. (1969). How much can we boost IQ and scholastic achievement? *Harvard Educational Review, 39*, 1–123.

Jensen, A.R. (1985). Compensatory education and the theory of intelligence. *Phi Delta Kappan, 66*, 554–558.

Johnson, P. (1983). *A cognitive basis for the assessment of reading comprehension*. Newark, DE: International Reading Association.

Johnson, P. (1984). Assessment in reading. In P.D. Pearson (Ed.), *Handbook of reading research*. New York: Longman.

Johnston, P.H. (1984). Assessment in reading. In P.D. Pearson (Ed.), *Handbook of reading research* (pp. 147–182). New York: Longman.

Johnston, P. (1987). Assessing the process, and the process of assessment, in the language arts. In J. Squire (Ed.), *The dynamics of language learning: Research in reading and English*. Urbana, IL: ERIC and National Conference on Research in English.

Jones, L.V. (1983, November). *White-black achievement differences: The narrowing gap*. Washington, DC: Science and public policy seminars of the Federation of Behavioral, Psychological, and Cognitive Sciences.

Jones, R. (1972). *Black psychology*. New York: Harper & Row.

Jones, V.C. (1981). *Cognitive style and the problem of low school achievement among urban black low SES students: Grades 2, 4, and 6*. Unpublished doctoral dissertation, University of California, Berkeley.

Kamin, L.J. (1974). *The science and politics of IQ*. New York: Wiley.

Keats, E.J. (1970). *Hi, cat!*. New York: Macmillan.

Keats, E.J. (1971). *Over in the meadow*. New York: Scholastic Books.

Keogh, B., & Kornblau, B. (1980). *Techniques for assessing teachers' views of pupil teachability*. Project REACH report. Los Angeles: University of California.

Kifer, E. (1977). The relationship between the home and school in influencing the learning of children. *Research in the Teaching of English, 11*(1), 5–16.

King, E.M. (1980). Literacy begins at home. In G. Bray & T. Pugh (Eds.), *The reading connection* (pp. 46–53). London, England: United Reading Association.

Laosa, L. (1985). Social policies toward children of diverse ethnic, racial and language groups in the United States. In H.W. Stevenson & A.E. Siegel (Eds.), *Child development and social policy*. Chicago: University of Chicago Press.

Lazar, I., & Darlington, R. (1982). Lasting effects of early education: A report from the consortium for longitudinal studies. *Monographs of the Society for Research in Child Development, 47*(2–3, Serial No. 195).

Leinhardt, G., Zigmond, N., & Cooley, W. (1981). Reading instruction and its effects. *American Educational Research Journal, 18*, 343–361.

Lionni, L. (1968). *Swimmy*. New York: Pantheon.

Lippmann, W. (1922). The reliability of intelligence tests. *The New Republic*.

Loughlin, C.E. & Martin, M.D. (1987). *Supporting literacy: Developing effective learning environments*. NY: Teachers College Press.

Lubeck, S. (1985). *Sandbox society: Early education in black and white America — A comparative ethnography*. Philadelphia, PA: The Falmer Press, Taylor & Francis.

Lyons, C.A. (1987). *Helping readers make accelerated progress: Teacher responses and knowledge*. Paper presented to the National Reading Conference, St. Petersburg, Florida.

Lyons, C.A., Pinnell, G., Short, K., & Young, P. (1986). *The Ohio reading recovery project: Vol. VIII year one, 1986–1987*. (Technical report). Columbus: The Ohio State University.

Lyons, C.A., Pinnell, G.S., Young, P., & DeFord, D. (1987). *Report of the Ohio reading recovery project: Year 1, Implementation* (Technical Report). Columbus, OH: The Ohio State University.

Mahoney, E., & Wilcox, L. (1985). *Ready, set, read: Best books to prepare preschoolers*. Metuchen, NJ: Scarecrow Press.

Martin, B. (1967). *Brown bear, brown bear*. New York: Holt, Rinehart & Winston.

Martinez, M., & Teale, W.H. (1987). The ins and outs of a kindergarten writing program. *The Reading Teacher, 40*, 444–451.

Martinez, M., & Teale, W.H. (1988). Reading in a kindergarten classroom library. *The Reading Teacher, 41*, 568–572.

Mason, J. (1977). *Reading readiness: A definition and skills hierarchy from preschoolers' developing conceptions of print* (Tech. Rep. No. 59). Urbana, IL: University of Illinois, Center for the Study of Reading.

Mason, J. (1980). When do children begin to read? *Reading Research Quarterly, 15*, 203–227.

Mason, J. (1985). Acquisition of knowledge about reading: The preschool period. In D. Forrest, G.E. MacKinnon, & T.G. Waller (Eds.), *Metacognition, cognition and human performance*. New York: Academic Press.

Mason, J.M., & Allen, J. (1986). A review of emergent literacy with implications for research and practice in reading. In E.Z. Rothkopf (Ed.), *Review of research in education* (Vol. 13). Washington, DC: American Educational Research Association.

Mason, J., & McCormick, C. (1981). *An investigation of prereading instruction from a developmental perspective: Foundations for literacy* (Technical Report No. 224). Urbana, IL: University of Illinois, Center for the Study of Reading.

Mason, J., & McCormick, C. (1983). *Intervention procedures for increasing pre-school children's interest in and knowledge about reading*. American Educational Research Association Convention, Montreal, Canada.

Mason, J., & McCormick, C. (1985). *Little books for early readers*. Charleston, IL: Pintsize Prints.

Mason, J., McCormick, C., & Bhavnagri, N. (1986). Lesson negotiation between a teacher and preschool children. In D. Yaden, & W.S. Templeton (Eds.), *Metalinguistic awareness and beginning literacy: Conceptualizing what it means to read and write*. Portsmouth, NH: Heinemann.

McConnell, B. (1980). *Effectiveness of individualized bilingual instruction for migrant students*. Unpublished doctoral dissertation, Washington State University.

McConnell, B. (1981). *Long term effects of bilingual education* (ED 206 203). Pullman, WA: Bilingual Mini Schools.

McCormick, C., & Mason, J. (1986). Intervention procedures for increasing pre-school children's interest in and knowledge about reading. In W. Teale & E. Sulzby (Eds.), *Emergent literacy: Writing and reading*. Norwood, NJ: Ablex.

McDermott, (1976). *Kids made sense: An ethnographic account of interactional management of success and failure in one first-grade classroom*. Unpublished doctoral dissertation, Stanford University.

McNett, I. (1983). *Demographic imperatives: Implications of education policy*. Washington, DC: American Council on Education.

MDC, Inc. (1985). *The state's excellence in education commissions: Who's looking out for at-risk youth?* Report prepared for the Charles Stewart Mott Foundation. Chapel Hill, NC: Author.

Meek, M. (1982). *Learning to read*. London: The Bodley Head.

Michaels, S. (1981). "Sharing time": Children's narrative styles and differential access to literacy. *Language in Society, 10*, 423–442.

Minarik, E.H. (1957). *Little bear*. New York: Harper & Row.

Mitchell, J. (1982). Reflections of a black social scientist: Some struggles, some doubts, some hopes. *Harvard Educational Review, 52*, 27–44.

Morrow, L.M. (1987). The effect of one-to-one story readings on children's questions and responses. In J.E. Readence and R.S. Baldwin (Eds), *Research in Literacy: Merging Perspectives*. Rochester, NY: National Reading Conference.

Morrow, L.M. (1987) Promoting inner-city children's recreational reading. *Reading Teacher, 41*(3).

Morrow, L.M. (1988). Young children's responses to one-to-one story readings in school settings. *Reading Research Quarterly, 23*, 89–107.

Morrow, L.M., & Weinstein, C.S. (1982). Increasing children's use of literature through program and physical design changes. *Elementary School Journal, 83,* 131–137.

Nagy, W., Herman, P.A., & Anderson, R.C. (1985). Learning words from context. *Reading Research Quarterly, 20,* 233–253.

National Coalition of Advocates for Students. (1985). *Barriers to excellence: Our children at risk.* Boston, MA: Author.

Ninio, A. (1980). Ostensive definition in vocabulary teaching. *Journal of Child Language, 7,* 565–573.

Ogbu, J. (1978). *Minority education and caste.* New York: Harcourt Brace Jovanovich.

Ogbu, J. (1981). Origins of human competence: A cultural-ecological perspective. *Child Development, 52,* 413–429.

Orfield, G. (1986). Hispanic education: Challenges, research, and policies. *American Journal of Education, 95,* 1–25.

Ornstein, A.C. (1982). Baby boom: Bad news for city schools. *Principal, 62,* 9–13.

Owens, L.H. (1976). *This species of property: Slave life and culture in the Old South.* New York: Oxford University Press.

Paley, V. (1981). *Wally's stories.* Cambridge, MA: Harvard University Press.

Pappas, C., & Brown, E. (1987). Learning to read by reading: Learning how to extend the functional potential of the language. *Research in the Teaching of English, 21,* 160–184.

Pellicano, R.R. (1987). At risk: A view of "social advantage." *Educational Leadership, 44*(6), 47–49.

Peterman, C., & Mason, J. (1984). *Kindergarten children's perceptions of the form of print in labeled pictures and stories.* St. Petersburg, FL: National Reading Conference.

Peterson, Paul E. (1985). *The politics of school reform, 1870–1940.* Chicago: University of Chicago Press.

Pflaum, S.W. (1986). *The development of language and literacy in young children* (3rd ed). Columbus, OH: Charles E. Merrill.

Pillar, A.M. (1987). Resources to identify children's books for the reading program. In B. Cullinan (Ed.), *Children's literature in the reading program* (pp. 156–164). Newark, DE: International Reading Association.

Pinnell, G.S. (in press). Interviewing in holistic ways to help children at risk in reading. *Elementary School Journal.*

Pinnell, G.S., Huck, C.S., DeFord, D., & Lyons, C.A. (1987). Proposal for the Early Literacy Research Project. The Ohio State University.

Pinnell, G.S., Short, K., Lyons, C.A., & Young, P. (1986). *The reading recovery project in Columbus, Ohio: 1985–1986* (Technical Report). Columbus: The Ohio State University.

Preston, E.M. (1976). *The temper tantrum book.* New York: Penguin.

Price, G.G., Hess, R.D., & Dickson, W.P. (1981). Processes by which verbal-educational abilities are affected when mothers encourage preschool children to verbalize. *Developmental Psychology, 17,* 554–564.

Raspberry, W. (1985, September 16). Why the low test scores?. *The Washington Post,* p A–1.

Resnick, M.B., Roth, J., Aaron, P.M., Scott, J., Wolking, W.D., Laren, J.J., & Packer, A.B. (1987). Mothers reading to infants: A new observational tool. *The Reading Teacher, 40,* 888–894.

Reuning, C., & Sulzby, E. (1985). Emergent reading abilities in high and low literacy background children. In J. Niles & R. Lalik (Eds.), *Issues in literacy: A research perspective.* Rochester, NY: National Reading Conference.

Rhodes, L.K. (1981). I can read! Predictable books as resources for reading and writing instruction. *The Reading Teacher, 34,* 511–518.

Riddle, W.C. (1986). *Education for disadvantaged children: Federal aid* (Updated 3/26/86). Washington, DC: Congressional Research Service.

Rist, R. (1973). *The urban school: A factory for failure.* Cambridge, MA: MIT Press.

Rosen, R. (1959). Race, ethnicity, and the achievement syndrome. *American Sociological Review, 24,* 47–60.

Rosenshine, B. (1986). Synthesis of research on explicit teaching. *Educational Leadership, 43,* 60–69.

Roser, N., & Martinez, M. (1985). Roles adults play in preschoolers' response to literature. *Language Arts, 62,* 485–490.

Ross, A. (1976). *Psychological aspects of learning disabilities and reading disorders.* New York: McGraw-Hill.

Rubin, L. (Ed.). (1980). *Critical issues in educational policy: An administrator's overview.* Boston: Allyn and Bacon.

Scheffler, I. (1984). On the education of policy makers. *Harvard Educational Review, 54*(2), 152–165.

Schlesinger, B. (1982). Functioning families: Focus of the 1980's. *Family Perspectives, 16*(3), 111–116.

Sendak, M. (1963). *Where the wild things are.* New York: Harper & Row.

Shanahan, T., & Hogan, V. (1983). Parent reading style and children's print awareness. In J.A. Niles & L.A. Harris (Eds.), *Thirty-second yearbook of the National Reading Conference* (pp. 212–218). Rochester, NY: National Reading Conference.

Shavelson, R. (1983). Review of teachers' pedagogical judgments, plans, and decisions. *Elementary School Journal, 83,* 392–413.

Shavelson, R., & Stern, P. (1981). Research on teachers' pedagogical thoughts, judgments, decisions and behavior. *Review of Educational Research, 51,* 455–498.

Shaw, C.G. (1947). *It looked like spilt milk*. New York: Harper & Row.

Shepard, L.A., & Smith, M.L. (1985). *Boulder Valley kindergarten study: Retention practices and retention effects*. Boulder, CO: Boulder Valley Public Schools.

Shipman, V. (1976). *Notable early characteristics of high and low achieving black low-SES children*. (Report #PR-76—21). Princeton, NJ: Educational Testing Service.

Shor, I. (1986). *Culture wars: School and society in the conservative restoration 1969—1984*. Boston: Routledge & Kegan Paul.

Short, K.G. (1986). *A study of teacher/student interactions supporting literacy*. Paper presented to the National Reading Conference, Austin, TX.

Shuey, A.M. (1966). *The testing of Negro intelligence*. New York: Social Science Press.

Slaughter, D. (1982, March). What is the future of Head Start? *Young Children*, pp. 3—9.

Slaughter, D. (1983). Early intervention and its effects on maternal and child development. *Monographs of the Society for Research in Child Development, 48* (4, Serial No. 202).

Slaughter, D., & Schneider, B.L. (1986, February). *Newcomers: Blacks in private schools* (Grant No. NIE-G-82—0040, Project No. 2—0450). Final report to the National Institute of Education.

Slavin, R.E. (1987). Making Chapter 1 make a difference, *Phi Delta Kappan, 69*, 110—119.

Slobodkina, E. (1947). *Caps for sale*. Reading, MA: Young Scott Books.

Snow, C.E. (1983). Literacy and language: Relationships during the preschool years. *Harvard Educational Review, 53*, 165—189.

Snow, C.E., & Goldfield, B.A. (1983). Turn the page please: Situation specific language acquisition. *Journal of Child Language, 10*, 551—570.

Snow, C.E., & Ninio, A. (1986). The contribution of reading books with children to their linguistic and cognitive development. In W. Teale & E. Sulzby (Eds.), *Emergent literacy: Reading and writing*. Norwood, NJ: Ablex.

Snow, C.E., Perlmann, R., & Nathan, D. (1987). Why routines are different: Toward a multiple-factors model of the relation between input and language acquisition. In K.E. Nelson (Ed.), *Children's language* (Vol. 6, pp. 65—97). Hillsdale, NJ: Lawrence Erlbaum.

Sowell, T. (1970, Spring). Patterns of black excellence. *The Public Interest*, p. 53.

Sowell, T. (1981). *Ethnic America: A history*. New York: Basic Books.

Spewock, T. (1988). Training parents to teach their preschoolers through literature. *Reading Teacher, 41*(7), 648—652.

Spindler, G. (Ed.), (1987). *Doing the ethnography of schooling*. Prospect Heights, IL: Waveland Press.

Strahan D. (1983). The teacher and ethnography: Observational sources of information for educators. *Elementary School Journal, 83,* 195–203.

Strickland, D. & Taylor, D. (1988). *Family storybook reading: For children, families and curriculum.* Unpulished manuscript, Teachers College, Columbia University.

Sulzby, E. (1985a). Children's emergent reading of favorite storybooks: A developmental study. *Reading Research Quarterly, 20*(4), 458–481.

Sulzby, E. (1985b). Kindergarteners as writers and readers. In M. Farr (Ed.), *Advances in writing research, Vol. 1: Children's early writing development* (pp. 127–199). Norwood, NJ: Ablex.

Sulzby, E., & Teale, W.H. (1985). Writing development in early childhood. *Educational Horizons, 64,* 8–12.

Sulzby, E., & Teale, W.H. (1987). *Young children's storybook reading: Longitudinal study of parent-child interaction and children's independent functioning.* Final report to the Spencer Foundation. Ann Arbor, MI: University of Michigan.

Taylor, D. (1983). *Family literacy: Young children learning to read and write.* Portsmouth, NH: Heinemann.

Taylor, D. (1986). Creating family story. In W. Teale & E. Sulzby (Eds.), *Emergent literacy: Writing and reading.* Norwood, NJ: Ablex.

Taylor, D. (1987). The (con)textual world's of childhood. In B. Fillion, C. Hedley, & F. DiMartino (Eds.), *Home and school: Early language and reading.* Norwood, NJ: Ablex.

Taylor, D. (1988a, Winter). Ethnographic educational evaluation for children, families and schools. *Theory into Practice,* pp. 67–76.

Taylor, D. (1988b). *Conversations on family talk.* Unpublished manuscript.

Taylor, D. (1988c). [Working parents and their children: A study of family literacy and learning.] Research proposal submitted to the International Research Committee.

Taylor, D., & Dorsey-Gaines, C. (1988). *Growing up literate: Learning from inner-city families.* Portsmouth, NH: Heinemann.

Taylor, D., & Strickland, D. (1986a). *Family storybook reading.* Portsmouth, NH: Heinemann.

Taylor, D., & Strickland, D. (1986b). Family literacy: Myths and magic. In M. Sampson (Ed.), *The pursuit of literacy: Early reading and writing.* Dubuque, IA: Kendall/Hunt.

Teale, W. (1986a). The beginnings of reading and writing: Written language development during the preschool and kindergarten years. In M. Sampson (Ed.), *The pursuit of literacy: Early reading and writing.* Dubuque, IA: Kendall/Hunt.

Teale, W.H. (1986b). Home background and young children's literacy development. In W.H. Teale & E. Sulzby (Eds.), *Emergent literacy: Writing and reading* (pp. 173–206). Norwood. NJ: Ablex.

Teale, W.H. (1987). Emergent literacy: Reading and writing development in early childhood. In J.E. Readence & R.S. Baldwin (Eds.), *Research in literacy: Merging perspectives*. Rochester, NY: National Reading Conference.

Teale, W.H. (1988, November). Developmentally appropriate assessment of reading and writing in the early childhood classroom. *Elementary School Journal*.

Teale, W.H., & Martinez, M. (1986). Teachers' storybook reading styles: Evidence and implications. *Reading Education in Texas, 2*, 7–16.

Teale, W.H. & Martinez, M. (in press). Getting on the right road to reading. *Young Children*.

Teale, W.H., & Sulzby, E. (Eds.), (1986). *Emergent literacy: Writing and reading*. Norwood, NJ: Ablex.

Teale, W.H., & Sulzby, E. (1987). Access, mediation, and literacy acquisition in early childhood. In D.A. Wagner (Ed.), *The future of literacy in a changing world* (pp. 111–130). New York: Pergamon Press.

Tharp, R., Jordan, C., Speidel, G., Au, K., Klein, T., Calkins, R., Sloat, K., & Gallimore, R. (1984). Product and process in applied developmental research: Education and the children of a minority. In M. Lamb, A. Brown, & R. Rogoff (Eds.), *Advances in developmental psychology*, Vol. III (pp. 91–144). Hillsdale, NJ: Erlbaum and Associates.

Thomas, K. (1985). Early reading as a social interaction process. *Language Arts, 62*(5), 469–475.

Thomas, W.I. (1966). *On social organization and personality: Selected papers*. (M Janowitz, Ed.). Chicago: University of Chicago Press.

Tobin, A.W. (1981). *A multiple discriminant cross-validation of the factors associated with the development of precocious reading achievement*. Unpublished doctoral dissertation, University of Delaware.

Tompkins, G.E., & McGee, L.M. (1983). Launching nonstandard speakers into standard English. *Language Arts, 60*, 463–469.

Tompkins, G.E., & Webeler, M. (1983). What will happen next? Using predictable books with young children. *The Reading Teacher, 36*, 498–502.

Tulkin, S. (1972). An analysis of the concept of cultural deprivation. *Developmental Psychology, 6*, 326–339.

Tyack, D. (1976). Ways of seeing: An essay on the history of compulsory schooling. *Harvard Educational Review, 46*(3), 355–389.

Ulibarri, D.M. (1982). *Cognitive processing theory and culture-loading: A neo-Piagetian approach to test bias*. Unpublished doctoral dissertation, University of California, Berkeley.

U.S. Department of Education. (1983, April). *A nation at risk*. Report prepared by the National Commission on Excellence in Education. Washington, DC: Author.

U.S. Department of Education. (1984, October). *Involvement in learning: Realizing the potential of American higher education*. Report prepared by the Study Group on Conditions on Excellence in American Higher Education. Washington, DC: National Institute of Education.

U.S. Department of Education. (1986, September). *First lessons: A report on elementary education in America*. Washington, DC: Author.

Viorst, J. (1972). *Alexander and the terrible, horrible, no good, very bad day*. New York: Atheneum.

Vygotsky, L.S. (1978). *Mind in society*. Cambridge, MA: Harvard University Press.

Walker, A. (1984). *Horses make a landscape look more beautiful: Poems by Alice Walker*. New York: Harcourt Brace Jovanovich.

Washington, V. (1985). Implementing multi-cultural education: Elementary teachers' attitudes and professional practice. *Peabody Journal of Education, 59*, 190–200.

Washington, V. (1985). Social and personal ecology influencing public policy for young children: An American dilemma. In C.S. McLoughlin & D.F. Gullo (Eds.), *Young children in context: Impact of self, family and society on development* (pp. 254–274). Springfield, IL: Charles C. Thomas.

Washington, V., & LaPoint, V. (1988). *Black children and American institutions*. New York: Garland.

Washington, V., & Oyemade, U.J. (1987). *Project Head Start: Past, present, and future trends in the context of family needs*. New York: Garland.

Washington, V., & Woolever, R. (1979). Training teachers for diversity: An urban necessity. In W.J. Wicker (Ed.), *Perspectives on urban affairs in North Carolina* (pp. 57–66). Chapel Hill, NC: University of North Carolina Urban Affairs Institute.

Weaver, C. (1988). *Reading process and practice*. Portsmouth, NH: Heinemann.

Weinberg, M. (1977). *Minority students: A research appraisal*, Washington. DC: Government Printing Office.

Wells, G. (1981). *Learning through interaction: The study of language development*. New York: Cambridge University Press.

Wells, G. (1985a). *Language development in the preschool years*. New York: Cambridge University Press.

Wells, G. (1985b). Preschool literacy-related activities and success in school. In D.R. Olson, N. Torrance, & A. Hildyard (Eds.), *Literacy, language, and learning: The nature and consequences of reading and writing* (pp. 229–255). Cambridge, England: Cambridge University Press.

White, S., & Buka, S. (1987). Early education: Programs, traditions, and policies. In E. Rothkopf (Ed.), *Review of Research in Education*, Volume *14*, 3–41.

William T. Grant Foundation Commission on Work, Family, and Citizenship. (1987). *Current federal policy and programs for youth*. New York: The William T. Grant Foundation.

Williams, D., & Loertcher, K. (1986, April). *Teachers as naturalistic inquirers: A case study*. Paper presented at the annual meeting of the American Educational Research Association, San Francisco, CA.

Woolsey, D. (1986). *The constructive child: First steps in Reading Recovery*. Unpublished doctoral dissertation, The Ohio State University, Columbus.

Wyman, A. (1987, December 14). Stressed for success in suburban schools. *The Boston Globe*, pp. 25, 26.

Yaden, D. (1988). Understanding stories through repeated readalouds: How many does it take? *The Reading Teacher, 41*(6), 556–561.

Youth and America's Future. (1988, January). *The forgotten half: Non-college youth in America*. An interim report on the School-to-Work Transition Committee. Washington, DC: The William T. Grant Foundation.

Zolotow, C. (1965). *Someday*. New York: Harper & Row.

Indexes

AUTHOR INDEX

SUBJECT INDEX